The Poor and Their Possessions

The Poor and Their Possessions

Possessions and the Poor in Luke-Acts

DAVID PETER SECCOMBE

WIPF & STOCK · Eugene, Oregon

THE POOR AND THEIR POSSESSIONS
Possessions and the Poor in Luke-Acts

Copyright © 2022 David Peter Seccombe. All rights reserved. Except for brief quotations in critical publications or reviews, no part of this book may be reproduced in any manner without prior written permission from the publisher. Write: Permissions, Wipf and Stock Publishers, 199 W. 8th Ave., Suite 3, Eugene, OR 97401.

Wipf & Stock
An Imprint of Wipf and Stock Publishers
199 W. 8th Ave., Suite 3
Eugene, OR 97401

www.wipfandstock.com

PAPERBACK ISBN: 978-1-6667-1003-8
HARDCOVER ISBN: 978-1-6667-1004-5
EBOOK ISBN: 978-1-6667-1005-2

May 12, 2022 8:43 AM

Unless otherwise indicated, Bible references are from the Revised Version of the Bible (with Apocrypha) published by Oxford University Press, 1895.

Scripture quotations marked (Phillips) are from J. B. Phillips, "The New Testament in Modern English", 1962 edition, published by HarperCollins.

Scripture quotations marked (JB) are from *The Jerusalem Bible* © 1966 by Darton Longman & Todd Ltd and Doubleday and Company Ltd.

Scripture quotations marked (NEB) are from the New English Bible, published by Oxford University Press, 1970.

Scripture quotations marked (NIV) are from the The Holy Bible, New Internationalal Version®, NIV®. Copyright © 1973, 1978, 1984, 2011 by Biblica, Inc.™ Used by permission of Zondervan. All rights reserved worldwide. www.zondervan.comThe "NIV" and "New International Version" are trademarks registered in the United States Patent and Trademark Office by Biblica, Inc.™

Scripture quotations marked (RSV) are from the Revised Standard Version of the Bible, copyright © 1946, 1952, and 1971 National Council of the Churches of Christ in the United States of America. Used by permission. All rights reserved worldwide.

Possessions and the Poor in Luke-Acts. Studien zum Neuen Testament und seiner Umwelt (SNTU). Linz, 1982.

Contents

Preface | vii

Preface to the 1982 Edition | ix

Abbreviations | xi

INTRODUCTION TO THE NEW EDITION | 1

Chapter 1	QUESTIONS AND PROCEDURES	12
Chapter 2	THE POOR AND THE SALVATION OF ISRAEL	23
Chapter 3	RENUNCIATION AND DISCIPLESHIP	103
Chapter 4	POSSESSIONS AND THE CHRISTIAN LIFE	142
Chapter 5	FELLOWSHIP AND THE CHURCH	201
Chapter 6	LUKE'S MESSAGE	227

Appendix | 233

Bibliography | 263

Index of Modern Authors | 297

Index of Scriptural and Other References | 305

Preface

THE NUMBER OF STUDIES of money-matters in Luke and Acts, which have appeared over the past forty years is sufficient evidence of the continuing importance of this theme. Nothing that has appeared has seriously challenged the conclusions I reached in my 1982 monograph. My solution to the question of the identity of the poor in Luke-Acts has been noted, and largely ignored, but the attempts to reach different conclusions have, in my judgement, not succeeded. On the question of Luke's view of how possessions should be used, there has been general convergence on what I argued forty years ago.

My thanks go first to William Taylor, Vicar of St Helen's Bishopsgate in London, for urging the importance of making this work available to Christian preachers. I am especially grateful to Dr Albert Fuchs, Professor of the Theological Faculty of the University of Linz, and editor of Studien zum Neuen Testament und seiner Umwelt, for encouraging me to proceed with the new edition. Of special help with this were my wife, Lorraine, who did much of the word processing, and Christine O'Neil, who checked the translations from German and French. Next, I thank Sam Rae and those who helped with the crowdfunding. I am grateful too for Wipf and Stock's willingness to republish my work, and for the help of Matt Wimer, Griffin Edwards, and the rest of the team in the process.

I also wish to acknowledge the institutions that have encouraged and supported my work, among them, George Whitefield College in Cape Town, Moore Theological College in Sydney, Trinity Theological College in Perth Western Australia, the Faculty of Theology of North-West University in South Africa, the Faculty of Protestant Theology of the University of Tübingen, and Oak Hill College in London. The churches that have extended their fellowship are too many to name, though St Matthew's in Shenton Park, and St Peter's in Fish Hoek cannot go unmentioned.

I dedicate this work to preachers who work hard at understanding the Scriptures, and equally hard at explaining them to their congregations.

Preface to the 1982 Edition

WHAT IS A CHRISTIAN APPROACH to money and possessions? What should be the Christian's reaction to wealth and to poverty? Is there an essential connection between the gospel and the poor? These questions have never been more urgently debated than they are now, aware as we are of the widening gulf between rich nations and poor. Economic and social thinkers from the extreme right to the extreme left sometimes appeal to the Bible for support for their views.

Christian thinking, as opposed to thinking which simply seeks to bolster itself by appealing to this or that biblical statement, must begin with a clear understanding of what the various biblical writers are saying. At once we meet a complex and diverse set of writings each of which must be analyzed with regard to its life-setting and purpose before any kind of overall synthesis is possible. On the principle that one should concentrate attention where the issue of concern is highlighted, this study explores the outlook of Luke-Acts, since Luke has plainly collected a disproportionate amount of material reflecting on wealth and poverty, the rich and the poor. Why? What is he saying? And to whom?

There are many indications that Luke-Acts is a work addressed, not as is often said, to the poor, but to the wealthy about the poor. The results of this study are therefore peculiarly appropriate to Westerners in the twentieth century. They should provide a number of important considerations to those seeking a Christian theology of possessions. Ranging as it does over Gospel and Acts it provides insight into the theory and practice both of Jesus and the post-Easter community.

This study was undertaken as a doctoral dissertation at Cambridge University (1978). It was supervised first by C. F. D. Moule and later by J. P. M. Sweet. Their guidance and encouragement as well as their Christian kindness over a period of some difficulty is something I could not think to repay. The thesis was examined by E. Bammel and G. B. Caird. *Possessions and the Poor in Luke-Acts* was originally published as a monograph by Studien zum Neuen Testament in seiner Umwelt (Linz). The late Professor Fuchs's eagerness to bring this work to light has been no little encouragement to me.

Thanks go also to the folk at Christ Church Claremont who inspired me to think in this direction, the Australian Fellowship of Evangelical Students for its financial support of my studies, to the Sydney Diocesan Education and Book Society, and to Archbishop Geoffrey Sambell and those who carried out his wishes after his death for generous help toward the cost of publication.

I would also thank the many, especially those men at Tyndale House Cambridge (1975–78), who know that their stimulus and encouragement had a hand in this book. To all who seek "the Way of the Lord" I dedicate this study.

David Peter Seccombe
June 1982

Abbreviations

ABenR	*American Benedictine Review*
ABR	*Australian Biblical Review*
AG	William F. Arndt and F. Wilbur Gingrich. *A Greek-English Lexicon of the New Testament and Other Early Christian Literature*. Cambridge, UK: Cambridge University Press, 1959.
AGSU	Arbeiten zur Geschichte des Spätjudentums und Urchristentums
AJBI	*Annual of the Japanese Biblical Institute*
AJP	*American Journal of Philology*
AnBib	Analecta Biblica
AncB	The Anchor Bible
ASTI	*Annual of the Swedish Theological Institute*
AThANT	Abhandlungen zur Theologie des Alten und Neuen Testaments
AThR	*Anglican Theological Review*
BC	F. J. Foakes-Jackson and K. Lake, eds. *The Beginnings of Christianity*. 5 vols. 1922–39. Reprint, London: Macmillan, 1976.
BDB	Francis Brown, S. R. Driver, and Charles A. Briggs, eds. *A Hebrew and English Lexicon of the Old Testament*. Oxford: Clarendon, 1976.
BETL	Bibliotheca Ephemeridum Theologicarum Lovaniensium
BhTh	Beiträge der historischen Theologie
Bib	*Biblica*

BiLeb	*Bibel und Leben*
Billerbeck	Paul Billerbeck and Hermann Strack. *Kommentar zum Neuen Testament aus Talmud und Midrasch.* 4 vols. 1924–28. Reprint, München: Kessinger, 1969.
BJRL	*The Bulletin of the John Rylands Library*
BNTC	Black's New Testament Commentaries
BS	*Bibliotheca Sacra*
BTS	*Bible et Terre Sainte*
BVC	*Bible et Vie Chrétienne*
BW	*Biblical World*
BWANT	Beiträge zur Wissenschaft der Alten und Neuen Testament
BZ	*Biblische Zeitschrift*
BZNW	Beihefte zur Zeitschrift für die Neutestamentliche Wissenschaft und die Kunde der Älteren Kirche
Cath	*Catholica*
CBQ	*The Catholic Biblical Quarterly*
CBQ MS	Catholic Biblical Quarterly—Monograph Series
CleR	*Clergy Review*
CNT	*Coniectanea Neotestamentica*
Conc	*Concilium*
CSR	*Covenant Seminary Review*
CTM	*Currents in Theology and Mission*
CUOS	Columbia University Oriental Studies
CV	*Communio Viatorum*
Diss.	Dissertation
DJD	Roland de Vaux et al. *Discoveries in the Judaean Desert.* 40 vols. Oxford University Press: Oxford, 1955–77.
DoLi	*Doctrine and Life*
DR	*Downside Review*
DThC	Alfred Vacant et al. *Dictionaire de Théologie Catholique.* Paris: Letouzey and Ane, 1923–50.
ed(s)	editor(s)
EeT	*Eglise et Théologie*

ERE	James Hastings, ed. *Encyclopedia of Religion and Ethics*. 12 vols. Edinburgh: T. & T. Clark, 1908–26.
ER	*Ecumenical Review*
ET	English Translation
ETL	*Ephemerides Theologicae Lovaniensis*
ETR	*Etudes Théologiques et Religieuses*
EvQ	*Evangelical Quarterly*
EvTh	*Evangelische Theologie*
Exp	*The Expositor*
ExpT	*The Expository Times*
Fs.	Festschrift
FRLANT	Forschungen zur Religion und Literatur des Alten und Neuen Testaments
GNT	Grundrisse zum Neuen Testament
Greg	*Gregorianum*
GuL	*Geist und Leben*
HbNT	Handbuch zum Neuen Testament
HeyJ	*Heythrop Journal*
HThK	Herders Theologische Kommentar zum Neuen Testament
HTR	*The Harvard Theological Review*
HTS	Harvard Theological Studies
HUCA	*Hebrew Union College Annual*
ICC	The International Critical Commentary
IEJ	*Israel Exploration Journal*
IER	*Irish Ecclesiastical Record*
Interpr	*Interpretation*
IThQ	*Irish Theological Quarterly*
JAAR	*Journal of the American Academy of Religion*
JBL	*Journal of Biblical Literature*
JBR	*Journal of Bible and Religion*
JE	Cyrus Adler and Isidore Singer. *The Jewish Encyclopedia*. New York: Ktav, 1903.
JEvThS	*Journal of the Evangelical Theological Society*
JJS	*The Journal of Jewish Studies*

JpTh	*Jahrbücher für protestantische Theologie*
JQR	*Jewish Quarterly Review*
JSJ	*Journal of the Study of Judaism*
JSNTSuppl	Journal for the Study of the New Testament Supplement Series
JTCh	*Journal for Theology and the Church*
JTS	*The Journal of Theological Studies*
Jud	*Judaica*
KAT	Kommentar zum Alten Testament
KEK	Kritsch-Exegetischer Kommentar über das Neuen Testament
KNT	Kommentar zum Neuen Testament
KuD	*Kerygma und Dogma*
LD	Lectio Divina
LexTQ	*Lexington Theological Quarterly*
LQR	*London Quarterly Review*
LUA	Lunds Universitets Arsskrift
MarSt	*Marian Studies*
MNTC	The Moffatt New Testament Commentaries
MO	*Le Monde Orientale*
Moulton	J. H. Moulton. *A Grammar of New Testament Greek*. 3 vols. Edinburgh: T. & T. Clark, 1930–63.
MüThSt	Münchner Theologische Studien
MW	Muslim World
NBl	*New Blackfriars*
NCeB	New Century Bible
n.d.	No date
NIDNTT	Colin Brown, ed. *The New International Dictionary of New Testament Theology*. 3 vols. Grand Rapids, MI: Zondervan, 1975–79.
NKZ	*Neue kirchliche Zeitschrift*
NovTest	*Novum Testamentum*
NovTestSuppl	Supplements to Novum Testamentum
NRT	*Nouvelle Revue Théologiques*
NTD	Das Neue Testament Deutsch

NTS	*New Testament Studies*
ÖTK NT	*Ökumenischer Taschenbuchkommentar zum Neuen Testament*
OTS	*Oudtestamentische Studien*
Pauly	August Friedrich von Pauly. *Real-Encyclopädie der classischen Altertumswissenschaft.* 83 vols. Stuttgart: J. B. Mertzlersche Buchhandlung, 1894–1980.
PNTC	*The Pelican New Testament Commentaries*
PRefR	*Presbyterian and Reformed Review*
PrJ	*Preussische Jahrbücher*
PrM	*Protestantische Monatshefte*
PTR	*Princeton Theological Review*
RB	*Review Biblique*
RechSR	*Recherches de science religieuse*
RefJ	*The Reformed Journal*
REJ	*Revue des études juives*
RevQum	*Revue de Qumran*
RExp	*Review and Expositor*
RGG	Kurt Galling, ed. *Die Religion in Geschichte und Gegenwart.* Tübingen: Mohr 1961
RHLR	*Revue d'histoire et litérature religieuse*
RHPhR	*Revue d'histoire et philosophie religieuses*
RNT	Regensberger Neuen Testament
RRef	*Revue reformé*
RThPh	*Revue de théologie et philosophie*
SBFLA	*Studii Biblici Fransiscani Liber Annuus*
SBL MS	Society of Biblical Literature—Monograph Series
SBL SP	Society of Biblical Literature—Seminar Papers
SBS	Stuttgarter Bibelstudien
SBT	Studies in Biblical Theology
ScEs	*Science et Esprit*
SCH	Studia ad Corpus Hellenisticum Novi Testamenti
Scrip	*Scripture*
SJ	Studia Judaica
SJLA	Studies in Judaism in Late Antiquity

SJT	Scottish Journal of Theology
SNTS MS	Society for New Testament Studies—Monograph Series
SNTU	Studien zum Neuen Testament und seiner Umwelt
SPB	Studia Post-Biblica
StANT	Studien zum Alten und Neuen Testament
StudEv	Studia Evangelica: Papers presented to the First through Seventh International Congresses on New Testament Studies, Christ Church, Oxford, 1957.
StudTheol	Studia Theologica
StudTheol (Riga)	Studia Theologica, Riga
StUNT	Studien zur Umwelt des Neuen Testaments
SVTP	Studia in Veteris Testamenti Pseudepigrapha
TDNT	Gerhard Kittel, ed. Theological Dictionary of the New Testament. 10 vols. ET. Grand Rapids, MI: Eerdmans, 1964–76
TDOT	G. J. Botterweck and H. Ringgren, eds. Theological Dictionary of the Old Testament. ET. 11 vols. Grand Rapids, MI: Eeerdmans, 1974–76.
TheolColl	Theological Collections
THK NT	Theologische Handkommentar zum Neuen Testament
ThRu	Theologische Rundschau
ThStKr	Theologische Studien und Kritiken
ThViat	Theologia Viatorum
TLZ	Theologische Literaturzeitung
TQ	Theologische Quartalschrift
TS	Theological Studies
TU	Texte und Untersuchungen zur Geschichte der altchristlichen Literatur
TynB	Tyndale Bulletin
TZ	Theologische Zeitschrift
USQR	Union Seminary Quarterly Review
VC	Verbum Caro
VetTest	Vetus Testamentum

ABBREVIATIONS

VetTestSuppl	Supplements to Vetus Testamentum
VigChr	*Vigiliae Christianae*
VoxEv	*Vox Evangelica*
VS	*Vie spirituelle*
WUNT	Wissenschaftliche Untersuchungen zum Neuen Testament
ZAW	*Zeitschrift für alttestamentliche Wissenschaft*
ZKG	*Zeitschrift für Kirchengeschichte*
ZkTh	*Zeitschrift für katholische Theologie*
ZNW	*Zeitschrift für die Neutestamentliche Wissenschaft und die Kunde der älteren Kirche*
ZSTh	*Zeitschrift für systematische Theologie*
ZThK	*Zeitschrift für Theologie und Kirche*
ZwTh	*Zeitschrift für wissenschaftliche Theologie*

Introduction to the New Edition

WHEN A CHURCH LEADER asked me to republish my 1978 dissertation on Jesus' teaching about rich and poor I was energized by the thought that my conclusions and the evidence I had collected could still be of use to a working preacher or teacher.

My study of this question began in 1975. The Ethiopian famine of 1973 stirred the conscience of the West. Harrowing pictures of skeletal children stumbling through the dust and rows of shrouded bodies brought about a new consciousness of poverty in "the third world." Each night television screens brought the poor into our well-provisioned homes. In the name of the third-world's poor Schumacher's book, *Enough is Enough*, challenged our excessive consumption of the world's dwindling resources. The Vietnam War provided another face to poverty.

Working through possible topics for PhD studies with Cambridge's Professor C. F. D. Moule, we agreed on the need for a detailed study of Luke's teaching on wealth and poverty, and I was privileged to study under him in the last year before his retirement. His colleague, Mr. John Sweet, took me on for the last two years.

Possessions and the Poor in Luke-Acts was published as an academic monograph in 1982, and is now available only in libraries. If it is to be useful again, I need to say a few things by way of introduction. When, in 1975, I set out on what for me was an adventure of exploration, it was as a Christian preacher who had come to believe in Scripture as the word of God and normative for Christian life. This was Jesus' view, and I continue to hold to it, and believe that proclaiming the divine message is the most privileged of all callings.

Hans Conzelman's work on Luke's reason for writing (*Die Mitte der Zeit*, 1954) was translated into English in 1960 as *The Theology of St. Luke*, and "redaction criticism" soon became a preferred method of study in the

New Testament scholarly world. *Redaktion* is German for "editing." This method puts the spotlight on the author, in this case Luke, and seeks to determine the shape of his individual thinking, given that he employed sources that other writers also utilized, sometimes in different ways. The goal of redaction criticism is to understand what *Luke* wrote, and why he wrote it. As a research project I could side-step the question of how far this corresponded to the actual teaching of Jesus, though I have never thought the Gospel writers falsified their Lord's teaching, nor that the product of their labor was not guided by the hand of the Almighty.

STUDY OF THE BIBLE

For as long as the Scriptures have existed they have been the object of intense study, and many are the ways of reading them carefully. One person may look for devotional insights, another for doctrine, and yet another for historical information. Someone may wish to construct a biblical worldview; another may be seeking ammunition to demolish the truth of Christianity. The Bible is often trawled for ethical insight. Over the last century sociology has become a favored discipline, so it is not surprising to find the New Testament books scrutinized for their correspondences to this or that sociological insight. There is no end to people's motives for studying the Bible.

For our Christian forebears Scripture was a doctrinal quarry, where every statement is of equal worth (being all of God), the goal being to construct a comprehensive understanding of Christianity. This common approach has yielded, and continues to yield, many true answers, and resulted in the confessions of faith of various church traditions. But it overlooked an amount of profound biblical knowledge. Few today would doubt that a knowledge of Paul's background and the nature of his opposition illuminates his writings in a way that brings them alive and also clarifies some obscure texts. This is important for the preacher. It may also bring to the surface truths that otherwise remain invisible. It is so with the writings of Luke. We might liken the doctrinal reading of Scripture to an aerial photograph. What it reveals of the terrain below will be true, but a three-dimensional model will display much more.

Biblical Criticism

During the so-called Enlightenment there was a revolt against the church in Europe. One form this took was an attempt to undermine the theological foundation of Christianity by close scrutiny of the biblical documents. The church was no longer trusted as interpreter; suspicious scholars wanted to examine the founding documents for themselves and make of them what they would. Some wished to undermine faith; others believed there was a kernel of truth that could form the basis of a new Christianity. In 1788 (an easy date for Australians) Herman Samuel Reimarus wrote his subversive account of Jesus and the origins of Christianity.[1] When it was published early in the nineteenth century by G. E. Lessing it planted the idea that the "real Jesus" might be different to his portrayal in the canonical Gospels. So began an avalanche of attempts to recover the so-called "historical Jesus." At the turn of the twentieth century Albert Schweitzer showed up many of these as laughable, and added his own account of the "real" Jesus. From the beginning of the nineteenth century techniques for the study of ancient writings were applied to the Bible, and new techniques are still being invented. Some of them can be helpful; in the wrong hands some are poisonous to faith.

In Germany, where many state-funded universities have faculties of theology, there was a movement to make the study of theology a scientific discipline. This gave rise to "the historical critical method," which soon established itself in Germany and elsewhere as the proper scientific approach to study of the Bible.

The Historical Critical Method

It was believed that only by uncovering the historical background of the various scriptural writings could their true meaning be seen. However, this carried with it a problem: the normal rules of historical study do not allow God or the supernatural to be considered as part of the chain of cause and effect. This is legitimate for the study of most science and history, because in nature and history God operates at a different level to what we call the natural. For example, we may believe that God led the Allies to victory in the war against Nazism, but a historian will not expect to find points when he "interfered" with the course of things. Jesus

---

1. Reimarus, *Fragments*.

explained that not even a sparrow falls to the ground without the decision of God, how much more the outcome of a global war! The sovereign God oversees everything, but not normally by upsetting the regularities he himself has established. However, in the case of Jesus and in much of the Bible's history we find God doing just that; miracles are an integral part of the story. Where historical criticism disallowed this as an axiom of method, it is not surprising that it came to anti-Christian, sometimes atheistic, conclusions. A good example is Albert Schweitzer. He did not regard miracles to be a possibility, so he overlooked the very evidence Jesus gave for the presence of the kingdom, and ignored the resurrection. According to Schweitzer, Jesus regarded the kingdom as entirely future and set out to achieve it. He followed his belief in the kingdom of God to the bitter end, but discovered on the cross that God was not going to intervene. In his final cry, "My God, my God, why have you forsaken me?" he admitted his mistake. His hope for the promised kingdom proved false. Though Jesus was mistaken, Schweitzer saw him as a hero, who by his "discovery" laid the foundation of the secular world. Since Schweitzer had no place for miracle or resurrection, his conclusion followed surely on his original premise.

What then are we to make of historical criticism? Eta Linnemann, a student of the leading New Testament scholar of the German world in the mid-twentieth century (Rudolf Bultmann), researched and wrote within that world, but later renounced the method as atheistic and destructive. She was responding to the unbelieving scholarship in her circle, but historical criticism has come to mean different things to different people and has been embraced and used as much by believers as by others. As soon as someone "discovers" that some part of the biblical history did not happen and launches an attack on Christian faith, other scholars join in the fray, and are often able to find fault in the critic's thesis. It is difficult to see how Christian scholars can do other than employ the same method as their opponents. Careful historical study, albeit without its atheistic or deistic underpinnings, seems to me essential to a historical faith in a world where its claims are always controversial. It is noteworthy that more than two hundred years of critical attacks on the historical basis of Christianity have not succeeded in their aim. Careful historical study, while it cannot "prove" Christianity, has certainly disproved many of the claims against it. Furthermore, the positive results of historical investigation have brought to light dimensions of the New Testament that are otherwise lost to us.

Textual Criticism

"Text criticism" seeks to establish what was written by the original author. It is an essential handmaid to exegesis and historical criticism, and deserves the "scientific" label. With many thousands of ancient manuscripts of all or parts of the New Testament, most containing some scribal errors, this is an essential foundation discipline for which we all have much to be grateful. Not that any text fails to convey the overall message of the New Testament, but it is good to know how reliably they have come down to us. Thanks to the work of many text critics we can be confident that the current Greek New Testament along with its critical apparatus gives us the words of the original New Testament writers with a very high degree of accuracy.[2] Variations in different manuscripts are mostly small and those that are not can readily be accounted for.

Source Criticism

"Source criticism" tries to identify the sources, written and oral, that underlie writings like the Gospels. Historical criticism assumed (falsely) that whichever Gospel came first would be superior historically to the others. Each of the Gospels comes from within the memory period of some of the first witnesses, so there is every reason to think they all contain valuable information.

Nevertheless, to know which was written first, and who copied whom, assists with exegesis and any attempt at a history of early Christianity. The results of source criticism are tentative; my own work followed what is still widely accepted as most probable, that Mark wrote first, and was used by Matthew and Luke, both of whom also used a now-lost document conveniently labelled "Q" ("*Quelle*" is German for source). Luke also used other sources, written and oral. His material additional to Mark and Q is commonly labelled "L." Many think he employed Mark as a framework, because of its authority as essentially Peter's Gospel. Acts has Luke coming with Paul to Jerusalem about AD 58, and departing with him to Rome in AD 60. He had two years to collect additional material for his Gospel and Acts. Some of it must have been in the form of

---

2. Revision of the text of the New Testament on the basis of ancient manuscripts is an ongoing enterprise. The Bible Society's *Greek New Testament* (edited by Kurt Aland and others) is up to its fifth revised edition, published in Stuttgart in 2014.

"verbatims" of participants in the "Jesus affair"; in Luke 1:1–4 he writes of others who had attempted written accounts.

Form Criticism

"Form criticism" took its rise from the realization that Jesus' teaching and the story of his life were preached before they were ever written down. The separate "pearls" (sayings, miracle stories) which make up Mark's Gospel look like they were originally preached by early Christian evangelists and teachers. This much can be freely admitted, but the conclusion that was frequently drawn, that they were *creations* of the early church, has always seemed to me to be silly. To believe that the first Christians, who worshipped and adored Jesus, had no interest in his actual life story, and in a matter of thirty years had so overlaid his teachings with their own that what we see in the Gospels is not him, but them—well, that is a theory which to me beggars belief, and it has hardly stood the test of time.

Redaction Criticism

Form criticism was in its heyday when I did my first studies in theology. It was a great relief when redaction criticism eclipsed it and focused attention on the message of the individual evangelists. It is their finished works which we have received from the early church as canonical Scripture, and to study their total message matters more than quarrying them for primitive material. Although at its beginning redaction criticism of the third Gospel tended to focus on the ways Luke had altered his sources (Mark and Q), scholars soon saw the illogicality of this. Luke's message is to be seen just as much in what he did *not* change as in what he did— and in the way he has arranged his material, and in his emphases and major and minor themes, and, of course, in the way the Gospel coheres with Acts. Some now prefer to speak of "composition criticism." This is a more mature version of redaction criticism (or redaction criticism is an incomplete version of composition criticism). Luke-Acts is a rich field for redaction critical work, as is evidenced by the many studies that have appeared in recent decades. I think it is here to stay and will outlast even the current interest in narrative criticism. It is a useful tool for uncovering the particular theological interest of the individual evangelists.

Narrative Criticism

"Narrative criticism" pays attention to the way the Gospels and Acts are structured as stories. That the Bible contains much narrative is obvious, yet sometimes the narrative is not taken with full seriousness. The story is seen as a veil for general life-truths or as a mine for timeless theological principles. If this were the author's intention, one wonders why he did not simply state those truths in the manner we find in many works of systematic theology. Thus the "rediscovery" of the importance of biblical narrative is a welcome development. Christianity is its story. Preaching which overlooks this goes astray.

However, stories are told for different reasons, and it is important to pay attention to the *purpose* of the Gospel narratives. An author may write purely to entertain, another to create a fictional representation of life. Luke's prefaces make clear his desire to relate a matter of great significance that happened in the recent past. He is interested in facts and their meaning. Richard Pervo thinks he wrote Acts to entertain.[3] New Testament documents were designed to be read out loud to gatherings of people, so it is not surprising that an author will pay some attention to telling the story as interestingly as he can—without necessarily entailing any departure from truth. Luke makes it clear at the outset that he is committed to truth as well as providing an orderly (well-structured) narrative.

We need also to exercise caution using tools developed for the analysis of fictional writings when reading history—or these strange writings we call Gospels, that speak of a real past. Narrative critics are often quick to insist that the historicity of narratives is not their concern. But if the author intended to relate events that happened, as was the stated aim of Luke, reading the story as though it were fiction must distort its meaning.

The author of a novel or short story is a "creator," in full control of his or her story. Authors can do what they like with setting, characters, plot, and point of view. Writers of nonfiction are constrained by an external reality. With the Gospels and Acts, as with most history, there are many details that are neither followed up nor explained. They are there because they happened. There is a real history which the evangelist is drawing on, but is never able to represent fully, which inevitably leaves loose ends. The Gospels are full of these loose ends, which may be important for what they reveal, though they actually distract from the

---

3. Pervo, *Profit with Delight*.

narrative's plot. Nowhere is this more obvious than in the "central section" of Luke's Gospel (chapters 9–19), which is mostly a collection of Jesus' teaching in the contrived setting of his last journey to Jerusalem. Narrative analysis is ineffective here. Luke's intention is to teach, mostly about Christian living. The preacher, like the interpreter, must give heed to the nature of the material.

Rhetorical Criticism

When we move beyond the "methods" we have already discussed there are a number of "angles" or "interests" an interpreter may use with a text. Rhetoric and sociology are two. Rhetorical criticism recognizes the importance of rhetoric and rhetorical training in the Greco-Roman world. Learning to write and deliver speeches in various settings was an important part of a classical education. A convincing speech had to contain a convincing argument. None of our New Testament documents are speeches, but they do present arguments, and it would not be surprising to find correspondences with contemporary rhetorical principles. However, it is debatable how much this recognition helps us in our task of interpretation. We can recognize and analyze an argument quite well without reference to classical rhetorical training. C. J. Classen[4] points out that one of the basic rules of speech-making was to disguise the fact that you were following rules; this hardly detracted from the argument being presented!

Social-Scientific Criticism

The current interest in sociology is reflected in the way the New Testament is now being studied. Formerly, history writing was primarily about kings and queens, the rise and fall of governments, wars, generals, and other great people. Today there is interest in general populations and conditions of the times. Social-scientific criticism tries to illuminate biblical writings from current theories about how societies function. It is of interest to the sociologist to see to what extent the events of the past related in the Gospels and Acts correspond to modern theories. However, whether this helps with interpretation is doubtful. To my mind, the degree to which Mediterranean communities have been influenced by

---

4. Classen, *Rhetorical Criticism*.

fifteen hundred years of Islam, and sociological thinking by Marxism makes this a problematic discipline for understanding the New Testament. It is a different matter with historical sociology.

Socio-Historical Criticism

Attempts to better understand social conditions in New Testament times are to be welcomed, so long as they are firmly grounded on the literary and archaeological evidence from the period. Preachers want, as much as possible, to bring to life the passages they are explaining. Socio-rhetorical analysis is actually another facet of historical criticism, paying special attention to the way ordinary people in New Testament times lived and thought.

Straightforward Exegesis

The various tools of criticism should never eclipse plain exegesis. They can give false results when they do. By plain exegesis I mean paying attention to the meaning of words, the grammar which connects them, the author's structure, and the flow of thought (or argument) which emerge—all in the immediate and wider context of the writing we are considering. This is how we understand any writing, and should be the main task of the preacher. What is this passage about, and what does it say about what it is about? These are the questions we should be asking. In the present study I was seeking Luke's message and meaning. To achieve this, I needed to attend to the whole of the Gospel and to Acts. In some cases comparison was needed with other books of the New and Old Testaments and with contemporary ancient literature. The goal was a fuller understanding of Luke's message.

With regard to preaching, William Taylor puts it like this:

> If preaching is to carry real pastoral weight then the preacher must follow the structure and the organisation of ideas of the original author as they are applied for his original pastoral purpose within the book that is being studied. The biblical authors are, after all, the church's primary theologians. They have organized their theology in order to drive home major pastoral goals. The key to what I call "grown up" preaching or "weighty" preaching is to understand the original purpose of the author,

within its biblical context, and why the author has deployed the particular theological points for that particular goal within that particular book. Insofar as a preacher fails to grasp the big issue that the original author is addressing and why he has lined up his theology to drive that point, so far will the preacher's sermon lack credibility. Insofar as the preacher has understood the author's original aim, and how his theology drives that application, so far will the preacher's sermon carry weight.

PRESUPPOSITIONS AND METHOD

The Poor and Their Possessions fits broadly into the genre of redactional critical studies and generally proceeds with respect for the historical critical method. But there is more to say on the question of method (or "methodology," as aspiring scholars like to call it). Many of the analytical tools mentioned above became useful to me at one point or another in my study; my approach was eclectic. I read all I could on every relevant passage of Luke and Acts and noted anything that was illuminating, whatever its method. I was forever following up references in one author's work to another; the trails were often fruitful.

I came to the subject of wealth and poverty with a measure of fear. Having grown up with a businessman father in a middle-class home in an affluent country, I doubted my ability to be impartial. I wondered what I would do if I came to conclusions about Jesus' teaching which I considered impractical or impossible. I knew people who were deeply troubled by aspects of the Gospels. One man I knew took his life worrying about the rich ruler and what was required of him. I decided the best way to proceed was first to identify all the passages in Luke and Acts which touched on the theme of wealth, poverty, and the poor and rich. Second, I would make a detailed study of each of these in isolation from the others. I feared that if I carried the results of one into the next and the next, any mistakes or biases would magnify themselves. Only when I had done all these preliminary studies did I inquire into the relationship between them. Thus it was only in the last year of my studies that any "thesis" began to emerge, and as the reader will see, it was actually a number of *theses*. Not all the material belongs to one topic.

The dissertation is much as it was in 1978, and then published in 1982. To help non-specialist readers I have provided a translation of the foreign language quotations. To assist smooth reading, I have also removed as many references as possible to footnotes. An appendix reviews some of the important studies that have emerged since my own.

Chapter 1

Questions and Procedures

1.1 THE PROBLEM

We begin our study of possessions and the poor in Luke-Acts by considering briefly the past one hundred years' scholarly attention to these themes.

1.1.1 The Question of Origin

In the Jowett Lectures for 1906 F. C. Burkitt made the following statement: "It appears to me that the two tendencies which are really characteristic of the writings of S. Luke are a tendency towards voluntary poverty and a tendency towards asceticism. Neither of these ideals, as I understand the matter, belonged by nature and choice to the earliest form of the Christian movement."[1]

It is understandable that in the late nineteenth and early twentieth centuries discussion of this alleged *Tendenz* should have concentrated on the question of its source. Some, like Burkitt, saw it as a tendency of Luke

---

1. Burkitt, *Gospel History*, 210.

himself,[2] others attributed it to one of his sources,[3] and some insisted that it went back to Jesus himself.[4]

It can hardly be said that the source question has ever been finally settled. All three solutions continue to be canvassed. It may be that a concern with possessions and the poor was shared by Jesus, and the early Palestinian church, and by Luke. In any case, the sheer quantity of material that Luke has preserved on these subjects makes it impossible to avoid the conclusion that he has a special interest in this area.[5]

Many scholars, however, have wanted to question the appropriateness of speaking of an ascetic or Ebionite tendency in Luke.[6] They are able to point to much which indicates a non-ascetic outlook, and many indications of interest in, and favor towards, the well-to-do. In fact, it was the existence of this contrary picture which formed the most convincing argument for attributing Luke's "Ebionism" to a source.[7]

This allows us to formulate an important question, which it is hoped the present study will resolve: How is it possible to reconcile the existence in Luke-Acts of two apparently contradictory pictures? For on the one hand there is material which appears to glorify poverty, condemn the rich, and demand the renunciation of all possessions, but on the other, the well-to-do are shown receiving favor from Jesus, and in Acts the Christian movement is portrayed making its way among socially and economically advantaged people. The modern emphasis on the active role of the evangelist as selector and editor of his material forbids our concluding—at least without further serious inquiry—that Luke has simply piled up material without regard to its self-consistency.

---

2. Campbell, "Its Ebionite Tendency."

3. Keim, *Jesus of Nazara*, 101–03; Feine, "Texte der Bergpredigt bei Matthäus und Lukas," 15–16; *Vorkanonische Überlieferung*, 140–45; Feine, *Theologie*, 524; Behm, "Kommunismus und Urchristentum," 286–87; Hauck, *Stellung des Urchristentums zu Arbeit und Geld*, 82–83; Hauck, *Lukas*, 205–06; Rezevskis, "Makarismen," 164–65; Schoeps, *Jewish Christianity*, 102.

4. Pfleiderer, *Primitive Christianity*, 294; Goguel, "Luke and Mark," 4; Percy, *Botschaft Jesu*, 89–106.

5. Approximately 27 percent of the approximately six hundred verses of teaching material in the Gospel (Luke 3–22) relates to this theme. To this should be added Luke 1:46–55, 19:1–10; Acts 2:42–47, 4:32–5:11.

6. Plummer, *Luke*, xxv–xxvi; Koch, "Wertung des Besitzes in Lukasevangelium," 151–69.

7. See Behm, "Kommunismus und Urchristentum," 286–87.

Our method, then, cannot be to play off one lot of material against another. Each piece must be considered in its own light for what it says in the total context of Luke-Acts. Only then will it be possible to say Luke does, or does not, have a consistent outlook.

1.1.2 The Question of Destination

If the early part of this century was dominated by the question of the source of Luke's possessions theme, the time since then has been increasingly concerned with the question of its destination. The rise of redaction criticism has concentrated attention on the evangelist as a creative theologian writing with certain definite objectives to a particular group of readers. The objectives of the evangelist are closely related to the problem situation of his readers. Once again, the apparent diversity of outlook within Luke-Acts has led to diametrically opposite approaches.

Despite the observations of influential scholars that the quantity of teaching in Luke on the use of possessions implies a greater interest in the rich than the poor,[8] the dominant view continues to see Luke as the "evangelist of the poor," addressing a message of hope and encouragement to the downtrodden of the earth. A second question therefore suggests itself: For whom did Luke write? For rich, for poor, or for both?

Having formulated questions relating to the self-consistency of Luke's material, and to its *raison d'être*, we will now look briefly at the more important studies which have appeared recently on the question of the poor and possessions in Luke-Acts.

1.1.3 Hans-Joachim Degenhardt, *Lukas—Evangelist der Armen* (1965)

The title of this work is deceptive, for Degenhardt gives scant attention to the question of the poor. His study is devoted rather to the themes of renunciation and possessions. The tension between the demand for renunciation and the material which presupposes an ongoing relationship to

---

8. Zahn, *Introduction*, 74; Cadbury, *Making of Luke-Acts*, 260–63. This position has been revived recently by Karris, "Lukan Sitz-im-Leben," 219–33. He thinks Luke wrote to a church with rich and poor members, chiefly to address the anxiety of the rich over whether their wealth precluded their being genuine Christians. He thinks Luke's approach is to attack their attitude to the poor and their belief that riches were a sign of God's favor.

possessions is neatly solved by referring these teachings to two separate groups. Renunciation is demanded only of office-holders in the church (missionaries, evangelists, teachers, etc.): the rank and file of the church may continue with their possessions. Luke indicates this by supplying for each part of Jesus' teaching a key to its application in the form of a superscription directing it to "disciples" (μαθηταί: *mathētai*); or "people" (λαός: *laos*), "crowd" (ὄχλος: *ochlos*) or "multitude" (πλῆθος: *plethos*). Degenhardt thinks Jesus demanded renunciation of possessions only of his band of traveling companions (*mathētai*). By directing such demands to *disciples*, Luke indicates that they apply to the "professional" ministry of the church of his day. Teaching for the wider membership of the church is directed to the *laos*, etc. The situation of the church he addresses is best expressed in Degenhardt's words:

> The enthusiastic spirit of the first generation seems to be past and the attempt of the office-bearers to establish themselves comfortably in this world has become an acute danger. Luke wants to confront this and to encourage full commitment and dedication in the service of the gospel.[9]

But is Luke-Acts really addressed primarily to the leadership of the church, as Degenhardt implies?[10] The prologue certainly does not give this impression. One would hardly set out to answer the problems of church leaders with a Gospel.[11]

The besetting weakness of Degenhadt's work, which inevitably leads to the above conclusion, is his seeing *disciples* and *people* as figures for church leaders and ordinary Christians respectively. Later, it will be shown that *mathētai* (μαθηταί) in Luke denotes a wider group than the semi-professional band that followed Jesus on the road, and that there is a

---

9. "Die enthusiastische Begeisterung der ersten Generation scheint voibei zu sein und die Versuchung der Amtsträge, sich in dieser Welt behaglich einzurichten, ist eine acute Gefahr geworden. Ihr will Lukas entgegentreten und zu vollem Einsatz und zur Ganzhingabe im Dienst des Evangeliums ermuntern." Degenhardt, *Evangelist der Armen*, 216.

10. Luke 16:1-9, for example, is directed to μαθηταί, though in Degenhardt's opinion it is part of a series of ethical preconditions for attaining salvation (therefore hardly appropriate only to leaders). To solve this dilemma he calls the whole section "ein 'ethisches Kompendium', dass dem christlichen Amtsträger für seine ethische Unterweisung Material in die Hand gibt (an 'ethical collection' which gives the Christian office-holder material for his use.)" Degenhardt, *Evangelist der Armen*, 113.

11. For a more realistic appraisal of the general purpose of the Gospels see Moule, "Intention of the Evangelists," 165-79.

natural continuity between the disciples of the Gospel and the Christians in Acts (whom Luke calls disciples).[12] For all this, Degenhardt's attention to audiences as an important clue to Luke's understanding and application of the gospel material is valid, and I have made extensive use of this insight in the present study.

1.1.4 Jacques Dupont, *Les béatitudes*, Vol. III (1973) 17–206

Dupont devotes a large section of the third part of his three-volume work on the beatitudes to a consideration of Luke's redaction of the beatitudes in the light of the rest of his material on wealth and poverty. He argues that the beatitudes and woes envisage two quite distinct groups, the persecuted church of Luke's day and the persecuting Jewish unbelievers.[13] Luke writes to encourage poor and persecuted Christians. When Dupont comes to consider the woes in relation to the rest of Luke's teaching on riches, he extends this primary thesis to include Luke's condemnation of wealth as such. The wealthy receive their consolation now, and will have nothing in the age to come; they are in bondage to the god "Mammon." Nevertheless, he reasons, the woes against the rich cannot be read without taking into consideration the emphasis Luke places on charity as the way in which the rich may ensure that they are, after all, received at death into eternal bliss.

Much of Dupont's argumentation and exegesis is searching and cogent but his overall thesis entails some glaring difficulties. If, as he claims, Luke is writing to encourage a poor and persecuted church, and the woes are directed against complete outsiders, why is such attention given throughout Luke-Acts to the dangers of wealth and to its proper use? Why is there no expansion of the poverty theme such as we might expect if it is the problems of the poor he addresses? Dupont's thesis also fails to account for the gentile orientation of Luke-Acts. Would gentile Christians have faced persecution from the synagogue?[14]

---

12. Further, see Degenhardt's thesis on pages 153–54, below.
13. According to Dupont, *Béatitudes*, III.299–342, the woes were Luke's creation.
14. Further to Dupont's thesis see pages 35–36, 93–96, below.

1.1.5 Walter Schmithals, "Lukas—Evangelist der Armen" (1975)

Schmithals also defines the problem in terms of the apparent internal contradiction:

> ... that Luke emphasizes the danger of riches for faith, and wants, on the one hand, to encourage renunciation of possessions for the sake of confession of Christ, while on the other he calls for responsible use of possessions, for giving alms and for feeding the needy, which has as its presupposition possessions and striving for possessions.[15]

He reasons from the Beatitudes that the solution to this contradiction lies in the fact that Luke addresses a persecuted community in which Christians had to be prepared for the loss of all (family, possessions, etc.) if they were to confess Jesus. The demand for renunciation is to be understood, therefore, as the requirement for *readiness* to surrender all. Even the demand for radical charity is explained from the persecuted state of the brotherhood, which made the retention of possessions doubtful. Those who gave to the needy would find goodwill and help when it came their turn to suffer. This constituted a better security than riches.[16]

Thus, in Schmithals's view Luke's teaching on possessions is strictly conditioned by the situation he faces and has limited application outside the persecuted community:

> In an extreme situation—the little flock suffers menacing persecution—he commends, relative to this situation, behavior as radical as it was realistic, which, however, apart from the situation presupposed, ceases to be practical, and therefore cannot be timelessly imitated.[17]

---

15. "... dass Lukas einerseits die Gefahren des Reichtums für den Glauben unterstreicht und zum Besitzverzicht um des Christusbekenntnisses willen ermuntert, andererseits zum verantwortlichen Umgang mit dem Besitz, zum Almosengeben und zum Speisen Bedürftiger auffordert, was Besitz und Besitzstreben gerade zur Voraussetzung hat." Schmithals, "Lukas—Evangelist der Armen," 164.

16. He hardly substantiates this connection. In fact, Luke never grounds the unreliability of possessions on the likelihood of losing them through persecution.

17. "In einer extremen Situation—die kleine Herde leidet unter bedrohlicher Verfolgung—fordert er ein dieser Situation angemessenes, ebenso radikales wie realistisches Verhalten, das aber abgesehen von der vorausgesetzten Situation aufhört, realistisch zu sein, und deshalb nicht zeitlos imitiert werden kann." Schmithals, "Lukas—Evangelist der Armen," 165.

One frequently meets with the suggestion that Luke is addressing a persecuted community,[18] and this is understandable when it is recalled how much of Luke-Acts touches, in one way or another, upon the theme of suffering and persecution. However, the mere presence of such material does not decide the question of whether Luke's community was currently under persecution. One can easily point to material that seems to indicate a quite different background.[19] Even more telling are passages where Luke has toned down or erased references to persecution in Mark,[20] and where he has added to Mark's apocalyptic discourse a warning against surfeiting, drunkenness, and cares.[21] It is also suggestive that in Paul's warning to the Ephesian elders of future troubles there is no mention of persecution, but only of heresy, internal disorder, and greed.[22] I am skeptical, therefore, as to whether Schmithals has provided a defensible solution to the problem he formulates.

1.1.6 Luke Timothy Johnson, "The Literary Function of Possessions in Luke-Acts" (1977)

Johnson declines to enter into historical questions and decides to treat Luke-Acts as a "story" whose main theme is the appearance of the prophet like Moses and his "prophetic" successors (the apostles) to divide Israel. The outcome of the story is the rejection of Israel's leadership and its replacement by the twelve apostles. The poor and possessions have symbolic roles in relation to the main lines of the story. The poor are the outcasts; the prophet comes to them and they receive him. The rich are those who are accepted by men; they reject the word of the prophet

---

18. Argued by Schütz, *Leidende Christus*, 11–20; Schmithals, "Lukas—Evangelist der Armen."

19. Luke 12:45-46; 17:26-37.

20. Compare Luke 8:13 with Mark 4:17, and Luke 18:29-30 with Mark 10:30. Schmithals, "Lukas—Evangelist der Armen," 161–62, uses the reference to διωγμῶν (persecutions) in Mark 10:30 to establish that persecution lies in the background of Luke's understanding of the rich ruler story! Note, too, the absence from Luke of the story of John's martyrdom (Mark 6:17-29).

21. Luke 21:34-36. Note also Luke's addition of ἐν ὑπομονῇ (with patience) in Luke 8:15. *Bearing fruit* with *patience* betokens more a situation of declining enthusiasm than of persecution.

22. Acts 20:29-35.

and are rejected. In short, the poor and the rich are the people and their rejected rulers.[23]

Possessions for Luke are "a primary symbol of human existence, an immediate exteriorization of and manifestation of the self."[24] Accordingly, they indicate a person's response to, or rejection of, the prophet. Acceptance of Jesus is exteriorized in renunciation, rejection by clinging to possessions. Possessions also have a symbolic role with respect to human relationships. Unity is shown by sharing, alienation by each having his own.[25] Having disposal of another's possessions represents having personal authority over him.

Putting these ideas to work, Johnson reaches some interesting conclusions: Judas's field represents his rejection of apostolic office;[26] the sharing of possessions in the early church is Luke's way of representing their unity;[27] the laying of possessions at the apostles' feet is a way of representing their spiritual authority;[28] the charitable journey of Paul and Barnabas from Antioch to Jerusalem is to establish Paul's submission to the Jerusalem apostles.[29]

Johnson has made a bold and imaginative attempt to unify the poor-possessions theme in Luke-Acts. There is, however, an obvious danger of artificiality. It is true that possessions can exteriorize attitudes and relationships, but whether this means they have become a fixed symbol, which Luke has systematically carried through his whole work, is doubtful. Johnson has been misled here by what is the chief weakness of his thesis, the decision to treat as *"story"* that which for Luke is much more. Because Luke gives a partial account of things external to his own imagination, reference outside his "story" will be required for the full elucidation of his categories. Nevertheless, Johnson's literary study makes a valuable contribution, and uncovers relationships which a more "historical" study may elucidate and refine.[30]

---

23. Compare the observations of Hauck and Kasch in *TDNT* VI.328.
24. Johnson, "The Literary Function of Possessions in Luke-Acts," 221.
25. Johnson, "The Literary Function of Possessions in Luke-Acts," 20.
26. Johnson, "The Literary Function of Possessions in Luke-Acts," 174.
27. Johnson, "The Literary Function of Possessions in Luke-Acts," 183.
28. Johnson, "The Literary Function of Possessions in Luke-Acts," 200.
29. Johnson, "The Literary Function of Possessions in Luke-Acts," 217.
30. Johnson has a stimulating analysis of the parable of the Prodigal Son along these lines (Johnson, "The Literary Function of Possessions in Luke-Acts," 159).

1.2 PURPOSE AND PLAN OF THIS STUDY

The foregoing sketch of previous work relating to the theme of the poor and possessions has raised the question of whether there is any consistency in the outlook of Luke, and the question of the destination and purpose of the large amount of material he has included on these subjects. Both questions, however, are only handmaidens to the fundamental concern of this study to discover what it is that Luke is saying with this material. The problem besetting most studies of the theme is that the quantity of material limits the attention that is given to the component pericopes.[31] Degenhardt's work is by far the most detailed and comprehensive in this respect, but he gives such attention to isolating the original teaching of Jesus that his time for Luke is necessarily curtailed.[32] It is, of course, legitimate and useful to have attempted a comparison of Luke and Jesus, despite the inevitable hazards in reconstructing sources. Nevertheless, I have not sought to make such a distinction in this present study.

My aim has been to treat Luke-Acts as a whole as an expression of the theology and viewpoint of Luke. This has enabled a great deal more time and space to be devoted to detailed exegesis of the separate pieces of Luke's material. Perhaps, however, this approach requires some justification in the light of the usual redaction critical procedure of concentrating attention where the editor has altered his sources.

The problem with this method is that it fails to give sufficient attention to the main bulk of the evangelist's material. True, he did not create this material, and it bears the stamp of another mind and another situation. Nevertheless, the mere fact that he felt free to modify it to his own ends argues in favor of his being happy with what he has incorporated unmodified. This overstates the case somewhat since it is quite feasible that an evangelist might incorporate traditions, unaware that they present a view in tension with his own. However, when, as in the present case, we are dealing with an author who has made a special collection of material relating to certain themes, and when there are definite thought links between the components of this collection, there is a strong presumption in favor of his having understood and *intended* the meaning which each pericope conveys within the framework he has provided. It will be clear from this that I am viewing Luke, at least in reference to the individual

---

31 Johnson devotes more than half of his dissertation to an elucidation of the prophet theme, which barely touches the question of possessions.

32. He has no treatment of the story of Zacchaeus or the parable of the pounds.

stories, parables, etc. which related to his theme of possessions and the poor, less as an innovator who has quarried existing material to the ends of his own distinctive theology than as one who has understood and accepted the traditions which reached him and seeks to represent them and commend them to others. Their synthesis into an overall theme or themes, if such there be, will be his own achievement. However, even in transmitting traditional material he does introduce emphases and interpretations of his own, and for this reason I have employed the redaction critical method where I have judged it to be applicable. Following Degenhardt I have given special attention to audience and setting, since Luke has been so assiduous in providing them. However, I have not thought it useful to enter into comparison of Luke with sources which cannot be reconstructed without an appreciable measure of uncertainty.

A second problem with studies of the possessions theme in Luke-Acts is an over-readiness to lump the material together under inappropriate classifications. There is a common tendency to treat all Luke's material on possessions and the poor as the expression of a single theme. A major concern of this study has been to make an appropriate classification of the material and to discern which themes are operative in the mind of Luke as he uses it. To achieve this my method was to study each passage as much as possible in isolation from the others to determine its thrust purely in relation to itself and its literary context. Only at a later stage did I permit the different units to interact and link up. The result has been an arrangement of the material in four thematic categories which seem to me to be distinct, but also related.

Chapter 2, "The Poor and the Salvation of Israel," argues that in a number of key passages Luke uses "the poor" as a soteriological term characterizing Israel in her great need of salvation. Chapter 3, "Renunciation and Discipleship," examines passages which deal with the renunciation of possessions and concludes that they are not intended to teach a general ethic of renunciation, but to inculcate a certain view of "limitless" discipleship. Chapter 4, "Possessions and the Christian Life," gathers materials directly relevant to the Christian's ongoing attitude to and use of possessions and seeks to discern the theological presuppositions of this teaching. Chapter 5, "Fellowship and the Church," examines the meaning of and motive behind Luke's description of the early community's activities with respect to possessions, and explores its relationship to the outlook of the Gospel. In the course of the whole study it will appear that the poor-possessions material in Luke is not self-contradictory, and valuable light will be thrown on its destination and purpose.

Insofar as it is I, not Luke, who has made this classification, the objection may be raised that I am imposing it on Luke. My defense would be that I have sought the classification from the material, and that it does seem to represent four foci of Luke's thinking. I trust it will aid a clearer apprehension of the evangelist's message.

Chapter 2

The Poor and the Salvation of Israel

2.1 INTRODUCTION

Luke's interest in the poor is widely noted. Some, as we have seen, attribute this to his Ebionite tendencies; i.e., they think Luke holds a poverty ideal. Most others tend to group the poor with the tax collectors and sinners, women and children, Samaritans and gentiles, for whom Luke seemed to have such affection, and attribute his interest either to a natural sympathy for all underprivileged groups or to his "universalism."

It is worth inquiring, however, whether these latter explanations are sufficient to account for the centrality Luke gives to the poor in his portrayal of Jesus' mission. Jesus has been anointed to "evangelize" the poor.[1] Does Luke mean that *even* the poor, or that the poor *too*, or *only* the poor are evangelized? Or is there something which marks them out from other underprivileged groups? That there may be something special about them is suggested by their reappearance in Luke 6:20 and 7:22.

It is a matter of some importance, therefore, to determine at the outset whom Luke means by "the poor" and why he has given them such prominence.

We will look first at some commonly-held views about the identity of the poor in Luke. Then I will present what I believe is the relevant background for a solution of the problem—in the Old Testament,

---

1. Luke 4:18.

intertestamental literature, Qumran, and the Rabbis—laying the groundwork for my thesis that Luke uses "the poor" as a characterization of Israel in her need of salvation,

Following this we will look closely at the imagery of the quotation from Isaiah 61:1–2 in Luke 4:18–19 to see how well such a view fits the Nazareth Sermon. The Magnificat (Luke 1:46–55) will confirm that we are thinking in the right direction, and we will finally apply our results to elucidating the Beatitudes and Woes. In this manner the basic thesis will be confirmed and refined, and its implications for the theology of Luke explored.

2.2 WHO ARE THE POOR?

Some see the poor as the pious, some as a particular social group. Some see them as those who have voluntarily abandoned their possessions, and others emphasize the condition of those afflicted with literal poverty. Still others see the poor in the light of the Old Testament, as the designated heirs of salvation. My own thesis, which builds out from this last position, is that "the poor" is a characterization of the nation of Israel.

2.2.1 The Poor Are the Pious

In an initial discussion of poor and rich, Martin Dibelius argues in his commentary on James (1921)[2] that by the time of Jesus "poor" had become a religious self-description for certain groups of "messianic pietists." He traces the development of this stream of piety from the Psalms through the Hasidim of the Maccabean period and the Pharisees of the Psalms of Solomon to the pious ʿammē haʾaretz,[3] or small landholders and craftsmen among whom Jesus was at home.

A further step is taken by W. Sattler,[4] who sees them as an organized party called the ʿanawīm (the humble). However, he adduces no positive evidence for the existence of such a party in New Testament times, but simply postulates it to fill a gap in the historical sources and to provide a

---

2. Dibelius, *James*, 39–42.
3. "People of the land."
4. Sattler, "Anawim," 1–15.

bridge from the Old Testament to the religion of Jesus. Nevertheless, his view has found some acceptance.[5]

Others, while not claiming the existence of a party, have followed Dibelius in thinking the term "poor" is virtually synonymous with "pious," though frequently with the qualification that such piety thrived chiefly among the literally poor.[6] Matthew's "poor in spirit" in 5:3 is then seen as a suitable rendering of Luke's "poor" in 6:20.

However, the foundation upon which this identification stands is far from firm. Even in the Psalms it is doubtful that "poor" can be treated as a synonym for "pious." Dibelius and Sattler lean heavily on the work of Alfred Rahlfs,[7] who argued that whereas ʿani (עָנִי) has the objective "secular" sense of being in a position of inferiority with respect to another,[8] ʿanaw (עָנָו) has the subjective religious sense "humble." Rahlfs isolated a group of eleven psalms which, he thought, came from a party of the late exilic and early restoration period. They called themselves the ʿanawim (עֲנָוִים), the purified remnant who had been humbled and converted through the experience of the exile.[9] Some scholars have preferred to think of a movement rather than a party,[10] but Rahlfs's general position that ʿanaw described a religious disposition (the meek, humble) rather than an objective state (the poor, afflicted, lowly) has won considerable acceptance and has found its way into the interpretation of the New Testament, as we have seen.

This position has been challenged, however, by Harris Birkeland,[11] who denies that any distinction can be drawn between ʿani and ʿanaw and finds no evidence for the use of ʿanawim as a party-designation.

---

5. Bultmann, *Synoptic Tradition*, 126n1; Isaacs, "Mary in the Lucan Infancy Narrative," 80–95; Brown, *Birth of the Messiah*, 350–55.

6. οἱ πτωχοὶ τῷ πνεύματι. Harnack, *What is Christianity?* 94–95; Kittel, *Palästinischen Spätjudentums*, 54; W. Manson, *Luke*, 64; T. W. Manson, *Sayings of Jesus*, 47; Geldenhuys, *Luke*, 216; Schniewind, *Matthäus*, 41; Morris, *Luke*, 126–27.

7. Rahlfs, *Psalmen*, 92.

8. Rahlfs, *Psalmen*, 73. On the meaning of עָנִי see also Birkeland, *ʿAni und ʿAnaw*, 8; Kuschke, "Arm und reich," 31–57, 49–50; Munch, "Bemerkungen," 13–26, 18–20.

9. For a recent exposition of this theory and its extrapolation into the NT see Gélin, *Poor of Yahweh*.

10. E.g., Baudissin, "Die alttestamentliche Religion und die Armen," 193–231, 219–20. Munch, "Bemerkungen," thinks of upper- and lower-class conflict. For a summary of the debate see Van der Ploeg, "Pauvres," 236–70, 237–42.

11. Birkeland, *ʿAni und ʿAnaw*. Also Percy, *Botschaft*, 47–63.

Arguments from context aside, the subjective interpretation of ʿanawim has in its favor the meaning of ʿanawah (עֲנָוָה—humility) and the fact that in later Judaism the ʿanawim were sometimes understood as the humble.[12] On the other hand, although seven times in the Psalms ʿanaw is rendered as praus (πραΰς—meek), it is also rendered five times as penēs (πένης—poor), and once as ptōchos (πτωχός—poor). Outside the Psalms praeis is never used to translate ʿanawim.[13] Instead we find tapeinoi (ταπεινοί—lowly) three times[14] and ptōchos (poor) twice. In Isaiah 11:4, 29:19, 61:1, and Amos 2:7 ʿanawim occurs in parallel with words or ideas which show that an objective condition of abasement is meant.[15] Only in Zephaniah 2:3 might ʿanawim possibly be rendered as "humble."[16]

This suggests that ʿanawim normally signified those with an objectively inferior position, and, only by way of metaphorical extension, those of a humble disposition. It may be that the Septuagint translators spiritualized the poverty language in some of the Psalms.

Be that as it may, what is of most importance for the present study is the understanding of Luke and of the New Testament. If a self-conscious ʿanawim piety existed, and if they regarded themselves as the humble, it is surprising that they should be represented by ptōchoi in the New Testament. We would surely expect praeis (meek). The New Testament, therefore, does not assist us towards an identification of "poor" with "humble" or "pious." Neither does Qumran, for although the sect identified itself with the ʿanawim of Psalm 37:11, it lays claim to this scripture under the name ʾebiōnim (אביונים—poor).[17] This juxtaposition demonstrates that at Qumran, at least, ʿanawim was taken to mean "the poor" or "needy," not "the humble." That the sect referred to itself as the ʾebiōnim also suggests there was nothing especially attractive about the term ʿanawim in the first century.

---

12. See Lauterbach, *Mekilta de-Rabbi Ishmael*, II.273; *b. AZ* 20b. Rahlfs argues that the Massoretes distinguished ʿani and ʿanaw. See, e.g., the *Qere* reading Prov. 3:34.

13. Except for the *Ketibh* Job 24:4. Πραΰς renders ʿani in Zeph 3:12; Zech 9:9; Isa 26:6; Sir 10:14, though not in the Psalms. See Kuschke, "Arm und reich," 51–52.

14. Leivestad, "ΤΑΠΕΙΝΟΣ—ΤΑΠΕΙΝΟΦΡΩΝ," 36–47, argues that ταπεινός (tapeinos) normally denotes objective lowliness (*gering, elend*).

15. Cf. the *Qere* readings of Prov 14:21, 16:19; Isa 32:7; Amos 8:4.

16. Compare *Qere* Prov 3:34. The only singular occurrence of ʿanaw in the OT (Num 12:3) is probably a scribal corruption; Birkeland, *ʿAni und ʿAnaw*, 19; Bammel, "Πτωχός," 885–915, 888; Kuschke, "Arm und reich," 52.

17. 4QpPs37 1:8–10; cf. 2:9–12.

THE POOR AND THE SALVATION OF ISRAEL

Turning from specific words to the wider semantic field, one cannot deny that poverty language has a strong religious coloration in the Psalms. This, together with the frequency of reference to the poor in the Psalms, suggests the possibility of influence on the New Testament, so it will be useful at this point to consider what religious significance the poor did have in the Psalms.

'Ani, 'anaw, and 'ebiōn (אביון, ענו, עני) are used in the Psalms principally to describe the socially deprived, people in great need, and the nation Israel. In Israelite religion God was seen as the defender of those with an inferior social or economic position.[18] Poor or not, they were his people and enjoyed his protection. The king, as God's vice-regent, came thus to have a special responsibility for the poor.[19] This inevitably gave the poor a religious value even when they were seen in a purely social light, but their poverty was in no sense a virtue.

Because God is pledged to uphold the poor and the needy, who have no other defender, it is natural that a person in trouble should plead his poverty and need before God.[20] Therefore, poverty terminology in the Psalms comes to refer to a whole range of need and suffering in addition to literal poverty.[21] Persecution in particular leads the Psalmist to cry to God that he is poor and needy.[22] It is striking how many such Psalms are ascribed to David.[23] People familiar with these would be unlikely to understand such language automatically as referring to literal poverty. This does not mean, however, that "poor" had a religious meaning akin to "pious." It is a description of need. The religious dimension of this language lies in God's known character as a Savior who rescues those who are in need.[24] There is nothing positive about suffering except that it leads a person to call on God, who saves him from evil.

---

18. Ps 12:5; 113:7. Bolkestein, *Wohltätigkeit*, 19–21, 47, 180, shows that the concept was characteristic of Israel and Egypt but totally foreign to Greece and Rome.

19. See Ps 72. Further, van Leeuwen, *Le développement du sens social*, 212–14; Dupont, *Béatitudes*, II.53–90.

20. Ps 34:6, 86:1.

21. In Ps 88:16 a sick man calls himself 'ani; in 25:16 both enemies and sins contribute to the condition of the 'ani.

22. Ps 22:24, 35:10, 69:29, 33, 70:5, 109:16, 22, 140:12. The dominance of this idea led Munch, "Bemerkungen," 18–20, to think 'ani literally meant "oppressed" ("vergewaltigt").

23. Thirty-five of the sixty-nine uses of 'ani according to Gélin, *Poor of Yahweh*, 22.

24. Martin-Achard, "Yahwé et les 'anawim," 349–57, stresses the need of the 'anawim; their joy results from their distress coming to an end.

The third use of poverty terminology is to describe the nation Israel.[25] It is clear in Psalm 9 that it is Israel, over against the nations that oppress her, that is described as "poor."[26] In Psalm 68:10 the congregation which God saved from Egypt is called "the poor" (*'ani*).[27] It is also possible that many of the personal psalms, being seen as prayers of the king for salvation from his enemies, contain this national dimension.[28]

Thus, the dominant idea behind the poverty vocabulary of the Psalms is need,[29] most frequently the need which arises from the attacks of enemies, be they rich oppressors or enemies of the king or the enemies of the nation. The "poor" are saved in the Psalms not because "poor" or "pious" have any inner relation, but because only those in need have anything to be saved from.

Later literature presents us with much the same picture. The Psalms of Solomon have been quoted as evidence of the continuance of "the piety of the poor" among the early Pharisees,[30] but this can hardly be substantiated considering the few references to *ptōchoi* in these psalms compared with the constant repetition of the *hosioi* (holy ones). The Psalms of Solomon simply echo the Old Testament conviction that God is the refuge of the poor.[31] Psalms of Solomon 5 is a magnificent expression of the idea that God responds to human need: when a person is in distress they call to God and their need is met. In this case the psalmist's need is economic; he fears lest through necessity he be led to sin; he beseeches God for moderate means. There is no glorification of poverty in these psalms; it

---

25. See Baudissin, "Die alttestamentliche Religion und die Armen," 215, who includes Ps 72 in this category. Also Gélin, *Poor of Yahweh*, 35; Birkeland, *'Ani und 'Anaw*, 101; Dahl, *Volk Gottes*, 26.

26. See also Percy, *Botschaft*, 60. All three terms are used.

27. Further Ps 74:19, 21, 76:9, 149:4. Also perhaps 132:15, 147:6, and compare 102:17.

28. Cf. Frisch, *Jewish Philanthropy*, 15–16.

29. This is entirely in character with the Pentateuch, for, whereas van Leeuwen, *Le développement du sens social*, 25, defines the poor Israelite as the landless who must sell his labor to others, one gains the impression from Deut 15:7-11 that even a landed Israelite could be considered poor (*'ebion*, *'ani*) if he fell into financial need. This is certainly the case in the prophets where the poor are the small farmers being squeezed by the expansion of rich land-owners (van Leeuwen, *Le développement du sens social*, 71).

30. Dibelius, *James*, 40; Charles, *Apocrypha and Pseudepigrapha*, II.628-29; T. W. Manson, *Sayings of Jesus*, 47; cf. *TDNT* VI.896.

31. Ps. Sol. 15:1, 18:2.

is prayed that it will come as judgment upon the wicked!³² In Psalms of Solomon 16:13–15 it is seen as a chastisement for the righteous which can only be borne with the strength of God.

In Psalms of Solomon 10:6 the pious and the poor are in parallel not because the terms are synonymous or closely related, but because, having suffered the affliction of conquest and having bared their backs to chastisement, the pious have become "poor and needy" and thus specially qualified to receive God's help.

The argument for the identity of the poor and the pious is, therefore, misconceived. It mistakes the obvious religious significance of poverty in the Psalms for an ethical quality, whereas, in fact, it is God's character as the savior of those in real need which gives poverty (= need) this value. Luke shows that this is his understanding of the "poor" by grouping them with prisoners, the blind, the oppressed, the hungry, and the weeping.

2.2.2 The Poor as a Particular Social Grouping

H. L. Strack and Paul Billerbeck³³ identify "the poor" with the 'ammē ha'aretz (people of the land) of rabbinical literature³⁴ and note that this group consisted of more than just the economically poor; rich men were also numbered among them.³⁵ Their poverty consisted in the fact that they did not know or practice the law in the way the Pharisees did. The converse is that the rich are the Pharisees.³⁶ In a similar manner S. Agouridès sees the poor as those who do not belong to the established religious order, but to various sects looking for the fulfilment of the Old Testament promises to the poor. The rich are those who do belong to the establishment.³⁷

---

32. Ps. Sol. 4:6, 15, 12:4.

33. Billerbeck I.190.

34. See also Jeremias, *Theology*, 109–13; Frankemölle, "Makarismen," 52–75, 60. Batey, *Jesus and the Poor*, 2, 9–11.

35. This is important. If we are thinking of the 'amme ha-aretz we cannot think in terms of an economically deprived class. Many were poor, but many must have prospered, freed as they were from scruples over buying, selling, and tithing. M. Hor. 3:8 can conceive of the High Priest being an 'am ha-aretz. Further see Oppenheimer, 'Am Ha-aretz, 20–21.

36. See also Rienecker, *Lukas*, 172: "Die Pharisäer vertraten die Auffassung: wer ganz genau das Gesetz erfüllt, der ist reich bei Gott (The Pharisees represented the view: whoever fulfills the law completely is rich with God.)."

37. Agouridès, "La tradition des béatitudes," 9–27, 17–18.

Such views have gained wide acceptance though they are pure supposition. At this point I would simply make a few observations.

'Am ha'aretz[38] is a term we do not encounter in any form in the New Testament (or anywhere before the Mishnah) and it is questionable whether the unbridgeable gulf separating them from the *haberim* (comrades) of the Tannaitic and Amoraic periods can simply be read back into the New Testament. Alexander Guttmann thinks the separation did not occur until after AD 70, when the Sadducees, the common enemy of the Pharisees and 'am ha'aretz, were removed.[39] He points to Josephus's picture of the Pharisees as a party in contact with the common people.[40]

Joachim Jeremias calls the whole non-Pharisaic population of Jesus' time ("the masses") 'ammē ha'aretz,[41] despised and rejected by the Pharisees.[42] But this is an improbable reconstruction and assumes a continuity in the relationship between Pharisees and people in periods when the Pharisees were a minority sect and when they represented the only legitimate viewpoint and were in a position of "theocratic" authority over the whole nation. Adolf Büchler's study of the Galilean 'am ha'aretz confirms this.[43] The Galileans in the period when the temple was still standing were generally faithful in the payment of tithes. It was only in the later period that strong exhortations were necessary to ensure this. It is likely, then, that in the early period the 'ammē ha'aretz were a much smaller group. Perhaps the "sinners" of the Gospels were a closer equivalent.[44]

---

38. On the 'am ha-aretz see the appendix by Moore in *BC* I.439-45; Büchler, *Der galiläische 'Am-ha'Ares*; Zeitlin, "Am Haarez," 45-61; Oppenheimer, *'Am Ha-aretz*.

39. Guttmann, *Rabbinic Judaism*, 172-73.

40. Josephus, *War* 2.166: "The Pharisees are affectionate to each other and cultivate harmonious relations with the community." See also Oppenheimer, *'Am Ha-aretz*, 228-29.

41. Jeremias, *Jerusalem*, 259, 266-67.

42. As *JE*, I.484-85; Scroggs, "Earliest Communities," 1-23, 9-13.

43. Büchler, *'Der galiläische 'Am-ha'Ares*, esp. 31-32. He argues that the uncleanness of the 'am ha' aretz arose from the need to protect priestly offerings, and that the stringent laws on the defilement of the 'am ha' aretz which are usually associated with the time of Jesus, were not enacted until after AD 136 in Usha (212). Oppenheimer, *'Am Ha-aretz*, questions much of this (4-10), but agrees that the opposition to the 'am ha-aretz was especially prevalent in the Jabneh and Usha periods (114-117).

44. See also Dibelius, *James*, 41. He thinks Jesus came from another more scrupulous group (42). Derrett, *Jesus' Audience*, 61-65 sees the "sinners" as the often-wealthy collaborators with Roman-Hellenistic culture. Büchler's description of Rabbi Meir's 'ammē ha'aretz is almost the same (Büchler, *'Am-ha'Ares*, 190)

It is important to remember that *'am ha'aretz* was a term of abuse almost equivalent to "gentile."[45] Büchler points out that in Judea they were defined not in terms of non-payment of tithes, but of neglect of basic religious duties such as saying the *Shema'*.[46] I find it difficult, therefore, in the light of such things as the piety of Jesus' home and Peter's protestation about never having eaten anything unclean,[47] to accept the judgment of G. F. Moore that Jesus and his disciples would have been considered *'ammē ha'aretz* simply because of their neglect of hand-washing rituals.[48] Jesus was accepted as the guest of Pharisees, a thing forbidden if he was an *'am ha'aretz*, according to *M. Dem.* 2:3.

To see "the poor" as the *'ammē ha'aretz* is to opt for a metaphorical meaning of "poor" which is entirely conditioned by a Pharisaic viewpoint. But in a time when other parties existed, when the Pharisees, whatever their influence, were a minority, and when a large population of pious non-Pharisees practiced their traditional faith, paid their tithes, and made their pilgrimages to the temple, to think that all but the Pharisees were regarded as despised outcasts and regarded themselves so seems unrealistic.[49] The identification of "poor" with the *'ammē ha'aretz* must therefore be judged to be quite improbable.

Other scholars think rather of the literal poor: the economically deprived classes. Edwin Hatch thinks the *ptōchoi* are "the poor of an oppressed country, the peasantry or fellahin."[50] Albert Nolan comments, "Today some might refer to this section of the population as the lower classes; others would call them the oppressed."[51] Raymond Brown thinks Luke is writing to gentile churches, the majority of whose members were poor: "they [the beatitudes] concern the privileged role of the physically poor and needy in Jesus' evaluation of men."[52]

---

45. Moore, *Judaism*, I.321.

46. *b Ber.* 47b. Büchler, *'Am-ha'Ares*, 22–23.

47. Acts 10:14.

48. Moore, *BC*, I.445.

49. Sanders, *Paul and Palestinian Judaism*, 152–57, argues that the *'amme ha'aretz* were never regarded as cut off from Israel.

50. Hatch, *Essays*, 76.

51. Nolan, *Jesus before Christianity*, 21. This is the position taken by proponents of "liberation theology." See Cone, *God of the Oppressed*, 78–79; "Structures of Captivity," 44–47. Cf. Wrege, *Bergpredigt*, 12–15; Braun, *Radikalismus*, II.73.

52. Brown, "Beatitudes," 270 (265–71). See also Koch, "Wertung," 169. Weiss, *Schriften*, I.444–45, thinks Luke's "poor" theme arose from conflict between poor

There is need for caution here. Ideas about what constitutes poverty differ with time and place. In the Poor Law Commissioners' Report of 1834 poverty is defined as the state of one who, in order to obtain mere subsistence, is forced to have recourse to labor.[53] This definition is quoted seriously in an early-twentieth-century encyclopedia; its inappropriateness to modern conditions should warn us against unthinkingly reading our own definitions back into New Testament times.

Leaving to one side the special cases of the use of *ptōchoi* which we are presently considering, Luke gives the impression that the *ptōchos* was someone unable to live without charitable assistance: a poor widow with only one sixty-fourth of a denarius or a beggar at a rich man's gate.[54] He is the recipient of alms, on a level with the maimed, the lame, and the blind, who are unable to make any repayment for what they are given.[55]

This picture is consistent with what we find elsewhere in the New Testament.[56] There is nothing that would support an identification of the *ptōchoi* with the peasantry. This leads to an important observation which has been largely overlooked: in the New Testament the *ptōchoi* are regarded as a group apart from Jesus and his disciples.[57] The former are alms-takers, the latter are almsgivers.[58]

Thus, if we are to regard the *ptōchoi* of Luke 4:18, 6:20, and 7:22 as a particular social group, it is of the destitute we should think, and Jesus and at least some of his disciples do not belong to it.[59] It is improbable that Luke thought of Jesus' mission in such limited terms.

---

despised Christians and Pharisees.

53. *ERE* X.139.

54. Luke 21:2, 16:20–21.

55. Luke 14:13–14, 21. This is noted by Dupont, "Introduction aux Béatitudes," 97–108.

56. Jerusalem contained many Christian *ptōchoi* who needed outside support for their maintenance (Rom 15:26; Gal 2:10). In Jas 2:2 the *ptōchos* is dressed in filthy clothes (cf. Rev 3:17).

57. This is most strikingly illustrated in Mark 14:7 ESV: "For you always have the poor with you, and whenever you want, you can do good for them."

58. John 13:29. The support received by Jesus' party during their mission (Luke 8:3) is not alms: it is more akin to modern-day support of missionaries.

59. Jesus came from an artisan family. James and John were part of a family business employing labor. Theissen, *First Followers*, 33–34, is wrong to speak of the "social rootlessness" of Jesus and his disciples. Buchanan, "Jesus and the Upper Class," 195–209, goes beyond the evidence when he argues that Jesus may have been a rich person (a contractor employing carpenters) who voluntarily surrendered his wealth (taking

2.2.3 The Poor as Those Who Have Left All

Kurt Schubert understands "the poor" and "the poor in spirit" of the Sermon on the Mount against the background of the Essenes' contempt for wealth: "Jesus called those blessed to whom worldly goods were nothing."[60] Similarly Degenhardt thinks that in the beatitudes Luke is not praising the poor in general, but particularly those who have become so in order to be with Jesus.[61]

These possibilities will need to be considered further when we come to look at the beatitudes. For the present I would simply question Schubert's appeal to the Essenes. He thinks the Qumran sect called themselves the 'ebiōnim (poor; beggars) because they practiced community of possessions and were contemptuous of money.[62] There is nothing in the literature of the sect, however, which gives any basis for this explanation. Community of possessions need not mean poverty; for some it probably meant the end of poverty. H. J. Kandler points out that nowhere is the impression given that the new member gives up his possessions in order to be without property: "Just as infrequently does one find clues that the community saw in personal poverty and modesty an ascetic ideal to be striven for."[63] Though he himself then goes on to draw a connection between the sect's designation of itself as the 'ebiōnim and the new member's surrender of property, it is, as he admits, pure inference.[64]

The "mingling" of property is to be seen not in the light of an ascetic ideal, but in connection with the ritual purity of the community. Community

---

2 Cor 8:9 literally). However, his observations on the character of Jesus' teaching and friends are a useful corrective to the common idea that Jesus was penniless.

60. Schubert, "Sermon on the Mount," 122 (118-28). See also Ellis, *Luke*, 113.

61. Degenhardt, *Evangelist der Armen*, 51. Though he also says Luke is thinking of an economically and socially depressed group (50-51).

62. Cf. Thiering, "Qumran Asceticism," 431.

63. "Ebensowenig finden sich Anhaltspunkte dafür, dass die Gemeinschaft in persönlicher Armut und Anspruchslosigkeit ein erstrebenswertes asketisches Ideal sah." Kandler, "Armut," 205-06.

64. He is influenced by his understanding πτωχοὶ τῷ πνεύματι (poor of spirit) (1QM 14:7) as "freiwillig Arme" (voluntarily poor) (Kandler, "Armut," 179), i.e., those who are voluntarily poor (as Schubert). The preceding descriptions ("the discouraged heart," "the dumb," "feeble hands," "them whose knees stagger," "those whose back is bent") suggest that "faint-hearted" may be closer to the meaning (as Best, "Matthew 5:3," 255-58); but see Légasse, "Pauvres en esprit," 340-41. Cf. Dupont, "Les pauvres en esprit," 53-64; Degenhardt, *Evangelist der Armen*, 199-200; Flusser, "Poor in Spirit," 1-13, esp. 6.

members could deal with one another without fear of ritual defilement.[65] It may be true that the Qumran sect, like the Essenes spoken of by Philo and Josephus, lived a simple life, but we should hesitate before labelling this as poverty, since both Josephus and Philo tell us that they lived free from necessity.[66] I will return later to the question of why the sect called themselves 'ebiōnim.[67]

2.2.4 The Poor Understood in Terms of Their Poverty

A number of scholars focus attention on the actual condition of poverty as something which conditions people to virtue or makes them receptive to the message of the kingdom of God. Thus, Alfred Plummer says, "Actual poverty, sorrow, and hunger are declared to be blessed (as being opportunities for the exercise of internal virtue)."[68] But here one must question whether the blessedness of the poor in fact resides in their poverty; is not their blessedness rather that the appearance of the kingdom will *end* their poverty?[69] As G. B. Caird aptly comments: "It is only in the presence of a magnificent banquet that the hungry man is more blessed than the well-fed."[70]

More in harmony with the eschatological setting of the beatitudes, B. S. Easton[71] paraphrases Luke 6:20 as "your poverty has disposed you towards a reception of the blessings."[72] Accordingly, it is often suggested that Jesus' (and Luke's) experience of mission was that whereas the poor were open to the gospel, the rich were too involved with their possessions to respond.[73]

Even this, however, is not without difficulties. One can quote the case of the rich ruler, but one must also consider the cases of Levi, the

---

65. Steiner, "Warum lebten die Essener asketisch?" 17–19. Priests were dominant in the community and the whole sect lived in levitical purity.

66. Philo, *Quod omn.* 77, 87; Josephus, *War* 2.122.

67. See pages 43–45, below.

68. Plummer, *Luke*, 179. See also Godet, *Luke*, I.312.

69. See Luke 6:21.

70. Caird, *Luke*, 102.

71. Easton, *Luke*, 83.

72. Similarly, Bartsch, "Feldrede und Bergpredigt," 10; Percy, *Botschaft*, 89; Koch, *Wertung*, 159–61.

73. See Degenhardt, *Evangelist der Armen*, 52; Schürmann, *Lukasevangelium*, 327.

centurion in Capernaum, Jairus, and Zacchaeus, as well as the evidence of Acts, which indicates that, at least in Luke's experience, the gospel made headway among more than the lower classes.

2.2.5 The Poor as Heirs of Salvation

The biggest problem with the foregoing views is their failure adequately to consider the dependence of our three passages on Isaiah 61:1. A. R. C. Leaney,[74] Jacques Dupont,[75] and Heinz Schürmann[76] all point to the importance of this connection.

Dupont argues in detail that behind the first three beatitudes lies the prophetic picture of comfort of Isaiah 40–66, particularly its idea of blessing for the poor.[77] This becomes the key to his interpretation of the beatitudes. Schürmann holds that in declaring the beatitudes, Jesus acts as the "messenger of joy and bringer of salvation," proclaiming the gospel in its most primitive form.[78] He objects therefore to any interpretation that sees positive value in poverty, hunger, and tears:

> Therefore, the poor, hungry, and weeping are not praised as such ... but because poverty hunger and tears shall soon be taken from them, and instead of these they will be granted in the near future an overwhelming eschatological gift.[79]

Similarly, Dupont comments on the first beatitude in the light of Isaiah 61:1:

> In the line of thought of this prophecy, happiness is promised to the unfortunate, not because they fulfil certain moral conditions, by their poverty itself or their moral disposition, but

---

74. Leaney, *Luke*, 83.
75. Dupont, *Béatitudes*, passim, esp. I.293, II.91–93.
76. Schürmann, *Lukasevangelium*, 326–28.
77. Dupont, *Béatitudes*, II.91–99.
78. "Freudenbote und Heilbringer." Schürmann, *Lukasevangelium*, 326–27. This was also argued by Percy, *Botschaft*, 40–42.
79. "Die Armen, Hungernden und Weinenden werden also nicht als solche gepreisen ... sondern weil Armut, Hunger und Tränen nunmehr von ihnen genommen und sie darüber hinaus in Bälde eschatologisch-überschwenglich beschenkt werden sollen." Schürmann, *Lukasevangelium*, 328–29.

because God has decided to save them: he sends the Messiah whose mission concerns them in particular.[80]

To the question of who are the poor, Schürmann answers that for both Jesus and Luke literal sufferers are meant; in particular, Jesus' persecuted disciples.[81] Luke's understanding has been conditioned, he feels, by the early Christian experience that the poor "found faith before the possessors, who were always endangered by their wealth" (and also Jesus' experience).[82] Dupont thinks the message of Jesus was a proclamation of salvation to all who suffer,[83] and that Luke, in casting the beatitudes into the second person, restricted them to Christians.[84]

These studies are important in bringing to our attention that in Isaiah "the poor" are a group with a definite eschatological destiny, and that Luke is thinking along these lines when he quotes Isaiah 61:1-2. However, when they come to the task of identifying the poor, they run into the same problems I have raised in relation to other views (the problem of seeing the *ptōchoi* as other than the destitute; that of assuming Luke saw little response from the rich) as well as the glaring problem of what could have been meant by Jesus' offering salvation unconditionally to all sufferers (and to no others) or even by Luke's characterization of all Christians as poor. To reach a solution of these problems we will turn to Isaiah as a likely influence on Luke's understanding of the poor.

2.2.6 The Poor as Israel

The fact that the three passages under consideration are interrelated and take their rise from a common Old Testament prophecy (Isaiah 61:1) is a presumption in favor of looking to Isaiah for help in understanding the meaning of "the poor."[85] Care is needed, for it is possible for a New

---

80. "Dans la ligne de pensée de cette prophétie, le Bonheur est promis aux malheureux, non pas parce qu'ils remplissent certaines conditions, par leur pauvreté même ou leurs dispositions morales, mais parce que Dieu a décidé de les sauver: il leur envoie le Messie dont la mission les concerne tout particulièrement." Dupont, *Béatitudes*, I.293.

81. Schürmann, *Lukasevangelium*, 327-28.

82. "... eher zum Glauben fanden als die durch ihren Reichtum immer sehr gefährdeten Besitzenden." Schürmann, *Lukasevangelium*, 327.

83. Dupont, *Béatitudes*, II.50.

84. Dupont, *Béatitudes*, III.28, cf. 96.

85. This approach is followed by Stonehouse, *Witness of Luke*, 76-85; Crockett, "Old Testament in Luke," 99-101; and Jones, "Who Are the Poor?" 62-72.

Testament writer to use an Old Testament text with very little regard to its origins, meaning, or context. Nevertheless, there are many signs which point to a more considered use of Isaiah by Luke.

Elsewhere I have argued that Luke was uncommonly influenced in writing the Gospel and Acts by the book of Isaiah.[86] Not only does he quote from it extensively, but he has also drawn from it many of his theological categories (Spirit, Anointed One, *euaggelizomai* [evangelize], doing good, the servant, the poor). He displays a special consciousness of the relationship between the ministry of Jesus and the theological patterns of Isaiah. In that study I concluded that in approaching Luke's quotations and allusions to Isaiah there is a presumption in favor of his having been aware of their context and wider meaning within Isaiah as a whole.

This does not mean that a certain understanding of "the poor" in Isaiah can be guaranteed to have been adopted by Luke. Some references to "the poor" in Isaiah can be viewed in more than one way.[87] Nor am I suggesting that the Septuagint version of Isaiah was the sole source of Luke's understanding of the poor. He stood within the Christian tradition and in close proximity to Jewish thinking. His way of looking at Isaiah may have been influenced by what was traditional in these circles. Nevertheless, the fact that he has chosen from Isaiah a key text which mentions the poor makes it worth investigating what that term might have conveyed to him and his contemporaries, viewed in the context of the book to which it belongs.

In fact, there is no unified view of the poor in Isaiah, but there is a relationship between the parts which is best understood by looking in turn at the three periods which the book as we have it covers: the pre-exilic period, the exile, and the post-exilic period.

The prophet of the first period confronts a disintegration of the social order of Israel and Judah. He protests against a prosperous upper class, which is encroaching upon the ancestral lands of the peasant farmer, forcing him off his land and into a condition of serfdom, or into a growing landless class.[88] The poor are landowners who have fallen into need, and are being victimized and dispossessed by the wealthy.[89]

86. Seccombe, "Luke and Isaiah," 252–59.
87. E.g., Stonehouse, *Witness*, 81, sees Isaiah's poor as "the meek," "a transformed people."
88. See van Leeuwen, *Le développement du sens social*, 90.
89. Isa 3:14–15, 10:1–2. Cf. Isa 5:1–8.

In Isaiah 3:15 there is a striking parallel between the poor (*'aniīm*) and God's people, which led van Leeuwen mistakenly to identify the *'aniīm* with the godly.[90] It is rather that in attacking the poor, the rich are attacking Israel in no less serious a manner than an invader would. The prophet is protesting against more than social injustice; the whole structure and organization of the theocratic society, where each family holds its property on trust from God is being destroyed.[91] He warns the rich that the poor are God's people and God will defend them; if they persist in their attacks they will suffer the same fate as the heathen who attack his people. Isaiah has no illusions about the piety of the poor; in his eyes "everyone is profane and an evil-doer," even the fatherless and widows.[92] What he demands is a return to the brotherliness and care which God demanded of his people in the law;[93] the God-ordained structure of land and people must be restored. In the absence of this repentance, which is demanded but never expected, the prophet declares that God himself will act, and, in the person of the messianic ruler, will establish a new order of true justice, for the poor in particular.[94] One of the distinctive ideas of Isaiah is the place which is given to the "poor and needy" in that age of salvation. The outcome of the judgment will be a new era of peace where Zion will be a secure habitation for the poor and afflicted.[95] Again the idea is not that the poor are righteous and therefore deserving of salvation, but that the conditions of the new age, unlike the present, will be such that the poor can live safely; there will be no oppression, since the Davidic king will be there to exercise judgment on behalf of the weak.

In Isaiah 40–55 the people of Israel are seen languishing in exile, awaiting God's intervention to judge their oppressors and rescue them from captivity. The situation of oppression is seen no longer in terms of the poor Israelite being exploited by his rich overlords; the whole nation is now poor and suffers oppressive captivity among the gentile nations.[96] The prophet announces the end of judgment, the comforting of God's people, and their return from captivity. In Isaiah 49:13 (MT) "the poor"

---

90. Van Leeuwen, *Le développement du sens social*, 90.

91. Wright, "Family, Land and Property," shows the importance in ancient Israel of the family's land in its relationship to God and to society,

92. Isa 9:17; cf. Jer 5:1–5.

93. Isa 1:17.

94. Isa 11:1–5; cf. 32:1–8,

95. Isa 14:29–32; cf. Isa 29:17–21.

96. See Isa 42:22. Kittel, *Psalmen*, 287.

are explicitly identified with the nation returning from captivity: "For Yahweh has comforted his people; and will have compassion on his poor."⁹⁷ Here "the poor" equals Israel.⁹⁸ The same is true in Isaiah 41:8-20: "the poor and needy"⁹⁹ are "you worm Jacob, you men of Israel,"¹⁰⁰ who have suffered at the hands of the nations but are now to be redeemed.

Poverty is seen here not in economic terms at all, but, as in some of the Psalms,¹⁰¹ in connection with the great need into which the nation has fallen through her sin and its judgment. The answer to this need is God's salvation, and the thirsty and penniless are urged to come, buy, and eat, without money and without price.¹⁰²

This understanding of "the poor" as Israel in exile is taken up and applied to Luke by Larry Crockett: Luke thinks of "Israel in its post-crucifixion situation" as being metaphorically in a state of exile, and qualified, therefore, to be addressed as the *ptōchoi*.¹⁰³ In his exceedingly complex treatment of the Nazareth story Crockett argues that Luke has Jesus deliberately contrive his rejection in order to put the Nazarenes (Israel) among those who may receive salvation in the post-resurrection period:

---

97. כי נחם יהוה עמו וענייו ירחם. This identification is not so clear in the LXX (ὅτι ἠλέησεν ὁ θεὸς τὸν λαὸν αὐτοῦ καὶ τοὺς ταπεινοὺς τοῦ λαοῦ αὐτοῦ παρεκάλεσεν). Crockett, "OT in Luke," I.100-101, thinks the LXX translator took up the notion of the poor as Israel in exile and applied it to his own community, away from Jerusalem. Be that as it may, in Isa 25:1-5 the LXX translator has introduced a reference to "ὁ λαὸς ὁ πτωχός (the poor people [of God])," clearly Israel in the latter days (cf. v. 5); cf. Isa 18:7 where a description of the Ethiopians has been transformed into a description of Israel's salvation from exile in the last days ("ἐκ λαοῦ τεθλιμμένου καὶ τετιλμένου (καὶ ταπεινούς) καὶ ἀπὸ λαοῦ μεγάλου ἀπὸ τοῦ νῦν καὶ εἰς τὸν αἰῶνα χρόνον") ("from a people afflicted and plucked [poor], and from a people great from henceforth and forever").

98. This was argued by Baudissin, "Die alttestamentliche Religion und die Armen," 211-15. He thinks the identification of poor and Israel began with I-Isaiah (209-11), and that D-Isaiah used '*anawim* as a religious term to denote those who were humble because of the experience of captivity.

99. העניים והאביונים, οἱ πτωχοὶ καὶ οἱ ἐνδεεῖς.

100. LXX has "Jacob, Israel few in number."

101. The emphasis on need, especially persecution, in the Psalms' use of "poor" terminology will be recalled, as well as its frequent application to the nation Israel (pages 27-29, above).

102. Isa 55:1.

103. Crockett, "OT in Luke," I.99-101.

"Jesus makes the people become poor, bound, blind, oppressed, just so they too can be among those who are forgiven."[104]

However, the need for such a difficult solution evaporates when we come in Isaiah to the period following the exile and to the passage which most concerns us. For it can readily be seen that the situation of Israel in the restoration period is in many ways analogous to the state of affairs at the time of Jesus.

The setting of Isaiah 61:1 presupposes that the people are once again in Jerusalem (61:3). Still the awaited salvation has not arrived. Injustice and oppression have already reappeared,[105] but more than this, the whole nation is subject to heathen powers,[106] and many are still in exile.[107] No doubt even the land was obstinate, having been so long deserted.[108] It is natural, by analogy with the exilic situation, to understand "the poor" (*ptōchoi*, *'anawīm*) to whom the Spirit-anointed prophet announces salvation as suffering Zion: Israel humiliated in her subjection to the nations and in the miserable state of her inner life. The poor are "those who mourn in Zion," understood not as a group among the people but as the people itself. Of course, the prophet hardly thinks of oppressors and the unjust sharing in this salvation; they will fare like the heathen.[109] His attention here, however, is not on the division between the righteous and the wicked, but on Zion itself,[110] and it is her children that are characterized as "the poor." The prophet declares God's answer to the need of the people, and no reference is made to moral qualities predisposing them to salvation.[111]

---

104. Crockett, "OT in Luke," II.344. His thesis is complicated by further "nuances" in Luke's understanding of "the poor." He derives these by using the parable of the Banquet as the key to interpreting Luke's use of Isa 61:1–2. As well as "Israel in exile," "the poor" are the outcast (tax collectors, etc.), those literally poor who are open to the gospel, and the gentiles (II.352–55).

105. Isa 58:4–7.

106. Isa 62:8.

107. Isa 60:4.

108. Isa 62:4. Further, see Everson, "Isaiah 61:1–6," 69–70.

109. Isa 61:8; 65:13–14. See Dahl, *Volk Gottes*, 46–48.

110. See also the two adjacent chapters (60:1–3, 14–21, 62:1–12).

111. Against van Leeuwen, *Le développement du sens social*, 125–26, who sees the "broken-hearted" of 61:1 as an indication of the humility to which the poor are better adapted than others. This is ruled out by the fact that the "broken-hearted" are "healed" (ἰάσασθαι) or "bound up" (לחבש).

Thus, the book of Isaiah presents us with three pictures of the poor: the peasants of the pre-exilic period being squeezed off their lands by the rich and powerful, the captives of the exile, and the dispirited nation of the restoration. In each case the people is in some sense under attack, and the conviction which characterizes the whole book is that in the latter days God will execute a great salvation for "the poor" and make them the heirs of his blessing.

The thesis which I wish to present and defend is that Luke has carried into his Gospel this understanding of the poor as the nation Israel suffering and in great need. As far as I am aware no modern exegete has sought to do this in any consistent manner, though some have drawn attention in passing to the possible relevance of this Old Testament motif.[112]

We have seen this concept in Isaiah and the Psalms, two books which had a disproportionate influence on Luke.[113] There is evidence of a direct line of influence from Isaiah to Luke, though it would be unwise to rule out Jesus and the early church as intermediaries. There are, in fact, even further areas of possible influence; to these we will now turn.

The only other place in the Old Testament where we find anything comparable to what we have uncovered in Isaiah and some of the Psalms is in Zechariah. Although it lacks anything like Isaiah's vision of a glorious eschatological future for the poor, the poor do occur, and in a context where it is possible to take them as the nation Israel, oppressed by her overlords, be these unscrupulous Israelite governors or the gentiles.[114] The "flock" (Israel) is poor because it is destined for slaughter. Admittedly these ideas are not found in the Septuagint, which in 11:7 reads, "and I will tend the flock of slaughter in the land of Canaan,"[115] and in 11:11, "and the Canaanites will know the sheep who are being guarded."[116] Because of the obscurity here, many would amend the Hebrew text, "thus the poor" to "to the Canaanites,"[117] removing any reference to the poor. However, even if this was the original reading of the Hebrew, CD 19:7–9

---

112. Boehmer, "Erste Seligpreisung," 298–99; Navone, *Luke*, 103–04; McHugh, *Mother of Jesus*, 76; cf. Leaney, *Luke*, 135.

113. Holtz, *Alttestamentlichen Zitate bei Lukas*, shows that Luke probably had access to Isaiah, Psalms, and three Minor Prophets in a version of the LXX.

114. Zech 11:7, 11. Rabbi Johanan bar Nappaha identifies "the poor of the flock with Israel (*Midr. Ps.* 12. See page 45 below for text)

115. καὶ ποιμανῶ τὰ πρόβατα τῆς σφαγῆς εἰς τὴν Χαναανῖτιν.

116. καὶ γνώσονται οἱ Χαναναῖοι τὰ πρόβατα τὰ φυλασσόμενα.

117. לכנעניי to לכן עניי.

shows that the Massoretic reading goes back at least to New Testament times[118] and proves that in at least one first-century Palestinian group "the poor of the flock" was a recognized eschatological category.[119] Thus, although here we cannot postulate direct influence from the Septuagint on Luke, it is quite possible that the Hebrew text of Zechariah could have contributed to a Judeo-Christian understanding of the poor as the downtrodden remnant of Israel in the last days.

Apart from the Psalms of Solomon, the apocryphal and pseudepigraphal literature shows little trace of the themes or motifs we are seeking.[120] In Psalms of Solomon 10:6 and at Qumran, however, we do encounter the idea of salvation for the poor.

It has already been pointed out that Psalms of Solomon 10:6 does not necessarily imply an equivalence of meaning between *ptōchoi* and *hosioi* (poor and devout). However, it clearly does show knowledge of the idea that the poor are the heirs of Israel's salvation:[121]

> Just and holy (ὅσιος) is our Lord in his judgments for ever, and Israel shall praise the name of the Lord in gladness (εὐφροσύνῃ), and the pious (ὅσιοι) shall give thanks in the assembly of the people (ἐν ἐκκλησίᾳ λαοῦ), And on the poor (πτωχούς) shall God have mercy in the gladness (ἐν εὐφροσύνῃ) of Israel, For good and merciful is God for ever, and the assemblies (συναγωγαί) of Israel shall glorify the name of the Lord. The salvation of the Lord be upon the house of Israel unto everlasting gladness (εἰς εὐφροσύνην αἰώνιον).

It is possible that at the same time as the psalmist identifies the salvation of the poor with the salvation of Israel he also restricts it to the pious, viewing his own community as the true Israel because of their piety and as the poor because of the chastening they have willingly accepted (10:1-3). Nevertheless, it is *Israel's* salvation which is the focus of his attention,[122] and this is coterminous with the salvation of the poor.[123]

---

118. See also Aquila (πτωχοὶ τοῦ ποιμνίου μου), and the comment of Jerome in Field's *Hexapla* (II.1025).

119. Matt 26:31, 27:9-10 (possibly Luke 12:32) show that the early Christians took this part of Zechariah in reference to events of the end.

120. What there is, is gathered in a section on references to the poor in an eschatological setting in *TDNT* VI.895-96.

121. See Percy, *Botschaft*, 64-65.

122. See Ps. Sol. 2:22, 7:8, 10, 9:11, 11:1-9, 12:6, 14:5, 17:21-22, 45.

123. Ps. Sol. 18:1-5 is probably also to be understood this way.

On the basis of the above Ernst Bammel, suggests a connection between the Psalms of Solomon and a Qumran-type community;[124] it is indeed striking that we encounter the same way of thinking in the writings of the Qumran sect.

Earlier I disputed Kandler's and Schubert's view that the sect called themselves the *'ebiōnim* because of the individual's surrender of his property to the community.[125] The positive suggestion I wish to make is that the sect seized upon a preexisting soteriological theme which saw the salvation of Israel in terms of the salvation of the poor, and, as with all the Scriptures, applied it to themselves. In thus laying claim to Israel's salvation for themselves alone, it was probably necessary that they should seek in some way to convince themselves that they really were the poor of promise. This justification is to be seen not in their community of possessions, nor in their contempt for riches, but in the experience of persecution and suffering which marked the early life of the community[126] and in the weakness they later felt in the face of the great nations of the world, which they saw it as their destiny to destroy.

The origins of the former understanding are probably to be seen in the experience of the Teacher of Righteousness and the early community.[127] Repeatedly throughout the Qumran Hymns the Teacher, in the manner of the Old Testament psalmist, describes himself as "the poor one," using the whole range of terms which the Old Testament provides. It is his experience of persecution which lies behind this language,[128] not anything economic or ascetic.[129] Nor does he suffer alone; the community are included with him in his "poverty":

> And thou hast set my foot in the sweepings, in the midst of the poor (*'anawim*), and in the midst of them that are quick unto

---

124. *TDNT* VI.896n92.

125. Pages 33-34.

126. Cf. Légasse, "Volontaires," 343.

127. I agree with those scholars who think the Hymns at least reflect the experience of the Teacher of Righteousness.

128. 1QH 2:31-37, 3:23-28, 5:11-15, 20; for the sufferings of the teacher at the hands of the wicked priest see 1QpHab.

129. Against Thiering, "Suffering and Asceticism," 393-405, who thinks much of the language of the Hodayot describes the community's ascetic efforts to inaugurate the messianic age.

righteousness, to cause all the poor of Grace (אביונים חסד) to arise from the tumult together.[130]

This is similar to the picture of 1QpHabakkuk 12, where Habakkuk 2:17 is peshered in terms of the attack of the Wicked Priest on the poor. In verse 10 he is said to have stolen their goods. Although such language as is found in the Hymns may initially have meant no more than an appreciation of the use of "poor" terminology in the Old Testament Psalms to describe need of all kinds (especially the need of the persecuted one), 1QHodayot 18:12-15 shows that at some point it was also connected with the prophetic eschatological theme of salvation for the poor.

In the War Rule attention is less on persecution, and more on the amazing contrast between the mighty nations of the earth and the complete powerlessness and insignificance, humanly speaking, of the 'ebiōnim whom the mighty God is going to use to destroy them.[131] This may reflect a later stage in the sect's life when overt persecution had ceased. The 'ebiōnim are the "smitten in spirit" (נכאי רוח), those "bent in the dust," those with "feeble hands," "knees that stagger," and "bent back"; they are the "poor in spirit" (ענוי רוח), in this context surely those who are at the end of their human resources.[132] We could sum all this up as weakness and need, accentuated by the apparent might of their enemies. The deciding factor in the confrontation will be the mighty God.

Thus, the sect can identify with the 'anawim of Psalm 37:11 ("But the 'anawim will possess the earth . . . ."), taking a name ('ebiōnim) which makes them recipients of the promise.[133] Their justification for taking this name was that they had accepted the "time of affliction,"[134] which, we recall, is very like the thought of Psalms of Solomon 10. Isaiah 61:1 is itself appropriated by the community in 1QHodayot 18:12-15,[135] where the Teacher of Righteousness sees himself in the role of the anointed one, "evangelizing" the 'anawim, consoling the "crushed of spirit" (לנדכאי ריח) and bringing the "mourners" (אבלים) to eternal joy. Though this passage

---

130. 1QH 5:21-22. Note Lam 3:45 where Israel is called "offscouring and refuse among the peoples." Cf. 1 Cor 4:13, where Paul calls his missionary party the "sweepings" because of their experience of rejection and persecution.

131. 1QM 11:7-13, 13:13-16, 14:4-8.

132. 1QM 14:5-7. See pages 33n64, above.

133. 4QPs37 1:8-10; cf. 2:9-12.

134. מועד התענית (time of humiliation); cf. 1QS 5:6; 8:4.

135. Compare 11QMelch.

refers to the present experience of the community, it has an eschatological dimension: in being enlightened, the community member already tastes the powers of the age to come. The sect also identified itself with the "poor of the flock" of Zechariah 11:11, seeing themselves as the heirs of salvation at the time of God's final visitation.[136]

The Qumran writings certainly do not see "the poor" as Israel as it was in their own day, but rather as the remnant,[137] in a way which flows naturally from Psalm 37:10-11: The wicked (gentiles and unfaithful Israelites) would be destroyed and the poor would inherit the earth. What is evident is that they did not see the poor as one group, among others, who would also be saved; *only* the poor would be saved. They claim to be the Israel which is to inherit salvation; therefore, they must be the poor.

Thus at least two groups (perhaps related) in the intertestamental period seemed to have understood that salvation was the property of the poor and of no others, and therefore had to see themselves as the poor, since they were laying claim to Israel's salvation as their own.

In concluding this section it is of interest to note that R. Johanan bar Nappaha, the reputed editor of Midrash Psalms, who died in AD 279 in Tiberias, taught:

> Whenever such phrases as "We are brought very low," "the oppressed," "the impoverished," "the neediest among men," "he that is waxen poor," "the poor of the flock," "the bruised," and "the helpless" occur in Scripture, they refer to Israel.[138]

Having seen the origin of this stream of interpretation in Isaiah and the Psalms and various uses of it in the intertestamental period, at Qumran, and among the later rabbis, it is possible now to turn to Luke to ask whether this understanding of the poor fits the passages under consideration, and if so, how it functions.

---

136. CD 19:9-10.

137. See 11QPsa 154:18 (*DJD* IV.64-65). CD 3:4-19 describes the relationship of the remnant to the wider nation. See Steiner, Warum lebten die Essener asketisch?" 4-6: "Die Sektengemeinde von Qumran versteht sich vom AT her als *Gottes Bundesgemeinde, Trägerin der göttlichen Verheissungen*" (5). (The members of the Qumran sect understood themselves as God's covenant community, bearers of the divine promises.)

138. *Midr. Ps.* 9:12; cf. *Gen. Rab.* 71:1 on Gen 29:31; *Midr. Ps.* 60:3, 68:11; *Num. Rab.* 11:1; *Pes. Rab.* 36 (162a); *Prot. Jas.* 20:2.

2.3 THE NAZARETH STORY, LUKE 4:16-30

The commanding position of the Nazareth story in the Gospel of Luke is commonly recognized, and justifies beginning here our inquiry into the meaning and significance of the poor for Luke.

Jesus emerges from the desert into Galilee in the power of the Spirit. The description of his Galilean ministry in Luke 4:14-15 shows that Luke does not imagine the sermon at Nazareth to be chronologically the start of Jesus' ministry. In terms of declaring the context and character of his mission, however, it takes pride of place, and there is little doubt that this is why Luke has advanced it to this position.

In order to determine whether the meaning of "the poor" suggested above is indeed Luke's meaning, it will be necessary to enter in some detail into his use of Isaiah 61:1-2 in Luke 4:18-19. To determine how he might have taken the passage, we will seek first to understand its leading motif, and then the various other terms which occur in connection with "the poor" ("captives," "blind," etc.). Only then will it be possible to see that our identification of "the poor" fits naturally and harmoniously into place. Finally, we will relate the quotation to its wider context in the Nazareth story. First, however, we must consider to what extent the story may be regarded as Luke's.

2.3.1 Tradition and Redaction

Matthew, Mark, and Luke each record a story about Jesus coming to his home town. Matthew probably used Mark as his basic source, and some have argued that Luke has too, transposing and enlarging it (supplying the reading from Isaiah 61), perhaps from other traditions, perhaps from his own imagination.[139] Though possible, this view cannot be plausibly demonstrated for the following reasons:

a. There is no argument from coincidence in the order of successive pericopes in Luke and Mark, though Luke could have transposed the story from its position in Mark for theological reasons.

b. There are no verbal connections between the two stories, which might betray their dependence. The operative word in the proverb is rendered differently, though again Luke may have had theological

---

139. Loisy, *Évangiles synoptiques*, 839-40; Tannehill, "Mission," 52; Drury, *Tradition and Design*, 66-67, 85-86.

reasons for such a change.[140] Other dissimilarities point away from dependence.[141] Tim Schramm argues that Luke would hardly have added "amen I say to you" in verse 24 when his normal custom is to remove or replace it.[142]

c. The similarities in the structure of the story do not require that Luke used Mark as his basic source, so long as it is admitted that the occasion described in each case is the same. The similarities are then attributable to tradition.

d. It has been inferred by some scholars that since Luke 4:23 implies a previous ministry in Capernaum which is related in Mark, but not in Luke until afterwards, it betrays knowledge of Mark. However, this need not mean Luke has used Mark as his source for the story itself.

We cannot be certain that Luke did not use Mark's story, but I can see nothing to suggest that he did, and, since there are certain pointers to independence, it would be foolish to proceed on the assumption that Mark is Luke's main source, and that the Isaiah reading is therefore Luke's work. As to other possible sources for the story we can only guess. Schürmann argues from the occurrence of *Nazara* in Matthew 4:13 and Luke 4:16 and nowhere else in the Gospels, that the story was originally part of a "Bericht vom Anfang" (report about the beginning) followed by Matthew, Mark, and Luke.[143] In another article he reasons from the tension between 4:22a and 23–29 that the Isaiah reading (also 25–27) was a secondary insertion into the original Markan story.[144] However, it was not an invention of Luke, and, according to Schürmann, stood in Q,[145] so that even were his reconstruction accepted (and it is tenuous),[146] it would afford no justification for attributing Jesus' scripture reading to Luke.

---

140. Luke 4:24: ἄτιμος to δεκτός: "dishonoured" to "not acceptable." See pages 48–55, below. Note, however, that *GospThom* 31 supports Luke's version (also POxy 1:6).

141. ἐξεπλήσσοντο—ἐθαύμαζον; "astounded"—"amazed."

142. Schramm, *Markus-Stoff bei Lukas*, 37n2. Note, however, O'Neill, "Six Amen Sayings," 1–4.

143. Schürmann, "Bericht vom Anfang," 242–58.

144. Schürmann, "Nazareth-Perikope," 187–205.

145. Schürmann, "Nazareth-Perikope," 191–94.

146. See the critique of Stanton, "Christology of Q," 27–42, 32–33, who is doubtful whether Luke 4:16–30 stood in Q.

It is wisest, therefore, to take the story as it stands, to see what it yields of itself. Its commanding position in the Gospel assures us that its meaning, be it mediated through traditional materials or through the author's modifications, will be peculiarly expressive of Luke's aims and intentions.

2.3.2 The Reading

Whatever may have been the regular practice of the synagogue in Jesus' time, Luke indicates that the reading was Jesus' own choice. What he reads, however, is curious, consisting not of a single passage, but of Isaiah 61:1–2a with one line missing and a line supplied from Isaiah 58:6. A number of explanations of this oddity are possible.

a. Luke could have transcribed the passage from memory and unconsciously introduced the discrepancy.[147] This is unlikely for the following reasons:

1. There are in fact two alterations. The clause about the healing of the brokenhearted has been omitted and that about freeing the oppressed added, but in another place. It is not simply a case of substitution.

2. The passage has otherwise been transcribed so accurately that a written source seems probable. The only variations from the A text of the Septuagint are "announce" for "call" and "to send" for "send" (demanded by the context).[148]

3. Other major quotations in Luke-Acts make it clear that Luke had access to a Septuagint scroll of Isaiah.[149]

b. Luke could have deliberately conflated Isaiah 61:1–2 with Isaiah 58:6 in the interests of his own theology. Erich Klostermann explained the association of the two texts on the basis of the word *aphesis* (release, forgiveness),[150] and Tannehill argues that, since the two passages share this common word only in Greek, the association is

---

147. Plummer, *Luke*, 120.
148. κηρύξαι for καλέσαι and ἀποστεῖλαι for ἀπόστελλε.
149. Page 41n113, above.
150. Klostermann, *Lukasevangelium*, 63.

Lukan.[151] G. W. H. Lampe says it introduces "Luke's favorite theme of 'release', a word generally used in the sense of 'forgiveness' (of sins), which is for him of the essence of the gospel."[152]

This is an attractive solution to the problem which, if correct, would undoubtedly point to the centrality of forgiveness in Luke's understanding of Jesus' mission. Nevertheless, we should hesitate before ascribing to Luke such a radical rearrangement of a scripture reading simply on the basis of a catch-word, especially when in neither place does it have the sense of forgiveness. Though the word does not occur elsewhere in Isaiah there are other places where the concept of forgiveness occurs; one wonders why he could not have made something of one of these if this was his chief thought.[153] It is also questionable that forgiveness is for Luke the essence of Jesus' mission. This is not to dispute its importance, nor to deny that Luke has it in mind among other things in his double use of *aphesis* in the composite reading.

c. It is possible that Jesus read a number of Old Testament passages which Luke (or his source) abridged and combined.[154] What lies behind Luke's account could, therefore, be more complex than meets the eye. Normally one would expect the reading from the Prophets (*haphtarah*) to be followed by an Aramaic paraphrase (targum) and perhaps a sermon.[155] It was not essential that the *haphtarah* be a single passage.[156] Texts could be strung together in a manner characteristic of midrash ("pearl stringing"—*haruzīn*),[157] so long as one did not change books (even this was possible in the Minor Prophets).[158] According to Billerbeck it was forbidden to jump

---

151. Tannehill, "Mission," 66. The Masoretic Text has דרור חפשים.

152. Lampe, "Luke," 828. Haenchen, *Weg Jesu*, 217, sees the composite text as proof that we are not dealing with early tradition: "Sondern einen späteren Versuch, Jesu erste Predigt inhaltlich zu bestimmen."

153. Isa 1:18, 33:24, 55:7.

154. Though note that according to Büchler in *JE* VI.136 in the oldest times *haphtaroth* consisted of only two or three verses. Cf. *pMeg* 4:3. Also Leaney, *Luke*, 53; Caird, *Luke*, 87.

155. Billerbeck, "Synagogengottesdeinst," 155–57. Billerbeck IV.167.

156. Billerbeck IV.167.

157. *Meg*. 4:4. See also Cave, "Sermon at Nazareth," 232, who thinks v. 18 was not the *haphtarah* but the text of Jesus' sermon.

158. *TMeg* 4:18.

backwards in such a reading,¹⁵⁹ but this rule does not appear in the Mishnah. It is likely, therefore, that it was not well established, and its very existence is evidence for the currency of the practice at an earlier period. Charles Perrot notes that the reading is like a targum.¹⁶⁰ However, the omission of a line from the major text is hard to account for on this theory.

To explore and to test this line of approach it will be necessary to enquire how Isaiah 58:6 might have come to be associated with 61:1-2. Perrot thinks Isaiah 57:15–58:14 was read on the Day of Atonement, and that 61:1-2 belongs naturally to the Day of Atonement which inaugurates a Jubilee:

> In this precise context one understands now how an element drawn from Isa 58:6—to return the oppressed into freedom—has been able to join itself easily to the quotation of Isa 61:1 made by Luke.¹⁶¹

However, Perrot fails to justify his association of Isa 58:6 with the Day of Atonement. It belongs here in the modern synagogue lection, and this practice is no doubt old, but simply to assume that it was so in New Testament times is inadmissible. The reading is not given in connection with Yom Kippur in R. G. Finch's ancient lectionary tables.¹⁶² Nor is there any evidence that Isaiah 61:1-2 was a reading for Yom Kippur. Finch,¹⁶³ following Büchler, gives it as *haphtarah* to Deuteronomy 15:7, the *seder* for a sabbath in Cheshvan, but Büchler does not think the *haphtaroth* were fixed in the first century.¹⁶⁴ Bengel associated it with the Day of Atonement, but only on the basis of its association with Isaiah 58:6 in Luke 4:18. Jacob Mann¹⁶⁵ inferred from the content of the Midrash

---

159. T. Meg. 4:19. Billerbeck IV.167

160. Perrot, "Luc 4:16-30," 173.

161. "Dans ce contexte précis, on comprend déjà comment un element tiré d'Is 58:6: *renvoyer des opprimes en liberte* ait pu s'agreger facilement à la citation d'Is 61:1 faite par Lc." Perrot, "Luc 4:16-30," 178.

162. Finch, *Synagogue Lectionary and the New Testament*, 22-32. On 32 he gives Isa 57:15 as an early reading for the Day of Atonement.

163. Finch, *Synagogue Lectionary and the New Testament*, 54.

164. Büchler, *JE* VI.136. Morris, *New Testament and the Jewish Lectionaries*, Crockett, "Luke 4:16-30 and the Jewish Lectionary Cycle," 13-46, and Finkel, *Pharisees and the Teacher of Nazareth*, 14-149, also urge caution in this area.

165. Mann, *Bible in the Old Synagogue*, 282-87.

Tanhumah that Isaiah 61:2–62:2 was the underlying *haphtarah* for *seder* 33 (Gen 35:9–10), though the one set is Isaiah 43:1–21. He too denies that his results can be extrapolated into the New Testament period,[166] though they have been used nonetheless by Aileen Guilding[167] and C. H. Cave.[168]

Perrot bases his argument on the association of ideas in 11QMelchizedek, which contains reference to Isaiah 61:1–2, as well as to ideas of atonement and Jubilee. Isaiah 58, however, is conspicuously absent from 11QMelchizedek. Arguments from synagogue lectionaries are too uncertain to be useful. Besides, the rules about skipping in *haphtaroth* imply that even in the Tannaitic-period prophetic lections were not fixed,[169] and *b. Megillah* 31a shows that at a later period even the readings for feast days were a matter of variation and dispute.

However, it is not necessary to invoke the occasion of the Day of Atonement to explain 11QMelchizedek or Luke 4:18–19. Thoughtful midrashic exposition of Isaiah 61:1–2 could have achieved the same results.[170] Each of the passages combined in Luke 4:18–19 deals in its original context with an "acceptable" time,[171] the similarity this time being more apparent in Hebrew than in Greek. This provides a possible alternative to the catch-word *aphesis* (forgiveness), which would carry the association behind the Greek stage.

Following Perrot, it is possible to go deeper. Isaiah 58 does contain allusions to Yom Kippur, described in Leviticus 23:27 as a day for "afflicting the soul."[172] The same expression occurs twice in Isaiah 58 (verses 3 and 5). Isaiah 58:6, however, reminds us not simply of Yom Kippur but of the Jubilee. A release was to be proclaimed throughout the land, everyone was to return to his ancestral lands, and all slaves were to go free. It is

---

166. Mann, *Bible in the Old Synagogue*, xvii.

167. Guilding, *Fourth Gospel and Jewish Worship*, 125–26.

168. Cave, "Sermon at Nazareth," 231–35.

169. *Meg.* 4:4, 4:18–19.

170. Miller, "Isa 61:1–2 in 11QMelchizedek," 467–69, argues that Isa 61:1–2 stands behind the whole of 11QMelch: "The three major Scripture texts quoted from the Torah, the Prophets, and the Writings (Lev 25:13; Isa 52:7; Ps 82:1-2) unfold their inner relation and meaning for the community with reference to Isa 61:1–2" (469).

171. Is 61:2: ἐνιαυτὸν κυρίου δεκτόν – שנת רצון ליהוה. Is 58:5: νηστείαν δεκτήν – יום רצון ליהוה.

172. ועניתם את נפשתיכם. Compare Lev 23:29, 32, 16:31. In pre-exilic times Yom Kippur was the only regular fast day, celebrated on the tenth of Tishri (Lev 16, 23:23–32); see van Goudoever, *Biblical Calendars*, 36–42. For post-exilic fast days: Zech 7:1–7, 8:18–19; van Goudoever, *Biblical Calendars*, 45–48.

significant that it is the verse which is most characteristic of the provisions of the Jubilee which is carried into Jesus' reading.

The presence of Jubilee ideas in Isaiah 61:1–2 is frequently noted. Most obvious is the occurrence of the word "freedom" (דרור); in this context "year of favor" naturally denotes a year of Jubilee.

The two passages can be related conceptually in a way which finds verbal expression in the "day of favor of Yahweh" (the Day of Atonement) which introduces the "year of favor of Yahweh" (the great eschatological Jubilee).[173] However, a glaring problem is encountered in the association of these two passages: Isaiah 58:6 is part of what Yahweh is demanding by way of behavior from his people, but Isaiah 61:1–2 tells what Yahweh himself is going to do when he comes to save. In Luke 4:18 the former passage has been recast into the pattern of the latter. Is it possible to justify such exegetical violence?

One necessarily enters the realm of speculation, but closer consideration of Isaiah 58 does suggest an understanding of what has taken place. God is condemning the people not because they are irreligious, but because they combine outward religion with injustice and inhumanity. They complain that God takes no notice of them when they fast. The reason, says God, is that their fast day is a day for doing their own pleasure and for doing wickedness. It is not necessary to think of the Day of Atonement at this point, though it may be in mind. God's answer to them, however, is in terms of the Day of Atonement, the one, in fact, which inaugurates the Jubilee. "Is such the fast that I choose," asks the Lord—outward show? "Will you call this a fast, and a day acceptable to the Lord [a day of favor of Yahweh]?" (Isa 58:5 RSV). At this point Yahweh describes the day he has chosen in terms reminiscent of the Jubilee Day of Atonement: a day for freeing all the victims of oppression, untying all unjust decrees, and helping all the victims of misfortune. The prophet points out the nature of Yahweh's fast day to show them that theirs is the exact opposite; if they were to act in a manner appropriate to his fast day he would surely hear them and salvation would dawn.[174] It is for this presumably which they fast.

In Isaiah 61 we find an anointed Spirit-filled one proclaiming the "year of favor of Yahweh," a "release" for captives and a general emancipation from all the evils besetting the people. Yahweh's salvation of his

---

173. שנת רצון ליהוה and יום רצון ליהוה.

174. Notice the similarity in the picture of salvation in Isa 58 and 61. Esp. compare 58:12 and 61:4.

people is being described, but in terms of his Jubilee, a period in which he intervenes to bring freedom to his people. It is easy to see in the light of this how the day of favor of Yahweh of Isaiah 58:5–7 could be conceived not simply as God's specification for how his people should behave, but as a description also of how he himself will act when he comes to put into effect the Jubilee-release of his people. Yahweh's day is contrasted with *their* day to bring them to repentance.

If this explanation is anywhere near the truth, for the person who made the midrashic association of these passages, the leading theme must have been the time of God's favor. But is this something of which Luke could have been conscious? That he ends the quotation with "to announce the acceptable year (the year of favor) of the Lord" suggests that it was, for the emphasis naturally falls on this last statement.[175]

A number of scholars have also wondered about the double appearance of *dektos* (δεκτός—acceptable) in Luke 4, once to render *ratsōn* (v. 19) but also in the proverb, "No prophet is *dektos* in his own homeland (*patris*)."[176] The form of the proverb is different in Mark and Matthew where the operative word is *atimos* (ἄτιμος—without honor). I have hesitated to build anything on the Markan dependence of Luke's story, but a proverbial saying is unlikely to have circulated in different forms even in oral tradition, so Luke may well have deliberately recast the proverb to highlight the contrast between God's willingness to "accept" the Nazarenes and their unwillingness to "accept" his messenger.

Tannehill and Perrot also point out that Luke's only other use of *dektos* occurs in Acts 10:35, also in connection with Isaiah 61:1–2.[177] As we shall see later, Peter's speech to Cornelius contains a number of parallels to the Nazareth story.[178] Grounds exist, therefore, for thinking that Luke was fully aware of the importance of the "acceptable year" in his quotation. Could he also have been aware of the sort of exegetical procedure which has been suggested for the transportation of Isaiah 58:6 into the quotation from Isaiah 61:1–2?

---

175. This is so whether or not Jeremias, *Jesus' Promise to the Nations*, 44–46, is correct in thinking the omission of "the day of vengeance of our God" is significant.

176. De la Potterie, "L'onction du Christ," 232; Tannehill, "Mission," 57–58; Perrot, "Luc 4:16–30," 173, 178–79; Hill, "Rejection at Nazareth," 169; Crockett, *OT in Luke*, II.342.

177. See previous footnote.

178. Pages 65–66, below.

At the outset it is clear that Luke was aware of the source of the intruding line for he transcribes it accurately from the Septuagint with only one change to fit it to its new function. This alone indicates that he saw the association of Isaiah 58 and 61 to be important.

Second, his portrayal of John's demands of those who signified their willingness to repent seems to rest on Isaiah 58[179] and shows that Luke understood the passage also in a moral context. To the question of the crowds, "What must we do?" John answers, "He that has two coats let him impart to him that has none; and he that has food, let him do likewise." In Isaiah 58:7 the description of the fast which is acceptable to God continues: "Is it not to share your bread with the hungry, and bring the homeless poor into your house; when you see the naked to cover him . . ." John's instructions to tax collectors and soldiers, to avoid extortion and wrongful exaction and violence, also remind us of the things demanded by God on his fast day.[180]

Whether the account of John's requirements is Luke's own composition or comes from an earlier source, he can hardly be unaware of the connection of thought with Isaiah 58, when it is clear he copied from it.[181] It is therefore safe to conclude that he knew two applications of the passage, one moral and the other eschatological.[182] This suggests an interesting possibility.

John's ethical demands stand in the same relationship to the announcement at Nazareth as Isaiah 58 does to Isaiah 61. What God demands of his people who fast (presumably for salvation)[183] is that they anticipate salvation by doing towards each other what he will do for them in his Jubilee year. In like manner, John requires that those who are coming for baptism (being prepared for salvation) should do the sorts of things which Jesus announces are about to be realized in the kingdom (viz. the end of oppression and the satisfaction of need).[184] We seem to

---

179. Luke 3:11-14. Creed, *Luke*, 52.

180. Isa 58:6.

181. Bammel, "Baptist," 105-06, thinks Luke composed 3:10-14 and "hung" them on something much more radical in Q.

182. Isa 58:6 is also used in Acts 8:23 where σύνδεσμον ἀδικίας (bond of unrighteousness) describes Simon Magus's bondage to Satan.

183. See also Isa 59:1.

184. Luke 4:18-19; cf. 6:20-21

be dealing here with the seeds of an ethic of anticipatory realization of kingdom conditions, about which I will say more at a later point.[185]

We have wandered a little from the main line of our inquiry, but in so doing have succeeded in uncovering the leading thought in Luke's quotation of Isaiah 61 and 58. We will continue to explore the quotation in the direction of the year (day) of favor of Yahweh.

2.3.3 The Time of Favor

There exists in the Old Testament a potentially fruitful field for midrashic exegesis based on the key concept of the time of God's favor. Apart from Isaiah 58:5 and 61:2 there is also Isaiah 49:8, 60:10,[186] and Ps 69:14.[187] The literature of the Qumran sect shows that at least one first-century Palestinian group seized upon it.[188]

Thus in 1QHodayot 15:14-17 (7:19) the Psalmist says that God has created the just man "for the time of good-will (favor) . . . and that he may unloose all the distress of his soul to (possess) eternal salvation and perpetual peace."[189] The wicked, on the other hand, have been created for the time of God's Wrath and the Day of Massacre. The time of favor stands opposite the day of wrath as the time of eschatological salvation.[190] André Dupont-Sommer[191] and Svend Holm-Nielsen[192] both point to

---

185. Pages 187-91, 224-26, below.

186. The Septuagint destroys the connection by translating it as διὰ ἔλεον (because of mercy).

187. Though more personal in tone than the Isaiah passages, this lament too has eschatological dimensions. The psalmist is praying ultimately for the salvation of Zion (Ps 69:35). Note the similarity of Ps 69:33-34 to the Isaiah passages: "For the Lord hears the 'ebiōnim and despises not his prisoners (אסיריו) . . . For the Lord will save Zion and build the cities of Judah." This psalm was much used by the early Christians (John 2:17; 15:25; Rom 15:3; Acts 1:20; Rev 3:5).

188. רצון is a favorite word in the DSS. It is used of human will (CD 2:21, 3:3, 11:4). Sometimes it has sacrificial overtones (1QS 8:10, 9:4; 1QM 2:5). It is used of the pleasure of God, becoming a technical expression for his will (e.g., 1QS 5:1, 9, 10, 9:13, 15) It expresses more than his desire; it is his sovereign *fiat* without which nothing exists or can be known (e.g., 1QS 11:18; 1QM 18:14; 1QH 1:8, 10, 15, 5:4, 10:2, 6, 9). It is the predestinating pleasure of God by which men are elected to salvation (1QS 8:6; 1QH 14:13) becoming "sons of his good pleasure" (בני רצונו – 1QH 4:32-3). Cf. 1QH11:9).

189. "For the time of good-will (favor)" = למועד רצון

190. "Day of wrath" = יום הרגה

191. Dupont-Sommer, *Essene Writings from Qumran*, 246n4.

192. Holm-Nielsen, *Hodayot Psalms from Qumran*, 230n13.

Isaiah 49:8 for the origin of this concept. The clause "that he may release all the distress of his soul" also probably goes back to the thought of the catena of Isaiah passages dealing with the time of favor. 1QHodayot fragment 9,[193] and 11Q Melch 9,[194] also refer to the time of favor (the year of favor in the latter) where it is clear that the final age of salvation is in view. In 1Q34bis 1–6, the time of favor is already operative in the election of the community.[195]

Thus the Qumran sect was able to describe the time of salvation, whether they regarded it solely as future, or as present to some degree, as the period of God's (Melchizedek's) favor.[196] The fact that *ratsōn* had become something of a technical term for them is evidence of an interest at some stage of their history in the Old Testament passages from which the concept is derived, and probably indicates some sort of midrashic exposition of one passage in terms of others.[197] This being so, it cannot be held at all improbable that Jesus or the Palestinian church should also have associated such passages as we find in the Nazareth Sermon. It is not easy to imagine Luke as the originator of such an association, though, as we have seen, he does seem aware of what has happened. He may well have been indoctrinated with such exegesis.

At this point we may conclude that the term "acceptable year" (ἐνιαυτὸς δεκτός—*eniautos dektos*) is the Septuagint equivalent of a known Palestinian expression for the time of God's intervention to save his people. Its connection with the Jubilee has already been noted and must now be examined more closely.

---

193. קץ רצונכה. Sukenik, *Dead Sea Scrolls*, plate 55, fragment 9; translation: Holm-Nielsen, *Hodayot Psalms from Qumran*, 268.

194. הקץ לשנת הרצון. It is partially obliterated and was read by van der Woude, "Melchisedek als himmlische Erlösungsgestalt," 358, as הקק לשנת הרצון, but later as ... הקץ (Jonge and van der Woude, "11QMelchizedek," 302). Horton, "Melchizedek Tradition," 70–71, follows the latter suggestion.

195. קץ רצונך. *DJD* I.154; translation in Vermes, *Dead Sea Scrolls in English*, 206.

196. מועד, קץ, שנת   year, end, time.

197. Though I know of no example of this specifically for "the time of *ratsōn*," we find it in related areas in 11QMelchizedek; Ps. Sol. 11.

2.3.4 Literal Jubilee?

André Trocmé argues that in his sermon Jesus was proclaiming a literal Jubilee, from which much of his ethics, particularly those relating to possessions and the poor, can be explained:

> In his speech, Jesus suddenly demanded that the law be put into effect immediately. This implies among other things expropriating the lands of the wealthy and liquidating the usurious system from which the ruling classes lived.[198]

He is followed by John Howard Yoder,[199] and some support for their ideas might be derived from August Strobel,[200] who calculated that AD 26/27 (which he argues was the year Jesus began his ministry)[201] was a Jubilee year, the tenth after that instituted by Ezra.[202] He links this with the 490 years prophecy of Daniel,[203] and thinks that it was amidst the high expectations associated with this time that Jesus began his ministry. He sees interest in the time reflected in Mark 1:14–15 and in Luke's Nazareth story, and points to 11QMelchizedek 7 for confirmation that great expectations were attached to the time of the tenth Jubilee.[204] However,

---

198. Trocmé, *Jesus and the Nonviolent Revolution*, 27–30.

199. Yoder, *Politics of Jesus*, 34–40.

200. Strobel, "Apokalyptische Terminproblem," 251–54; Strobel, "Ausrufung des Jobeljahrs," 38–50.

201. Normally the beginning of John's ministry is given as 28/29 or 27/28 on the basis of Luke 3:1. Strobel solves this by reckoning the first year of Tiberius from his association with Augustus in ruling the provinces (AD 12).

202. On the authority of Maimonides and others he begins from 464 BC (he supports his case from Eusebius, TestLev, and rabbinic sources). AD 26/27 is thought by others to have been a Sabbath year (Prat, *Jésus Christ*, 491). Cf. Cave, "Sermon at Nazareth," 235, who thinks Jesus "took advantage of the end of a *Schemittah* year, a year which would end on the Day of Atonement, to proclaim his gospel." He thinks the Jubilee was only a memory at this time, but thinks it could have been such a year.

203. Lemoine, "L'année jubilaire," 281–82 counts the seventy weeks prophecy of Daniel as one of the OT passages in which the Jubilee idea is active.

204. Further to Strobel's calculations note those of Dupont-Sommer, *Essene Writings from Qumran*, 121n2. To the 390 years from the Babylonian Captivity to the foundation of the sect, he adds the 20 years to the coming of the Teacher, the 40 years (approx.) of his generation and the 40 years from his disappearance to the Visitation. The total of 490 years gives the reason for the belief of the community that the End was near. Dupont-Sommer thinks the numbers are essentially symbolic.

Strobel does not see the Jubilee as an economic reality, but, at the time, a religious and chronological event.²⁰⁵

11QMelchizedek certainly links the idea of Jubilee with that of salvation. The fragmentary text is introduced by a quotation from Leviticus 25:13 about the Jubilee. This is amplified from Deuteronomy 15:2 which specifies procedure for Sabbath years. In line 4 it is given an interpretation for "the end of days": "Its meaning for the end of days concerns those taken captive whom . . ." In line 6 it appears that these captives are to be liberated,²⁰⁶ and in line 7 the time is specified as the last year of Jubilee, the tenth Jubilee year. Line 9 makes this "the time of the acceptable year of Melchizedek." It is to be a time of judgment and conflict, which culminates in, or is the subject of, the proclamation of peace and salvation (Isaiah 52:7) by the Anointed One mentioned by Daniel. In line 26 the idea of Jubilee returns.

It is clear that we are dealing here with a tradition which understood the Jubilee, or in particular the tenth Jubilee, as the time of ultimate salvation and judgment. A connection with the 490 years of Daniel 9:24-27 is probable. We have no evidence that they were looking towards a particular date. 1QpHabukkuk 7:2 even suggests that they rejected the idea of an exactly revealed moment, and 7:12 recognizes that the time of the End might delay.

We may conclude then that the quotation in the Nazareth sermon probably evoked the idea of Jubilee, at least in the Palestinian realm. If Strobel's authorities are thought to preserve reliable tradition, it may even be that Jesus' mission began in proximity to a Jubilee year. The evidence of Qumran suggests, however, that even if this were so, the moment of God's Jubilee may not have been mechanically tied to the literal Jubilee year. For all this, the thesis of Trocmé and Yoder is open to severe criticism. For there is no indication that Jesus demanded the most important and characteristic provision of the Jubilee: return to ancestral property. Nor is the rejection of Jesus in any of the accounts of the Nazareth episode connected with any demands he made: it is a reaction to his person. Trocmé says that the disciples' leaving all was Jubilee-obedience,²⁰⁷ but the tradition uniformly impresses us with the fact that for Jesus property

---

205. See also van Goudoever, *Biblical Calendars*, 269. The importance of Jubilees as a reckoning of time, in some circles at least, is shown by the Book of Jubilees (see CD 16:3). See 1QS 10:8 for the ceremonial importance of the Jubilee for the Qumran sect.

206. דרור—*derōr*. *derōr* is also associated with Jubilee in 1QS 10:8.

207. Trocmé, *Jesus and the Non-Violent Revolution*, 32.

was a matter of no importance in comparison with the kingdom.²⁰⁸ In a literal Jubilee only those who were holding the lands of others would be required to leave them; the dispossessed would be returning to their homes. Thus, a literal Jubilee cannot be the explanation for the renunciation of property.²⁰⁹

What then are we to make of the idea of Jubilee in the Nazareth sermon? The important thing is to realize that Luke makes nothing of it in a literal sense.²¹⁰ He gives no indication that there was anything special about the Sabbath or the year. The phrase "according to his custom" (κατὰ τὸ εἰωθὸς αὐτῷ) suggests indifference to the identity of that Sabbath.²¹¹ Even Mark's statement, "the time has been fulfilled" (πεπλήρωται ὁ καιρός) is absent from Luke;²¹² only the Scriptures are being fulfilled.

If it is not a literal Jubilee with all its economic stringencies which is being proclaimed, and if Luke is not interested in the actual time of Jesus' sermon, we are thrown back to understanding the Jubilee motif of the reading as part of the traditional imagery of the *eschaton* such as is encountered in 11QMelchizedek and probably in Psalms of Solomon 11.²¹³ It is also to be found in the tenth of the Eighteen Benedictions: "Sound with the great trumpet to announce our freedom; and set up a standard to collect our captives . . . Blessed art thou, O Lord, who gatherest the outcasts of thy people Israel."²¹⁴ The time of salvation is the time of God's Jubilee.²¹⁵ In proclaiming the latter Jesus proclaims the former.

---

208. In Luke 12:14 Jesus refuses to arbitrate in the matter of an inheritance, preferring to warn his listeners against greed.

209. Yoder, *Politics of Jesus*, 74–77, transforms the return to one's ancestral lands into "redistribution of capital," and in that way relates it to Jesus' demand for renunciation.

210. See also van Goudoever, *Biblical Calendars*, 269. He thinks Luke is describing a year of "ministry" (favor) (it turns out to be longer), which opens with the sermon and closes with the sword saying (Luke 22:35–56). Such a view was countered earlier by Holtzmeister, "Angenehme Jahr des Herrn" 272–82.

211. Luke 4:16.

212. Mark 1:15.

213. Ryle and James, *Psalms of Solomon*, 101, translate "Blow ye the trumpet in Sion, yea the holy trumpet of Jubilee."

214. Schürer, *History of the Jewish People*, II.455–63 for translation and history. Also *JE* XI.270–83; Zeitlin, "Shemoneh Esreh," 238–49; further discussion, Légasse, "Volontaires," 339n7.

215. Our first witness to this idea is, of course, Isa 61:1–2. Schürmann, *Lukasevangelium*, 230.

2.3.5 Captive Zion

We have elucidated the leading thought in Luke's description of Jesus' mission: Jesus has come to announce the great Jubilee of God's final deliverance of his people. Now we must examine those who, along with the poor, are the special objects of this proclamation: the captives, the blind, and the oppressed. We will discover that these are three alternative descriptions of a single reality: Israel's captivity.

2.3.5.1 *To Announce Release to Captives—* κηρύξαι αἰχμαλώτοις ἄφεσιν—לקרא לשבוים דרור

Aichmalōtoi (αἰχμάλωτοι) strictly means "captives of war" as does *shebuim* (שבוים). It is most naturally understood in relation to Isaiah 40–55 as captive exiles. Even here, however, the idea of captivity has been applied to Israel as a whole.[216] Thus it may be that the *aichmalōtoi* of Isaiah 61:1 should be taken not as those still in exile, but as a characterization of Jerusalem, inhabited, but still captive to foreign powers and to a host of other evils.[217]

There were times in Israel's history when exiles loomed large in people's minds, and when salvation was conceived in terms of their return,[218] but one wonders whether this concept would have had great relevance in New Testament times. The Qumran scrolls show no interest in the idea of return from exile as an object of their eschatological expectations.[219]

In 11QMelchizedek, however, captives (השבויים) are mentioned in an eschatological setting. Unfortunately, the fragmentary nature of the text does not allow us to see exactly who is meant, and in what sense they were thought of as captive.[220] Isaiah 61:1 is certainly in view, and

---

216. "Captive daughter of Zion"; שביה בת ציון; ἡ αἰχμάλωτος θυγάτηρ Σιών. Isa 52:20. Compare Ps 79:11; 102:18–22.

217. It is often difficult to tell whether the OT is speaking of exiles, or of the captivity of the nation, or both. In any case, captivity is something in which the whole nation is involved. See Ps 13(14):7, 69:32–36, 84(85):1, 102:18–22, 125(126):1; Isa 1:27 (LXX); Zech 9:11–12.

218. Ps. Sol. 11:1; 1 Bar. (esp. ch 5); *Tg. Isa.*, which intensifies references to captivity and return.

219. At one stage they saw themselves as exiles in the land of Damascus but this did not call forth eschatological hopes. Their residing in the desert is not envisaged as an exile, but as a voluntary "going out" to prepare the way of the Lord 1QS 8:13–14.

220. It is tempting to read 1QH 9:8 (אסיר עד קץ רצונכה . . .) as ". . . a prisoner until

no doubt the sect members are included in some way. James A. Sanders thinks "captives" is "an epithet for the Covenanters like 'poor' or 'pure' or 'good' in other Qumran texts."[221] The emphasis on atonement and rescue from Belial points to the likelihood that sin and demonic bondage were part of their understanding of captivity. This is strengthened when we find a similar notion in the Testaments of the Twelve Patriarchs, writings which share much in common with the outlook of Qumran. Testament of Dan 5:10-13 reads:

> And there shall arise unto you from the tribe of *Judah and of Levi the salvation of the Lord;* and he shall make war against Beliar, and execute an everlasting vengeance on our enemies; And the captivity (αἰχμαλωσίαν), he shall take from Beliar, *the souls of the saints,* And turn disobedient hearts unto the Lord . . . And no longer shall Jerusalem endure desolation, Nor Israel be led captive.[222]

We must take care, however, not to read our own dichotomy between "spiritual" and "political" into these passages. The demonic bondage into which the nation had fallen was manifested in sin, suffering, and political subjugation. In Testament of Levi 5:6 an angel says: "I am the angel who intercedeth for the nation of Israel that they may not be smitten utterly, for every evil spirit attacketh it." The Assumption of Moses, a writing from about the time of Jesus, says of the coming of God's kingdom: "And then his kingdom shall appear throughout all his creation, and then Satan shall be no more, and sorrows shall depart with him."[223]

It is clear, then, that by the New Testament period captives are more likely to have been seen in terms of the overall spiritual-political oppression of Israel, than as literal prisoners or exiles.

---

the time of thy favor," though אסיר could mean "I shall withdraw," but see line 6, "cords of the spirit" בעבותי רוח). Text: see page 56n193, above.

221. Sanders, "Isaiah 61 to Luke 4," 92.
222. Probable Christian additions in italics. Cf. *T. Zeb.* 9:8.
223. *Ass. Mos.* 10:1.

2.3.5.2 Send Forth the Oppressed in a Release—
ἀπόστελλε τεθραυσμένους ἐν ἀφέσει—ושלח רצוצים חפשים

Thrauō (θραύω) occurs only here in the New Testament. Its literal meaning is "to break (in pieces)" and metaphorically "to oppress."[224] In Isaiah 58:6 it is used of the oppression of the weak by the strong, but most frequently it is used of God's judging his enemies,[225] or of his delivering Israel to oppression by foreign powers.[226]

In the Damascus Document the overseer of the camp is to carry out the provisions of Isaiah 58:6: "He shall unloose all the bonds which bind them that there may no more be any oppressed or broken among his congregation."[227] Dupont-Sommer thinks this is a reference to spiritual bonds.[228]

Thus "to send the oppressed in freedom" is open to the same breadth of interpretation as "to proclaim release to captives."

2.3.5.3 And to the Blind (Prisoners) the Opening of the Eyes—
τυφλοῖς ἀνάβλεψιν—ולאסורים פקח קוח

On the surface, giving sight to the blind seems somewhat removed from releasing captives, but this is only because we are unaccustomed to this kind of imagery. In fact, the Masoretic Text speaks of opening the eyes of prisoners (literally, "those bound"). The Septuagint has evidently had difficulties with this metaphor and has translated it by analogy with Isaiah 42:7 as opening the eyes of the blind.[229]

Exile was characterized as darkness,[230] so it is logical that freedom should be symbolized by the return of sight. This is not so strange when it is considered that dungeons were very dark places.[231] Light and darkness were also images for the presence or absence of God,[232] and thus absence

---

224. רצוץ is similar in function.
225. Exod 15:6; Num 24:17; Isa 2:10; Jdt 13:14; Ps. Sol. 17:22.
226. Esp. Deut 28:33 (τεθραυσμένος); Num 16:46 (17:11–15); 2 Chr 6:24.
227. עשיק ורצוץ. CD 13:9–10. Compare Hos 5:11 (MT).
228. Dupont-Sommer, *Essene Writings from Qumran*, 157n4.
229. For further discussion see BDB, 824; France, *Jesus and the Old Testament*, 252–53; Sanders, "Isaiah 61 to Luke 4," 80–82.
230. Isa 42:7; Compare *Tg. Isa.* 42:7.
231. Joseph describes his prison as "the abode of darkness"; *T. Jos.* 8:5; also 2:4, 9:1.
232. Isa 60:19–20.

from the land was conceived as dwelling in darkness. The targum has caught the force of the image when it renders Isaiah 61:1 "(and to say) to the prisoners, 'Be revealed (or Reveal yourselves) to the light.'" Thus, the Hebrew text could be dealing here with the concept of salvation from exile.

However, it was possible for Zion herself to become a land of darkness, in need of the light. In the depressed situation of the post-exilic community, the people cry out: "We look for light, and behold darkness, and for brightness but we walk in gloom. We grope for the wall like the blind, we grope like those who have no eyes."[233] This is not simply a description of lack of spiritual knowledge. It is a situation of hopeless mourning, where judgment and salvation are far away. It expresses the frustration and Godforsakenness of the people: "We have become as they over whom thou never barest rule."[234] Zion's salvation, the coming of God to rule in their midst, is described as the dawning of light.[235]

At Qumran we see a further development of the light-darkness concept. For them it is not so much Israel and the nations which are symbolized as the place of light and darkness; rather have light and darkness become symbols of the ultimate division between God and Belial, a division which manifests itself everywhere and in everyone. Israel itself is in darkness; only in the community does the light shine. The Teacher of Righteousness "uncovered the eyes" of those who for twenty years groped in darkness.[236] Light is the truth and grace which comes from God.

However, in the experience of the Teacher, recounted in the Hymns, another application of light-darkness imagery is encountered, this time to describe the misery resulting from his persecution. 1QHodayot 5:32–34 reads:

> And the light of my face darkened to thick night
> and my brightness changed into blackness . . .
> And to (my) distress they added still more.
> They shut me up in the darkness
> And I ate the bread of groaning . . .

---

233. Isa 59:9–10.

234. Isa 63:19.

235. Isa 58:10, 60:1–3, 19–20, 62:1. Also 9:1–2 on Galilee under occupation. For the later equation of light and salvation see *Tg. Isa.* 9:1; 60:1; *Midr. Ps.* 27:1; *Pes. Rab.* 36; 1 En. 1:8, 5:6g, 38:4, 45:4, 58:4–6.

236. CD 1:9–10, 2:14. Cf. 1QH 4:5–6, 27; 18:19; 1QS 11:3–5. See also *T. Levi* 19:1; *T. Ash.* 5:3; 1 En. 90:35.

> For my eyes were darkened because of sorrow
> And my soul (was plunged) in bitterness every day.

This comes close to a description of suffering and bitterness as blindness.[237] Significantly, he adds a new metaphor, that of being bound in prison:

> For (I was) bound with unbreakable cords
> and with chains impossible to sunder,
> and a stou(t) wall (held me shut up)
> (and) bars of iron and door(s of bronze).
> And my prison was like the Abyss without (...)
> (and the bonds of Be)lial bound my soul without any (escape ...).[238]

In both of these passages suffering is symbolized as enclosure in a dungeon, and if, as seems probable, it is "light" that the Abyss is without,[239] both see this prison as a lightless place.

Thus, in the Qumran literature not only are light and darkness used as symbols of the realm of God and Belial, and hence of salvation and perdition; they also signify truth and ignorance, blessedness and suffering. The opening of the eyes might indicate spiritual enlightenment or deliverance from anguish. In this last case we find a natural blending of ideas of darkness and blindness with those of imprisonment and bondage, just as we find in the quotation from Isaiah 61:1. Admittedly, in the Hymns it is used of an individual, but such imagery is equally applicable to the nation.[240] May it not be that the Teacher has taken imagery which originally applied to Zion and reapplied it to his own suffering?

It is possible that even a reader of the Septuagint, as Luke was, might, if he was familiar with Palestinian symbolism, have understood opening the eyes of the blind as something more than a miracle of healing.[241]

---

237. Also 1QH 9:26-28; cf. *T. Jos.* 2:4; 1 Bar. 1:12, 2:18; 2 Bar. 48:50. This notion is also to be found in the OT: Job 11:16-17, 17:7; Isa 8:22–9:2, 53:11 (LXX, DSS); Lam 3:1-2, 5-7; cf. *Tg. Isa.* 50:10; *Gen. Rab.* 97 on Gen 49:13.

238. 1QH 5:36-39 (13:36-9).

239. Gen 1:2.

240. Isa 8:22—9:2.

241. For contact points with classical Greek conceptions see Bultmann, "Lichtsymbolik," 1-36, and especially 4-10, where death is darkness and life and all that makes it worthwhile is symbolized as light. Combrink, "Structure and Significance of Luke 4:16-30," 31, suggests that opening the eyes of the blind and freeing captives may be synonymous, purely on the basis of their structural parallelism.

What we have disclosed is a possible unity in the three images: "captives," "oppressed," and "blind." Israel suffers captivity and oppression. She is in bondage to Satan, a state of affairs which manifests itself in inner disorder, and, outwardly, in the foreign yoke. The people walk in a darkness of ignorance, shame, and suffering. The light of God's presence is far away. But Jesus announces that all this is ended.[242]

2.3.5.4 Realities behind the Metaphors

It is now possible to test these findings by examining how Luke portrays the fulfilment of the prophecy whose "today" Jesus announces in the Nazareth Synagogue. How does Jesus go about freeing Israel and bringing them forth to the light?

Luke 24:21 and Acts 1:6–7 make it clear that Luke understands the political dimensions of Israel's salvation but sees them belonging to the future.[243] Nevertheless, something does happen which justifies him seeing the presence of salvation in Jesus. Peter's speech to Cornelius reveals what it is.[244] The speech is peculiarly revealing because 10:37–42 is like a summary of the Gospel of Luke, with the allusion to Isaiah 61:1 in its Luke 4:18 position. It begins with John's baptism, next comes the anointing (Luke 3:22; 4:18), and then follows a description of what Jesus did: "who went around doing good and healing all who were oppressed by the devil."[245] The sequence of thought—anointed with the Spirit, healing all those oppressed/overpowered by the devil—is a strong indication that Luke understood the imagery of releasing the captives and

---

242. Some support for this "national" interpretation of Luke 4:18 might be gleaned from Luke's curious omission of ἰάσασθαι τοὺς συντετριμμένους τῇ καρδίᾳ. Its inclusion would not destroy the picture, but if Luke had been thinking of suffering individuals, rather than the nation, its omission would have been absurd. However, this hardly constitutes an explanation for the omission. Nor do I know of any convincing explanation. Further see Toy, *Quotations in the New Testament*, 78–79; Dupont, *Béatitudes*, II.132n1; Maillot, "Réparer les coeurs brisés." 97–103. Reicke, "Jesus in Nazareth," 49, supports the inclusion of the line on metrical grounds.

243. Cadbury, *Making of Luke-Acts*, 278, says of Luke's awareness here that it "portrays either accurate information or accurate imagination." Wainwright, "Luke and the Restoration," 76–79, thinks Luke is influenced by Jewish expectations. Cf. W. Manson, *Luke*, viii.

244. Acts 10:34–43.

245. ὃς διῆλθεν εὐεργετῶν καὶ ἰώμενος πάντας τοὺς καταδυναστευομένους ὑπὸ τοῦ διαβόλου. If Stanton, *Jesus*, 70–75, is correct in seeing the influence of Ps 107:20 here, it may indicate another source of captivity-darkness imagery (Ps 107:10, 14).

the downtrodden in terms of Jesus' conflict with and victory over the demonic forces which held the people in captivity.[246]

"Oppressed" (καταδυναστευόμενος) is practically synonymous with "broken" (τεθραυσμένος), being used once in the Septuagint to translate רצץ (crush).[247] Moreover, the combination of "healed" (ἰώμενος) with the devil shows that more than exorcism is intended. All Jesus' ministry is seen as undoing the works of the devil.[248]

Once we grasp the significance for Luke of Jesus' conflict with Satan, and that this is in mind as he presents Jesus proclaiming liberty to the people, then it appears more than fortuitous that the Nazareth Sermon falls between two stories which also deal with Jesus' conflict with Satan. Is there not an integral link between Jesus' own victory over Satan's temptations, and his appearance in Nazareth to declare the end of Satanic bondage?[249] Following the sermon his very first work is to cast the demon from a man in the synagogue at Capernaum.

Two sayings in the Gospel are also indicative of the direction of Luke's thought. At the return of the seventy Jesus says: "I saw Satan fallen like lightening from heaven."[250] The saying is modelled on Isaiah 14:12. The king of Babylon has become Satan in the thinking of Luke, and probably originally in the thinking of Jesus. Thus, not only has Old Testament prophecy relating to the physical captivity of Israel been applied to the Satanic captivity of the people, but the king of Babylon, "the oppressor,"[251] who is to be cut to the ground, has become Satan.[252]

The Q parable of the Strong Man stands within the same framework of thought.[253] It is inspired by Isaiah 49:24-25, and again the king of Babylon has become Satan. Luke did not invent this idea but has understood

---

246. See also Caird, *Luke*, 36; Glöckner, *Verkündigung des Heils*, 134-36; Franklin, *Christ the Lord*, 24-25; Thompson, *Luke*, 30-31.

247. 1 Kgdms 12:4 (1 Sam 12:4); cf. Amos 4:1; Hos 5:11; it is used in Jas 2:6 of the rich oppressing the poor.

248. See Luke 13:16.

249. Cf. Betz, "The Kerygma of Luke."

250. ἐθεώρουν τὸν σατανᾶν ὡς ἀστραπὴν ἐκ τοῦ οὐρανοῦ πεσόντα. Luke 10:18

251. Isa 14:4.

252. On the power of the seventy to cast out demons as a sign of the presence of salvation, see *T. Sim.* 6.6. "Then shall all the spirits of deceit be given to be trodden under foot, and men shall rule over wicked spirits." Also *T. Levi* 18:12; cf *T. Benj.* 5:2.

253. Luke 11:21-22.

it. In 11:22 God "will divide up his spoils"²⁵⁴ (not in Matthew), which takes up Isaiah 49:25 which is probably then associated midrashically with Isaiah 53:12.

Finally, Acts 26:18 shows how Luke equates the receiving of sight with coming to the light, and sees both in terms of rescue from satanic captivity. Luke 22:53 shows how closely associated are darkness and the activity of Satan in the mind of Luke (only he records this saying).

Having confirmed in this section that the previous course of the inquiry has led in the right direction, we are now able to gather together this understanding of Luke 4:18-19.

Claiming for himself the role of the anointed one who is to "evangelize" the poor, Jesus announces the final Jubilee of God, which is the long-awaited time of Israel's salvation. He spells it out in terms of release from captivity and oppression, and opening of the eyes of the blind, images which to a Palestinian audience (and, as we have seen, to Luke also) meant the end of Israel's subjugation to Rome and the breaking of the satanic oppression of sickness, possession, sin, and ignorance.

Bammel has suggested that the images we have examined are summed up in advance by the expression "to evangelize the poor" (εὐαγγελίσασθαι πτωχοῖς).²⁵⁵ If this should prove true, we will be able to conclude that Luke understands "the poor" in the Nazareth Sermon as suffering Israel.

2.3.6 To Evangelize the Poor— εὐαγγελίσασθαι πτωχοῖς—בשר ענוים

When we compare him with Philo and Josephus we find something of an oddity on the part of Luke: an absolute use of εὐαγγελίζεσθαι (*euaggelizesthai*) anterior (at least logically) to the use of the word for Christian evangelism.²⁵⁶ In Josephus we find only one use of the verb without an

---

254. καὶ τὰ σκῦλα αὐτοῦ διαδίδωσιν.

255. *TDNT* VI.906.

256. On Luke's "unterminologisch" use of the word see Stuhlmacher, *Paulinische Evangelium*, 229-30.

object (accusative or with *peri*) and here it is clearly understood.[257] Philo has three such cases but each time the object is supplied from the context.[258]

We are thrust back, therefore, to the Septuagint, where we find an absolute use of *euaggelizesthai* (בשר) to describe the work of a (professional) herald.[259] On its own, however, this is no solution to the problem posed by Luke; the explanation lies in an extension of this use in Isaiah.

In Isaiah *euaggelizesthai* is used absolutely and with an object. In Isaiah 52:7 the "evangelizer" (εὐαγγελιζόμενος—מבשר) proclaims "peace" and "good." Babylon has fallen and the herald proclaims a new era of peace. However, the dimensions of this peace transcend the historical situation. The fall of Babylon is to be the final act of God to redeem his people and to establish Jerusalem in everlasting peace. The herald, then, is more than a messenger of a battle won and peace attained. He announces ultimate deliverance, proclaiming to Zion, "Your God reigns," which the targum renders, "The kingdom of thy God has been revealed." The picture in Isaiah 40:9–11 is similar. In Isaiah 41:27 (Hebrew only) the object of the "evangelizer's" proclamation is uncertain because of the difficulty of the text. The targum is probably correct in seeing it as the fulfilment of former prophecy: "The words of comfort that the prophets prophesied afore-time concerning Zion, *they have come to pass* (אתר הא)." In any case he is proclaiming salvation and it is natural to link him with the messengers of Isaiah 40:9 and 52:7.

Thus, when we come to Isaiah 61:1 we are well prepared for an absolute reference to one who "evangelizes" in Yahweh's name, and it is natural to understand that his message is final salvation. Not that the "evangelizer" has necessarily become a technical term at this stage (see Isaiah 60:6), but in certain contexts it is recognizably a reference to the proclamation of salvation (comfort) to Israel. In such contexts it is important to understand that this "evangelizer" is not a "long-term predictor" like the prophets. He is bound up in the salvation he announces, for he announces its presentness, that God has won the battle, and that peace is already on its way.

Thus, in Psalms of Solomon 11:1, "the voice of the evangelizer" is a recognizable symbol for the dawning of Israel's salvation. The sound of

---

257. Josephus, *Ant.* 18.228; there are eleven more occurrences of the word in Josephus.

258. *Ios.* 250; *Virt.* 41; *Legat.* 231 (seven more occurrences).

259. 2 Kgdms 4:10, 18:20, 26 (2 Kgdms = 2 Sam).

his voice is the trumpet which inaugurates the Jubilee.[260] The mere hearing of this "voice of the evangelizer" (φωνὴν εὐαγγελιζομένου) means that "God has had mercy on Israel in their visitation."

The picture at Qumran is somewhat different. They expected Melchizedek to proclaim liberty to them at the final (tenth) Jubilee.[261] This would be the time of their salvation. The *mebassēr* (מבשר—courier) of Isaiah 52:7 and 61:1, however, seems to have been identified as the Teacher of Righteousness.[262] He is the one who prepares them for eternal joy. Nevertheless, insofar as they saw the work of the Teacher as part of the end-time, and because of his teaching lived in expectation of an imminent salvation, they have not entirely lost sight of the close connection between the *mebassēr* and final salvation.

At the end of the first century Jose the Galilean identified the *mebassēr* with the Messiah.[263] Here the "evangelizer" is the Savior, and his message actualizes salvation.

Thus, there is sufficient evidence to show that *euaggelizomai—bissēr* had salvific connotations in Palestinian Judaism of Jesus' day.[264] In its absolute form it would have been readily understood, especially when there were other suggestions of its Isaianic derivation. It meant "to proclaim salvation," not in the long-term predictive sense, but in the sense of announcing a salvation which was already dawning. As Friedrich puts it, "The message actualizes the new time (of divine rule)."[265]

Once it is seen that *euaggelizesthai* carries with it the idea of salvation it can be seen that the rest of the quotation in Luke 4:18–19 in a sense says no more than is implicit in this single word. To "evangelize" in effect means to proclaim (and effect) release for the captives, sight for the blind, and freedom for the oppressed; in short, to inaugurate the Jubilee of God's salvation of his people Israel. The equation of "the poor" with captive-blind-oppressed Israel is then demanded by the context. The conclusion of section 2.2, that "the poor" as the objects of God's salvation

---

260. Page 59, above.
261. לקרא להמה דרר 11 QMelch 6.
262. 11QMelch 15–20, esp. 20; cf. 1QH 18:14–15 (21:14–15).
263. *Perek Hashshalom* 59b (*Sonc.* 600); *TDNT* II.715–16.
264. Also, perhaps, 2 Bar. 46:6.
265. *TDNT* II.718.

could be understood as "suffering Israel," is found to make perfect sense in Jesus' sermon at Nazareth.²⁶⁶

At this point the objection could be raised that "the poor" (= captives-blind-oppressed) might refer to a remnant, as at Qumran, rather than to the whole people. This possibility may be tested by asking with respect to Luke's other uses of *euaggelizesthai*,²⁶⁷ whom he understands to be addressed by this "evangel."

In fact, we find no restriction in Luke's Gospel on the scope of "evangelization." Jesus is anxious to preach in *all* the cities of Judea.²⁶⁸ He preaches in the synagogues—hardly where one would go to find an outcast remnant. He places no restriction on the twelve when he sends them out. Luke stresses the comprehensiveness of their mission when he says they "evangelized" "everywhere."²⁶⁹ In Jerusalem Jesus teaches "the people (*laos*)" in the temple.²⁷⁰

The only change in Acts is that the scope of "evangelization" is widened to include the gentiles. The only example in Luke-Acts of an individual being "evangelized" is the Ethiopian eunuch.²⁷¹ He is scarcely a representative of an economically or socially deprived class (though his being a eunuch is probably significant).

The clearest expression of Luke's mind on this matter comes in Acts 10:36, where strong links with the Nazareth Sermon are apparent. The "word" was sent "to the sons of Israel evangelizing peace through Jesus Christ."²⁷² For Luke, then, the recipients of the "evangel," i.e., "the poor," are "the sons of Israel" understood in terms of their great need of healing, understanding, forgiveness, freedom, and peace; in short, their need of

---

266. Bammel, "Israels Dienstbarkeit," 295–305, explains the proverb "Poverty befits Israel like red trapping a white horse," which occurs in various forms in rabbinic literature, in terms of the notion that the Messiah would come riding a white horse (Israel). He attributes this saying to Akiba. Poverty (עניות, מסכנות), which he interprets not simply as economic hardship, but as Israel's bondage to Rome ("Dienstbarkeit"), predisposes Israel for salvation, and is thus a precursor to the Messiah's coming. This accords well with the picture I have presented.

267. Luke's fondness for εὐαγγελίζομαι is best explained from the influence of Isa 61:1 (Stuhlmacher, *Paulinische Evangelium*, 233).

268. Luke 4:43–44, 8:1. Influence of the Nazareth Sermon is apparent in Luke's redaction of 4:43.

269. πανταχοῦ—Luke 9:6.

270. Luke 20:1.

271. Acts 8:35.

272. τοῖς υἱοῖς Ἰσραὴλ εὐαγγελιζόμενος εἰρήνην διὰ Ἰησοῦ Χριστοῦ.

salvation.²⁷³ We will now carry these conclusions into the story of Jesus' rejection at Nazareth.

2.3.7 Rejection at Nazareth

Luke sees Jesus as the Spirit-endowed Christ,²⁷⁴ announcing the release of the people of Israel from their bondage to Satan—hence from all suffering and need. Jesus' only comment on the reading, "Today this scripture has been fulfilled in your hearing," is almost demanded by the nature of the prophecy. For it is one which when proclaimed by the legitimate "anointed one" must come into effect at the time of its proclamation.²⁷⁵ The drama of the "today" is that it transforms a mere reading of Scripture into a divine proclamation of the age of salvation. To what extent Luke gives the "today" at Nazareth an absolute significance is more difficult to decide.²⁷⁶ He has already given a summary of Jesus' Spirit-empowered ministry in Galilee and so is not thinking that it began in Nazareth. For the people of Nazareth, however, when they hear the liberating word proclaimed by the anointed one ("in your ears"),²⁷⁷ it is the beginning. Luke may see the "today" in a double sense: within the story itself it means the coming of salvation among the Nazarenes themselves in the person of Jesus, but in the light of the programmatic significance of the story, it represents the coming of salvation to Israel.

This means that any interpretation of the story which sees Jesus to be offering salvation to some group other than the people of Nazareth (or Israel)²⁷⁸ and excluding those whom he addresses must be rejected. Luke calls the message "words of grace" because the hearers are Israelites,

273. See also Luke 2:10.
274. See van Unnik, "Jesus the Christ," 113; Thompson, *Luke*, 25–28.
275. Noack, *Gottesreich bei Lukas*, 48.
276. On σήμερον (today) see Rice, "Fulfilled in Your Ears," 45–46; Flender, *Theologian of Redemptive History*, 147–52; Grundmann, "Komposition des lukanischen 'Reiseberichts,'" 253–54; Drury, *Tradition and Design*, 70–71. Against the view of Conzelmann, *Theology of St Luke*, 28, 36, that σήμερον represents the inauguration of a "Satanless" period (also Robinson, *Way of the Lord*, 38–42), see Marshall, *Luke: Historian and Theologian*, 119–21, and Glöckner, *Verkündigung des Heils*, 132–33.
277. Compare 2 Cor 6:2. Flender, *Theologian of Redemptive History*, 152, says "Each one present is individually gripped by the word and compelled to make a 'decision.'"
278. E.g., Hill, "Rejection at Nazareth," 169–70; Haenchen, *Weg Jesu*, 219; Crockett, *OT in Luke*, II.343–44.

there and then receiving the word of salvation and grace.[279] They are understandably amazed.

This is perhaps the best point at which to appreciate the difference between the outlook of Qumran and that of Jesus, as Luke presents him. J. A. Sanders ascribes two axioms to the Qumran sect: they live in the end time, and all the blessings of the Old Testament apply to them, and all the woes to those outside the community.[280] Jesus, he thinks, holds to the first but not the second. The ire of the Nazareth synagogue is aroused because Jesus challenged their covenantal self-understanding and brought his prophetic criticism to bear on them. Sanders is right to deny the second axiom to Jesus, but his manner of deducing this from the Nazareth story is incorrect. There is no challenge to their covenantal self-understanding; Jesus proclaims to them their salvation. It is not his refusal to limit salvation to them which establishes his non-sectarian outlook and raises their ire, but the fact that *he* can stand in a synagogue and offer Israel's salvation to all present. His rejection is related to the fact that it is *he* who offers it to them.

Thus, Glöckner is correct to see "Jesus' human lowliness" as a motive for his rejection.[281] He is wrong, however, to see "his mission to the lowly and poor" as a second motive.[282] For the people of Nazareth are "the downtrodden and poor," and would hope to be thought so.[283] The fact that Jesus addresses them as such with the message of salvation is a measure of his openness to *all* Israel.

Though some scholars have declined to see a negative response in the words, "Is not this Joseph's son?" in its Lukan context it surely is.[284] For it is vital to realize that the "today" which transformed the scripture reading into a divine proclamation also transformed the reader into a divine messenger. It makes him the Messiah who inaugurates the salvation of God.[285] Admittedly Luke does not have the offensive "son of Mary" in

---

279. Violet, "Nazareth-Perikope," 264–66, thinks χάρις (grace, favor) was used to translate רצון (favor) (Aram. רעות, רעותה). This is a further indication that we have grasped the right "Leitgedanke."

280. Sanders, "From Isaiah 61 to Luke 4," 75–106.

281. "Die menschliche Niedrigkeit Jesu": Glöckner, *Verkündigung des Heils*, 145.

282. "Seine Sendung zu den Erniedrigten und Armen."

283. "Die Erniedrigten und Armen."

284. Luke 4:22.

285. In my view it is pointless to talk about a lost sermon. More could not have been said. Luke never suggests that Jesus gave a conventional address. It is a story of

his account.²⁸⁶ Nevertheless, they clearly baulk at his person. How can the son of Joseph be the one to inaugurate the age of salvation? It is not necessary to see this as a hostile reaction;²⁸⁷ that comes later. For the moment it is simply a refusal to believe "that anything good could come out of Nazareth."²⁸⁸ Jesus anticipates the rest of their response: a defiant challenge to prove himself,²⁸⁹ which he rejects as non-acceptance.

The following biblical illustrations show that when a prophet is rejected he may go elsewhere: those who might have been thought to have first claim on the blessings he carries may find themselves bypassed in favor of others. Admittedly, there is no mention of rejection of the prophet in the stories themselves, but in the context of the proverb, "No prophet is acceptable in his own country," and the known apostasy of the Elijah period, this may be assumed. Thus, the people of Nazareth are denied any share in salvation because they deny the one who brings it to them. Salvation goes elsewhere with the prophet.

The same thought is expressed in Jesus' answer to the disciples of John the Baptist.²⁹⁰ Many mighty works characteristic of the age of salvation are witnessed, and the poor are having salvation proclaimed to them, but there is a danger that people will stumble at the messenger; "the outward appearance is not what one would expect in 'the Coming One.'"²⁹¹ Jesus, therefore, ends with the beatitude: "blessed is whoever

---

action and reaction. Finkel's theory that the Beatitudes constitute the text of the lost sermon is without foundation ("Sermon at Nazareth," 112-14; *Pharisees*, 155-58). Nor is there reason to think, as does Bajard, "Péricope de Nazareth," 170, that the sermon goes on after an interruption by Luke to show us what reaction Jesus was receiving.

286. See Lightfoot, *History and Interpretation*, 197.

287. Nor to follow Violet, "Nazareth-Perikope," 256-57, and Jeremias, *Jesus' Promise to the Nations*, 44, in thinking that they bore witness *against* him. For a critique of these see Hill, "Rejection at Nazareth," 163-65; Anderson, "Rejection at Nazareth Pericope," 266-70.

288. John 1:46. Compare George, "Prédication inaugurale," 21-22; Brun, "Besuch Jesu in Nazareth," 9; Glöckner, *Verkündigung des Heils*, 146-47.

289. Nolland, *Luke's Readers*, 13-26, thinks 4:23 contains two challenges. The former is a direct challenge to Jesus' person: if he is who he says, why hasn't he done something for himself? The latter is a challenge for authenticating signs: what he has allegedly (ἠκούσαμεν—we have heard) done in Capernaum, he should do here.

290. Luke 7:22-23. For views on this pericope see Dupont, "L'ambassade de Jean-Baptiste," 805-21, 943-59.

291. Van Unnik, "Jesus the Christ," 115. Compare Stanton, "Christology of Q," 29-32, for a discussion of ὁ ἐρχόμενος (the coming one).

does not take offense at me."²⁹² It is the response to Jesus' person which finally decides whether salvation "stays"²⁹³ or departs.²⁹⁴

In the Nazareth story Luke wishes to tell his readers that Jesus the Messiah proclaimed salvation freely to all Israel but that from the very beginning his ministry encountered refusal. From the moment that the gracious words announcing the time of salvation were heard, the one who bore them was rejected. Because he is the one who brings the actualization of his message, rejection of him means also the rejection of salvation. He will go elsewhere and the mission will go on, but the position and importance of this story shows that for Luke it goes on under the shadow of rejection.²⁹⁵

2.4 THE SONG OF MARY, LUKE 1:46-55

The Magnificat has frequently been grouped with the passages we have been studying as evidence of Luke's concern for the poor and downtrodden and antipathy towards the rich. It has also been grouped with the Beatitudes and Woes and the parable of the Rich Man and Lazarus to manifest a doctrine of reversal (περιπέτεια).²⁹⁶ Those who are poor now will be rich then, and vice versa. It will concern us to keep both these possibilities in mind as we examine the Magnificat. First, however, we must make some inquiry into the literary origin of this poem.

2.4.1 Literary Character

The Magnificat is one of a number of poetic pieces set within the matrix of Luke's infancy narrative. The character of this prologue has been much debated over the past century, views ranging from those who see

---

292. καὶ μακάριός ἐστιν ὃς ἐὰν μὴ σκανδαλισθῇ ἐν ἐμοί.

293. μακάριος—happy. Dupont, "L'ambassade de Jean-Baptiste,"952, says "En regle générale, μακάριος vise le Bonheur de deux qui sont admis à participer au salut messianique (As a general rule *makarios* envisages the blessedness of those who are admitted to participate in the messianic salvation)." Dupont's view differs from my own in that he sees those who do not take offense at Jesus as a further group who, though not of the "poor," are offered a share in the blessings of the poor. In my view it is the danger of refusing the kingdom through stumbling at the messenger which is the point.

294. Compare Luke 10:5-6.

295. Further, Schütz, *Leidende Christus*, 42-46.

296. E.g., Dodd, "Beatitudes," 4-6.

the whole as a unified source which Luke has translated and attached to the start of his Gospel,[297] to those who see the whole (including the canticles) as a free composition of Luke.[298] Most scholars have avoided these extremes. Nevertheless, J. Gresham Machen, after a thorough critique of Harnack's position,[299] was still persuaded that Harnack was correct in assigning to Luke a large role in the construction of the infancy narratives.[300] There has been a trend in this direction in recent times, too, in the recognition of the importance of the prologue to an understanding of Luke's theology.[301] One might sum up the results of a century of attention to the source question in the prologue thus: we must allow that Luke may have used sources, though it is not possible with any certainty to isolate or identify them; nor is it possible even to decide whether they were written or oral, or in which language they existed before Luke used them. The difficulty arises because Luke has reproduced whatever he has used in his own style. Whatever sources may have been used have been thoroughly edited, or even digested and re-expressed, before being incorporated in his infancy story.[302]

The case of the longer canticles, however, is different. Harnack sought to demonstrate for the Magnificat that, when the influence of the Septuagint is allowed for, the residue is Lukan.[303] However, he confined his attention only to a small group of Septuagint passages, which he thought formed the basis of the hymn. Machen[304] showed that when all septuagintalisms were removed nothing remained to be identified as

---

297. Hillmann, "Kindheitsgeschichte," 192–261; Schmid, *Lukas*, 33.

298. Harnack, "Magnifikat der Elisabet," 62–85; Harnack, *Luke the Physician*, 97–102, 199–218; for Harnack this did not mean Luke had no recourse to traditional and historical sources. A more radical position is taken by Goulder and Sanderson, "St Luke's Genesis," 12–30, who see the prologue as a "pious meditation" and a "piece of Haggadah" of Luke.

299. See also Machen, "Hymns," 1–38; Zimmermann, "Hilgenfeld und Harnack," 247–90.

300. Machen, "Origin of the First Two Chapters of Luke," 256.

301. Oliver, "Lucan Birth Stories," 202–26; Minear, "Luke's Use of the Birth Stories," 111–30; Tatum, "Epoch of Israel," 184–95; McHugh, "Mother of Jesus," 3–10; Gaston, "Lucan Birth Narratives," 209–17; Franklin, *Christ the Lord*, 80–87; Glöckner, *Verkündigung des Heils*, 68–90, 114–24.

302. Compare the conclusions of Dupont, *Sources of Acts*, 166–67, in relation to Acts.

303. Harnack, "Magnifikat der Elisabet," 62–85.

304. Machen, "Hymns," 1–38.

Lukan style. Machen concludes: "The author of such a hymn must have lived in the atmosphere of the Old Testament, and must have been familiar from earliest childhood with its language. Only so could elements derived from so many sources have been incorporated without artificiality in a single poem."[305]

Working from a different direction Hermann Gunkel came to conclusions similar to Machen's.[306] Comparing the form of the Lukan canticles with Old Testament and later parallels he was able to classify the Magnificat and Benedictus as "eschatological hymns" and concluded: "The author, therefore, lived so much in the old tradition that to him the genres were fully trusted."[307]

On the grounds of both form and content, therefore, it seems unlikely that we should see the Magnificat as Luke's work. Nevertheless, his choice of such a hymn must be counted as significant, especially when he has underlined it by including another similar hymn (the Benedictus). Moreover, although it is generally felt that traditional materials such as this are of less relevance to the theology of the Gospel writer than his own compositions, the likelihood of influence in the other direction should not be ignored. Luke may have been strongly influenced by the piety and theology of such hymns as the Magnificat, and might well have carried their ideas and concepts into areas where his own authorship is more apparent.[308] It is also possible that Luke translated the Magnificat and edited it for its place in the Gospel.[309]

2.4.2 Context and Speaker

In his analysis of the structure of the prologue, René Laurentin, mistakenly, it seems to me, sees Mary's visit to Elizabeth as an additional separate section sandwiched between the parallel annunciation stories

---

305. Machen, "Hymns," 23.

306. Gunkel, "Lieder in der Kindheitsgeschichte Jesu," 43–60.

307. "Der Verfasser lebte also so sehr in der alten Ueberlieferung dass ihm die Gattungen noch völlig vertraut waren." Gunkel, "Lieder in der Kindheitsgeschichte Jesu," 52.

308. Compare Machen, "Origin of First Two Chapters of Luke," 255–56.

309. Various scholars have argued for a Semitic original: Wood, "Magnificat," 48–50; Aytoun, "'Ten Lucan Hymns," 274–88; Winter, "Maccabaean Psalms?" 328–47; Laurentin, "Traces d'allusions étymologiques," 1–23; Gryglewicz, "Herkunft der Hymnen des Kindheitsevangelium," 265–73.

THE POOR AND THE SALVATION OF ISRAEL

and the parallel birth stories.[310] In fact, the annunciation to Mary and her visit to Elizabeth are closely connected through the angel's announcement about Elizabeth. Though not requested, this is granted to Mary as a sign, and her departure "in haste" to witness it is an integral part of the annunciation story.[311] The Magnificat thus comes as the climax of this annunciation-sign story.[312]

Once this is seen it becomes clear, first, that the Magnificat stands in close relationship to the revelation to Mary that she is to bear the Davidic Messiah, and secondly, that Mary is the natural speaker of the hymn.[313]

---

310. Luke 1:39–56. Laurentin, *Structure et théologie de Luc 1–2*, 32–33. Cf. Wilkens, "Theologische Struktur," 1–2.

311. Luke 1:36. Creed, *Luke*, 21.

312. Note the parallel in the annunciation to the shepherds: a sign is given (2:12) and the shepherds come σπεύσαντες (hurrying) to witness it (2:16) and then return glorifying God (2:20). The muteness of Zechariah is probably to be viewed in the same way.

313. The controversy over whom Luke saw to be the author of the Magnificat takes its rise from the existence of the variant reading "Elizabeth" instead of "Maria" in three North Italian mss, a, b, 1* (fourth or fifth century, fifth century, eighth century). The whole Greek ms tradition has "Mariam" (Mary). Zahn, *Lukas*, 746, reckons the earliest witness as the *Prot. Jas.* (before 150 AD). The debate does not appear to have begun until the supporting evidence of Niceta of Remesiana's "De psalmodiae bono" was published in 1897, though Burkitt, "Who Spoke the Magnificat?" 220, admits that Niceta's evidence does not add to that of a, d, 1*. The reading "Elizabeth" is supported by Irenaeus, *Adv. Haer.* 4.7.1 (two mss; the other has Mary), but in 3.10.2 all mss read Mary. The evidence of Irenaeus is variously evaluated (Burkitt, "Who Spoke the Magnificat?" 221; Bardenhewer, "Ist Elisabeth die Sängerin?" 192–93. Origen (in *Lucam Hom.* 7) says "Non enim ignoramus, quod secundum alios codices et haec verba Elisabeth vaticinetur (For we are not ignorant, that according to other books here words are placed in Elizabeth's mouth)." However, this only exists in Jerome's translation, and Zahn, *Lukas*, 748–51, argues that it should be attributed to him, not to Origen. Barns, "Magnificat in Niceta of Remesiana and Cyril of Jerusalem," 449–53, summoned Cyril as a further witness, but was refuted by Brightman in an editorial note at the end of Barn's article. Jacobé, "L'origine du Magnificat," 424–32, Harnack, and Burkitt in 1897, 1900, and 1906, respectively, argued independently on textual grounds and on the basis of internal contextual evidence that "Mary" was not original. The internal evidence alleged was: the flow of the conversation (Μαριὰμ σὺν αὐτῇ [Mary with her]) in v. 56; analogy to the Song of Hannah, where the problem was barrenness; that Elizabeth is described as "filled with the Holy Spirit" (v. 41), not Mary; Luke's discreet handling of Mary and Joseph. All these are said to have made it unlikely that he would put the song in Mary's mouth. Harnack argued that the original reading was simply καὶ εἶπεν (and she), but that Luke understood Elizabeth as the speaker.

Jacobé drew a counter-attack from Durand, "L'origine du Magnificat," 74–77, and in 1901 Bardenhewer, "Ist Elisabeth die Sängerin?" gave a much fuller answer to the arguments of Jacobé and Harnack. Bardenhewer proposed that the reading "et ait Elisabeth" arose through the accidental dropping of "Maria" and the supplying of

In Luke's understanding the Magnificat is her response to becoming the mother of the Messiah. To have here Elizabeth's praise for the gift of her son would do violence to the context.[314]

One expects to find, therefore, that the Magnificat according to Luke will be a song of praise celebrating the coming of the Messiah.[315] The following analysis will confirm this expectation and show that his coming is conceived in terms of the salvation of Israel,[316] and not of any particular group within Israel.

2.4.3 Israel's Salvation

For the purpose of this discussion the Magnificat is divided into three sections: Luke 1:46-49, 54-55, and 51-53. I have inverted the order of

---

"Elisabeth" from the context (199-200). He refers to four mss prior to Jerome cited by Tischendorf with neither Mary nor Elizabeth (199). Harnack's contextual arguments are answered point for point. Bardenhewer's most telling argument (repeated by many others) is that v. 48b suits the mother of the Messiah only, and is quite inappropriate on the lips of Elizabeth. Burkitt was opposed by Bernard, "Magnificat," 193-206, and Emmet, "Should the Magnificat Be Ascribed to Elizabeth?" 521-29. Emmet accepted the emendation καὶ εἶπεν, but argued that Luke understood Mary as the speaker. Harris, "Mary or Elizabeth?" 266-67; Harris, "Again the Magnificat," 188-90, argued for the reading "Elisabeth" on the basis of an allusion to the name Zechariah in the phrase "in remembrance of his mercy" (v. 54). However, Laurentin, "Traces d'allusions étymologiques," finds allusions to Zechariah, Elizabeth, John, Jesus, Gabriel, and Mary in both the Magnificat and Benedictus. Davies, "Ascription of the Magnificat to Mary," 307-08, also accepts the reading καὶ εἶπεν and suggests that "Mary" was introduced, though the context implies that Elizabeth is the speaker, because of the word δούλη (maidservant—vv. 38, 48). However, his argument is as strong for the reverse case: that Mary was intended by Luke. In 1967 Benko, "History of the Controversy," 263-75, produced a review of the debate in which he concludes "the so-called 'external evidence' is overwhelmingly in favor of the reading 'Mary said.' But the so-called internal evidence supports very strongly the opposite view. The two sides just about balance each other out" (271). It seems to me, however, that he underestimates the "internal evidence" against ascribing the song to Elizabeth (δούλη in vv 38, 48, the unsuitability of v. 48b on Elizabeth's lips ("eine unerträgliche Übertreibung [an unbearable exaggeration]," Schmid, *Lukas* 54), the lack of any hint of former barrenness (cf. 1 Sam 2:5b), and, more seriously, he ignores the total context.

314. Perhaps recognizing this, some who ascribe the hymn to Elizabeth suggest that it has been dislocated from another point in the story. See Sahlin, *Messias und Gottesvolk*, 159-61; Leaney, "Birth Narratives," 158-63; Krafft, "Vorgeschichten des Lukas," 217; compare Schmid, *Lukas*, 53.

315. Rengstorf, *Lukas*, 30-31. Schnackenburg, "Magnifikat" 344-45.

316. As in Creed, *Luke*, 23.

the last two sections in the belief that verses 54–55 give a more prosaic and straightforward statement of what is expressed figuratively in verses 51–53 and because verses 51–53 contain the terms which are of real interest to this study. It will be shown that in the setting of the Magnificat the *tapeinoi* (ταπεινοί—lowly) and *peinōntes* (πεινῶντες—hungry) are to be understood most naturally as Israel, and the *ploutountes* (πλουτοῦντες—rich) as her gentile oppressors.

2.4.3.1 Luke 1:46–49

Though verses 46–49 relate ostensibly to Mary's personal situation there are various suggestions that more is involved. Some scholars see her as "the Daughter of Zion," a personification of Israel.[317] Others see her as a representative or symbol of the ʿanawim and of God's raising them up.[318]

While these views seem to me to go well beyond what evidence we have, there is some point in seeing Mary's words in a wider frame of reference than that of her personal triumph. Her role in the Magnificat is unique: all generations will call her blessed.[319] Nevertheless, she stands among her people as one of those whom the Messiah comes to save. In describing God as her "Savior" she is not just pointing to her individual blessing as mother of the Messiah. Nor is she expressing a notion of personal salvation.[320] Rather, she is identifying herself with the people whom God is pledged to save through his Messiah. The annunciation is the signal to her of the salvation of the people, in which her own

---

317. Argued independently by Sahlin, *Messias und Gottesvolk*, 149–50; Laurentin, *Structure et théologie de Luc 1–2*, 64–68, 148–61. Also, Hebert, "Virgin Mary as Daughter of Zion," 403–10; Thurian, *Mary: Mother of the Lord*; Vogels, "Magnificat, Marie et Israël," 279–96. McHugh, *Mother of Jesus*, 29–52, 150–53, is more cautious; though well-disposed to the identification, he hesitates to affirm that Luke made it. The idea is criticized by Isaacs, "Mary," 92–93; Jones, "Background and Character of the Lukan Psalms," 22; and Brown, *Birth of the Messiah*, 320–28.

318. Isaacs, "Mary"; Brown, *Birth of the Messiah*, 353. Brown thinks Luke took a hymn composed and used among the ʿanawim and attributed it to Mary, a perfect embodiment of their piety. Compare Tannehill, "Magnificat as Poem," 274; Gélin, *Poor of Yahweh*, 91–98 ("perfect and living expression of the ʿanawim," 94); Navone, *Themes of St. Luke*, 104.

319. Schnackenburg, "Magnifikat," 355.

320. All Luke's references to Jesus as "Savior" have in view the nation (Luke 2:11; Acts 5:31, 13:23).

salvation is bound up.³²¹ It is probable, therefore, that the word *tapeinōsis* (ταπείνωσις—poverty, lowliness) describes more than Mary's inferior economic and social position.³²² For it was the *tapeinōsis* of the people that called forth God's salvation in the Exodus and would call it forth in a new Exodus.³²³ Thus W. Vogels argues that the Exodus provides the main background for the salvation language of the Magnificat,³²⁴ and R. Le Déaut suggests a conscious parallel between Miriam and the Song of Moses, and Mary and the Magnificat.³²⁵ The seventh of the eighteen Benedictions says: "Look we beseech Thee upon our affliction (בעניינו) . . . and redeem us . . . Blessed art Thou, O Lord the Redeemer of Israel."

It might be objected that the obvious source of verse 48a is Hannah's prayer for a child in 1 Kingdoms 1:11—"If indeed you should look upon the poverty (downtroddenness) of your maidservant and remember me."³²⁶ It is important to realize, however, that such language had undergone development and by New Testament times had richer associations than just those of childbirth. This was facilitated by such language passing into liturgy to describe Israel's salvation.³²⁷ In 4 Ezra 9:38–10:59 the barren woman is seen in her affliction as a figure of Jerusalem before sacrifice was offered there.³²⁸ Probably the image could function in various ways and it would not be surprising to find Hannah's affliction being used as a symbol of the affliction of Israel. In fact, the targum to Hannah's prayer does just this:

---

321. Marshall, *Luke: Historian and Theologian*, 98.

322. Schmid, *Lukas*, 54; Isaacs, "Mary," 88; and Schoonheim, "Lukas 1:51," 245-46, see it as her humility. This is contrary to NT and LXX usage. Koontz, "Mary's Magnificat," 342; Scheele, "Maria in der Gemeinschaft and Geschichte Israels," 103; Schnackenburg, "Magnifikat," 345-46; Mussner, "Anfänge der Marienverehrung," 289; and Flood, "Magnificat and Benedictus," 205-10, see it as her objective state.

323. Deut 26:7; Neh 9:9; Isa 40:2; 1 Kgdms 9:16; Ps 135(136):23; 4 Kgdms 14:26; Jdt 6:19 (LXX); 13:20.

324. Vogels, "Magnificat, Marie et Israel," 279-96.

325. LeDéaut, "Miryam et Marie," 216.

326. ἐὰν ἐπιβλέπων ἐπιβλέψῃς ἐπὶ τὴν ταπείνωσιν τῆς δούλης σου καὶ μνησθῇς μου.

327. Psalm 135(136):23; cf. 9:14 (LXX), 24(25):18)

328. 4 Ezra 9:45: "And it came to pass after thirty years, God heard thy handmaid (*ancilla*) and looked upon my affliction (*humilitatem*); and considered my distress (*tribulationi*) and gave me a son." (Eth. and Arab. have "humiliation"; Violet, *Esra-Apokalypse*, 282-83).

So Jerusalem who is like a barren woman will in future be filled with the people of her captivity. And as for Rome which is full and abounding in people, her camps shall cease; she shall be desolated and laid waste.[329]

Thus, Mary's *tapeinōsis* should be seen in connection with the humiliation and affliction of Israel.[330] The coming of the Messiah means salvation both for her and for Israel.

2.4.3.2 Luke 1:54–5

The last two verses of the Magnificat explicitly identify the object of salvation as Israel, and do so using national salvific language.

Ἀντιλαμβάνεσθαι (to help) occurs frequently in the Old Testament, often in the Psalms, to describe the help which the king (representing his people) receives from God,[331] and in Isaiah 40–66 of the salvation which God provides for his exiled and afflicted people.[332] The occurrence of "his servant Israel" in association with "helped" (*antelabeto*) in 1:54 and *brachiōn* (βραχίων—arm) in 1:51 draws special attention to this last picture. Harnack was right to point to Isaiah 41:8 to explain Luke 1:54, though it should be remembered that the terms involved are enriched by their occurrence elsewhere.[333] Behind their appearance in the Magnificat lies the rich background of the new and final exodus: God's poor and afflicted people have no helper until he comes to their aid and sets them up as the wonder of the whole earth.

It is striking that it is in just this section of the Old Testament that the "prophetic aorist" is most apparent.[334] The prophet seems to describe salvation as a past event, though it still lies in the future. This suggests that the *antelabeto* (helped) of the Magnificat (also the aorists in 1:51–53)

---

329. *Tg. 1 Sam.* 2:5.

330. Sahlin, *Das Messias und das Gottesvolk*, 164, thinks the original reference was not to Mary or Elizabeth but to "erniedrigte Zion" (degraded [humiliated] Zion). He thinks in "Proto-Luke" Zechariah was the speaker. Glöckner, *Verkündigung des Heils*, 122, goes beyond the thought range of the Magnificat in seeing *tapeinōsis* as the situation of *humankind*.

331. Ps 19(20):2, 62(63):8, 68(69):29, 117(118):13; cf. 88(89):43.

332. Isa 41:8–9, 42:1; 49:26, 51:17–20, 59:16–20, 63:5; cf. 41:13–14.

333. Harnack, "Magnificat der Elisabet," 68, 72.

334. Isa 41:8–9, 13–14, 51:22, 59:16, 63:5; in 42:1 the tense is future but the idea is the same.

should also be seen this way.³³⁵ Luke 1:54a is an affirmation that God has fulfilled the Isaianic hope of salvation and restoration of the people. This proleptic use of language is especially appropriate because God has already begun to act. Israel is, as it were, already saved, because the Savior is at last in their midst.³³⁶ It is this intensity and immediacy which distinguishes the Magnificat from other Old Testament psalms and prayers.³³⁷

"To remember mercy" (μνησθῆναι ἐλέους), then, does not mean that God has perpetually had his people in mind, but that he has made himself aware of their plight and is about to act. When his people in Egypt cried because of their bondage, God remembered his covenant with Abraham, Isaac, and Jacob, and began to act.³³⁸

Thus, in this last section of the Magnificat, even more obviously than in the first, attention is on salvation, understood in terms of the paradigms of exodus and new exodus. Now, as then, this is seen to embrace the nation Israel.

2.4.3.3 Luke 1:51-3

This is the most figurative part of the poem, as well as being of most interest to our study. What it describes, however, is simply what is expressed in more prosaic terms in verses 54-55.

The reference to the "arm of the Lord" shows that the Exodus paradigm of salvation is still to the fore. In a few cases *brachiōn* (arm) is used generally of God's power, but in most of its Old Testament uses thought of the Exodus, when God stretched forth his arm and by acts

---

335. A few scholars see the aorists as gnomic and would therefore translate with the simple present (Schmid, *Lukas*, 55; Vogels, "Magnificat, Marie et Israel," 281). The existence of such an aorist is questioned by others (Plummer, *Luke*, 32-33). Turner in Moulton, *New Testament Greek*, 73-74, gives instances, but Moule, *Idiom Book*, 12-13, disposes of some of these. Turner suggests that the aorists in the Magnificat may be gnomic, but most of his examples are quite different to those in the Magnificat. The case for the prophetic aorist in the Magnificat was argued by Gunkel, "Lieder in der Kindheitsgeschichte," 53: praise is conceived from the standpoint of "that day" when all has been accomplished.

336. English knows a similar use of language. People in great danger, seeing someone coming to the rescue will say, "We are saved!" or even "We've been saved!"

337. Barrett, *Holy Spirit and Gospel Tradition*, 17; Warfield, "Messianic Psalms of the New Testament," 307-08.

338. Exod 2:23-25; compare Isa 63:11 (note the "arm of the Lord" in v. 12).

of power redeemed his people, is near at hand.³³⁹ The fact that such language passed into liturgical descriptions of the Exodus no doubt ensured its transmission in relation to the theme of salvation.³⁴⁰ In Isaiah, and to a lesser extent Ezekiel, it is used to describe the new Exodus.³⁴¹ In Isaiah 40 the *zeroaʿ Yahweh* (זרוע יהוה—arm of Yahweh) is even hypostasized and seen as God's conquering servant, his ruler in the new age.³⁴² It is not impossible that the *brachiōn* of Luke 1:51 is a figure for the Messiah himself.³⁴³

Other motifs show that the focus of attention in the Magnificat is on Israel's salvation vis-à-vis the nations rather than any sectarian notion of salvation for a distinct remnant within Israel. Admittedly *hyperēphanoi* (ὑπερήφανοι—arrogant) could be overweening Israelites,³⁴⁴ but the term is much more likely to have been used to describe gentiles. *Hyperēphania* (ὑπερηφανία—arrogance) can even be thought of as the distinctive gentile sin. Thus, in Psalms of Solomon 2 the word and its cognates are used repeatedly in relation to the desecration of Jerusalem by Pompey and his forces:

> 31(28)   He reflected not that he was man
> 35(31)   (It is He—God—) who setteth me up in glory, And bringeth down the proud (*hyperēphanous*) to eternal destruction in dishonor, Because they knew him not.³⁴⁵

Because the gentiles do not know God they are naturally prone to arrogance. Thus Psalms of Solomon 17:15(13) says of Rome: "In his

---

339. Exod 6:6, 15:16; Deut 3:24 (LXX), 4:34, 5:15, 6:21 (LXX), 7:8 (LXX), 19, 9:26 (LXX), 29, 11:2, 29:2 (A, Bs); 4 Kgdms 17:36; Jer 39(32):21; Dan 9:15; Wis 16:16, Bar. 2:11. The LXX accentuates this theme.

340. Ps 43(44):3, 76(77):15, 135(136):12, compare 88(89):10, 13.

341. Isa 52:9-10; Ezek 20:33-34; cf. Isa 40:10, 59:16, 63:5, 12.

342. Isa 40:10, 51:5, 9, 53:1. The LXX makes Moses the arm of God's glory in Isa 63:12.

343. Compare John 12:38.

344. Isa 2:12; 29:20 (LXX); compare Job 40:7(12); Prov 3:34; Jas 4:6; 1 Pet 5:5; Mark 7:22; 2 Tim 3:2.

345. This psalm is similar in many ways to the taunt over the King of Babylon (Isa 14:4-20). Johanan ben Zakkai probably applies it to Titus (b. Hag. 13a; b. Pes. 94a). See also the descriptions of Antiochus Epiphanes in 2 Macc 9:11; 4 Macc 4:15, 9:30; and cf. 3 Macc 1:27, 5:13, 6:4.

alienness the enemy did arrogance and his heart was alien from our God."³⁴⁶

In the Palestinian targum tradition God's triumph over Pharaoh is seen as triumph over his pride and arrogance.³⁴⁷ This tradition is preserved even in Onkelos.³⁴⁸ In Romans 1:30 idolatrous gentiles are characterized as *hyperēphanoi*. Thus, although Luke 1:51b could refer to proud Israelites, it is more natural to take it of Israel's proud and godless overlords. They are to be scattered³⁴⁹ in the midst of their plans.³⁵⁰ This understanding is confirmed by the next line.

Dunastai (δυνάσται) could be any kind of ruler from a minor official to the emperor, but the fact that they are to be put down from their thrones suggests that the Magnificat is thinking less of the petty harassment of the people and more of those who hold ultimate sway, keeping them a subject and oppressed people. The *tapeinoi* are then naturally to be understood as the humbled nation, identical to the *ptōchoi* we have already discussed.

Thus in the messianic Psalm 17(18) the oppressed people is set over against the arrogant enemies: "because you will save an afflicted people."³⁵¹ Midrash Psalms 18:23 commenting on this explains the "afflicted people" as "the people of Israel afflicted in exile"³⁵² and "the haughty eyes" as "Edom (Rome) and Ishmael who walk in arrogance on the earth." Ben Sirach (10:14-15) no doubt has the occupation of Canaan in mind when he says as an example of God's abhorrence of the proud:

> Thrones of rulers has the Lord thrown down
> And established (the) meek in their place.
> Roots of nations has the lord plucked up

---

346. ἐν ἀλλοτριότητι ὁ ἐχθρὸς ἐποίησεν ὑπερηφανίαν καὶ ἡ καρδία αὐτοῦ ἀλλοτρία ἀπὸ τοῦ θεοῦ ἡμῶν.

347. TJ I&II on Exod 15:1, 21.

348. TO Exod 15:21. Compare *Num. Rab.* 11:1 where the Edomites (Romans) (insolent) are contrasted with Israel, the *'anawim*; compare 4 Ezra 11:42-43; Shemoneh Esre 12.

349. Note especially Num 10:35, where Moses prays for the scattering of all who oppose Israel's entry into Canaan. Compare Ps 67(68):1.

350. Compare Isa 14:13 where the King of Babylon plans ἐν τῇ διανοίᾳ σου (in your thoughts) to ascend into heaven. Compare 2 Bar. 67:7.

351. ὅτι σὺ λαὸν ταπεινὸν (עַם עָנִי) σώσεις. Ps 17(18):27.

352. Isa 14:32, 26:6, 49:13, 54:11.

And planted (the) poor in their stead.³⁵³

Luke 1:52 and 53 of the Magnificat are in chiastic parallelism:

The hungry and rich are not further groups, but an alternative characterization of the *tapeinoi* and the *dunastai*. The needy nation stands over against the oppressive heathen.³⁵⁴ Salvation means the satisfaction of the needs of the hungry and the destruction of oppressors. Jones suggests that the background to this imagery is to be found in the gift of an abundant land to Israel.³⁵⁵ It is a constantly recurring theme of the Old Testament that God feeds the hungry. This is grounded in his providence, but is also seen as a manifestation of his salvation.³⁵⁶ God fed his people in the wilderness when they cried to him, and he will do the same in the new Exodus.³⁵⁷

Isaiah 62:8–9 shows how close could be the connection between literal hunger and gentile domination, but even in the Old Testament hunger has come to mean more than just lack of food. It is the condition of the person in great need, and can function much as the poverty language.³⁵⁸ Thus, in Baruch 2:18, in a prayer for salvation which looks back to the Exodus, the survivors of the destruction of Jerusalem are described as "the soul that is greatly vexed which goeth stooping and feeble, and the eyes that fail, and the hungry soul."

It is thus traditional and natural that those who suffer and wait for God's salvation should be portrayed as hungry (and thirsty and poor) and that salvation should be seen as the satisfaction of their needs. The

---

353. θρόνους ἀρχόντων καθεῖλεν ὁ κύριος
καὶ ἐκάθισεν πραεῖς ἀντ᾽ αὐτῶν·
ῥίζας ἐθνῶν ἐξέτιλεν ὁ κύριος
καὶ ἐφύτευσεν ταπεινοὺς ἀντ᾽ αὐτῶν·

354. See also Winter, "Maccabaean Psalms?" 341. Sy^cs read "the poor" for "the hungry."

355. Jones, "Lukan Psalms," 26.

356. For the combination of themes see Ps. Sol. 5, but especially TJ I&II on Exod 15:2.

357. Ps 107:4–9; Isa 49:9–10.

358. Isa 28:12 (LXX) has πεινῶντι for עיף. Compare Isa 55:1–3, 32:6; Sir 4:2.

quotation from Isaiah 49:10 in Revelation 7:16-17 shows that such imagery remained alive in the early church.[359] The author of the Paraleipomena Jeremiou is able to summarize the ministry of Christ: "He shall fill the hungry souls" (9:20).

The turning away of the rich is a natural corollary. That the rich are opposed to the hungry, and equivalent (in the chiasmus) to the rulers shows that we are not dealing in this context with a rejection of the rich or of wealth as such.[360] It is the oppressors of God's people, the heathen overlords, who are to be driven away. They are characterized as rich because, from the point of view of the exploited nation, they are rich, and at Israel's expense.

In the targum to the Song of Hannah there is an interesting combination of the concepts we have been considering which lends considerable support to the case I have advanced. The influence of this song on the Magnificat has often been noted, though, significantly, there is no evidence of influence from the Septuagint (Greek) version. The targum treats Hannah's Song as a series of prophecies of God's victories over those who at various stages oppressed his people (the Philistines, Sennacherib, Nebuchadnezzar, the Greeks, Haman, Rome). It closes with an affirmation that God will wreak vengeance on Magog and the armies of the nations of captors and establish the kingdom of the Messiah. The "full" and the "hungry" of 1 Samuel 2:5 are associated respectively with Haman, and Mordecai and Esther:

> Of the sons of Haman she prophesied and said: "Those who were full of bread and proud in wealth and great in mammon have been impoverished. They have returned to be hired for bread, for the food of their mouth. Mordecai and Esther who were poor have become rich and have forgotten their poverty. They have returned to be the children of free men. So, Jerusalem who is like a barren woman, will in future be filled with the people of her captivity. And as for Rome which is full and abounding

---

359. Also Matt 5:6; John 6:35.

360. So far as I am aware there is no condemnation of wealth or the wealthy *per se* in the OT or in the Jewish intertestamental literature. In both we find strong condemnation of those who gain their wealth at another's expense, and of those who set their hearts on their wealth and forget God, but potentially, at least, wealth is a blessing. There was a growing resentment of the wealthy in the intertestamental period but it never amounted to a condemnation of wealth as such. See Sir 13:19 and Hengel, *Judaism and Hellenism*, 136-38. Also 1 En. 46:7-8, 94:6-10, 97:9-10, 102:9-10. The LXX inserts "rich" into Ps 9:29(10:8) and 33(34):11, which deal with wicked men.

in people, her camps shall cease; she shall be desolated and laid waste."[361]

The motif of the rich being made poor does not occur in 1 Samuel 2:5; it has been introduced into the targum, probably from Esther 5:11.[362] No doubt 1 Samuel 2:7 influenced this.

The uncertainties in dating the targums make it impossible to argue for dependence of any kind, but the similarity of outlook and imagery is striking, and is no doubt to be attributed to a common fund of traditional Jewish understanding of the Old Testament. The targum associates the hungry and poor with Israel, and the rich and full with her oppressors, just as we find in the Magnificat.

2.4.4 Song of a True Israelite

According to the way Luke has presented it, the Magnificat is a song of exultation over the salvation of Israel, which is imminent because of the Messiah's conception. This salvation is pictured in traditional terms, especially those drawn from the patterns of exodus and new exodus in the Old Testament. God has remembered his covenant with the patriarchs and is about to shatter the proud enemies of his people and set the afflicted nation high.[363]

The Magnificat contains nothing to indicate a sectarian interest. It cannot be claimed for the so-called *'anawim*, as J. Massingbird Ford claims.[364] As a messianic hymn in a messianic setting, it is only natural that it should share common ground with the Zealots. The hope of every true Israelite was that afflicted Israel should be exalted and her oppressors scattered. The distinctive Zealot philosophy was that this should be achieved by active revolutionary violence. Of this the Magnificat has no trace. It is neither a Zealot nor an *anawistic* hymn; it is an Israelite hymn.

This does not mean, however, that the Magnificat envisages the salvation of every Israelite. Luke 1:50 makes this clear; only those who fear him will receive his mercy. Nevertheless, the imagery which it employs is not meant to define a group of God-fearers within Israel, like the Qumran

---

361. *T. Jon.* on 1 Sam 2.
362. In *b Meg.* 15b Esther 5:11 is expounded midrashically with the aid of 1 Sam 2:5.
363. The message is identical with that of the Benedictus (Luke 1:68-75).
364. Ford, "Zealotism and the Lukan Infancy Narratives," 280-92.

sect. It is a traditional characterization of suffering Israel, and would have been meaningful to any Israelite who felt the pressure and humiliation of being part of a subject people. Such feelings would have been appropriate under Herodian rule as well as under the later procurators.

We may now answer the problems raised at the beginning of this analysis, and say that there is nothing in the Magnificat to justify speaking of Luke as a champion of the cause of the lower classes, nor to indicate any antipathy on his part towards the well-to-do. The poor are saved not because they are without possessions, but because they are God's chosen people, trodden down by the nations. Nor are the rich scattered because they are wealthy, but because they are the proud oppressors of Israel. The only doctrine of reversal to be found is the conviction that Israel, which at present is humbled and afflicted, will be raised to a state of power and glory.

I will now take it as demonstrated that in the passages so far discussed, *ptōchoi*, along with *tapeinoi* and *peinōntes*, is a way of characterizing Israel in her desperate need of salvation.

2.4.5 Purpose of the Magnificat

In addition to giving expression to Mary's joy at the confirmation that she is to be mother of the Messiah, the Magnificat serves the purpose of spelling out in traditional terms the content of this salvation, which the Messiah has come to achieve. However, because of the Jewishness of this picture of salvation, and, indeed, of the whole of chapters 1 and 2, it has generally been isolated from the rest of the Gospel and Acts. This is inadmissible in the light of recent studies emphasizing the integral relationship of the first two chapters to the rest of Luke's work.[365]

In my opinion these chapters are meant to function in somewhat the same manner as the prologue of the fourth Gospel.[366] Having read it, the reader is equipped from the outset with an understanding of the identity and mission of Jesus which will provide an interpretative key to the particular events of the Gospel. Accordingly, some scholars have seen in Luke's "prologue" a rehearsal of some of the themes of the main work. In the words of Heinz Schürmann: "The mountain grandeur of

---

365. See page 75n301, above.

366. On the Gospel prologues in general see Gibbs, "Gospel Prologues," 154–88; Seitz, "Gospel Prologues," 262–68.

the Gospel with its heights and depths is reflected in this contemplative, peaceful pre-history as in the clear lake at its foot."[367]

If this is so, Luke must mean his readers to carry this Jewish concept of salvation with them into the rest of the Gospel and Acts. The complementarity between this picture and that of the Nazareth sermon confirms this is so.

We can only be impressed with Luke's faithfulness to traditional Palestinian Jewish hopes,[368] but are caused to wonder how they fit with the generally non-political outlook of Luke-Acts. For he must have written at a time when such nationalistic expectations were the subject of some controversy. No doubt the answer lies in the identity of his readers. If the imagery of the Magnificat and the Nazareth sermon was to be intelligible to them they would need to have had some understanding of (hence, perhaps, some sympathy with) Judaism. If, however, they were gentiles, as is widely thought, they may have had suspicions about the political innocence of Judaism (and Christianity?). Presumably the gentile God-fearers of the first century accepted the notion of God's ultimate establishment of a messianic kingdom, and perhaps even the primacy of Israel within it, but armed revolutionary activity to inaugurate that kingdom must have seemed another matter, and could not fail to have generated antagonism towards Judaism.

If it was Luke's intention to demonstrate that Christianity was true to Judaism, and that Jesus was the legitimate fulfiller of Israel's promised salvation, this would have necessitated his being straightforward about the future "political" aspirations of the Jews. At the same time, as the character of Jesus emerges, as the Jews reject their Messiah, and as the political dimension of salvation recedes into the future, Christianity is cleared of the suspicion of being a revolutionary movement (if that is the problem) or, if such antagonism is directed more against the Jews, is seen to answer all the aspirations of Judaism, while remaining politically innocent.

---

367. "Das Gebirgsmassiv der Evangelienschrift mit seinen Hohen und Tiefen spiegelt sich in dieser besinnlich—friedvollen Vorgeschichte wie im klaren See zu dessen Fuss." Schürmann, *Lukasevangelium*, 21. Compare Schürmann, *Nazareth-Perikope*, 201–02; Marshall, *Luke: Historian and Theologian*, 97.

368. See page 65n243, above.

2.5 BLESSED ARE YOU POOR, LUKE 6:17-49

The task of this section will be to see how well our understanding of the poor harmonizes with the Beatitudes and Woes, and with the rest of Luke's Great Sermon. It will be necessary to give attention to the function of the complete sermon, and then of the beatitudes and woes within it. Finally, we will consider the application of the beatitudes and woes to Luke's readers.

2.5.1 Tradition and Redaction

Matthew's Sermon on the Mount and Luke's Great Sermon stand on the border between where we affirm on the basis of similarities an underlying written source, and where on the basis of dissimilarities we deny it. The order of pericopes suggests an underlying literary source.[369] The fact that both sermons are preceded by a description of Jesus' ministry, and followed by the healing of the servant of the centurion in Capernaum, links this with the larger source Q.[370]

However, the differences within the individual units which make up the sermons raise serious doubts about these conclusions, and have led other scholars to the view that Matthew and Luke are dependent on divergent oral or written traditions.[371]

Both views need correcting from one another. Overlapping sources probably account for some of the difficulties.[372] The letter of James witnesses to the fact that material from the "sermon" was in use in different forms in the church at an early stage. Thus, the recovery of a common *Vorlage* against which Lukan redaction can be measured may be a vain pursuit. This is especially so for the beatitudes and woes.[373]

It is necessary, therefore, to be careful about using the Matthaean parallels to judge Luke's redaction. More telling are such things as the

---

369. For arguments for a literary source see Loisy, *Évangiles synoptiques*, 534–36; Dupont, *Béatitudes*, esp. I; Jeremias, *Sermon on the Mount*; Schürmann, *Lukasevangelium*, 323–25.

370. See Manson, *Sayings*, 46–48; Grundmann, *Lukas*, 139–40; Easton, *Luke*, 81.

371. Bartsch, "Feldrede"; Wrege, *Bergpredigt*.

372. Caird, *Luke*, 101.

373. See Knox, *Sources of the Synoptic Gospels*, II.12–13, and Rezevskis, "Makarismen," 162. For an attemped recovery of the alleged common source of the Beatitudes see Dupont, *Béatitudes*, I.343.

setting of the sermon, the place Luke has given it in his Gospel, the audience to which he directs it, and obvious redactional touches such as Luke 6:20a, 27a, 39a, and 7:1.

2.5.2 Function of Luke's Sermon

Frédéric Godet argued that the sermon is to be seen in relation to the call of the apostles as the inaugural discourse of the new people of God.[374] The relationship of the sermon to the calling of the apostles is obviously important, but this view attributes to Luke an ecclesiology which is foreign to him. He has no doctrine of a "new Israel," nor of a "new people of God." He of all the evangelists most stresses the continuity between Christianity and Judaism.[375] The public nature of the sermon also tells against it being the inaugural discourse for a certain group.[376] Nor is there any hint from within the sermon of a new Israel or a new law.

Bo Reicke sees the sermon as Luke's attempt "to show how [the] apostles were given special instructions for their mission in the world," and to make these instructions available to later Christians.[377] Again, it must be pointed out that the sermon is not addressed only to apostles, but also to the wider public. It also has little to do with mission, the only possible points of contact being the sayings about persecution and perhaps those about teaching.[378]

That Luke connects the solemn choosing of the Twelve with the sermon is plain, and on the most superficial level it is clear that the subject matter of the sermon has to do with discipleship. Nevertheless, it is not just a treatise on discipleship for disciples, for Luke stresses that others are present.[379]

Ernst Percy argues that the beatitudes should be seen as Jesus' original proclamation of the gospel.[380] Hans-Werner Bartsch goes further and sees Luke's sermon as a unified whole presenting Jesus' public

---

374. Godet, *Luke*, 294–96. Also Caird, *Luke*, 100–102.
375. See also Jervell, *Luke and the People of God*.
376. Luke 6:17.
377. Reicke, *Luke*, 36.
378. I have now come to think it is very much about mission.
379. Luke 6:17: καὶ πλῆθος πολὺ τοῦ λαοῦ (and a great multitude of the people).
380. Percy, *Botschaft*, 40–42. See also Schürmann, *Lukasevangelium*, 332. See pages 35–36, above.

proclamation, and the behavior which he demanded of those who heeded the message.[381] But Luke draws too much attention to the presence of the disciples for the sermon to be regarded simply as evangelistic.[382] The setting of the sermon in relation to the appointment of the Twelve is clearly important to him. If, then, the sermon is neither esoteric instruction of Jesus' followers nor open proclamation of the evangel to the crowds, what is it?

In my view the sermon is what it appears to be, a discourse on discipleship appropriate to the newly-appointed apostles, but also deliberately addressed to the people to challenge them to discipleship. It thus has an evangelistic character as well as being a treatise on discipleship. The sermon is intended to bring the people to a point of decision. This is particularly apparent in the concluding parable of the Two House-builders;[383] it is expected that some of those who hear Jesus' words will do them, but others will not. The parable is a warning to all that they should be doers.

I would suggest, therefore, that Luke 6:20a is not a description of those to whom Jesus addresses these words so much as Luke's attempt to show to whom the blessings ultimately refer. Similarly, the woes are not addressed to absent rulers and Pharisees,[384] but to the same crowd of disciples and others to whom the beatitudes are addressed.[385] They are promise and warning; which one applies to any particular individual is determined by his response. Verse 27 does not necessarily indicate a change of audience,[386] but could be an appeal to those in the crowd who are responding positively to Jesus' words.[387] Thus the last parable is addressed to all, and Luke concludes the sermon with the words, "After he had ended all his sayings in the hearing of the people . . ." (Luke 7:1).

Thus, the sermon is a discourse on discipleship addressed to disciples and potential disciples. That the people have come to Jesus to be

---

381. Bartsch, "Feldrede."

382. Note the absence of εὐαγγελίσασθαι (announce) and κηρύσσειν (proclaim) in connection with the sermon.

383. Luke 6:47–49.

384. As Godet, *Luke*, I.317; Wellhausen, *Evangelium Lucae*, 24–25; Schürmann, *Lukasevangelium*, 337, and others hold.

385. See also, Zahn, *Lucas*, 288; Ellis, *Luke*, 112–13; Minear, "Jesus' Audiences," 107–08.

386. As Minear, "Jesus' Audiences," 104–106, holds.

387. See also Flender, *Theologian of Redemptive History*, 25; cf. Luke 8:8, 9:35, 4:24, 7:9, 11:9, 12:4.

healed and taught qualifies them to be addressed in this way. They are, after all, the *laos*.[388] At the same time, their being addressed as disciples carries with it the challenge to make this real. The whole sermon is characterized by this dialectic: it is apparent in the contrasting beatitudes and woes, the challenge to hear (verse 27a), the challenge to transcend the ethics of the "sinners," to teach oneself before seeking to teach others, and to do in practice what one has heard from Jesus.

The sermon, therefore, has as its purpose to expound the privilege and destiny of the disciple, along with his responsibilities, for the sake of the newly-appointed apostles, but also of the crowds who are accorded the privilege of being addressed as disciples if they are willing to accept it and make it effective.

2.5.3 The Beatitudes and Woes

Luke is generally careful in his description of audiences, so the clear description in 6:17–19 is likely to be important for understanding the beatitudes. However, it is unnatural to see the audience as a typological key for decoding and applying the sermon;[389] it is better to follow the scene "historically," giving full weight to the manner in which Luke has presented it. Only when it has been understood in this light will it be possible to apply its meaning beyond its own setting with any degree of certainty.

The audience consists of the newly-appointed apostles, a great crowd of other disciples, and a great multitude of the people. They have come from "all of Judea and Jerusalem and the coast of Tyre and Sidon" (Luke 6:17).[390] It is not to be imagined there were gentiles among them. Those who come from the districts of Tyre and Sidon belong to the *laos*, although they live outside the Land. In calling these areas "coastlands" Luke probably alludes to Isaiah 8:23–24 in the Septuagint, and includes in Jesus' audience Jews from the "dark" gentile-dominated lands.[391] For Luke, writing to non-Palestinians, "all Judea" means *Eretz* Israel (i.e.,

---

388. Luke 6:17.

389. As in Godet, *Luke*, I.308; Degenhardt, *Evangelist der Armen*, 44. Compare Dupont, *Béatitudes*, III.24–25.

390. πάσης τῆς Ἰουδαίας καὶ Ἰερουσαλὴμ καὶ τῆς παραλίου Τύρου καὶ Σιδῶνος.

391. Compare Mark 3:8; Matt 4:25; and see Matt 4:15–16.

Galilee is included).³⁹² Thus, what he portrays is a representative gathering of the *laos* Israel (Jerusalem, Israel, diaspora),³⁹³ waiting for Jesus to teach and heal them.

Jesus, on the other hand, is strikingly portrayed as the Spirit-anointed Messiah.³⁹⁴ To the detail that the people sought to touch him, which in Mark need indicate no more than the excitement of the crowds, Luke adds the explanation: "because power came forth from him and healed all."³⁹⁵

Thus, Luke has given the sermon a striking setting: the Messiah stands before a representative gathering of the *laos* Israel, many of whom are already his disciples, manifesting his power and the presence of his salvation in a burst of wonder-working activity.

In seeking to understand Luke's beatitudes, their reference to the disciples is usually noted and the task then becomes to discover in what sense the disciples were poor (socially, economically, spiritually, through renunciation, persecution, etc.). This having been decided, the lesson usually drawn is that this "blessed state" should be imitated by later generations. I have already indicated difficulties with all of these identifications of the poor, and have given reason for thinking that *ptōchoi* is intended as a characterization of Israel in her need of salvation. "The hungry" was seen to be open to a similar interpretation and it can easily be demonstrated that the picture of "weepers" being comforted and having their mourning turned to joy is also part of the traditional imagery of national salvation.³⁹⁶ Nowhere is this clearer than in Isaiah 61. *Klaiein* (κλαίειν—to weep) is closely associated with *penthein* (πένθειν—to mourn),³⁹⁷ and in the present framework of thought should be seen in

---

392. Compare Mark 3:7-8; Luke 4:44, 7:17; and see Creed, *Luke*, 89; *TDNT* III.382.

393. See also Minear, "Jesus' Audiences," 104.

394. See Rienecker, *Lukas*, 170.

395. Mark 3:9-10. See Luke 4:14 and 7:21-22.

396. Derek Erez Rabbah 2:20 (56a) says: "Concerning them who sigh, grieve, and look forward to (national) salvation, and mourn for Jerusalem, Scripture declares, 'to appoint to them that mourn in Zion, to give them a garland instead of ashes.'" Compare Isa 61:2-3, 7, 66:10, 30:19, 35:10; Ps 125(126), 136(137):1; Jer 31(38):10-13. Compare 1QM12.13-15, 17.7-8, 1QH18.14-15; cf. 11:19-22, 9:23-26; 1QS 4:6-7; CD 20:27-34; see also *TDNT* III.722-25; Dupont, *Béatitudes*, II.97, III.65-78.

397. Luke 6:25. Dupont, *Béatitudes*, III.75-76; Wrege, *Bergpredigt*, 16.

terms of that mourning over the condition of Zion which will issue in laughter and dancing when God comforts his people.[398]

Taken together, then, the first three beatitudes give us a characterization of downtrodden Israel, which God is pledged to save. Salvation—the messianic kingdom—is seen as the answer to all needs, the end of all hunger, and as the joy and laughter which accompanies this liberation. Once it is seen that we are dealing with a poetic characterization in traditional images of the nation which God has promised to save, it becomes unnecessary and inappropriate to enter into detailed discussion of what exactly is meant by "the poor," "the hungry," and "the weeping." It also explains why Luke feels under no compulsion to portray Jesus and his disciples as literally impoverished, hungry, or miserable,[399] and why in Acts he can proudly present the Christians as joyful and without pressing need.[400]

The beatitudes in themselves express no more than Israel's prophetic hope. The new thing is that the one who utters them is manifested as the Spirit-endowed Messiah who is able to effect them; he does not prophesy, he "evangelizes."[401] And, ostensibly at least, the object of his proclamation is the whole people.

This raises the problem of what Luke means by verse 20a. I have suggested that it does not indicate the audience to whom Jesus' blessings are directed, and this was confirmed when we perceived that Luke pictures Jesus as the Messiah in the presence of the *laos* Israel. Nor do the words themselves suggest that Luke is describing Jesus' audience. What then does he mean?

According to Dupont, Luke has narrowed the scope of Jesus' message, which was originally directed to *all* sufferers, to the suffering and persecuted disciples of his own (Luke's) day, by recasting the beatitudes into the second person.[402] But this can scarcely be accepted when even

---

398. Laughter in this context is joyful, not derisive; see Dupont, *Béatitudes*, III.65–69, against Rengstorf, *TDNT* I.658–60. In PsSol εὐφροσύνη (gladness) has become almost a technical term for Israel's salvation (10:5, 6, 8, 11:3, 14:10, cf. 17:35).

399 Luke 5:33–34, 7:34, 6:1–5 hardly disturbs this judgment, and 9:3 describes a particular mission. Jesus' weeping (ἔκλαυσεν) over Jerusalem (19:41) comes closer to what the beatitudes are about.

400. Acts 2:46, 4:34–35.

401. Schweizer, "Seligpreisungen," 121–26, adds weight to this observation from a comparison of Luke's Beatitudes with other semitic blessings.

402. Dupont, *Béatitudes*, III.21–28, I.272–98.

Matthew 5:11–12 attests the fourth beatitude and other parts of the sermon in the second person, and when James is familiar with something like the woes in this form.[403] Thus Bartsch is correct to deny that Luke is the author of the second-person form of the beatitudes.[404] Dupont's theory is also unable to explain why Luke should have given the woes a second-person form. He refers them to absent opponents, hence to the Jewish unbelievers of his day.[405] Furthermore, the second-person form of address in Luke's beatitudes (and throughout the sermon) naturally refers not just to the disciples, but to the wider audience he has indicated. It cannot indicate a narrowing of the scope of Jesus' message.

The most likely function of verse 20a, then, is to indicate Luke's view that the salvation which Jesus declares openly to all Israel will ultimately rest only upon his disciples. This is similar to the pattern of Luke 10:5–6: salvation (peace) is to be declared to all, but it will return from those who are not worthy of it

However, this is not an interpretation Luke has imposed on the tradition; it is inherent in the fourfold beatitudes and woes. The form of the fourth beatitude is quite different to that of the other three. Three parallel poetic blessings give way to a longer prosaic one dealing with those who are persecuted for their loyalty to the Son of Man. Many scholars have dismissed it as an addition by the later church,[406] though there is no real substance to their objections beyond its obvious differences in form and content. It was certainly part of Luke's source.

As a fourth beatitude, in series with the other three, it fits very badly, but as an interpretative climax and explanation or application of the other three it suits remarkably well. Thus, in an essay devoted to this beatitude, David Daube concludes from similar arrangements in other Jewish poetry: "To give the last member of a series a strikingly different form from the others is a plausible course to take wherever it is to contain

---

403. Jas 4:9; 5:1.

404. Bartsch, "Feldrede." Also Strecker, "Makarismen," 256–57.

405. Dupont, *Béatitudes*, III.28–40.

406. Bultmann, *Synoptic Tradition*, 110; Schürmann, *Lukasevangelium*, 335; Degenhardt, *Evangelist der Armen*, 45–46; Dupont, *Béatitudes*, II.283. Manson, *Sayings*, 49, thinks it comes from a later stage of Jesus' ministry. For echoes of this beatitude in the epistles see Brown, "Synoptic Parallels," 30–31. Its Palestinian origin is argued for by Easton, *Luke*, 85; Schürmann, *Lukasevangelium*, 333; Dupont, *Béatitudes*, I.233–35; Black, *Aramaic Approach*, 158.

a summary of the whole, or wherever it is meant as the climax."[407] In the last beatitude blessing (salvation) is promised to those who identify themselves with the Son of Man. Thus, Luke's reference to disciples in verse 20a as the ultimate resting point of Jesus' blessings is seen to be inherent in the fourth climactic beatitude. This is seen even more clearly in the woes.[408]

The four woes are similar in form to the beatitudes. The first three stand together and are climaxed by the fourth. In the first three woes, those who are rich, satisfied, and laughing are warned of their future fate. It is important to realize that we are not dealing here with an Old Testament characterization of the wicked or the gentiles,[409] but with a studied reversal of the picture of needy Israel given in the beatitudes. The fourth woe identifies this "non-Israel" with those esteemed by men. In the light of verses 22–23 this can only mean those who refuse to identify with the despised Son of Man.[410] What then is meant by characterizing them as rich, full, and laughing? Verse 24b suggests they are those for whom this present age is sufficient comfort. They have no longing for salvation and therefore will not identify themselves with the one who brings it.

Once this is seen, it is impossible not to reflect back upon the "poor-hungry-weeping" of the beatitudes and modify the initial thesis that this is simply a characterization of Israel in need of salvation. What at first appeared to be an ontological characterization has begun to take on a cognitive and volitional dimension. In the beatitudes Jesus proclaims to Israel its salvation. But it is possible to refuse that salvation, for it is to be received by identification with one who for the moment is a rejected figure. Such identification promises to be painful and dangerous, and many will choose to grasp at what good they can in the present—to be rich, full, and cheerful now—rather than become followers of Jesus. Jesus warns such people that they are withdrawing themselves from the true suffering

---

407. Daube, *New Testament and Rabbinic Judaism*, 198–99. In addition to Daube's examples see Luke 1:51–53 and 1:54–55. Minear, "Jesus' Audiences," 107.

408. The woes should not be seen as creations of Luke, since something like them must have been familiar to James (5:1). Against Dupont, *Béatitudes*, I.299-342, and Michaelis, "Seligpreisungen," 160.

409. The woe in 1 En. 94:8 is directed not against the rich as such, but against those who have *trusted* in their riches and *forgotten* God.

410. Schwarz, "Lukas 6:22a, 23c, 26," 269–74, underlines the parallelism between vv. 22a, 23c and 26. He thinks an original unified saying has been divided between the beatitudes and woes.

Israel,[411] and forfeiting their coming salvation. Conversely, those who will stand with Jesus and suffer abuse on his account demonstrate both their desire for salvation (they recognize their need)[412] and their true membership of poor, hungry, weeping Israel. They are promised the kingdom.

It might be objected at this point that my interpretation of the beatitudes and woes produces a result which is at variance with my conclusions from the Nazareth story. In the latter it was possible to contrast the "universalist" outlook of Jesus as he proclaimed salvation to all present with the sectarian outlook of Qumran, which identified its own membership as "the poor" and limited salvation to itself. But in the beatitudes and woes Luke seems to have collapsed back into sectarianism, limiting salvation to disciples.

The apparent discrepancy is solved when the public character of the Sermon is considered. Luke is careful to show that the whole *laos* is assembled (representatively). The Messiah addresses his salvation to all. However, the coming to rest of that blessing is dependent on the non-rejection of the messenger. The difference between the Nazareth occasion and the Great Sermon is that whereas in the former rejection takes place in the course of the story, in the latter it is explicit in the message (the fourth beatitude and the woes). Thus, whereas at Nazareth Jesus is portrayed, initially at least, offering salvation to his people in a totally open way, in the Great Sermon he is already a rejected Messiah; it is presupposed that identification with him will be painful. The demand for costly discipleship has become part of the proclamation of the kingdom.[413]

---

411. Compare Leaney, *Luke*, 135. Is there a hint of a "suffering servant" concept of discipleship in Luke 6:29 (cf. Isa 50:6)? Note, however, that this is in Luke's source.

412. Schweizer, "Seligpreisungen," 126 says, "Sie sagen in einer grossartigen Weite jedem Hörer, der arm genug ist, um Ohren zum Hören zu haben, das Heil zu (With a marvelous expansiveness they promise salvation to every listener, who is poor enough to have ears to hear)."

413. If Jesus' proclamation of the kingdom is foreshadowed in the Magnificat, the idea of the Son of Man being unacceptable and rejected is foreshadowed in the story of the manger (Luke 2:7, 12, 16). Luke sees the birth of Jesus in a manger as a sign; i.e., as a significant pointer to the meaning of what was taking place. The incongruity between what the child is said to be (v. 11) and how he is actually manifested draws attention prophetically to his destiny. There is no τόπος (place) for Jesus in human habitations (v. 7). Luke must certainly have connected the story of Jesus' birth with the saying in Luke 9:57-58. He places the latter just after Jesus' decision to go to Jerusalem and his rejection by the Samaritans. Jesus warns a man who wants to follow him, that he has no real home in this world; i.e., identification with the Son of Man in this age will be difficult and dangerous.

Nevertheless, Luke does not approach the mentality of Qumran. Discipleship remains open. The border between disciples and "others" is never organizationally defined.[414] One could even say that, as the *laos* who have come to hear Jesus and be healed, the people are given the benefit of the doubt and addressed as disciples. But they must decide whether the blessing will "stick." The *laos* is being divided.[415]

In sum, the beatitudes and woes are a challenge to all, to disciples and to the crowds, to stand with the suffering Son of Man, and so to be a part of the true suffering Israel which will inherit the kingdom. They are not intended to define an in-group and a group of reprobates, but to bring all to an earnest desire for salvation which will lead them to identify with Jesus and his cause.[416]

2.5.4 Application to Luke's Readers

Having given close attention to the narrative which introduces the beatitudes and woes, and to the larger sermon of which they form part, as well as following up the interpretative "clue" which Luke provides in verse 20a, we have arrived at an understanding of the beatitudes which is in harmony with our previous findings about the meaning of "the poor" in Isaiah 61 and dependent contexts in Luke. This approach avoids an unnatural typological understanding of the audience, and does away with the need to appeal to an audience who are not present. The sermon can be regarded as addressed throughout to a single audience, without unnatural skipping from group to group. However, the interpretation I have suggested could hardly have been grasped by totally gentile readers, but only by those with sufficient understanding of Jewish eschatological ideas to recognize the character of the poetic imagery of the beatitudes.[417]

---

414. See Dupont, *Béatitudes*, III.22–25.

415. Compare Luke 2:34–35 (εἰς πτῶσιν καὶ ἀνάστασιν—for falling and rising); 6:47–49, and see Jervell, *Luke and the People of God*, 47–74.

416. Minear, *I Saw a New Earth*, 148–50, on the beatitude in Rev 15:16. "A beatitude had this advantage: only the hearer could determine by his action whether he accepted the promise (or warning) as applicable to himself" (149). Also, Guelich, "Matthean Beatitudes," 416–17; cf. Franklin, *Christ the Lord*, 170–71; Brun, *Segen und Fluch im Urchristentum*, 43.

417. Vielhauer, *Urchristlichen Literatur*, 405, says of Luke: "Er wendet sich also an Aussenstehenden, aber nicht an völlig Kenntnislose—denn ohne eine Gewisses Verständnis von Judentum und Christentum waren seine Bücher unverständlich—sondern an Sympathisanten und interessierte Nichtchristen (He devotes himself

Assuming they did have this understanding, it is not difficult to find an application of the beatitudes and woes to Luke's readers. Once they saw them as Jesus' challenge to the Jews of his day to identify with him in persecution and suffering and so inherit Israel's destiny, they could scarcely fail to apply this message to themselves. The application would have been simple if they were Jews, but also, taken in the wider context of Luke-Acts, if they were gentile God-fearers, or gentile Christians, or catechumens.

2.6 SUMMARY AND CONCLUSIONS

I began by posing the question, "Who the poor are in Luke's Nazareth Sermon, in the Beatitudes, and in Jesus' answer to John the Baptist?" After surveying previous approaches to the problem, I presented the thesis that "the poor" is a traditional characterization of Israel understood in terms of its suffering and humiliation at the hands of the nations, and as a result of its own disordered internal life. The source of this imagery was located in Isaiah and the Psalms, books which had a disproportionate influence on Luke. The notion of a glorious eschatological future for "the poor," as a way of describing Israel's salvation, was also seen to be operative in certain intertestamental groups and was known to later Judaism.

I then examined *ptōchoi* in its context in the Nazareth Sermon and found that this understanding harmonized perfectly with the other imagery found there. All this imagery was seen to be current in the "national" soteriological thinking of first century Palestinian Judaism.

In the synagogue Jesus announced to the Nazarenes the fulfilment for them of Israel's hopes, but they rejected the God-ordained "evangelizer" who was not only to announce but also to effect their salvation. In refusing him they forfeited their salvation and he turned to others. The same pattern was found in Jesus' answer to the disciples of John the Baptist: Israel's salvation is proclaimed and present in Jesus' words and deeds, but one must be careful not to take offense at the unexpected lowly appearance of the Messiah.

Turning back to the Magnificat I was able to confirm that Luke is portraying salvation in terms familiar to messianic Judaism of the first

---

therefore to outsiders, but not to those completely without knowledge—for without a certain understanding of Judaism and Christianity his books would be unintelligible—but to sympathizers and interested non-Christians)."

century. Again "the poor" (*tapeinoi*—wretched), who are about to be exalted were seen to be Israel vis-à-vis the oppressor nations.

The same interpretation was seen to fit Luke's beatitudes, and to harmonize with the additional imagery found there. Again, Israel's salvation is declared to the whole people, but a new factor makes itself felt. Discipleship becomes the focal point of Luke's attention. He draws attention to the fact that the ultimate resting place of the blessings of salvation is upon Jesus' disciples. The Messiah faces his people, challenging them through blessings and woes to a longing for salvation, which will cause them to identify with the Son of Man in persecution. Those who do may rightly be called "the poor-hungry-weeping" (they may be). Those who are satisfied with the good things of this age and decline this identification are characterized as the reverse. They are "the rich-satisfied-laughing" but only for now; for they forfeit their claim to Israel's salvation.

A number of overall conclusions may be drawn from this chapter.

a. There is nothing socio-economic or socio-religious about Luke's use of "poor" terminology in the passages we have considered. To seek to ground a liberation theology, or an ethic of poverty, upon these texts would be to misunderstand and misuse them. The poor are Israel, and the answer to their poverty is the messianic kingdom. Of course, it is possible to delve more deeply into this poverty characterization, to extend it to the condition of humankind (as Luke no doubt did) and to explore its existential dimensions, but that is beyond our task here.[418]

b. It is possible to affirm the "universalist" outlook of Luke and relate this to his teaching about "the poor," though not in the way this has generally been done. Luke is not affirming that the lower strata of society are the special heirs of Jesus' salvation (which is hardly universalist), or that even the poor (whom no one else considered) will be saved. He is telling the story of the way salvation came to all Israel, and then to the nations, in the person of Jesus. Elsewhere he will develop and illustrate this in terms of Jesus' fellowship with despised groups and the mission to the gentiles. In the passages we have considered, however, it can only be affirmed in general terms of Israel.

---

418. See Dibelius, "Motive for Social Action," 154–56; Barth, "Poverty"; Bürki, "Die geistlich Armen," 58–64; Metz, *Poverty of Spirit*.

c. A general concept of "reversal" is not to be found in the passages we have considered. The impression that Luke is propounding such a notion is based on a failure to appreciate Jewish soteriological imagery with its contrasting characterization of Israel and the nations, and the Gospel's characterization of non-disciples as "non-Israel."

d. Though the passages we have considered are soteriological and non-ethical, a concept of discipleship emerges which begins to move in an ethical direction. Since, in the main, Israel turns its back on its salvation because of the unacceptability of the one who offers it, the inheritance of "the poor" falls finally to disciples. Because the rest will not follow Jesus, preferring the present order to the salvation Jesus proclaims, they are characterized as rich and satisfied and laughing, though in socio-economic terms they may or may not have been wealthy. Discipleship thus emerges in a double aspect: On the one hand there is an all-consuming desire for the kingdom which leaves all the "comfort" of this age (νῦν—now) in the shadows and on the other a willing allegiance to the rejected Son of Man and an acceptance of the ostracism this entails. This is necessarily reflected back into the poor-hungry-weeping characterization of the disciples so as to portray them not just as those with an objective need of salvation (as all Israel) but also as intensely aware of their need (or the need of their people), and deeply involved now in the conflict with the anti-God forces which presently cause misery, but which God will overthrow "on that day." The extension of this pattern of discipleship is to be seen in the rest of the Great Sermon (love of enemies, acceptance of persecution, non-attachment to possessions) and elsewhere in the Gospel. We will have further cause to consider it in the next chapter, which deals with the theme of renunciation in Luke. In chapter 4 we will take up and pursue further the idea of an anticipatory realization of kingdom conditions, which we have had reason to think may lie behind Luke's use of Isaiah 58 and 61 in the Nazareth sermon and the preaching of John the Baptist.

Chapter 3

Renunciation and Discipleship

3.1 INTRODUCTION

EXAMINATION OF LUKE'S UNDERSTANDING of "the poor" has revealed nothing of an idealization of poverty. We must now inquire whether this notion is not to be found in some of the passages where an emphasis is placed on the renunciation of possessions, an emphasis which has understandably brought upon Luke charges of Ebionism and asceticism.[1]

Those who reject the ascetic solution are forced either to "spiritualize" Jesus' concrete demands[2] or to limit their application to a particular group (the Twelve, "professionals" of the early church, the religious orders).[3] The story of the rich ruler is often dealt with as a specific individual situation intended to establish neither a general nor a limited ethic of renunciation. In this chapter I will seek to show that this "situational" approach does most justice not only to the story of the rich ruler but also to Jesus' demands of his disciples in Luke 14:25–35. However, as we shall

---

1. E.g., Campenhausen, "Early Christian Asceticism," 98–100, who thinks Luke has given "the ascetic solution" to the interpretation of some of Jesus' teachings. Compare Braun, *Radikalismus*, II.74; *RGG* I.643.

2. Bultmann, *Theology of the New Testament*, 9–11; Dupont, "Renoncer à tous ses biens," 561–82.

3. Schulz, *Nachfolgen und Nachahmen*, esp. 79–97; Degenhardt, *Evangelist der Armen*, esp. 41; Stanton, *Gospels as Historical Documents*, II.233–34; Galot, "Voeu religieux de pauvreté," 441–67.

see, this does not mean Luke does not have an important message for his readers. I will argue that Luke 14:25–35 is intended to reveal the limitless character of true discipleship, and that 18:18–30 is meant to offer a serious warning to those with possessions not to let wealth stand in their way of becoming Christians. Finally, I will draw some important clues about Luke's readers from the story of Zacchaeus.

3.2 CONDITIONS OF DISCIPLESHIP, LUKE 14:25–35

The key to this study is Luke 14:33, which the RSV renders: "So therefore whoever of you does not renounce all that he has cannot be my disciple." However, the verse cannot be treated in isolation, since it is connected as a summary conclusion with its antecedent context.[4] The contextual unit begins at 14:25 with a change of scene such as is common in Luke. Verses 34–35 are loosely appended to verses 26–33. Chapter 15:1 begins a new section with another change of scene.

3.2.1 Tradition and Redaction

There is no synoptic parallel to the whole unit, though elements of it are paralleled elsewhere. Luke 14:26–27 is similar to Matthew 10:37–39. Though the similarity of idea and image speaks for some common origin, a common Q source is doubtful. Luke 14:26 has only two words in common with Matthew 10:37,[5] and the cross-saying is so short and memorable that it hardly requires a written source. The variation in two key words speaks against a common Greek source.[6] The primitiveness of Luke's version of these sayings is generally admitted,[7] though he is suspected of having amplified the list of relations the disciple must hate.[8]

---

4. οὕτως οὖν (so therefore).

5. πατέρα, ματέρα (father, mother).

6. βαστάζει, λαμβάνει (carry, take). Manson, *Sayings*, 131, suspects a common Aramaic source.

7. Bultmann, *History of the Synoptic Tradition*, 160; Percy, *Botschaft*, 169; Betz, *Nachfolge und Nachahmung*, 27; Schulz, *Spruchquelle*, 446. Μισεῖν (hate) cannot but be original (compare John 12:25–26) and ἔρχεται ὀπίσω μου (come after me) reflects its Semitic origins more closely than ἀκολουθεῖ ὀπίσω μου (follow after me). However, compare Linton, "Parallelismus membrorum," 489–507.

8. Knox, *Sources*, II.86. Luke also adds "wife" to the list in Luke 18:29. See page 136n207, below.

The two parables in 14:28–32 have no parallel, and it is pointless to speculate on their source. Luke clearly means them to be understood as part of a dominical discourse, for after them he returns to a summary conclusion, which gathers up verses 26–27. Anselm Schultz[9] and Dupont[10] have argued that verse 33 is a Lukan formulation, but their arguments seem to me to do no more than establish the possibility. In my view there is insufficient evidence to judge whether verses 25–33 have been brought into their present unity by Luke, or existed earlier as a unified discourse. I hope to show that they have a natural coherence which cannot lightly be dismissed as a synthesis of originally disparate elements.

The salt sayings have parallels in Matthew 5:13 and Mark 9:50, but the nature of the dependence is manifestly complex and the isolation of a primary saying out of the question. They are only loosely connected to the rest of the discourse and may well have been added to it by Luke.

The narrative introduction to the discourse is typical of Luke, who locates much of Jesus' teaching in relation to an audience and occasion.[11] Whether these are created from his own imagination or reflect genuine tradition cannot be answered here. What is important is that they be taken seriously as pointers to the context in relation to which Luke desires Jesus' teaching to be understood.

3.2.2 Luke 14:25-7

In Luke 14:26–27 Jesus insists that unless a person hates his nearest kin and even his own life, and unless he carries his cross and follows his master, he cannot be a disciple. Crucial to an understanding of these demands is the meaning we give to *mathētēs* (μαθητής—disciple): Does Luke imagine Jesus to be calling certain people to a special kind of "professional" following, or is he challenging the whole crowd to a total allegiance to himself? Once this question is answered we can turn to consider what Luke means by "hating one's kin" and "bearing one's cross."

---

9. Schulz, *Nachfolgen und Nachahmen*, 90.

10. Dupont, "Renoncer à tous ses biens," 568–70.

11. See Baird, *Audience Criticism*; Mosley, "Jesus' Audiences," 145–49; Minear, "Jesus' Audiences."

3.2.2.1 What Is a Disciple?

Schulz[12] opposes Bultmann's view that Jesus' *mathētai* were "a changing circle of followers"[13] and argues that they were like the *talmidīm* of the rabbis, a limited group committed to a regimen of living together with their teacher.[14] He thinks there were only twelve. Luke represents a stage in the development of a more general concept of discipleship.[15] Schulz is able to take such demands as Luke 14:26–27 as originally "initial requirements for a profession"[16] for the disciple who was entering a new "way of life,"[17] which Luke has generalized in the direction of an understanding of discipleship as a "community of destiny."[18]

Degenhardt[19] adopts Schultz's thesis about the original meaning of "disciples" (Jesus' *talmidīm*, though he does not restrict their number to twelve), and applies it directly to Luke. I have already outlined the main tenets of his thesis and expressed dissatisfaction with what it implies about the purpose of Luke, as well as taking issue with its fundamental proposal that Luke intends his descriptions of Jesus' audiences as "disciples" or "people" to guide the application of his teaching to church office-bearers or to general church members respectively.[20]

In the case of Luke 14:25–35, he notes that the teaching is directed to the crowds[21] and interprets verses 26–33 as Jesus' demands of those who wished to pass from the ranks of general adherents to the "professional" group of *talmidīm* who accompanied Jesus and assisted him in his mission. Luke's intention was to exhort Christians of his own day to a realistic appraisal of what was involved in joining the "professional"

---

12. Schulz, *Nachfolgen und Nachahmen*, 47–49.

13. Bultmann, *History of the Synoptic Tradition*, 345.

14. Schulz, *Nachfolgen und Nachahmen*, 21–23. Mark 2:15, 4:10 militates strongly against this view.

15. Schulz, *Nachfolgen und Nachahmen*, 49, 96, n. 87.

16. "Berufsvoraussetzungen."

17. "Lebensordnung."

18. "Schicksalsgemeinschaft." Schulz, *Nachfolgen und Nachahmen*, 89. Navone, *Themes of St. Luke*, 112–13, thinks the church was forced to modify the practice of renunciation because of its inability to participate any longer in the "resourceless itinerant existence of the master during the age of Jesus."

19. Degenhardt, *Evangelist der Armen*, 27–33.

20. λαός, ὄχλος, πλῆθος. pages 14–16, above.

21. ὄχλοι πολλοί—great crowds.

ministry of the church (evangelists, missionaries, etc.).²² Admittedly this gives a neat solution to many of the problems raised by the passage, but it is questionable whether it can be sustained.

Degenhardt argues that for Luke the *laos* was not a negative unbelieving audience but a sympathetic crowd of "the people of God."²³ The *"disciples"* on the other hand were Jesus' literal followers who were called to renounce career, possessions, and family to follow him on the road.²⁴

He is certainly correct in seeing that for Luke *laos* usually indicates God's chosen people (Israel, and on occasions Christians),²⁵ but it does not follow that they are always viewed in a favorable light. Frequently people are termed *laos* in a very negative context. The *laos* is thoroughly implicated in Jesus' being condemned to death, as well as in the attacks on Stephen and Paul.²⁶ In Acts 28:26 Luke quotes Isaiah concerning the hardening of the *laos*. Thus, in reality, Luke depicts the *laos* positively, neutrally, and negatively.²⁷ For although the *laos* is the historic people of God, it is being divided; some are believing in Jesus and proving to be truly God's people, but others are rejecting him.²⁸ It is highly improbable therefore that Luke would have employed a typology in which the people (crowds) represent the subsequent believing church. They more naturally represent those to whom the word of God is addressed and who are in the process of believing or rejecting.

The main pillar of Degenhardt's case is the analogy between Jesus' disciples and rabbinic *talmidīm*, the esse of discipleship being the companionship and common life of teacher and disciple. Karl H. Rengstorff,

---

22. Degenhardt, *Evangelist der Armen*, 105–13. Theissen, "Itinerant Radicalism," 84–93; Theissen, *First Followers*, 8–16, argues that Jesus' teaching on renunciation was preserved among the itinerant evangelists and missionaries ("wandering charismatics") such as the Didache mentions.

23. Also ὄχλος, πλῆθος. Degenhardt, *Evangelist der Armen*, 38: "[Er] steht schon in bejahrende Einstellung zu ihm [Jesu] (It [the people] already stands in a positive relationship to him)."

24. Degenhardt, *Evangelist der Armen*, 27–33.

25. See Lohfink, *Sammlung Israels*, 35; Minear, "Jesus' Audiences," 81–84. Of the eighty-two occurrences of λαός in the singular in Luke-Acts only two do not refer to Israel (Acts 15:14; 18:10). Even in these two cases, God's people (including gentiles) are denoted. The plural *laoi* in Acts 4:25, 27 refers to Israel; in Luke 2:31 it possibly connotes all faithful people (including gentiles).

26. Luke 23:13; Acts 6:12, 21:30, 40, 26:17.

27. See Lohfink, *Sammlung Israels*, 40–46.

28. See page 98, above.

however, points out that the pattern of discipleship found in the Gospels differs markedly from the rabbinic pattern both in the manner of calling and in the character of the relationship with Jesus.[29] Martin Hengel argues a similar case, denying that Jesus' disciples took their pattern from the rabbinic *talmidīm*.[30] Nevertheless, Hengel argues even more positively than Rengstorf (who raises the possibility of people attaching themselves to Jesus without a call)[31] that the essence of discipleship lay in Jesus' individual authoritative call, thus implying that the disciples were a small, select group, as Schulz and Degenhardt maintain.[32] Erich Fascher opposes this idea and points out that Jesus also differed from the rabbis in his open teaching of the crowds.[33] If he taught the crowds, it is to be expected that he had many disciples who remained in the crowds. The problem is complicated because the Gospels do not present a uniform picture. Jesus did have an "inner circle" who followed him on the road, and these are frequently termed "disciples."[34]

However, a much larger group are also called disciples by Luke, and it is not at all clear whether they had experienced a special call, nor whether they shared a common life with Jesus and the Twelve.[35] The problem with Hengel's study is that it assumes the identity of disciple and follower.[36] While what he says is valid for those whom Jesus called to follow him, he does not demonstrate that it was this call or this following which made a disciple. Luke's first mention of *mathētai* is in Luke 5:30, and Mark's is in Mark 2:15. Neither of them mentions the word in relation to the call of Simon and his partners or of Levi.[37] We cannot just assume that these are typical representations of the call to discipleship; they may be more closely connected with what Luke later describes as Jesus'

---

29. *TDNT* IV.444-50.
30. Hengel, *Nachfolge und Charisma*.
31. *TDNT* IV.444-45.
32. Also Bornkamm, *Jesus of Nazareth*, 144-52.
33. Fascher, "Jesus der Lehrer," 331-42.
34. Luke 9:49. Luke 8:22, 9:14, 18; cf. 8:1-3.
35. Luke 6:17, 19:37.
36. So does Otomo, *Nachfolge Jesu und Anfänge der Kirche*. This identification is almost universal and understandable when it is considered that the later church saw following Jesus on the way to his passion (and glory) as a paradigm of the Christian life. In the Gospels, however, one must be careful to enquire whether this identification is valid for every case.
37. Luke 5:1-11, 27-28; Mark 1:17-20, 2:14.

selection of apostles from among his many disciples.[38] The fact that for some, discipleship and literal following were co-extensive does not mean that it was so in all cases.[39] In Matthew 8:21–22, the passage on which Hengel's case is built, it is a disciple who is told, "Follow me," and in Luke's version two of the men who are subsequently challenged to "follow" address Jesus as Lord.[40] Thus it should be kept in mind that when Hengel bases his exposition of the distinctive character of Jesus' disciples on the Q original of these sayings, he does it in opposition to both evangelists' understanding of their material.

It makes more sense to see the disciples in Luke as all those who made a positive response to Jesus and regarded him at least as their teacher.[41] The Twelve are so named because they belong to a wider genus. As those who accompanied Jesus, they were disciples *par excellence*,[42] but the essence of their discipleship was not physical following but attention to his teaching.[43] Such a view is not inconsistent with first-century use of *mathētēs* or *talmīd*[44] and explains the curious fact that there is no other term in the Gospels for one who made a positive response to Jesus' teaching, but was not called to literal following. It also explains why in Acts Christian believers are termed "disciples" without the need to postulate a dramatic change in the meaning of common words.[45] Degenhardt holds the odd position that Luke employs *mathētai* as a typological symbol for church office-bearers in the Gospel, while in Acts it is one of his normal

---

38. Luke 6:13–14. This is not to deny that these stories may be intended as paradigms of response for later disciples.

39. Cf. Schweizer, "Disciples of Jesus and the Post-Resurrection Church," 243, 245; *Lordship and Discipleship*, 20.

40. Luke 9:50–62. Luke follows these three calls to follow, with the choosing of *others* to go before Jesus and preach (10:1).

41. Minear, "Jesus' Audiences," 88–89.

42. Zahn, *Lukas*, 405, and Lohfink, *Sammlung Israels*, 74, suggest there was an inner and outer group of disciples.

43. Note Luke 6:40, which Luke places in the context of open instruction of the crowds; also, Luke 6:46–9 par. It is probable that behind κύριε κύριε lies the title רבי רבי (master, master); see *TDNT* VI.965; Hengel, *Nachfolge und Charisma*, 46–47, with notes 19 and 20. Those who *do* his teaching may *rightly* call him Lord.

44. See *TDNT* IV.437, 439, for examples of disciples of Homer, Moses, Balaam, Aaron, and Hillel (after his death). Also, the discussion on μαθηταὶ τῶν Φαρισαίων (disciples of the Pharisees), 443.

45. As Degenhardt, *Evangelist der Armen*, 33–36, and Otomo, *Nachfolge Jesu und Anfänge der Kirche*, 206, are forced to do.

terms to describe a Christian. Much better with Schürmann to regard the disciples in Luke as "model and prototype of the original Christian community,"[46] or with Lohfink, as "not yet the church itself, but a preview of what it will become after Pentecost."[47]

This view makes good sense in Luke 14:25–35, which does not read naturally as an invitation to those in the crowds who would like to join the inner group of Jesus' traveling companions. The passage seems rather to suggest that those who crowded round Jesus were held, outwardly at least, to be his disciples, though perhaps only in their own eyes.[48] The point of the discourse is to make clear to them what else is involved if they are to be *true* disciples. The emphatic appeal of verse 35b stresses the public character of the discourse and calls for heart-searching on the part of the crowds to see whether their inward resolution matches their outward allegiance.

3.2.2.2 The Demand to Hate

Scholars are almost unanimous that Luke's word "hate" faithfully represents the word of Jesus,[49] and, since it therefore represents a Semitic original,[50] many are of the opinion that it should be treated as Semitic hyperbole and be understood in the sense of "love less."[51] Others would give it more force than this, but add the explanation "so far as they stand in the way of following Jesus."[52] Instances of such a meaning are given from the Old Testament,[53] but on examination these turn out to have to do with hatred of women, mostly by their husbands. As such they represent

---

46. "Vor- und Urbild der urchristlichen Gemeinde." Schürmann, *Lukasevangelium*, 320–21.

47. "Noch nicht die Kirche selbst, aber Präformation dessen, was nach Pfingsten geschehen wird." Lohfink, *Sammlung Israels*, 75; compare 71, 73–74.

48. εἴ τις ἔρχεται πρός με (if anyone comes to me). Compare Luke 19:37, 39.

49. μισεῖ (*misei*). Dodd, *Historical Tradition*, 338–43, argues that when John 12:25 is stripped of Johannine additions it reveals the tradition from which Luke 14:26 was also derived.

50. Hebrew שׂנא, Aramaic סני

51. Creed, *Luke*, 194; Caird, *Luke*, 178–79; *TDNT* IV.690–91; Grundmann, *Lukas*, 302; Degenhardt, *Evangelist der Armen*, 106; Schulz, *Nachfolgen und Nachahmen*, 80–82; Lagrange, *Luc*, 409 (in times of persecution); Kittel, *Probleme*, 54–55.

52. Easton, *Luke*, 231; Plummer, *Luke*, 364; W. Manson, *Luke*, 175; Leaney, *Luke*, 215; Zahn, *Lucas*, 555.

53. E.g., Gen 29:31, 33; Deut 21:15–17; Isa 6:15; Prov 30:23.

a special case[54] from which it would be unwise to draw conclusions about a weakening of the force of "hatred." The feelings that lead to divorce are rarely without passion![55]

The Old Testament concept of "hate" differs from the modern concept in two ways.

First, the word does not carry the connotations of evil it does today. God is more frequently spoken of as "hating" than "being hated." Hatred of things is used in a good sense (e.g., dishonest gain) as often as in a bad sense (e.g., reproof), and the righteous are described as hating the wicked as often as the reverse. Thus, hatred in itself is not viewed as evil in the Old Testament. This may have had some influence on Jesus and the early church.[56]

Second, in the Old Testament the word "hate" often carries a more objective meaning than it does in modern speech. Where we might say, "He acted as though he hated him," the Old Testament simply says, "He hated him." Thus, in Proverbs 13:24 RSV ("He that spares the rod hates his son") it is not that the father dislikes his son, but that his actions are as though he did; he harms him.[57] Attention could thus be focused on the harmful action rather than on the psychological condition which generated it. It is in this sense that God's love of Jacob and hatred of Esau should be understood. His hatred of Esau consists in his having "made his mountains a desolation."[58]

The only extrabiblical example which is given meaning "to love less" is Exodus Rabbah 51:8. Sinai (סיני) was so named "because (it was on that mount) that God showed that he hates (שנא) the angels, and loves mankind." However, the fact that this follows a discussion about the humiliation of the Angel of Death at Sinai suggests that perhaps fallen angels may be meant. In any case, a single example of imaginative etymology such as this is no basis for establishing the sense of the word in the New Testament.

---

54. Whybray, *Isaiah 40–66*, 235–36, suggests that *sanē* was a technical term related to marriage and divorce.

55. See also Deut 22:13, 16, 24:3; Judg 14:16, 15:2, 2 Sam 13:15; Isa 54:6 (LXX); Sir 42:9.

56. See Rom 7:15, 9:13; Heb 1:9; Jude 23; Rev 2:6.

57. Also Prov 15:32, 29:24; cf. 19:18, 8:36.

58. Mal 1:2–3.

Thus, there is scant justification for taking *misei* in Luke 14:26 in the sense of "love less."[59] It should be accorded its normal intensity, implying strong dislike, or, as seems more appropriate to this context, behavior which would normally issue from strong dislike.

The difficulty now is that the saying appears to advocate what is elsewhere clearly condemned.[60] Is it not paradoxical that in the same Gospel disciples are commanded to love their enemies and to hate their own kin? Hengel explains this in terms of the final time of trial: "In the background stands the prophetic-apocalyptic motif of the shattering of families in the time of the final end-time *peirasmos* [trial]."[61] However, the references with which he supports this mostly relate to the unnatural inhumanity, which will break out in the last times. They give no hint that it might be virtuous or necessary to hate one's kin.[62] We are left with the question of why Jesus made such a strikingly offensive demand.

James Denny makes an interesting suggestion based on the context of the saying in Luke:

> In the situation presented to us by Luke there is something which it may be reverently said provokes Jesus to use strong language. Jesus was on his way to Jerusalem to die, and the attendance of great multitudes who were utterly without comprehension of him or sympathy with him, who were so far from being ready to die in the same cause that they could not find it in their hearts to do themselves the smallest violence for his sake, explains the passion with which he declares the conditions of discipleship.[63]

An attempt to recover the *Sitz im Leben* of this saying is beyond the scope of this study. The most we can do is examine whether such a view is consistent with the outlook and intention of Luke, and whether he means the saying to be understood in relation to such a setting.

---

59. Schütz, *Leidende Christus*, 18, notes that even when this is done, "doch bleibt auch dann ein gewisses Mass an Härte (yet there remains even then a definite amount of harshness)."

60. Luke 6:27–38, 11:11–13, 16:18, 18:20.

61. "Im Hintergrund steht das prophetisch-apokalytische Motiv des Zerbrechens der Familie in der Zeit des letzten endzeitlichen 'Peirasmos.'" Hengel, *Nachfolge und Charisma*, 14.

62. Compare Luke's portrayal of the ministry of John the Baptist: "to turn the hearts of the fathers to the children" (Luke 1:17).

63. Denney, "The Word 'Hate' in Luke 14:26," 41–42.

RENUNCIATION AND DISCIPLESHIP 113

Although verse 25 tells us only that great crowds went with him, the pericope is imbedded in the travel narrative, suggesting the possibility that Luke may have intended it to be understood in connection with the journey to Jerusalem, which clearly had historical significance for him.[64] At various points throughout the travel narrative there are clear indications that Luke has not lost sight of the journey[65] so that, although much of the teaching which he has included within it has no historical relation to the journey,[66] some of it clearly has.[67] It is important that we determine to which category 14:25–35 belongs.

The way Luke introduces the pericope strongly suggests a relation to the journey. That large crowds were accompanying him indicates both that Jesus was traveling and that he was surrounded by crowds. The concentration of occurrences of *poreuomai* (πορεύομαι—go) and its derivatives in relation to the journey is significant,[68] and the presence of crowds receives more emphasis than anything else in Luke's descriptions of the journey.[69]

Thus, Denney's suggestion about the "situational" character of Luke 14:25–35 is probably correct,[70] and we can now examine his suggestion about Luke's portrayal of Jesus' state of mind.

Luke consistently draws attention to Jesus' knowledge of his approaching death and a number of these predictions are characterized by an unusual intensity of feeling.[71] He anticipates this when he relates

---

64. See Gasse, "Reisebericht des Lukas," 293–99; W. C. Robinson, "Luke's Travel Narrative," 20–31; Robinson, *Way of the Lord*, 60; Marshall, *Luke: Historian and Theologian*, 150–53; Davies, "Purpose of the Central," 164–69; Stonehouse, *Witness of Luke*, 112–24.

65. Luke 9:51–10:24, 13:22, 17:11, 18:35, 19:11, 28.

66. E.g., Luke 10:38–42 probably belongs close to Jerusalem, but is associated with the story of the good Samaritan for didactic reasons (see pages 130–32, below). See Reicke, "Travel Narrative," 206–16; Schneider, "Analyse der lukanischen Reiseberichtes," 207–29.

67. Luke 13:22–35, 18:31–34, 19:11–27.

68. Luke 9:51–57, 10:38, 13:22, 33, 17:11, 18:36, 19:28, 36.

69. Luke 18:36, 19:37, 39; compare 11:29, 12:1, 13, 54.

70. Leaney, *Luke*, 214, and Schneider, *Lukas*, 320–21, also approach this passage from the angle of the journey. Cf. Lohse, "Lukas als Theologe der Heilsgeschichte," 260, and Wilder, *Eschatology and Ethics*, 165, on the situational character of Jesus' teaching in Luke.

71. Luke 12:49–50, 13:33–35.

that Jesus "set his face" to go to Jerusalem.[72] He portrays him journeying purposefully and with intense feeling towards his passion.

The crowds, on the other hand, have totally different expectations. Johannes Weiss comments on Luke 14:25:

> The masses who attach themselves to Jesus regard the procession to Jerusalem, according to Luke's interpretation, or that of his source, as a victory procession at the end of which the kingdom of God beckons.[73]

The Twelve are portrayed as uncomprehending, afraid to press Jesus for an explanation of his passion-prediction.[74] The crowds are enthusiastic,[75] expecting the inauguration of the kingdom at the end of the journey in Jerusalem.[76] In this situation strong words are certainly to be expected. But still it is necessary to ask why Jesus should demand that his followers should "hate" those dearest to them.

There is no doubt that Jesus' resolution to travel to Jerusalem and die there would have had serious implications for his family. In "setting his face" to go to Jerusalem he was in effect turning his back on his obligation to his own kin,[77] just as he was also setting himself in opposition to the demands of "his own life." "Hates his own mother, etc., and even his own life" would therefore have been an appropriate if intense description of Jesus on his last journey. The intensity is understandable in the situation Luke has described;[78] natural feelings are being denied for the sake of the mission; loved ones are being treated as though they were hated.

---

72. Luke 9:51, τὸ πρόσωπον ἐστήρισεν, is probably an allusion to Isa 50:7, therefore expressing a determination to suffer; not as Davies, "Purpose of the Central," 167, suggests a reference to judgment, as in Ezekiel.

73. "Die Massen, die sich Jesus anschliessen sehen nach der Auffassung des Lukas (19:11, 37) oder seiner Quelle den Zug nach Jerusalem als einen Siegeszug an, an dessen Ende das Reich Gottes winkt." Weiss, *Schriften*, I.465.

74. Luke 9:45. On the disciples' lack of understanding see Schütz, *Leidende Christus*, 20–25.

75. Luke 10:17, 12:1 (the size of the crowd is indication of their enthusiasm), 19:37.

76. Luke 19:1,; 9:46–50, 22:24–30; cf. Mark 10:35–45, and see Plummer, *Luke*, 363; Conzelmann, *Luke*, 74; Caird, *Luke*, 178; Schütz, *Leidende Christus*, 71–74; Elliot-Binns, *Galilean Christianity*, 33.

77. For what would be expected of a son see Derrett, *Jesus' Audience*, 34–36. Compare Theissen, *First Followers*, 11–12.

78. There is also an intentional, stark intensity in all the comparable OT examples of hate (page 111n57, above).

How, then, might the saying apply to disciples? Is it possible that Jesus was asking them to do exactly what he himself was doing: to turn their backs on all their loved ones, to treat them as though they hated them, to reject even their own lives, and to come with him to Jerusalem to die?[79] This is exactly what the second part of the saying—the demand that they bear their own cross—seems to be saying.

3.2.2.3 Bearing One's Own Cross

Although Bultmann suggests that the cross may already in Jesus' time have been a "traditional figure for suffering and sacrifice," no evidence of such an image exists prior to the Gospels.[80] Adolf Schlatter suggests that the saying came to Jesus' circle from the Zealot movement:

> Taking the cross had serious significance for everyone who held to Zealotism. As soon as the confession was accepted that there is only one Lord, and no other, the cross stood in view. This carried over to the disciples of Jesus.[81]

This possibility must clearly be granted.[82] However, the saying in its Lukan form could scarcely have been derived from the revolutionary movements. For it speaks not of the *possibility* of crucifixion, as might be expected in the exhortations of a revolutionary leader,[83] but of an *inevitability*. It is inconceivable that a rebel leader would exhort his followers with slogans indicative of the failure of his mission.

Bearing one's cross refers to the practice of making the condemned carry the horizontal cross-beam to the place of execution, during which

---

79. John 12:25–26 expresses the same thought. The demand to hate one's life (compare Luke 14:26) is followed by the words, "If anyone serves me, he must also follow me (compare Luke 14:27); and where I am, there shall my servant be also."

80. Bultmann, *History of the Synoptic Tradition*, 161. The only rabbinic parallel is *Gen. Rab.* 56:3. For Latin and Greek use see Hengel, *Crucifixion*, 64–68. There is no metaphorical use of the image of bearing the cross.

81. "Das 'Kreuznehmen' hatte für jeden, der sich zum Zelotismus hielt, ernsthafte Bedeutung. Sobald das Bekenntnis angenommen war, dass es nur 'einen Herrn' gebe und keinen zweiten, stand das Kreuz in Sicht. Das übertrug sich sofort auch auf die Junger Jesu." Schlatter, *Matthäus*, 350.

82. Crucifixion was the standard penalty for insurrectionists (Mommsen, *Römisches Strafrecht*, 565n1). It was well known in Palestine; Varus crucified two thousand in the rebellions after the death of Herod the Great (Josephus, *Ant.* 17.295).

83. Josephus, *Ant.* 18.23.

time he would suffer humiliation and physical abuse from the crowds.[84] The saying envisages Jesus already carrying his cross towards the execution site in Jerusalem. The crowds are told that the true disciple will be following behind the master bearing their own cross.[85] Thus the saying has an anti-Zealot tendency. Luke imagines the crowds in a revolutionary mood, expecting the kingdom at the end of the journey. Jesus, on the other hand, knows that he is already walking towards the cross and is deeply moved not only by his impending sufferings, but also by the evident lack of comprehension of the crowds. He warns his supporters therefore in strong and emotive terms that to follow him on this journey means to turn their backs on family and loved-ones, renouncing all further responsibility to them and treating them as though they were hated. They must even treat their own lives in this way and bear their cross behind him on the road to execution and apparent failure of the mission.

Three objections might be raised against this situational interpretation of Luke 14:26–27:

a. Luke 9:23, where Jesus challenges a would-be follower to deny himself and take up his cross "daily," seems to imply a generalized understanding of cross-bearing on the part of Luke.[86] The saying requires an attitude of mind such as is demanded of the Christian in the church, rather than demanding martyrdom in Jerusalem. All this may be granted without serious disturbance to the previous conclusion For the fact that the three synoptic evangelists are agreed in relating this demand to Jesus' first passion prediction suggests at least a tradition—perhaps even a recollection—associating it with Jesus' "journey" to his crucifixion.[87] This being so, it cannot be ruled out that the demand for martyrdom may originally have been

---

84. Pauly, *Real-Encyclopädie*, 768–70; but for variety in the manner of crucifixion see Hengel, *Crucifixion*, 25–26.

85. Bultmann, *History of the Synoptic Tradition*, 161, argues against the post-Easter provenance of this saying on the ground that ἑαυτοῦ (*his own*) does not envisage Jesus' cross. However, the fact that the disciple is to carry his own cross and follow Jesus surely implies that Jesus is also pictured carrying his (see Schulz, *Nachfolgen und Nachahmen*, 87). ἔρχεται ὀπίσω μου (comes after me) is part of the crucifixion image, not a reference to following a rabbi.

86. καθ' ἡμέραν. Also compare Luke's ἔρχεσθαι (to come—continuous) (9:23) with Mark's ἐλθεῖν (to come—aorist) (8:34).

87. Mark 8:31–38; Matt 16:21–28; Luke 9:22–27. The Johannine parallel (12:25–26) also occurs in relation to Jesus' consciousness of his passion.

connected specifically with Jesus' own consciousness of the danger that faced him in Jerusalem. It is not improbable that Luke should have generalized in a passage which serves him as a key statement on following and confessing Jesus,[88] all the while retaining a knowledge of the historical (situational) dimension and bringing this out in another place.[89] That the cross-saying occurs twice (without any generalization in Luke 14:27) is a pointer towards two different applications.

b. Could Jesus have anticipated death by crucifixion? It makes little sense to attribute to Luke a situational understanding of a saying which clearly implies that Jesus expected to be crucified unless there is some historical probability of this being so.[90]

There is certainly no improbability in Jesus having anticipated a violent death. The recent experience of the Baptist, and the opposition Jesus experienced in Galilee from the Pharisees and Herodians may well have warned him of this.[91] This would not be sufficient, however, to explain a cross-saying. Crucifixion was the penalty meted out by the Romans for crimes such as treason and insurrection, in addition to being their normal way of executing slaves.[92] It was not normally used against ordinary criminals.[93] For Jesus to have anticipated crucifixion he must have expected to be charged with something like treason in an area under Roman jurisdiction (like Jerusalem). As a matter of historical fact, we know that both these things occurred. If the traditions of Jesus' determination to journey to Jerusalem and his "messianic" activity there are reliable he might well have anticipated what in fact happened. For whereas

---

88. Lohmeyer, *Markus*, 171 thinks Mark has performed such a generalization by bringing the crowds into the picture (8:34).

89. Compare Schürmann, *Lukasevangelium*, 540-42.

90. Note that the fourth Gospel is aware of a tradition that Jesus expected death by crucifixion (John 12:32-33; 18:32).

91. Mark 1:14; 6:14-29; 3:6; Luke 13:31-33.

92. See page 115n82, above; also Hengel, *Crucifixion*, 46-63, and Bammel, "Crucifixion in Palestine," 162-65.

93. Indiscriminate practice of crucifixion against Jews would have been tantamount to treating the nation as slaves, and therefore highly inflammatory (note the horror of Josephus at Florus crucifying Jews of equestrian rank: *War* 2.308). Other penalties are attested (scourging, decapitation). Josephus notes that the brigands captured with Eleazar were crucified, while those convicted of complicity with them were merely punished (*War* 2.253).

in Galilee Pharisaic opposition to Jesus had to ally itself with the executive power of Herod in order to succeed, in Jerusalem any realistic attempt to eliminate him would have to be carried out in co-operation with the Sadducees and Romans, the latter being the only ones with capital power.[94] There are indications that Jesus was not an easy target,[95] and the presence of large crowds of sympathetic Galileans may have made a stoning impossible.[96] Hence crucifixion may have been the obvious thing.

c. Does Luke really imagine that Jesus wanted his disciples to face death with him? There is perhaps some tension in his thinking here, but there can be no doubt that such a thought was not foreign to him. In Luke 12:4-12 Jesus encourages his disciples not to be afraid of those who can kill the body, but to be loyal to him and to confess him. Those who fear for their lives and deny him, he warns, will themselves be denied by the Son of Man at his coming. Luke surely has this in mind as he describes the failure of the disciples to confess, and in particular Peter's denial.[97] At Gethsemane Jesus tells them to pray "that you not enter into temptation."[98] R. H. Lightfoot is no doubt correct in thinking they were to pray for the testing situation to be averted.[99] Nevertheless, it was to be a trial for them, not just for Jesus. In failing to pray, they also failed to stand when the trial broke. Luke does not record their flight, but it is assumed. It is the failure of the disciples to be disciples to the end which perhaps explains why Luke does not use the word "disciple" in the Gospel after 22:45.[100] It may also explain why, apart from the portrayal of Jesus himself, there is nothing in the Gospel which fully answers to the description "hate one's kin, one's life, and bear one's own cross." All the disciples failed at the point of testing and at the end Jesus was alone.

---

94. This is disputed (Winter, *Trial of Jesus*, 110-30) but the accuracy of John 18:31 has been ably defended by Sherwin-White, *Roman Society and Roman Law*, 24-47.

95. The story of the betrayal (Mark 14:10-11 par); cf. John 8:59.

96. Mark 14:1-2. Blinzler, "Jewish Punishment of Stoning," 147-61; 148-49 argues that stoning was a communal method of punishment.

97. Luke 22:57; compare 12:9.

98. ἵνα μὴ εἰσέλθητε εἰς πειρασμόν. Luke 22:46.

99. Lightfoot, *Message of St. Mark*, 53.

100. As in *TDNT* IV.446-47.

None of these objections, therefore, disallows a situational interpretation of the cross saying. Jesus warns the enthusiastic crowds who have failed to grasp the real direction of his mission that following him means journeying with him towards the place of execution, and that only those who have turned their back on family and even on the demands of their own life are truly his disciples.

The two parables follow in the same train of thought.[101] Jesus asks his would-be followers to consider whether they can fulfil the demands he is making of them. If not, it is better that they should not follow him at all, for in their failure to go all the way they will become a laughingstock.[102] In both parables the dominant thought is, "If you cannot see it through to the end, do not begin."[103] The tower builder must count the cost and the king must determine the relative strength of his army.[104] Each must take care not to begin unless he is able to complete the job. Jesus has indicated that on this journey the "end" of discipleship is death. It is not a matter of calculating one's general powers (Kräfte) for discipleship,[105] but of considering whether one is prepared to go the whole way (to death).[106]

---

101. Luke 14:28–32. γάρ (for—v. 28) may be taken in the sense, "The reason I tell you these things is this: Who of you . . ."

102. εἰς ἀπαρτισμόν, ἐκτελέσαι—to completion, to complete.

103. See also Jeremias, *Parables*, 196; cf. Derrett, "Towers and Wars," 243. Derrett relates the parables not to the disciples' need for forethought, but to Jesus' careful consultation with the Father on the course of his campaign. He seeks to inspire his followers with confidence that he would not ask them to do anything unless he had first planned everything carefully. The idea is interesting but does not seem to be what Luke was thinking. Sandwiched as these parables are between two appeals to disciples, the latter apparently logically connected to the parables (οὕτως οὖν—so therefore), they read most naturally as an appeal to disciples (ἐξ ὑμῶν—from you; compare v. 28 with v. 33). Moreover, the fate of the worthless salt (ἔξω βάλλουσιν αὐτο—they throw it outside—v. 35) seems to take up the idea of mockery (vv. 29–30), showing that the latter envisages the failure of the disciples.

104. If Derrett, "Towers and Wars," is correct in thinking the tower and the war are allusions to the new Jerusalem (the kingdom) and the messianic war, then Luke (Jesus?) has performed an interesting transformation of concepts: the kingdom is to be built, and the war against the hosts of evil to be won, not by arms, but by dying in Jerusalem.

105. Degenhardt, *Evangelist der Armen*, 110; compare Jülicher, *Gleichnisreden*, 208.

106. Lagrange, *Luc*, 412. Thus, there is no "strange contrast" between vv. 26–27 and 28–32, as Flender, *Theologian of Redemptive History*, 75–76, maintains.

3.2.3 Renunciation, Luke 14:33

Luke 14:33 sums up and concludes verses 26–32: "so therefore... he cannot be my disciple."[107] Lagrange remarks on the astonishing degree of softening in verse 33 with respect to verse 26; first one is commanded to hate those nearest and dearest, as well as one's own life, but later it is merely a matter of one's possessions.[108] It is probable, however, that in this context τὰ ὑπάρχοντα has the more general significance, "that which belongs to one," and should be understood to include not only inanimate possessions but family as well.[109]

The usual sense of *apotassesthai* (ἀποτάσσεσθαι) is "say farewell to" or "take leave of," though it is also used figuratively with impersonal objects to mean "renounce" or "give up."[110] It is used once in Mark, three times in Luke-Acts, and in 2 Corinthians 2:13 in the normal sense, and there seems no good reason why it should be given a different meaning in this one case.[111] Verse 33 might then be translated: "So, therefore, whoever does not say goodbye to all that is his cannot be my disciple."[112] As such it perfectly summarizes the thought of the preceding appeal. Disciples must "say goodbye" to family, possessions, and life as they shoulder their cross to follow Jesus to execution in Jerusalem.

3.2.4 Application

Degenhardt's direct application of the discourse to Christians who are considering whether they should enter the "professional" ministries of the church has already been rejected. His emphasis on the importance of the audience is sound, but points rather to an application to people faced

---

107. οὕτως οὖν... οὐ δύναται εἶναί μου μαθητής

108. πᾶσιν τοῖς ἑαυτοῦ ὑπάρχουσιν (all of his possessions). Lagrange, *Luc*, 412.

109. Technically one could take v. 33 in the sense of "whatever belongs to him." In Job 2:3-4 τὰ ὑπάρχοντα includes not only Job's estate but also his dead children. Compare Gen 13:6, 25:5, 39:4-6, 45:18 (Heb. בתיכם); Sir 41:1. In Luke 12:44 τοῖς ὑπάρχουσιν includes the household servants.

110. AG, 100.

111. Mark 6:46; Luke 9:61; Acts 18:18, 21. Against Dupont, "Renoncer à tous ses biens," 569, who argues that v. 33 is a Lukan creation because ἀποτάσσομαι has a Greek ascetic sense here.

112. J. B. Phillips has "says goodbye"; NEB, "taking leave."

with the decision whether to become Christians, or perhaps to those in danger of a hasty and shallow commitment to the Christian way.[113]

Dupont sees it as a message to a persecuted church, not that they should despoil themselves, but that they should be ready to be despoiled by their enemies; verse 33 was created by Luke to effect this application.[114] He wants to take *apotassetai* in the Greek ascetic sense of "renounce," but recognizes at the same time that Luke did not regard total renunciation as a demand for all Christians. He is forced, therefore, to take verse 33 in the sense of "whoever is not willing to renounce," arguing that the present indicative points to "a spiritual disposition."[115] It is doubtful, however, that so much should be pressed from a linear tense in a conditional clause such as this, and one wonders why, if Luke composed verse 33, he did not say, "willing to renounce," if that is what he meant. The most serious objection in seeing verse 33 as a direct application to the later church is that in effect it says no more or less than verses 26-27.

As with much of the teaching in Luke, application is much less mechanical than Dupont and Degenhardt are suggesting. Luke does not normally provide an independent interpretative word for the church extracted from the setting in Jesus' life which he provides. Whatever we may think about the historical form of the Gospel, Luke obviously means it to be taken seriously as a portrayal of the time of Jesus, not of the conditions of his own church. The reader is thus asked to be more imaginative in his application of Jesus' teaching. Application must proceed along the lines of discerning a congruence between the situation of the prototypical disciples and the later readers.

If my situational interpretation of Luke 14:25-33 is close to how Luke intended the passage to be understood, then he probably meant it to function as a paradigm of real discipleship, rather than as a direct command to the later church.[116] Luke gives a picture of discipleship at a

113. Dupont, "Renoncer à tous ses biens," 574, argues that since Luke uses εἶναι (to be), not γενέσθαι (to become) the reference is not to *becoming* but to *remaining* Christian. This is true for the imagined *Sitz* (outward adherents challenged to total commitment), but should not be pressed too hard in the application.

114. Dupont, ""Renoncer à tous ses biens," esp. 580-81.

115. "Une disposition d'ésprit." Dupont, "Renoncer à tous ses biens," 575.

116. Even commentators who recognize a situational element in these sayings often jump to a direct application; e.g., Schlatter, *Markus und Lukas*, 262-64. Others seek a congruence between Jesus' journey to the passion and the whole Christian life (Grundmann, "Fragen," 256). Though true, this does not help to interpret specific sayings.

time of great crisis. In this extreme situation the limits of discipleship are revealed.[117] Better still, it is revealed that discipleship has no limits. The disciple must continue with his Lord even to the point of turning his back on family, possessions, and life itself. In the extreme situation of the last journey to Jerusalem all this was literally necessary. Normally it will not be necessary, but at any moment it could be.[118] Having explained this, it is possible to agree with Dupont (though not with his method) that willingness to renounce all will be the ongoing Christian stance.

The concluding salt saying is loosely attached and has probably been brought into its present location by Luke. Its form lies somewhere between that of the parallel sayings in Mark and Matthew.[119] In Mark 9:49–50 salt denotes a quality which is induced in the disciple, while in Matthew 5:13 it denotes disciples themselves. In Luke it is not immediately clear to which it refers. Commentators vary in taking it as the spirit of self-sacrifice,[120] as the distinctive quality of a true disciple,[121] or as disciples themselves.[122]

Knox draws attention to the unusual use of *mōrainein* (μωραίνειν—make foolish) in Luke and Matthew.[123] The meaning "become insipid" is nowhere else attested, though *mōros* (μῶρος—foolish) can mean "insipid." He is doubtful, therefore, that this verb would have been used until the sayings had been taken to apply to disciples as the salt of the earth. Matthew Black comes to a similar conclusion on the basis of the Semitic *taphal* (תפל—insipid; foolish) which he thinks underlies both Mark's *analos* (ἄναλος—saltless) and Matthew's and Luke's *mōranthē*.[124] Black concludes: "The rendering of Q, μωρανθῇ, represents an interpretation; the 'insipid' salt refers to foolish disciples."[125]

---

117. Compare Dodd, *Gospel and Law*, 61.
118. There is therefore no conflict with the outlook of Acts.
119. Rengstorf, *Lukas*, 181.
120. Plummer, *Luke*, 366; W. Manson, *Luke*, 176.
121. Creed, *Luke*, 195; compare Finkel, *Pharisees*, 156.
122. De Wette, *Exegetisches Handbuch*, 90; Grundmann, *Lukas*, 303–304; Leaney, *Luke*, 215.
123. Knox, *Sources*, II.86–88.
124. חפלה = unsavouriness; foolishness. Black, *Aramaic Approach to the Gospels*, 166–67. He is following Lightfoot, *Horae Hebraicae et Talmudicae*, 152–53.
125. Black, *Aramaic Approach to the Gospels*, 166.

RENUNCIATION AND DISCIPLESHIP

Having decided that in Luke the reference is to disciples,[126] and not to some quality they possess, we can readily explain the parable in its present context. Salt is declared to be an excellent and useful commodity.[127] Its functions are proverbial: to preserve from putrefaction[128] and to improve taste. It is an agent which imparts its properties to the improvement of other things. If it loses its ability to do this—if salt itself becomes insipid—there is nothing that can season it, since it is the seasoning agent. It becomes totally worthless, being useful neither for fertilizer, nor even for the humus heap as potential fertilizer.[129]

The parable is appended to the discourse on conditions of discipleship to reinforce the point that disciples who cease to act as disciples (draw back from full identification with Jesus) are totally worthless. Its tone is similar to the rest of the discourse: not a friendly exhortation to more committed discipleship, but a passionate plea that it is useless to be a disciple unless one is prepared to persist to the end, whatever the cost. To be a disciple and then at some point to draw back (become foolish, insipid) is worse than never having begun ("they throw it away").

The relation of this theme to the preceding parable of the great banquet (Luke 14:16–24) is probably not accidental. The parable underlines the universality of the invitation to the kingdom; Luke 14:25–35 says to those who are entering that nothing less than a total commitment to Jesus, even to the point of death, is acceptable from those who wish to be disciples.[130] We have already seen these two themes emerging in chapter 2.

3.3 THE RICH RULER, LUKE 18:18-30

The history of the interpretation of the story of the rich ruler is long and varied.[131] Since Antony it has formed the basis of the monastic idealiza-

---

126. Billerbeck I.236 gives one example, which, if their interpretation is correct, points to the idea of Israel as salt (*b. Bek.* 8b)

127. καλόν—*kalon*. Sir 39:26 lists it as one of the essential commodities of life.

128. "The salt of money is diminution (or benevolence)." (*b. Ket.* 66b); "Shake off the salt and give the flesh to the dog." Salt = the soul which preserves the flesh from putrefaction (*b. Nid.* 31a).

129. εἰς γῆν (for the ground); εἰς κοπρίαν (or the dung heap).

130. Compare Wellhausen, *Lucae*, 79; Knox, *Sources*, II.86; Grundmann, *Lukas*, 301; Rengstorf, *Lukas*, 180.

131. See Haskin, *The Call to Sell All*.

tion of poverty,¹³² but has an equally strong and venerable tradition of non-literal interpretation dating from Cement of Alexandria's *Who Is the Rich Man Who Is Being Saved?* The task of this study will be to inquire whether Luke's use of this story indicates an ideal of poverty. Concentrating on Jesus' command to the ruler to sell all and give to the poor, we will ask whether Luke intended this to be followed literally by all of his readers,¹³³ or by some,¹³⁴ and if neither, what he did mean, and what effect he intended the story to have.

Examination of the triple tradition favors the common view that Luke has essentially followed Mark's version of this story.¹³⁵ The similarity of the two means that much help for elucidating Luke's story has been forthcoming from studies of Mark's.

3.3.1 The Command to Sell All, Luke 18:22

Before we can make any judgment about the application of this commandment we must be clear about its function in the story. A ruler asks Jesus how he may inherit eternal life and Jesus points him to the commandments. The ruler affirms that he has observed them from his youth, at which point Jesus tells him to sell all, give the proceeds to the poor, and come and follow him.

---

132. Athanasius, *Life of Antony*.

133. Lohmeyer, *Markus*, 212–14, argues from Mark that poverty is seen as an inescapable prerequisite for eternal life. The story is told from the standpoint of an original "Armenfrömmigkeit"; see also Haenchen, *Weg Jesu*, 355. Percy, *Botschaft*, 91–93, thinks Jesus made such a general demand. Légasse, *L'appel du riche*, 97–99, argues that Luke is demanding that rich Christians despoil themselves in favor of the church's poor. Franklin, *Christ the Lord*, 155, sees renunciation as an ideal, which Luke does not seriously expect his wealthy readers to heed.

134. Galot, "Voeu de pauvreté," 457–59, argues for the traditional doctrine of the "two ways," including Luke 14:33 in his analysis. Troadec, "Vocation de l'homme riche," 138–48 argues that Luke demands poverty of missionaries, etc.

135. As in the pericope before and after. See also Schramm, *Markus-Stoff*, 142; Taylor, *Behind the Third Gospel*, 92. Weiss, "Zum reichen Jüngling," 79–83, argued from the common omission by Luke and Matthew of a significant proportion of the Markan story (Mark 10:17a, 21a, 24, 30b) that they must have followed an "Ur-Markus" (similarly Hirsch, *Frühgeschichte des Evangeliums*, 110–13; Sanders, "Priorités et dépendances," 519 30, 537 40). It is more probable that the story circulated independently in oral tradition and that the elements omitted were clearly recognizable to both evangelists as Markan redaction.

The question which comes naturally to mind is how the demand to sell all and follow relates to keeping the law, which Jesus initially indicated as the answer to the ruler's question about life.

3.3.1.1 *The Law and the Command to Sell All*

Three views suggest themselves initially:

a. The nearby parable of the Pharisee and the tax collector invites a "Pauline" interpretation of the incident. Many commentators see the ruler's affirmation that he has kept the commandments as ignorant and uncomprehending. B. W. Bacon sees the man revealed as a representative of "the righteousness of the scribes and Pharisees" and interprets the story as an attack on legalistic righteousness.[136]

The demand to sell all is then seen as Jesus' attempt to expose the ruler's true condition.[137] Cranfield calls it "the sharp probe that will show the man his self-deception." The first commandment is at stake; the ruler must dispose of money which has become an idol.[138]

Behind such interpretation lies the assumption that the ruler was claiming to be sinless, or at least perfect according to the law. He is often compared to Paul, who, in accordance with Philippians 3:6, is thought to have believed before his conversion that he was perfect with regard to the law. However, Paul's assertion does not mean that he saw himself as perfect before God, but that he had *attained*[139] a standard of excellence in matters of the law (probably

---

136. Bacon, "Why Callest Thou Me Good?" 347. Similarly, Cranfield, "Riches and the Kingdom of God," 303–13; Geldenhuys, *Luke*, 457–59; Calvin, *Institutes* 4.13.13; Zahn, *Lucas*, 616; Rienecker, *Lukas*, 429. Plummer, *Luke*, 423, thinks the ruler's reply is sincere but wrong-headed.

137. Also in the Gospel of the Hebrews (or Gospel of the Nazaraeans) quoted by Origen in Commentary on Matt 15:14. Jesus says to the ruler, "How canst thou say, I have fulfilled the law and the prophets? For it stands written in the law, 'Love thy neighbour as thyself; and behold many of thy brethren, sons of Abraham, are begrimed with dirt and die of hunger—and thy house is full of many good things and nothing at all come forth from it to them!'" (Hennecke and Schneemelcher, *New Testament Apocrypha*, 148–49).

138. Cranfield, "Riches and the Kingdom of God," 309.

139. γενόμενος (having become) suggests not a steady state of fulfilment of the law, but arrival at a pinnacle of excellence. This is understandable if he is speaking of his advancement to the top of the Pharisaic system, but not if he is describing a state of imagined sinlessness before God. See also, Vincent, *Philippians and Philemon*, 99.

comprehending both fullness of understanding and exactitude of performance), such that he could neither be blamed,[140] nor bettered by his opponents, who prided themselves on their zeal for the law. This interpretation of Paul's words does not run into contradiction with Paul's other statements on the law.[141] Thus Paul cannot be invoked in support of a claim to perfection on the part of the ruler.

Billerbeck cites sufficient examples to demonstrate that perfect fulfilment of the law was conceived of as a possibility.[142] However, the persons cited are exceptional cases[143] and give the impression that sinlessness was thought to be very unusual, something that might be said of patriarchal figures and the occasional rabbi after his death, but hardly something that might have been claimed by the pious during their lifetime.[144]

Sources external to Luke, therefore, do not encourage us to think the ruler was claiming perfection,[145] nor does Luke himself. It is true that he omits the comment that Jesus looked at the man and loved him (Mark 10:21), but he gives no positive indication that he regards his reply in an unfavorable light. His description of him as an *archōn* (ἄρχων—ruler) cannot be so construed,[146] for he uses the term of Jairus whom he regards favorably.[147] He does not call the ruler a Pharisee, as he could easily have done had he wanted to forge a link with the self-righteous Pharisee of the parable. In fact, the

---

Compare Gal 1:14; Acts 22:3.

140. "'I omitted no observance however trivial' for μέμφεσθαι applies to sins of omission"; Lightfoot, *Philippians*, 148. Compare Plummer, *Philippians*, 72.

141. E.g., Rom 7:14–20.

142. Billerbeck I.814–16.

143. Abraham, Samuel, Elijah, Hezekiah, Moses, and Aaron (disputed), R. Hanina b. Papa (AD 300; manifestly legendary), Levi b. Sisi, and an unnamed *hasid*, R. Eliezer (where the point of the story is to show that he was not sinless).

144. Jesus challenges the Pharisees and scribes who bring the woman caught in adultery, "Let he who is without sin cast the first stone at her." No one accepts the challenge (John 8:3–11).

145. Lohmeyer, 210n5, mentions Mark 2:17 and 4 Ezra 3:35–6 but neither proves the point.

146. As by Johnson, "Possessions in Luke-Acts," 145, and Dupont, *Béatitudes* III.58–59.

147. Luke 8:41. ἄρχων denotes anyone in high office: *TDNT* I.488–89. Luke uses it of Beelzebul (Luke 11:15), judges (Luke 12:58; Acts 16:19), leaders of the Pharisees (Luke 14:1), leaders in Jerusalem (Luke 23:13, etc.), leaders of the Jews and gentiles in the diaspora (Acts 14:5), the high priest (Acts 23:5), and Moses (Acts 7:27, 35).

ruler's description of himself is not very different from Luke's own description of the piety of some of his Jewish characters; if anything, it is more modest than his portrayal of Zechariah and Elizabeth.[148] Such descriptions are not to be seen as avowals of perfect righteousness according to the law, but of piety and devotion.

There is nothing, then, except our preconceived theological understanding, to prevent us from thinking that Luke saw the ruler in a favorable light. He comes to Jesus with a vital question about eternal life, seeking neither to "tempt" Jesus nor, when pointed to the commandments, to "justify himself."[149] He replies sincerely that he has been an observer of the commandments since his youth.[150] "Still one thing is lacking to you" should therefore be taken seriously. Jesus is not speaking with tongue in cheek,[151] nor disputing the ruler's reply.[152] The view that the command to sell all is designed to expose the ruler's real failure to keep the law may be dismissed.

b. Ezra P. Gould agrees that the ruler was sincere in his confession, but thinks it related in the main to negative commandments: "So far in the path of righteousness the young man had gone. The thing which was lacking in him was the positive side, to contribute to his neighbor's good, and for this purpose to sacrifice his own."[153]

Against this view it must be objected that the ruler is hardly responding only to those commandments which Jesus quotes. The mention of others by Mark and Matthew (who includes love of neighbor) makes this clear. He is declaring that from his youth he has lived a God-fearing and pious life; one zealous for the traditions of his people and desirous of eternal life would hardly have failed to practice the almsgiving which was so important a part of Jewish

---

148. Luke 1:6. Compare Simeon (2:25), Joseph of Arimathea (23:50), and Ananias (Acts 22:12).

149. Compare Luke 10:25, 29.

150. See also Zimmerli, "Frage des Reichen," 96, who likens him to Nathaniel; Degenhardt, *Evangelist der Armen*, 140.

151. ἔτι ἕν σοι λείπει. Easton, *Luke*, 272.

152. Schniewind, *Markus*, 103, follows Luther in seeing the "one thing" as everything: "Dennoch ist das Eine, das dem Reichen fehlt, das Ganze (Therefore the one thing that the rich man lacks is everything)."

153. Gould, *Mark*, 191. Some commentators think Jesus was pinpointing an unmentioned commandment; e.g., worship of one God (Morris, *Luke*, 268) or covetousness (Ellis, *Luke*, 218).

piety. Moreover, the command to sell all is too extreme a course, if the intention is simply to teach charity. Thus, the view that Jesus is indicating some lack in the ruler's keeping of the commandments must be rejected; the action he demands is too far removed from them.

c. Some scholars, therefore, take the view that Jesus was indicating a further commandment or duty, additional to the law, which is a prerequisite to eternal life. For William Manson it is a demand "which Jesus has already imposed on the Twelve as part of what the gospel requires as the way to life."[154] To discern what is wrong with this view it is necessary to examine the first part of the story more closely.

Ernst Lohmeyer was probably correct in his view that Jesus' answer to the ruler's question about eternal life would have been unusual:

> What one wants to learn from a rabbi when one questions him is not the that, but the how of these commandments. For a rabbi, that is what it is to teach wisdom: how to practice these holy commandments in the presentness and diversity of life.[155]

Thus, when R. Eliezer (ca AD 90) is asked a similar question by his disciples to that put to Jesus by the ruler, he does not rehearse the commandments, but gives his own special advice.[156] Jesus however, simply refers the questioner back to God's existing law.

This suggests a solution to the problem presented by Jesus' repudiation of the ruler addressing him as "good teacher," which has frequently been considered in isolation from its context as a problem for Christology.[157] Some scholars have even argued that it should be treated as an isolated saying,[158] but it is exceedingly difficult to imagine Mark (or his source) joining such a problematical interchange to the story (nor Matthew and Luke following), unless there was some real basis for it in

---

154. Manson, *Luke*, 205.

155. "Was man von einem Rabbi lernen will, wenn man ihn efragt, ist nicht das Dass, sondern das Wie dieser Gebote. Das ist eines Rabbi Weisheit zu lehren wie diese heiligen Gebote in der Gegenwart und Mannigfaltigkeit des Lebens anzuwenden sind." Lohmeyer, *Markus*, 210.

156. b. Ber. 28b.

157. Wagner, "In welchem Sinne," 143–61; Warfield, "Jesus' Alleged Confession of Sin," 177–228.

158. Minear, "Needle's Eye," 163; Degenhardt, *Evangelist der Armen*, 138.

RENUNCIATION AND DISCIPLESHIP   129

history. Its relationship to the rest of the story is too abstruse for it to have originated in mere scene setting, yet the fact that Luke does not shrink elsewhere from describing people as "good" demands that it somehow be understood in relation to its context.[159] Recognition of a "psychological factor" in interpretation of this interchange is justified, therefore, and commentators are correct in seeing Jesus' reply as somehow conditioned by his apprehension of the ruler's unspoken assumptions.

The ruler's address is unusual and emphatic[160] and without any evidence of hypocrisy. Whatever else we might say, it is clear that he saw in Jesus a teacher whose competence was not in doubt, and to whom he could with confidence address the question about eternal life. Jesus' retort, therefore, is best regarded as a challenge to the rulers' view of him as a good teacher who should be able to provide a new answer to the question about eternal life.[161] He directs him to God, who alone is good,[162] in the sense that his competence reaches to defining the way to life, the good way.[163]

It is unnecessary to conclude with Lohmeyer that Jesus' answer constitutes a rejection both of the address and the question. The two are related, as are the two parts of his answer. What he does is underline very forcibly that he is neither teaching any new way to eternal life nor placing a new interpretation on the law. The commandments stand in their bare

---

159. Luke 6:45, 8;15, 19:17, 23:50; Acts 11:24.

160. Billerbeck II.24–25 gives one parallel where a rabbi is addressed as "good." The address is regarded as remarkable and taken as a portent (*b. Taan.* 24b). However, ἀγαθέ was a common enough address among the Greeks (Cranfield, *Mark*, 326) and a well-to-do "ruler" of this period may well have assimilated such manners. ἀγαθέ is in the predicative position: "O teacher, O good one!" Blake, "'Good Master,'" 334, wants to emend ἀγαθέ to ἀγαθόν.

161. In rabbinic literature "the good" is Torah (Billerbeck I.809). There is an interesting (though late) saying of R. Ezra which calls Moses "the good" in his function as dispenser of the law: "Let the good (sc. Moses) come and receive the good (sc. Torah) from the Good (God) for the good (Israel)." *b. Men.* 53b.

162. The epithet טוב (*tōv*—good) when applied to God in the OT refers more to his mercy and graciousness than to his moral purity (קדוש). Wagner, "In welchem Sinne," 157–61; compare Spitta, "Jesu Weigerung," 12–20. In a surprising number of cases where God is called "good," it is his activity as teacher which is in mind (Neh 9:20; Ps 25:8, 119:68, 143:10).

163. Complimentary to God being thought "good" as teacher is the picture of the "good way" (1 Sam 12:23; 1 Kings 8:36; 2 Chron 6:27; Jer 6:16; Mic 6:8). In 1 Kings 8:36 God is teacher of the "good way."

simplicity (in Luke their barest simplicity) as the God-ordained way by which a person may inherit eternal life.[164]

Such an attitude is consistent with Luke's presentation of the teaching of Jesus elsewhere. In Luke 10:25 the same question about eternal life is put to Jesus by a lawyer and the same answer given: Do the law and you will live! When pressed to go further Jesus will only challenge the questioner to real and total obedience. In the parable of the rich man and Lazarus Jesus insists that "Moses and the prophets" are sufficient to save a person from hell.[165] Thus, faced with the challenge to teach a new and better way to eternal life, Jesus declines to go beyond the published will of God.[166]

It can now be seen that to view the command to sell all as an additional commandment to which the promise of eternal life is joined would be to contradict the first part of the story. Jesus makes it crystal clear that he refuses to be seen in the role of a rabbi promulgating new interpretations, embellishments, or additions to the law, which stands in its simplicity as the God-revealed way to eternal life. That he would immediately after add a further requirement going beyond anything that the law demands is difficult to imagine. We are driven to the conclusion that the action Jesus demands must somehow transcend the commandments.[167]

3.3.1.2 Entering the Kingdom

The ruler's failure is seen not as a breach of the commandments, but as a decisive failure to enter the kingdom of God when it stood open to him. This is emphasized by Luke, who changes Mark's future tense to a present: "With what difficulty are those having possessions entering the kingdom,"[168] and it is consistent with his general theological attitude. The

---

164. Luke omits Mark's μὴ ἀποστερήσῃς (do not defraud); Matthew adds the love commandment.

165. Luke 16:29-31.

166. This is one of Luke's apologetic interests; the law-abiding nature of Jesus and his followers is stamped on the whole of Luke-Acts. See Jervell, *Luke and the People of God*, 133-51.

167. Not, however, in the way suggested by Ernst, *Lukas*, 501, that Jesus has appeared in place of Torah so that "Nachfolge ist die konsequente Aktuelisierung der Gebotserfüllung (Following is the consistent actualization of law-keeping)."

168. πῶς δυσκόλως οἱ τὰ χρήματα ἔχοντες εἰς τὴν βασιλείαν τοῦ θεοῦ εἰσπορεύονται. Luke 18:24; compare Mark 10:23.

kingdom is present with Jesus, and entry into fellowship with him is entry into the kingdom (salvation).[169] Jesus was not defining the way to life. His ministry was bound up with actually inviting people into the kingdom. Thus, in the parable of the banquet he castigates those who refused the invitation to the messianic banquet, which he was already celebrating with the tax collectors and sinners.[170] Thus his invitation to the ruler, "Come, follow me," which is manifestly a call to literal accompaniment,[171] is in reality an invitation to enter into the kingdom, the sphere in which eternal life is operative.[172]

Confirmation of this basic pattern—the sufficiency of the law to lead to life, transcended by the breaking in of the kingdom in Jesus[173]—may be seen in the juxtaposition of the parable of the good Samaritan and the story of Jesus in the home of Mary and Martha.[174] The former leaves us in approximately the same position as does the first part of the rich ruler story; to the question about eternal life the lawyer is pointed to the commandments and all attempt to evade their force is resisted. In the latter, however, Mary's sitting at Jesus' feet and listening to his word is judged to be of an entirely different (transcendent) order to Martha's

---

169. Babes are brought to Jesus with such words as strongly suggest their reception into the kingdom (18:15–17); Zacchaeus receives Jesus and is told, "Today is salvation come into your house" (19:9). See esp. 17:21, and Noack, *Gottesreich*; also Grundmann, "Reiseberichts," 253.

170. Luke 14:15–24.

171. This call formula is unusual, paralleled only by the call of the first disciples (Mark 1:17; Matt 4:19).

172. See also Zimmerli, "Frage des Reichen," 96–97; Bornkamm, *Jesus*, 148. Zimmerli, Frage des Reichen," 93–96, argues that the *Sitz im Leben* for the question about "life" was the pilgrim processions to the temple. In answer to the question of who might enter the Holy Place, which is the presence of God and the sphere of life, the commandments were rehearsed. If this idea were thought to be operative here, then Jesus' call to enter into his fellowship might be interpreted as entry into the sphere of life, by analogy to entry into the temple.

173. Also to be seen in Luke 16:16–17.

174. Luke 10:25–37. Goulder, "Lucan Journey," 195–202, thinks these two stories are in chiastic parallelism with the story of the rich ruler (197). Compare Flender, *Theologian of Redemptive History*, 10; Talbert, "Literary Patterns," 51–53.

service.¹⁷⁵ Jesus' answer to Martha, "One thing is needed," should perhaps be compared to his answer to the ruler, "You still lack one thing."¹⁷⁶

The one thing lacking, then, should be understood not in terms of the ruler's need to dispose of his possessions so much as in terms of his need to enter the fellowship of Jesus and hence into life itself. It is as if Jesus had said, "You have kept the commandment; now enter into life." Such an interpretation requires that the call to sell all be kept strictly subordinate to the invitation to follow Jesus.¹⁷⁷ This, however, can only be so if we understand "a treasure in the heavens" in some other way than as eternal life itself,¹⁷⁸ since it is joined to the selling and giving, not the following. I deal with this question at a later point,¹⁷⁹ and show that treasure in heaven is best understood as a figure for the favor of God, which is attained by good works, and is experienced in this age and in the age to come; it is not used in Luke for the kingdom itself.¹⁸⁰ There is perhaps a hint of the subordination of selling to following, in the way Luke has written Mark's "we have left . . . and we have followed," as "having left . . . we followed."¹⁸¹

3.3.1.3 Following and Renunciation

Having established that Jesus' call to follow him was seen by Luke as an invitation to enter the kingdom, and that the command to sell all and give to the poor was subordinate to this, it is still necessary to explore the relationship between following and renunciation if we are to reach an understanding of the call to sell all. For subordinate as it may be, this is what the story is all about.

---

175. The first teaching block (10:25-42) of the travel narrative follows directly on the aftermath of the return of the seventy where the presence of the kingdom is specially emphasized (10:17-24).

176. ἑνὸς δέ ἐστιν χρεία with ἔτι ἕν σοι λείπει. Compare Clement, *Rich Man*, 10.

177. As Degenhardt, *Evangelist der Armen*, 141, 144, who thinks the "one thing" is the whole package (selling-giving-following).

178. An in Plummer, *Luke*, 424; van Cangh, "Fondement évangélique de la vie religieuse," 636; Légasse, *L'appel du riche*, 57-60; Bornkamm, "Lohngedanke," 78.

179. Page 161-62, below.

180. See Lagrange, *Luc*, 481; Galot, "Voeu de pauvreté," 451-53.

181. Mark 10:28: ἀφήκαμεν . . . καὶ ἠκολουθήκαμεν; Luke 18:28: ἀφέντες . . . ἠκολουθήσαμεν.

The most obvious suggestion is that renunciation of possessions was an essential precondition for following Jesus on the road, which all the inner core of disciples had had to face, and which the ruler, therefore, could not evade.[182] The inadequacy of this suggestion appears more clearly in Luke than in the other Gospels. For Luke has intensified the degree of renunciation required of the ruler by adding "all" to Mark's "sell what you have"[183] and softened that of Peter and the others by replacing Mark's "everything" in 10:28 with "our own" in 18:28.[184] This, and the fact that the ruler is told to dispose of his possessions irrevocably, whereas the others merely "left" home[185] (perhaps to return),[186] makes the ruler's case very different from theirs. Luke evidently regards the demands made of the ruler as quite exceptional.[187] A further comparison illustrates this even more clearly. In the two brief encounters between Jesus and would-be followers in Luke 9:59–62, the point emphasized is that following must be immediate. Both men are denied permission to return home to set things in order. In contrast, the ruler is sent back to put his house in order, sell his belongings, and distribute them to the poor; the urgency is gone. It seems there is something about the ruler which makes his service unacceptable until he has disposed of everything he owns.

Thus, we are forced to the conclusion that Luke understood the command to sell all as something meant specifically for this man; we are dealing with a demand which can be related only to Jesus' understanding

---

182. See also W. Manson, *Luke*, 206; Schnackenburg, *Moral Teaching*, 48–49; Degenhardt, *Evangelist der Armen*, 142.

183. πάντα and ὅσα ἔχεις πώλησον.

184. Πάντα and τὰ ἴδια. see Lagrange, *Luc*, 484.

185. τὰ ἴδια could mean possessions, but in the present context (compare v. 29) almost certainly means "home"; compare Acts 5:18 (D); 14:18; 21:6; John 16:32, with Fascher, "Johannes 16:32," 186; John 1:11 with Field, *Translation of the New Testament*, 84, and Goodspeed, *New Testament Translation*, 88. Family and kindred alone would be οἱ ἴδιοι (95).

186. Lohmeyer, *Markus*, 216.

187. This disposes of Percy's assertion (*Botschaft*, 91–93) that the demand made of the ruler is general, because it is attached to a question about eternal life. There is nothing which obliges us to think Jesus led everyone to eternal life in the same way. Percy's argument does dispose of the common view of the "two ways": the normal way of obedience to the commandments and the special "counsel" of renunciation. On this, see Galot, "Voeu de pauvreté," who thinks the ruler turned his back on "treasure" but not on "life." Compare Troadec, "Vocation de l'homme riche." For Catholic criticism of this "two ways" interpretation see van Cangh, "Fondement évangélique de la vie religieuse"; Tillard, "Vie religieuse," 916–55; Légasse, *L'appel du riche*.

of his condition and to his sovereign authority over him.¹⁸⁸ Since none of the Gospels tells us anything about him other than he was rich, it is pointless to indulge in psychological speculations. What the story does allow us to observe is his reaction to Jesus' command. He became "deeply grieved" (Luke uses a strong word),¹⁸⁹ and he gives a simple explanation: "for he was exceedingly wealthy."¹⁹⁰ The power of his wealth is exposed. He comes wanting to know the way to eternal life, but, when it transpires that it will cost him his wealth, it is revealed that his love for the things of this world is greater than his desire for the kingdom.¹⁹¹

Given that this is the effect of the story, it is probable that we should also see it as the intention of the command to sell all. Not that it was desired that the ruler should fail, but Jesus is unwilling to have a follower with divided loyalties and interests.

3.3.2 Application

The story of the rich ruler is followed by two short interchanges between Jesus and those around him, which serve in some degree to generalize and apply the lessons of the story. Before considering these, however, it is important to consider what effect Luke might have wanted the action so far to have on his readers.

Simon Légasse argues that Luke has turned Mark's story into an appeal to the rich of the Christian community to dispose of their wealth in favor of the poor of the church.¹⁹² Apart from Luke's keeping the rich man "on stage" and the non-appearance of the disciples (for which I will indicate an alternative construction), he builds his case on the words *diados* (διάδος—divide) and *ta idia* (τὰ ἴδια—what is your own). From Luke 11:21–22 the victory of Jesus is seen as the conquest of a rich lord (Satan—"un riche seigneur") and the distribution of his goods to the poor of the Christian community as in Acts 4:35. Similarly the occurrence of *idion* (ἴδιον) in Acts 4:32 is thought to indicate that *ta idia* of Luke 18:28 suggests disposal of goods in favor of the Christian poor. But this is to

---

188. Campenhausen, "Early Christian Asceticism," 94. Compare Dibelius, "Social Action," 141–44.

189. περίλυπος.

190. ἦν γὰρ πλούσιος σφόδρα.

191. Compare the discussion of Luke 6:24–26 (page 97–98, above).

192. Légasse, *L'appel du riche*, 97–110.

read an impossible amount into two simple words. It also makes the distribution of possessions to the poor the main part of the story, which is hardly the case; in Peter's statement it does not even enter the picture.[193] Besides, Luke's omission of Mark's "fields" from the list of things which a person might need to leave for the sake of the kingdom makes Légasse's thesis highly suspect.[194] For if the example of the early Jerusalem church (therefore the story of Barnabas who sold a field)[195] was as much in Luke's mind as Légasse suggests, it is strange that he would have omitted such a clear parallel.[196]

A better explanation is possible for Luke's modified staging of the end of the story. Instead of having the ruler "depart sorrowing," he keeps him "on stage" so that in effect Jesus addresses the ruler himself about the difficulty of a rich person entering the kingdom.[197] He is kept suspended between obedience and refusal (though Luke never suggests that he is successful—in a sense he listens to his own judgment): a picture of the rich man experiencing difficulty entering the kingdom ("with what difficulty ... are they entering").[198] The disciples are kept out of the way until Peter's question in verse 28.[199] All this would make perfect sense if it were Luke's intention to speak not to church members but evangelistically to well-to-do people attracted to Christianity, but held back by certain misgivings related to money and social position.[200] The effect of this poignant portrayal of a rich nobleman whose wealth prevented him from taking hold of the kingdom when it came within his reach would be to warn these folk not to make the same mistake.[201]

At this point we should consider an objection arising from Luke 18:24–25. Haenchen thinks the only reason why it is impossible humanly speaking for a rich man to enter the kingdom is because complete renunciation of possessions is demanded of all, putting the rich in a very

---

193. Luke 18:28.

194. Luke 18:29; compare Mark 10:29–30.

195. Acts 4:36–37.

196. His motive for this omission possibly relates to the irrelevance of fields to his cultured urbanized readers. See page 138–39, below.

197. Mark 10:22: ἀπῆλθεν λυπούμενος.

198. πῶς δυσκόλως ... εἰσπορεύονται.

199. Compare Mark 10:23–24.

200. Perhaps this is why Luke says the rich man was an *archōn*.

201. Compare Luke 14:18–20.

difficult position.²⁰² His argument is based on the false assumption that in Mark 10:26 the disciples are asking which *rich* person can be saved,²⁰³ but he raises a challenging question nonetheless. For if total abandonment of possessions is not generally demanded, why should wealth constitute any barrier to entry into the kingdom?

The story does not set out to answer this question, but it is fairly clear that whether or not total renunciation was demanded generally, following Jesus did place a person's wealth at risk. It also placed his life at risk, of course, which is no doubt one of the reasons why Jesus pronounces it impossible (humanly speaking) for *anyone* to enter the kingdom.²⁰⁴ The greater a person's stake in this world, the harder it will be for them to take the decision to count this age as nothing in comparison to the kingdom. The rich constitute the extreme case, and the story of the rich ruler exposes their problem.

The final interchange between Jesus and Peter shows that this understanding is correct. Luke's significant weakening of the renunciation of the Twelve with respect to that demanded of the ruler has already been mentioned.²⁰⁵ More telling than this, however, is that Jesus promises a manifold reward not to those who leave *everything*, but to those who for his sake leave *anything* for the sake of the kingdom.²⁰⁶ Thus, it is not a question of total renunciation, but of decision for the kingdom in the face of the counter-pull of the world, from whatever source it comes.²⁰⁷

That Luke preserves the promise of a manifold reward "in this time," as well as eternal life "in the coming age," is the final demonstration that he intends no ideal of poverty by this story.²⁰⁸ It is evasive to

---

202. Haenchen, *Weg Jesu*, 352. Nolan, *Jesus before Christianity*, 50–53, has a similar view: Jesus demands that the rich divest themselves of possessions if they want to enter the "kingdom of the poor." Haenchen does not think such ascetic teaching came from Jesus or his immediate disciples, but from an ascetic Jewish-Christian group with gnostic tendencies.

203. Haenchen, *Weg Jesu*, 354.

204. Luke 18:26–27.

205. Page 133, above.

206. Luke 18:29.

207. Luke's addition of γυναῖκα (wife) to the list of people one might need to leave (compare Luke 14:26) probably reflects his knowledge of people who had lost their marriage partner through becoming Christians (compare 1 Cor 7:12–16), or who had forsaken marriage for the kingdom's sake (1 Cor 9:5) rather than being an ascetic demand for celibacy, as Legrand argues ("Christian Celibacy," 1–12).

208. ἐν τῷ καιρῷ τούτῳ—ἐν τῷ αἰῶνι τῷ ἐρχομένῳ.

limit this reward to spiritual things, as J. Lebreton does.²⁰⁹ Luke clearly has no objection to Mark's thought of a material recompense, even if he has abbreviated somewhat. If the disciple receives even in this age more than he can ever surrender, it is impossible that renunciation, for its own sake, or for the sake of a desired state of poverty, can be the point at issue. The ruler, having disposed of his possessions, might not necessarily have remained poor. What he would be, having decided for the new age by putting his past behind him and following Jesus, would be in Jesus' hands. It is this which is really the point.²¹⁰

The story ends as it begins, with the question of eternal life. It will be the inheritance of all who have had cause to leave *anything* for the sake of the kingdom of God (i.e., in order to follow Jesus), and have done it. "There is no one . . . who will not," stresses the absoluteness of this.²¹¹

3.3.3 The Wider Context, Zacchaeus, Luke 19:1–10

There can be little doubt that Luke has carefully framed the section 18:9–19:10 to represent various sides of the question of individual salvation.²¹² With the exception of the passion warning (18:31–34) each part deals

---

209. Lebreton, "Doctrine du renoncement," 404–05.

210. This would also seem to be the point in Luke 5:11, 28. In both cases Luke says the newly called disciples left all and followed Jesus (ἀφέντες πάντα ἠκολούθησαν αὐτῷ—καταλιπὼν πάντα ἀναστὰς ἠκολούθει αὐτῷ). We are not dealing here with paradigms of renunciation as Creed, *Luke*, 81, suggests, but with illustrations of radical turning and putting oneself totally at Jesus' disposal (Ellis, *Luke*, 102, and note the Western text of 5:11). There is no inconsistency in Luke making it even clearer than Mark that Levi's first action after his call was to make a great feast for Jesus in his house (5:29). It may be true that the disciples whose call is described here were entering into a special "vocation" which required them to leave home and join Jesus on the road (Degenhardt, *Evangelist der Armen*, 213–21). Nevertheless, the manner of their "turning" is related not as a paradigm of entry into professional church activity, but of entry into Christian life.

211. οὐδείς ἐστιν ὅς . . . ὃς οὐχὶ μή.

212. At 18:9 (or 18:15: Evans, "Central Section," 50) Luke reaches the point at which he wishes to rejoin Mark. With Mark 9:41–10:52 at his disposal he has omitted four pericopes (apart from this section, his only other omissions from Mark are 4:26–29, 6:17–29, 9:11–13, 11:12–14, 20–21, and 12:28–34). The great amount of omission in this section emphasizes his desire to present this theme at the close of the teaching section, and underlines the importance of the non-Markan pericopes he has included here (or the Markan pericopes he has included here according to the Proto-Luke theory).

with this theme.²¹³ By omitting the discourse on greatness he has brought the healing of the blind beggar into relationship with the rich ruler. The beggar is the exact opposite in economic terms to the ruler, but receives salvation because of his insistent faith in Jesus.²¹⁴ The story of Zacchaeus was probably introduced to complement the story of the blind beggar, but also to provide a contrast to the ruler, and to illustrate God's power to do the impossible.²¹⁵

The connection with the ruler is plain from Luke's vivid portrayal of both as rich men. The ruler is grief-stricken at Jesus' demand, because he was "exceedingly rich";²¹⁶ Zacchaeus is given a double description: "he was a chief tax collector and he was rich."²¹⁷ This can only be an intentional cross-reference. Despite the fact that Zacchaeus was rich, he was saved.²¹⁸ It is a fair inference, then, that Luke wishes to affirm, in relation to the story of the ruler, that salvation is open to the rich. This could be a significant clue for identifying at least a part of Luke's circle of readers.

B. E. McCormick concludes, quite apart from any consideration of the story of Zacchaeus, that one of Luke's characteristics is "a concern for the salvation of the rich."²¹⁹ He postulates that Luke's readers were

> inquiring gentiles, some at the doorway of the synagogue but perhaps most within the church, who live in an urban environment of Hellenistic life. They represent a well-to-do society who are enjoying a bourgeoisie-type prosperity.²²⁰

213. See Luke 18:14, 17, 24, 29, 42, 19:9.

214. 18:42 carries this double entendre: Marshall, *Luke: Historian and Theologian*, 95; Glöckner, *Verkündigung des Heils*, 93.

215. Luke 18:27.

216. Compare Mark 10:22—ἔχων κρήματα πολλά—having many possessions.

217. καὶ αὐτὸς ἦν ἀρχιτελώνης καὶ αὐτὸς πλούσιος. Luke 19:1.

218. It might be argued that as a tax collector he belonged to a class specially favored in the Gospels. This common sentiment is based on an unjustified romanticizing of tax collectors. The Gospels are interested in them because they show how comprehensive and far-reaching Jesus' forgiveness was (*TDNT* VII.104). Some have sought to make a hero of Zacchaeus by portraying him as unjustly excluded by the Jews. Godet, *Luke*, 217–18, thinks v. 8 is a revelation of Zacchaeus's habitual practice. Against this see Willcock, "St Luke 19:8," 236–37, and Watson, "Was Zacchaeus Really Reforming?" 282–85. It is hardly credible that a man could regularly distribute half his income to the poor without the city knowing of it. In fact, v. 8 is a confession of fraudulent practice (justifying ostracism, and the term τὸ ἀπολωλός—the lost) and vv. 9–10 are its absolution.

219. McCormick, *Social and Economic Background of Luke*, 206.

220. McCormick, *Social and Economic Background of Luke*, 206–07.

What we have seen in the stories of the rich ruler and Zacchaeus would fit this thesis. Two other features of Luke's redactional procedure also support it and draw further attention to the story of Zacchaeus. His omission of the name of the blind beggar ("the son of Timaeus, Bartimaeus")[221] combined with his naming of Zacchaeus gives evident weight to the latter story. At the very least it indicates that in Luke's mind Zacchaeus was someone of importance, and likely to be more significant to his readers than a "faceless" beggar. This could be because his readers had some knowledge of Zacchaeus,[222] or because he was the kind of person with whom they could identify. Luke has also altered the setting of the healing of the blind man so that instead of taking place as Jesus is leaving Jericho (Mark 10:46), it happens before his entry (Luke 18:35). This allows him to place the Zacchaeus story, which takes place in Jericho, after the healing of the blind man, and at the conclusion of his collection of salvation stories, thereby making it the climax of his presentation of aspects of individual salvation.[223] This demonstrates his concern with the salvation of the rich, and the seriousness with which he has transmitted 18:27.

If Luke means his readers to compare the ruler with Zacchaeus, what conclusion might be expected to emerge? We are not looking at the "proud Pharisee—humble tax-collector" pattern,[224] nor do these stories fit the pattern of the salvation of those who eagerly seek the kingdom and the rejection of the indifferent.[225]

The real contrast lies in the differing responses of the two men. No effort is made to explain this difference (each is rich; there is nothing prejudicial about the ruler's piety, nor commendatory about Zacchaeus's profession). The stories should, therefore, be treated as paradigms of response. Bound up in their response to Jesus is the manner in which each meets the offer of the kingdom.[226] The ruler meets it as demand, and

---

221. Mark 10:46.

222. *Clementine Homilies* 2.1; 3.63–65, 71–72, and *Recognitions* 3.65–71 preserve a tradition (or is it a fictitious romance?) that Zacchaeus was Peter's successor as Bishop of Caesarea. Compare Clement Alex., *Stomata* 4.6.35 who mentions a tradition that he was Matthias (Matthew). See Zahn, *Lucas*, 620, n.5.

223. Marshall, *Luke: Historian and Theologian*, 116, 118, points out that 19:10 climaxes and concludes the whole of Jesus' Galilean and Judean ministry.

224. As in Luke 18:9–14.

225. The reverse is almost the case. Compare Luke 7:29–30, 16:14–16, 18:38–43.

226. For Zacchaeus the offer of table fellowship with Jesus represents the coming

departs sorrowful; Zacchaeus meets it as gracious acceptance, and in his joy resolves to give half his possessions to the poor and to make fourfold restitution. The surprising thing is that no attempt is made to match the sacrifice demanded of the ruler. Renunciation, therefore, is not the issue. Presumably Zacchaeus remains materially in a comparable situation to where he began, though he has expressed his love and joy in a concrete manner.[227] This story, more than that of the ruler, provides some parallel to the early church where salvation was accompanied by spontaneous joy and generosity.

3.4 SUMMARY AND CONCLUSIONS

We began by asking whether Luke 14:25–35 and 18:18–30 imply an idealization of poverty on the part of Luke. In the former case, I argued, Luke portrays a "historical" situation in which Jesus warns the crowds, who, in expectation of the glorious manifestation of the kingdom, were following him to Jerusalem, that death, not glory, lay at the end of the journey. Those who wanted to be his disciples were told they would need to turn their backs on all further responsibilities for and feelings towards their families (treat them as though they hated them), to disregard even the demands of their own life, and to journey with him to crucifixion in Jerusalem. They were warned to think earnestly whether they were prepared to go the whole distance; not to begin was preferable to withdrawal before the end. In sum, they should literally say goodbye to all that was dear to them, and come with him to suffering and death.

Luke's object in this passage was to picture what discipleship meant in an extreme situation. If the crowds to whom Jesus spoke represent anything, it is folk at the door of the church (perhaps inside) being challenged with the demands of discipleship. In the extreme situation it is revealed that discipleship has no limits. One must not withdraw; not for the sake of family or possessions, nor even for the sake of life itself. Those

---

of the kingdom. See Luke 15:1–2 and the parables following; also, Jeremias, *Theology* I, 114–17; Bornkamm, *Jesus*, 80–81.

227. Against Navone, *Themes of St. Luke*, 106, who treats his giving as a precondition of salvation. Hoyt, *Poor in Luke-Acts*, 169–73, thinks Zacchaeus's response is the fulfillment of the commandment to the ruler. If this were the case one wonders why the ruler could not have offered to give half! If it is rather that Zacchaeus's joyful response to the entrance of Jesus proves his membership of the people of God (19:9), just as in 7:36–50, a woman's extravagant gesture towards Jesus proves her forgiveness.

who would be true disciples must be prepared to renounce anything or everything should the occasion arise; for the way to the kingdom is not a path leading directly to glory, but only by way of the cross. Discipleship means full identification with the suffering Son of Man; a disciple who withdraws is as worthless as saltless salt.

In the story of the rich ruler we began by seeking the relationship between the command to sell, distribute, and follow and the other commandments which Jesus indicated as the way of life. I argued that the command to follow was primary and should be construed, in the framework of Luke's thought, as an invitation to enter the kingdom. It therefore totally transcends the keeping of the law. The call to sell all was found to be subordinate to entry into the fellowship of Jesus. It was a unique demand, made only of the ruler, and its effect was to expose his greater love for wealth than for the kingdom.

I suggested that Luke intended this story as a warning to the well-to-do not to allow wealth to stand in the way of their coming to Jesus. Wealth is seen as a terrible obstacle to embracing the kingdom, for it intensifies the attachment to "this age" which is common to all people. Eternal life is promised to all who leave anything for the sake of the kingdom; far from their being any idealization of poverty, a manyfold reward is promised in this age to those who have cause to abandon anything for the kingdom.

Viewed in relation to the story of Zacchaeus, Luke 18:27 was seen to be very significant. Luke not only affirms the possibility of the rich being saved, but provides an example of a rich man who, unlike the ruler, joyfully embraced the kingdom when it met him in the person of Jesus. Taken together these two stories address the rich with warning and encouragement: they must not let their wealth keep them from adherence to Jesus; they should imitate the man who recognized God's grace when it came to him, and gave joyful expression to his newly found life in abundant generosity.

We may conclude that neither Luke 14:25–35 nor 18:18–30 contains any idealization of poverty nor general demand for renunciation of possessions. Instead we have uncovered a paradigm of the limitless character of discipleship and a warning against the insidious power of wealth to prevent a person laying hold of the kingdom when it comes within reach. Neither of these passages yields anything specific about the Christian's ongoing *use* of possessions, though the story of Zacchaeus begins to point the way.

Chapter 4

Possessions and the Christian Life

4.1 INTRODUCTION

IN THE PRECEDING CHAPTERS we have seen that Luke visualized the kingdom of God in traditional Jewish terms as the intervention of God to rescue his "poor" from all the evil forces which afflicted them. Captive Israel would be released, the hungry fed, tears would be wiped away, and "the poor" would inherit the world to come. However, Jesus' rejection by his own people results in a situation in which the kingdom can come only through suffering. From the beginning he ministers under the shadow of rejection and will eventually be delivered up to death by the leaders of his people. In this situation disciples are called to an unreserved commitment to being with their Lord, even if that should cost them family, possessions, and life itself. There was an ever-present danger, both in the time of Jesus and in the time in which Luke wrote, that people would choose the good things of the present age rather than that painful identification with the Son of Man which would have its glorious outcome in the coming kingdom.

We come now to the question of what positive guidance Luke has on the subject of possessions. However, we cannot divorce this from the deeper question of his worldview, for it is this which will determine his concept of the value of possessions and, consequently, his view of how they should be used.

According to Conzelmann, the determining factor in Luke's understanding is the so-called "parousia delay"; Luke's readers live many years after the period of Jesus' ministry, and still the awaited manifestation of the kingdom has not eventuated. The last few pages of *The Theology of St. Luke* is devoted to a consideration of the Christian life in the light of this problem. Luke no longer expects an imminent end, says Conzelmann; the "vita Christiana" has emerged. "Eschatology no longer has the immediate effect of a summons, for it has become an idea which now influences ethics indirectly, by means of the idea of judgment."[1] Flender has a similar outlook. He discusses Luke's ethics in the framework of the question, "How does Luke witness to the Christian message in a time no longer dominated by an expectation of the Lord but looking to a future in history?"[2]

Eric Franklin has a totally different conception of Luke's outlook: "Luke did not abandon the eschatological expectations of the early church. He reinterpreted them in such a way that hope in the End was not reduced, but was rather increased."[3] Thus the ethical teaching of the Gospel of Luke—and this applies to the teaching about possessions—is addressed to people in an urgent eschatological situation;[4] it is not intended as a guide for a continuing and developing church life.[5]

In this chapter we will examine the main passages of the Gospel which afford guidance on the Christian's ongoing use of and attitude towards possessions. We will begin with 12:13–34 and seek to locate greed, anxiety, and almsgiving in the pattern of Luke's thinking. Then we will turn to chapter 16 to discover his fundamental evaluation of possessions and their uses. Finally, we will draw together material on the themes of charity, the literal poor, and stewardship. From this it will be seen that Luke has a consistent ethic of possessions, determined at every point by the reality and imminence not only of the judgment but also of the age to come, but that he nonetheless expects a possible lengthy continuance of the present age.

---

1. Conzelmann, *Theology of St. Luke*, 232.
2. Flender, *Theologian of Redemptive History*, 88.
3. Franklin, *Christ the Lord*, 146.
4. Franklin, *Christ the Lord*, 151.
5. Franklin, *Christ the Lord*, 154.

4.2 GREED AND THE KINGDOM, LUKE 12:13-21

Though part of a larger discourse, this passage constitutes a manifest interruption and lends itself to being treated in isolation. The section is addressed to the crowd, no doubt because the problem it attacks is of universal importance. We begin with an analysis of verse 15 and go on to examine the parable of the rich fool.

4.2.1 Beware of All Greed, Luke 12:15

Having declined a request to mediate between two brothers in the matter of an inheritance, thereby underlining the spiritual character of his mission and warning us not to mistake him for a social reformer, Jesus addresses a strong warning to the crowds on the subject of greed. "Watch out and guard yourselves" is the strongest warning formula in Luke-Acts.[6] The only comparable double warning in the New Testament is the saying about the leaven of the Pharisees in Mark 8:15 and Matthew 16:6. This is remarkable since Luke has this saying close to the discourse we are considering, but with a single *prosechete* (προσέχετε—pay attention).[7] Evidently, he or his source considered that greed was even more insidious than Pharisaic hypocrisy!

Though often translated "covetousness," *pleonexia* is more properly "greed."[8] Plummer defines it as "the greedy desire to have more and more."[9] This fits verse 15 as well as the parable which follows, where covetousness in the sense of an illegitimate desire for what belongs to someone else does not enter the picture.[10] Thus Jesus is warning in the strongest terms against greed in all its forms and degrees.[11] It is an insidious and deceitful problem which easily disguises itself, perhaps even in the garb of a claim for justice.[12]

---

6. Ὁρᾶτε καὶ φυλάσσεσθε. Normally Luke uses προσέχω (pay attention) (12:1, 17:3, 20:46, 21:34; Acts 5:35, 20:28).

7. Luke 12:1.

8. πλεονεξία. *TDNT* VI.271.

9. Plummer, *Luke*, 323. Also *TDNT* VI.271.

10. Note the confusion in Oesterley's interpretation of the parable when he tries to relate "not being rich towards God" to covetousness (*Gospel Parables*, 172).

11. πάσης πλεονεξίας—all greed.

12. The brother's request lies in the background, but I cannot agree with Joüon, "Parabole du riche insensé," 487, that the parable is specifically addressed to the two

The remainder of the verse gives the reason why greed should be shunned. The translations of AV, RV, and RSV are faulty, rendering the verse as though it read "because a person's life does not lie in his possessions abounding."[13] Although this reading is found in Clement of Alexandria's *Stromateis* 4.6.34 and is defended by C. C. Tarelli,[14] it must be rejected in favor of the more difficult reading attested by the majority of manuscripts: ὅτι οὐκ ἐν τῷ περισσεύειν τινὶ ἡ ζωὴ αὐτοῦ ἐστιν ἐκ τῶν ὑπαρχόντων αὐτοῦ. The NEB translates this as "for even when a man has more than enough, his wealth does not give him life." The "even" is not found in the Greek but is a fair translation considering the emphatic position of ἐν τῷ περισσεύειν. Thus, the principle, *life does not come from possessions*, is stated in its strongest form: even when a person has an abundance, life does not come from possessions. How much more is this so when they are held in lesser quantities!

What then is meant by "life" and how might it be thought to derive from possessions? Some think of it in the sense of the preservation and prolongation of life, and therefore of the security which flows from possessions.[15] The strength of this interpretation is that it seems to fit the parable. It transpired in reality that the fool's life was "from God" and not "from his possessions," and the abundance of his possessions could not save him from the evil hour. But if this is the point of verse 15, it is a meagre one. It is true that possessions do not secure a person's life, but that does not destroy their value. Nor does it seem to be sufficient cause to frame such a strong warning against acquisitiveness. Most people are aware that they must die and that their possessions will not alter this fact, but it does not stop them accumulating what they can to improve what life they have.

Other scholars, therefore, think the saying has to do with quality of life.[16] This view is correct, for Luke would not use *zōe* but *psychē* if he was thinking of the termination of life.[17] He uses *psychē* in relation to the rich brothers.

13. ὅτι οὐκ ἐν τῷ περισσεύειν τινὶ τὰ ὑπάρχοντά ἐστιν ἡ ζωὴ αὐτοῦ.

14. Tarelli, "Luke 12:15," 260–62.

15. Godet, *Luke*, 97; Schlatter, *Lukas*, 310; Rengstorf, *Lukas*, 159; Rienecker, *Lukas*, 310n4. The Jerusalem Bible translates: "For a man's life is not made secure by what he owns, even when he has more than he needs."

16. Lagrange, *Luc*, 358; Caird, *Luke*, 163 ("abundance of life"). Plummer, *Luke*, 323, gives both meanings.

17. ζωή vs ψυχή.

fool and frequently elsewhere in this sense.[18] *Zōe* is "life" thought of in terms of its extension and quality.[19]

In verses 13–15 there is no thought of security or length of life. It is the quality and content of life that people hope to augment by greed. Security constitutes only a part of this. Even in the parable the rich man's harvest is not seen as a guarantee of long life, but as the promise of pleasure and ease. It is true that the fool dies, but what is illustrated is not the powerlessness of his possessions to save him, but the judgment of God on a worthless life—a greedy life which valued itself only in terms of its possessions.

Thus verse 15 negates the unspoken assumption of the avaricious person. He thinks that by increasing his possessions he will obtain "life," an ultimate quality of meaningful existence. But "life" is not from possessions, even when they abound.

Given that this is the principle enunciated in verse 15, why is it attached to such an urgent warning? The answer lies in the notion of *zōe*. Jesus is proclaiming the kingdom and offering *eternal* life.[20] For Luke this means more than an infinite extension of life. It is a new quality of existence lived in fellowship with God,[21] the entrance to which is to be found in painful identification with Jesus and his message. This is not to say that *"life"* in verse 15 means eternal life; the "his" precludes this. It is rather a rival form of self-fulfilment, which is pursued by the greedy.[22] For Luke, then, the danger of greed is that it seeks "life" in possessions, and fails to seek it where it is to be found, in the kingdom.

What we have uncovered in verse 15 is much more than an introduction to the following parable. It is a fundamental analysis of greed and its enmity to salvation, which must rate as a key statement of Luke's estimation of and attitude towards possessions.

---

18. Luke 6:9, 9:24, 12:22–23, 14:26, 17:33, 21:19; Acts 2:27, 20:10, 24, 27:10, 22.

19. Plummer, *Luke*, 323, calls it "the higher life," contrasting it with βίος. Compare *TDNT* II.834–37.

20. In most of its NT occurrences ζωή refers to eternal life, whether used absolutely or with αἰώνιος (eternal).

21. This is beautifully illustrated in the parable of the prodigal son: οὗτος νεκρὸς ἦν καὶ ἔζησεν (He was dead and has come alive—Luke 15:32). Compare Acts 2:28, 3:15, 5:20, 11:18; also John 10:10 and especially 1 Tim 6:19.

22. Ernst, *Lukas*, 398, thinks the saying originally referred to eternal life, but later changed to comprehend simply life on earth.

4.2.2 Greed and the Judgment, Luke 12:16–21

The parable of the rich fool skillfully depicts the greedy man. Faced with an abundant harvest his only thought is for the increase of his possessions, though he is already rich. He is happy because he imagines his abundance will provide for him the good life. But God intervenes.

The main problem is the meaning we are to give to the denouement in verse 20. Does the parable depict the death which inevitably falls on everyone, rendering all their efforts futile?[23] Or is his death a picture of God's judgment?[24] Various considerations point to the correctness of the latter view:

a. This parable has drawn deeply on the wisdom tradition,[25] and it must be admitted that the former of the above views is represented there. Since death is inevitable, hoarding is useless; what the greedy person gathers for himself will be enjoyed by others.[26] However, this theme is really a commonplace and is open to the objection, even in the wisdom literature itself, that since the same fate meets the wise and the foolish, there is no point in anything other than eating, drinking, and enjoyment.[27] Much more prevalent in the wisdom literature is the idea that the person who pursues wealth will meet with the judgment of God:

> Do not set your heart on your wealth,
> nor say, "I have enough."
> ...
> Do not say, "Who will have power over me?"
> For the Lord will surely punish you.[28]

b. The fool is consistently thought of as one worthy of judgment.[29] He rejects wisdom and goodness and allows himself to be ensnared by

---

23. Compare Rengstorf, *Lukas*, 159–160.
24. Following Jülicher, *Gleichnisreden*, 616–17; Jeremias, *Parables*, 165.
25. Jülicher, *Gleichnisreden*, 616, says of this parable, "Ein Weiser Israels könnte die Geschichte Lc 12:16–20 dann ebensogut wie Jesus vorgetragen haben (a wise man of Israel could have presented the story of Lk 12:16–20 just as well as Jesus)."
26. Ps 39:6; Sir 11:18–19, 14:11–19.
27. Eccl 2:14–17, 24.
28. Sir 5:1, 3; compare Job 27:8–23; Sir 11:23–28; 1 En. 97:8–10.
29. E.g., 2 Sam 13:13; Job 5:3–5, 30:8; Prov 9:13–18, 14–16, 19:29; Isa 32:5–8; Jer

evil. He is characterized by his godlessness.[30] Nabal, who may have had some influence on this parable, was thought of as a fool, and was judged by God in a manner which recalls the fate of the rich farmer.[31] Thus, when God addresses the rich farmer as a "fool," he speaks to him as a man devoid of piety towards God, care towards his neighbor, and interest in his own true wellbeing; therefore, a man worthy of judgment.

c. That it is God who tells the fool he is to die suggests that we are dealing with a sentence of judgment. There is also something ominous about the death sentence: "this night they are calling up your life."[32] Many suggestions have been made as to the subject of *apaitousin* (ἀπαιτοῦσιν—they are calling back).[33] Most commentators treat it as a variant of the "divine passive" though E. M. Sidebottom's warning against a too easy substitution of an active with God for the "divine passive" may apply here: "The passive is the language of destiny and of cause and effect."[34] Echoing the same thought, R. C. Trench suggested: "Why not render, 'This night they require thy soul of thee,' leaving who 'they' are who shall thus require it in the fearful obscurity of the original?"[35]

We may take it as established that the parable represents God's judgment on a greedy man. We have yet to discover what this signifies. Does it indicate death as the judgment of God and thus reflect "the perspective of an individual's death," as Dupont claims?[36] Or is the death of the fool simply a figure for some wider concept of judgment? It would be truer to the outlook of the Gospel to pose the question in a slightly different form:

17:11; 1 En. 98:9–10.

30. Ps 14:1, 53:1, 74:22.

31. 1 Sam 25:25, 38–39.

32. ταύτῃ τῇ νυκτὶ τὴν ψυχήν σου ἀπαιτοῦσιν ἀπὸ σοῦ.

33. Angels, the angel of death, robbers, Satan, God. Whoever is "demanding back" would seem to have a right to what is theirs (Luke 6:30). Thus, the demand must at least have the sanction of God. The clearest parallel is Wis 15:8 where God is obviously the giver of the soul. Epictetus, *Discourse* IV, 1.172; Epictetus, *Enchiridion* 11; 4 Ezra 7:75, 78.

34. Sidebottom, "Divine Passive," 202.

35. Trench, *Notes on the Parables*, 340.

36. "La perspective de la mort individuelle." Dupont, *Béatitudes*, III.117. Compare Ellis, *Luke*, 178; Navone, *Themes of St. Luke*, 109; Marshall, *Eschatology and the Parables*, 36.

What is Luke seeking to warn his readers about: their inevitable death, or the coming judgment? Jeremias answers this question for the case of Jesus. Speaking of this parable, he says:

> We are not to think that Jesus intended to impress upon his audience the ancient maxim, "Death comes suddenly upon man." Rather do all the appeals and parables of warning taken together show that Jesus is not thinking of the inevitable death of the individual as the impending danger, but of the approaching eschatological catastrophe, and the coming Judgment.[37]

Does Luke have a similar outlook, or can we detect some change of direction or emphasis? It would be foolish to deny that Luke (or even Jesus) saw the possibility of the judgment of God coming upon an individual in the form of death.[38] The question is whether this is what he seeks to warn his readers about. The generalization in Luke 12:21 and the larger discourse in which this parable is embedded suggest that it is not. Rather, Luke wishes to alert his readers to the inevitability of the eschatological judgment. Verse 21 promises the same fate as the fool to *all* who accumulate possessions.[39] He hardly imagined that all greedy people would meet with untimely death, and that those who are rich towards God would survive to old age. Similarly, in 13:5 he does not mean that the unrepentant will all meet with accidents, but that the judgment is coming which will sweep them all away. Furthermore, the discourse in which the parable is located majors on the inevitability and urgency of the coming judgment.[40] It uses a number of different images—the master's homecoming, the breaking in of a thief, being taken off to court—and reaches a crescendo in the parable of the fig tree. Admittedly this is all traditional material and probably reflects the outlook of Jesus first and foremost. Yet

---

37. Jeremias, *Parables*, 165.

38. The case of Ananias and Sapphira is sufficient to demonstrate this.

39. οὕτως ὁ. The absence of v. 21 from D, ita, b, d has led to doubt about its originality. Jülicher, *Gleichnisreden*, II.614, sees the obscurity of the saying as an argument against its introduction into the text, and Metzger, *Textual Commentary*, 160, says the omission "must be accidental, for the weight of external evidence attesting its inclusion is overwhelming." Some see it as the work of a post-Lukan redactor (Grundmann, *Lukas*, 258), some as Luke's moralizing addition to the parable (Michaelis, *Gleichnisse Jesu*, 224; Dupont, *Béatitudes*, III.115–17). Degenhardt, *Evangelist der Armen*, 78–79, thinks Luke found it in its present context, and Schürmann, "Sprachliche Reminiszenzen," 203, sees a memory of it in Matt 6:19–20 (thus in Q). Joüon, "Parabole du riche insensé," 488–89, argues that Jesus spoke it in conclusion to the parable.

40. 12:1—13:9.

there is no sign that Luke has tried to alter this; verses 35–48 especially, show the seriousness with which he contemplated the Lord's return, at the same time making it clear that he did not necessarily envisage an *immediate* parousia and judgment.

In summary we may say that the parable of the rich fool is a strong warning against greed. No suspicion of wrongdoing attaches to the manner in which the farmer acquired his wealth;[41] an abundant harvest is the blessing of God. His sin was "stockpiling."[42] He thought that the quality of life he desired lay in an abundance of possessions—in increasing his hold upon this age. But his greedy "life-in-possessions" attitude called down the judgment of God.[43] Luke wishes to warn all those who seek their wellbeing in the things of this world that the time for the judgment of God is rapidly approaching.

Thus, to the thought which I have suggested lies behind verse 15, that in seeking "life" in possessions one fails to look for it where it is to be found, is added the complementary warning that greed provokes the judgment of God. The alternative (being rich towards God) will be discussed at a later point.[44]

4.3 ANXIETY AND THE KINGDOM, LUKE 12:22-34

The setting in the wider discourse, 12:1–13:9, is of particular importance for understanding this passage. The "central section" of Luke's Gospel is made up, for the most part, of isolated or thematically related groups

---

41. Contrast this with 1 En. 97:8-10.

42. θησαυρίζων. Derrett, "Rich Fool," 139–48, thinks the parable contains a play on the double meanings in Hebrew and Aramaic of "fruit" and "goods." He points out that God's store chambers in heaven are often called "barns" (אפותיקי in Deut 32:34). The fool, who should have laid up interest-bearing capital in heavenly chambers was busy storing his goods in earthly barns, "Called suddenly to account he is bankrupt 'up there' precisely to the extent that he is rich 'down here'" (Derrett, "Rich Fool," 147).

43. It might be objected that Luke hardly thinks that greed will cause or hasten the parousia. There is a difficulty in his sources here. Luke 12:54–9 and 13:1–9 imply that the judgment can be averted if repentance is forthcoming. No doubt this faithfully represents the message of Jesus to the nation Israel (compare Caird, *Jesus and the Jewish Nation*), but hardly fits the outlook of post-Easter Christians for whom the parousia-judgment was to take place on an exactly-determined future day (Acts 17:31). However, reapplication of these passages is not difficult; the question is no longer one of averting the judgment altogether, but of encountering the unexpected parousia as salvation rather than judgment. The parable of the rich fool fits here.

44. Pages 160–62, below.

of pericopes, but 12:1–13:9 has the marks of being, at least in the mind of Luke, a connected teaching discourse belonging to a particular occasion in Jesus' ministry.[45] Much of the material found here is also found in different contexts in Matthew, but it is easy to see that Matthew has gathered this teaching into large thematically related sections of his own construction.[46] Luke's discourse, on the other hand, is not so much a thematic unity that we would be led to think he had regrouped it out of its original settings.[47] Rather, it moves from subject to subject with a logic more to be expected from occasional discourse than in a literary production. The interruption of someone in the crowd shifts the subject from persecution to the danger of greed. Jesus then returns to his original theme, though with the problem of greed also now in mind; then the subject changes to watchfulness, and the interruption of Peter occasions further teaching on stewardship and responsibility.[48] Following this Jesus switches his attention to the difficulties of his own mission,[49] which leads him to a crescendo on the theme of the judgment which is fast overtaking an unresponsive generation.[50] The whole is introduced by a vividly circumstantial description of the crowds trampling one another and is punctuated by references to the external setting.[51] The addresses to various parts of the audience are probably to be seen as Luke's attempts to indicate the audiences to whom the teaching is particularly relevant.[52]

The view of Hirsch that Luke 12 was a connected Q discourse to which verses 13–21 were later added runs into the problem of the severe discontinuity involved in the juxtaposition of 4–12 and 22–31.[53] For

45. Zahn, *Lucas*, 490–92.

46. In the mission discourse (Matt 10) we find Luke 12:1b-9, 51-53; in the Sermon on the Mount; Luke 12:22-31, 33-34, 57-59; and in the parousia discourse (Matt 24:25) Luke 12:35-38.

47. Against Klostermann, *Lukasevangelium*, 132: "Ein Musterbeispiel lukanischer Redaktion (a classic example of Lukan redaction)"; Loisy, *Évangiles*, 154–55; Pesch, "Exegese von Mt 6:19-21 und Lk 12:33-34," 359–60.

48. Moule, *Birth of the New Testament*, 147–48, argues that this interruption was part of the tradition prior to Luke's and Matthew's use of it.

49. Luke 12:49. Clarke and Collie, "Luke 12:41-58," 300, think the idea of stewardship leads Jesus to contemplate his own.

50. This theme pervades the whole discourse and is connected with the opposition Jesus encounters from the scribes and Pharisees (Luke 11:53–12:1).

51. Luke 12:1, 13, 41, 13:1.

52. Luke 12:1b, 15, 22, 54, 13:2.

53. Hirsch, *Frühgeschichte des Evangeliums*, II.114–16.

although the two passages have many points of connection which makes such a juxtaposition attractive,[54] the move from the life and death issue of confessing Christ under persecution and threat of death, to the mundane level of anxiety about food and clothing is difficult to credit, either in a dominical discourse or in a collection of discourses from various sources. The reverse order would be understandable, but the present order demands some sort of transition. This is provided by the interruption of the brother and the change of subject from persecution to greed. However, there are problems in the way of seeing this as a literary device. For if Luke or an earlier collector were composing the discourse, he is unlikely to have done it in this way. He would probably have begun with the rich fool, followed with the discussion of anxiety, and then the threat of persecution. The appeal for watchfulness would then have followed on nicely.

It seems more probable that verses 4–12, 13–21, 22–34 preserve, at least in outline, the memory of an historical unity where 13–21 provide a change of subject and 22–34 bring this new thought into relation to the original theme.[55] In line with this, Dupont has argued convincingly for the unity of 13–34 on the basis of similarities between the parable and the discourse on anxiety.[56]

4.3.1 Don't Be Anxious

Turning to the passage itself, it is noteworthy that it has received surprisingly little scholarly attention considering its great popularity in other circles. It is usually treated as a down-to-earth wisdom discourse on the avoidance of anxiety. Bultmann describes it as "the expression of a particular (common) piety" in contrast to secular wisdom, and wonders why there is no characteristically eschatological motivation."[57] E. G. Selwyn posed the same question and maintained that the usual understanding of the passage was mistaken. The passage is highly eschatological, the lesson

---

54. Manson, *Sayings*, 106, puts both passages under the heading "Disciples under Persecution." Compare Luce, *Luke*, 229, and pages 156–57, below.

55. We must then imagine the rich fool to have been in Q (see also Weiss, *Markus und Lukas*, 487–88). Matt 6:19-21 will then be a summary of the parable (Μὴ θησαυρίζετε ὑμῖν θησαυροὺς ἐπὶ τῆς γῆς—do not lay up for yourselves treasures on earth) and perhaps the concluding exhortation reflected in Luke 12:33-34; compare Schürmann, Sprachliche Reminiszenzen," 203.

56. Dupont, *Béatitudes*, I.74–79. Also Godet, *Luke*, 99; Plummer, *Luke*, 325.

57. Bultmann, *History of the Synoptic Tradition*, 104.

from the ravens being that God would provide "some higher kind of food for you"—i.e., the messianic banquet.[58] The lilies are pointers to "the garments of glory."[59] The whole is to be experienced after the resurrection of the dead. "The Christian is to cease from anxiety not because he is in a world which calls for none, but because, if he seeks the kingdom, he will be."

But this view wanders too far from the plain meaning of the passage. If the ravens are to teach that God will one day feed us in the kingdom, our anxiety about tomorrow remains unchecked. Nor would the command not to be anxious about food and drink make sense if "your Father knows that you have need of them" means only that he will satisfy your desires in the life to come.

We must return, therefore, to the plain meaning of the discourse and take up the main point which has aroused difficulties: the apparent impracticality of the carefree attitude Jesus seems to be advocating. One solution is to deny that the passage was meant for general application to all Christians. According to Degenhardt, it was intended historically for the "professional" disciples of Jesus. By addressing it to disciples Luke applied it to "full time church ministers:"[60]

> With the word of Jesus people are addressed who need not exercise the calling of farmer and who do not own their own home or storehouse. They do not need to care about all that, because God himself cares for them. It is not said that all are challenged to such lack of care and reliance on God's help instead of their own forethought.[61]

It is at this point that Degenhardt's audience theory produces the most attractive results; a particular group, called away from the cares of everyday life and guaranteed their sustenance by God, solves many of

---

58. E.g., Selwyn, "Luke 12:27, 28," 163–64.
59. Compare Minear, *Commands of Christ*, 145–46.
60. "Hauptberufliche Gemeindediener"
61. "Mit dem Wort Jesu müssen Menschen angeredet sein, die den Beruf des Bauern nicht ausüben sollen und die keine eigene Wohnung und Verratshäuser besitzen. Sie brauchen sich um das alles nicht zu kümmern, weil Gott selbst für sie sorgt. Es ist nicht gesagt, dass alle zu solcher Sorglosigkeit und solchem Vertrauen auf Gottes Hilfe statt der eigenen Vorsorge aufgefordert sind." Degenhardt, *Evangelist der Arme*, 80–88, esp. 81.

the difficulties which are normally encountered in the application of this passage.[62] Nevertheless, it is open to several objections:

a. It has already been shown that an audience of disciples does not necessarily indicate Jesus' permanent traveling party, and more naturally suggests an application to the church as a whole than to its ministerial class.[63]

b. That the passage occurs in an overall context in which Luke emphasizes the presence of crowds of onlookers does not favor the conclusion that he saw it applying to only to a limited group. His intention is rather that the crowds who hear what is demanded of disciples should themselves be challenged to allegiance.[64] Those who abandon worldly treasures to seek the kingdom will be counted as disciples.

c. A wider application than to a professional elite is indicated by "little flock," a characterization of the remnant of Israel.[65] Luke's only other use of "flock" is to describe the church.[66]

d. There is no indication in the passage itself that it addresses a select group of people called specially to give up normal occupations to spend all their time working for the kingdom. Contrary to what Degenhardt suggests, verses 24–27 need not imply this; they may simply underline the magnitude of God's care for the insignificant parts of his creation.

At the Sixth International Congress for Biblical Studies held at Oxford in 1978 David L. Mealand, in a paper entitled "'Paradisial' Elements in the Teaching of Jesus?" put forward the view that Luke 12:22–32 and its parallel should be understood with the mission charge (Luke 10:1–16

---

62. Sandegren, "Misunderstood Section," 134–38, has a similar view.

63. See also Olsthoorn, *Jewish Background of Mt* 6:25-33 *and Lk* 12:22-31, 19–20.

64. The same openness is seen in vv. 41–48. Any effort to restrict the scope of the teaching to the inner core (Peter's question) is resisted. All who take up the task and do it faithfully will be blessed, though more is expected of those to whom more is committed.

65. μικρὸν ποίμνιον. Luke 12:32. See 3 Kgdms 22:17; Ps 77(78):52, 70–72; Mic 2:12, 4:8, 5:3(4); Zech 10:3; Isa 40:11; Jer 13:17, 20; 23:1–6, 38(31):10; Ezek 34:12, 31; Bar. 4:26; Ps. Sol. 17:40; 4QpPs37 2:5–6; CD 13:9 (עדר); compare CD 19:7–9; Mark 6:34 (par).

66. Acts 20:28–29. Compare 1 Pet 5:2. In both cases leaders are addressed about the flock which is committed to their charge.

par.) in the light of the Jewish expectation of a return to the conditions of paradise in the last days. He drew attention to a saying of R. Simeon b. Eleazar in M. Kid. 4:14 in which man complains that he is unable to gain his sustenance without care, like the birds and the animals. The explanation is the fall: "But I have wrought evil and forfeited my sustenance."

The last point is illuminating, and may well point to the truth of Mealand's idea "that to live without such cares is to live in the new age."[67] However, the association with the mission charge is more problematical. In the discussion which followed the paper, attention was drawn to Luke 22:35-38. Whatever else these verses mean, they clearly show that Luke regarded the mission as in some way enjoying a special supernatural protection,[68] and that those conditions were no longer to apply after Jesus' betrayal.[69] From then on disciples would need to make normal preparations and take normal precautions for their work. The passage on anxiety, however, is part of a discourse which Luke clearly intends for direct application to his readers and is therefore unlikely to be linked too closely in his mind to the special conditions of a mission which was part of the completed history of the time of Jesus.

We must return to the more usual approach to the passage, which sees it as a general exhortation against anxiety.[70] "Be anxious" does not denote normal forethought and care, but the unnecessary anxiety and worry which only produces psychological disintegration.[71] The "do not seek" of verse 29 must be read with *mē meteōrizesthe* (μὴ μετεωρίζεσθε),

---

67. He points out that cares are associated with this aeon (1 Cor 7:32-33; Mark 4:19). Compare Luke 8:14; 21:34.

68. One may grant this without admitting the whole of Conzelmann's scheme. Also see Luke 10:17-20.

69. I am unable to agree with Minear's interpretation of these verses ("Luke 22:36," 128-34). He thinks they are a literary device to expose the transgressions of the disciples with whom Jesus is about to be reckoned. It can only be said that it is an exceptionally obscure device. Why is there mention of purse, wallet and cloak in v. 36? Why does v. 36 assume that some already *do* have swords? The natural sense of μετὰ ἀνόμων ἐλογίσθη (he was reckoned with law-breakers) is that Jesus is to be treated as a transgressor (rejected), and that from henceforth conditions would be different for his followers.

70. Zahn, *Lucas*, 500; Creed, *Luke*, 173-74; Geldenhuys, *Luke*, 357-58; Bienert, *Die Arbeit nach der Lehre der Bibel*, 213-23; Tannehill, *The Sword of His Mouth*, 60-67. Schlatter, *Lukas*, 533-34 thinks Jesus was telling disciples to worry about one day at a time.

71. μεριμνᾶν. Sir 30:24—31:2. Wisdom delivers from anxiety (Wis 6:15; 7:23).

which suggests anxiety and restlessness,[72] and against the background of the strivings of the nations of the godless world.[73]

However, to treat anxiety as a common human problem, as do most commentators, is to overlook an important point. As Minear points out, the context suggest that this exhortation is directed at the specific anxiety which arises from discipleship.[74] To confirm this we must look more closely at the relationship between verses 4–12 and 22–34. The following connections may be observed:

a. Both passages deal with fear and anxiety; in the former in respect of those who can kill the body and about what to say when put on trial; in the latter about what to eat and wear.

b. Both in verse 4 and in 32 Jesus addresses the disciples with the same intimate, encouraging, but somewhat unusual tone (also "little-faiths" in 28).[75]

c. In both passages the disciples' security is grounded in the care of God who looks after the humblest parts of his creation (sparrows, ravens, lilies). The reasoning in both cases is identical: Of how much more value to God are you: "you are more valuable than many sparrows"; "how much more valuable are you than the birds."[76]

d. It is clear that the first passage is an exhortation to disciples who are going to face those who have power to take their lives. Confession of Jesus will inevitably lead to anxiety, but they are encouraged that

---

72. A NT hapax whose meaning is disputed. In the LXX it means "to be arrogantly puffed up," and so it is taken in the Vulgate. However, it is attested in the sense "to be unsettled, anxious, restless," which is how the Old Latin and Syriac render it (Molitor, "Übersetzung von Lk 12:29," 107–108). Cox, "New Parable," 249–58, sees the word itself as a parable conjuring up the image of a boat tossing about on the open sea.

73. Τοῦ κόσμου (of the world) is not found in Matthew. It may be meant as an intentional contrast to the kingdom. Men of the world who have no heavenly Father to trust must necessarily be anxious about their future.

74. Minear, *Commands*, 132–34. He thinks the addressees were the inner core of disciples and suggests three possible settings for the teaching: the mission of the Twelve, the normal demands of Christian living, and the problem created by the expectation of unlimited almsgiving (143–45).

75. ὀλιγόπιστοι.

76. πολλῶν στρουθίων διαφέρετε; πόσῳ μᾶλλον ὑμεῖς διαφέρετε τῶν πετεινῶν. Luke 12:7, 24; compare v. 28. There is a further interesting parallel between Luke 12:12 ("The Holy Spirit can be trusted to give you in that hour what you need to say") and Matt 6:34 ("Leave tomorrow's anxieties until tomorrow"—no parallel in Luke).

the God who cares for the smallest parts of his creation will also be caring for them. The thought of verses 4–12 might be summarized: God will care for those who seek his kingdom (confess him). But this is exactly the thought of 22–31.

It is a fair inference then that verses 22–34 envisage the same situation of danger as in 4–12. This is confirmed by two further considerations:

a. Wilhelm Pesch has shown that the command not to fear has a rich Old Testament background, particularly with reference to the depressed and persecuted existence of Israel at the time of the exile.[77] Thus, the command not to fear in verse 32 (as obviously in verses 4 and 7) probably implies that persecution is in view.

b. "The little flock" also hints at persecution, for, as F. F. Bruce points out, it recalls "the poor of the flock" and "the little ones" of Zechariah 11:11 and 13:7 who are destined for persecution and slaughter.[78]

Thus, what is combatted is not general neurotic anxiety but the particular anxiety which arises when a person decides to seek the kingdom. For when confession of Jesus is likely to generate hostility the disciple is faced with a threat to his food and clothing. He may be tempted to play down his allegiance to Jesus (fail to confess) in the interests of security (life, food, drink, clothing) for himself and his family.

The solution to the disciples' anxiety is not to be found in putting first things first and caring more about the kingdom than about personal needs.[79] This is what generates the anxiety. The answer lies in considering God's providential care for the lesser parts of his creation and the infinitely greater worth of the disciple,[80] to whom it is the Father's good pleasure to give the kingdom. The promise to all who make the kingdom their first priority is that God will supply their needs, however he does it.

It is now clear that it is a serious misunderstanding of this exhortation to see it as a demand for cessation of labor, or even for a non-caring

77. Pesch, "Formsgeschichte und Exegese von Lk 12:32," 26–31.

78. Zech 11:4. Bruce, "Zechariah and the Passion Narrative," 342–49.

79. As Caird, *Luke*, 163.

80. The unclean κόραξ (raven) emphasizes the contrast. The lilies stress the magnanimity of God's care even for grass that is destined for burning next day anyway. The example of the lilies is difficult to reconcile with any ascetic interpretation of this passage. Note the change from θεός (God) in vv. 24, 28, where the creation is in view, to πατήρ (Father) in vv. 30, 32, where the disciples are in view. This pattern is not in Matthew (6:26).

attitude to one's livelihood. Nor again is it to be regarded as a general wisdom discourse on the avoidance of unnecessary anxiety. Rather, it is addressed to folk for whom "seeking the kingdom" threatened loss or diminution of livelihood and hence gave birth to anxiety. This is countered by an appeal from God's providential care for the world (*theos*—God) to his fatherly care for Jesus' disciples (*patēr*—Father). They are promised that they will receive their needs. Whether this is to be from their own labors cannot be decided from the passage;[81] only that the ultimate source is God.

4.3.2 Sell and Give Alms

Verses 32–34 follow on naturally from the preceding discourse, but are more than just a summary conclusion.[82] Whereas 22–31 deal with the anxiety of those who are seeking the kingdom, 32–34 go much further, encouraging them positively to break free of their possessions and make for themselves a heavenly treasure. The conclusion of the parable of the rich fool is recalled, and Jesus appears to recommend the reverse procedure to that employed by the farmer.[83] Verses 33–34 are frequently treated as a demand for total renunciation.[84] I declined to treat them in chapter 3, firstly because I do not think they are, and second because they belong properly with the discussion on possessions and the Christian life. It is necessary now to justify this procedure.

Three considerations suggest that we are not dealing here with a demand for complete renunciation:

---

81. Tannehill, *Sword of his Mouth*, 63, points out that birds spend their whole time gathering food. Bienert, *Die Arbeit nach der Lehre der Bibel*, 216, thinks Jesus shares the view of his contemporaries that animals do not work. Nevertheless, he argues strongly against deriving a non-work ethic from this passage. "Jesus fordert nicht: Arbeit nicht! Er fordert: Sorget nicht! (Jesus does not demand, Do not work! He demands, Do not be anxious!)."

82. It is questionable whether the appearance of ἐλεημοσύνη (almsgiving) in v. 33 requires that this conclusion be attributed to the pen of Luke. The dominical origin of v. 32 is defended by Pesch, "Lk 12:32." Vv. 33b, 34 probably come from Q (compare Matt 6:19–21). Something is needed with v. 33b.

83. διὰ τοῦτο (therefore) (v. 22) suggests that Luke sees the following discourse (vv. 22–34) as, in some manner, an alternative to the lifestyle of the fool.

84. E.g., *TDNT* III.138n1, who sees them in terms of Luke's poverty ideal.

a. The demand for renunciation is usually represented as a requirement of those entering the company of Jesus. This is manifestly not so here. Those addressed are already disciples and the kingdom is already theirs (verse 32b), yet they still appear to be experiencing problems with possessions. Thus, far from being an argument for a general requirement of total renunciation, in their Lukan setting these verses virtually rule it out.

b. I am inclined to think that had Luke been thinking in terms of complete renunciation he would have said "*all* your possessions" since in other places he makes such free use of this adjective.[85]

c. Verse 34 gives the rationale for what is being demanded: Treasure captivates the mind, whereas the disciple's mind must be free for the kingdom; thus he must convert his earthly treasure into heavenly treasure and so transfer his attention to the new age. The answer we give to the renunciation question hinges, therefore, on how we understand the term "treasure." In the New Testament *thesauros* (θησαυρός) does not necessarily, nor even naturally, express the idea of all that a person owns. It is rather that which is laid by, accumulated, and stored for future use, and therefore is not presently being put to use.[86] It is the bumper harvest which the farmer stores away in his barns so he can retire from life in ease; he exults over it and it fills his mind; it is his future.

If, therefore, verses 32–34 are not a call for complete renunciation of possessions, what is their function? It is important to notice in what spirit these words are said. The whole of 32–34 has the tone of a gentle

---

85. Percy, *Botschaft*, 90, sees v. 33–34 as a warning "allen ihren irdischen Besitz als Almosen zu verschenken (to give away all your earthly possessions as alms)."

86. Θησαυρίζω (store up) is used more commonly than we would use "treasure up" to express the thought "store up" or "lay by" (Luke 12:21; Rom 2:5; 1 Cor 16:2; 2 Cor 12:14; 2 Pet 3:7).

Θησαυρός frequently occurs outside the NT with the sense of "storehouse," "treasury." It may have this sense in Luke 6:45; Matt 12:35; 13:52; compare Philo, *Fug.* 79; *Leg. All.* III.104–06.

Philo, *Virt.* 90 says about the OT gleaning laws, "In this way he makes the well-to-do high-minded and liberal by sacrificing something of their own property instead of casting greedy eyes on the whole crop and stacking and carting it all home to be kept like a treasure" (θησαυροφυλακήσοντας—guarded as a treasure). In *Virt.* 140–41 the link between such thinking and Greek ideals is apparent. In *Quod Omn.* 76 he notes that the Essenes do not hoard (θησαυροφυλάκοντες) silver, gold, or property.

encouragement to apprehensive disciples.[87] In 22–31 Jesus shows them that their anxiety about material security is unnecessary since their Father can be trusted to give them what they need (handsomely—verse 27). Verses 32–34 go further, urging outgoing generosity and a positive, carefree approach to life. Because the Father stands as guarantor of their future, they are free to be liberal with their superfluity. "Sell . . . and give" should neither be taken as an entrance requirement to the kingdom, nor seen in any way as a rigorous *commandment*.[88] These folk are already in the path of discipleship, and are being encouraged to enter more fully into the freedom of complete trust in God and attachment to his kingdom. It would be strange if Luke (or Jesus) had sought to free disciples from anxiety, only immediately to lay upon them a demand which could only have generated the utmost anxiety. Thus, we might paraphrase verse 33a: "You are free now to sell your possessions (understood in a general, not a total sense) and give to the poor." Verses 22–34 are then saying: Don't be afraid to confess me—God has given you his kingdom and will care for your needs—you can afford to be generous—don't even be concerned to hang on to the possessions you already have—sell them and give alms.[89]

One obvious motive for such philanthropic activity is the desire that disciples should detach themselves from the false values and securities of the world and be more firmly rooted in the kingdom. Involved in this is probably a desire for the consistency of the witness of disciples: it is hardly straightforward to declare oneself for the new age while investing in the continuance of this one by stockpiling possessions. Conversely to act in the manner Jesus suggests is to bear witness to the reality of the coming kingdom.

There is also a positive motive for disposal of possessions: almsgiving makes the giver possessor of a treasure in the heavens. Here another wisdom theme makes its entrance, but again geared to Jesus' proclamation of the kingdom. If stockpiling possessions is seen as an investment in this age, in some sense almsgiving is seen as an investment in the age to come.

---

87. See also Godet, *Luke*, 102; Degenhardt, *Evangelist der Armen*, 87, 91; Rienecker, *Lukas*, 316.

88. Πωλήσατε . . . καὶ δότε.

89. This should not be "spiritualized." The aorists πωλήσατε and δότε (sell and give) show that Luke envisages a real act (perhaps repeated) of disbursement to the poor. A "detached attitude" without corresponding deeds would have been meaningless to him.

The nature of the heavenly treasure is frequently misunderstood because of a tendency to confuse first-century Jewish with later Christian eschatology. Jesus' eschatology is linear. Along with the Judaism of the first century he believed that the end of this evil age would usher in a new age in a transformed world.[90] Luke's view does not appear to be different.[91] In his way of thinking heaven is not the destination of the faithful, but the dwelling place of God, who stands as the guarantor and inaugurator of the new age.[92] "Treasure in the heavens" does not mean a pile of goods waiting to be enjoyed when finally one reaches heaven; it means to be in God's favor, to be rich towards God.[93]

This is confirmed by a study of the concept in intertestamental Jewish literature where treasure meant blessings in this life such as protection, forgiveness and deliverance from death.[94] The same concept is expressed differently in Tobit 4:7: "Turn not away thy face from any poor man, and the face of God shall not be turned away from thee." A parallel idea occurs in Tobit 12:12–14: Raphael brings the memorial of Tobit's prayers and good deeds before God, as a result of which healing is sent forth for him and his daughter-in-law.[95]

In later Jewish thought reward in the age to come became much more important,[96] until the point was reached where one was actively encouraged to avoid taking any recompense now for fear of losing it in the future world.[97] Luke's thinking lies somewhere between these views.[98] Both this age and the age to come are important to him; the disciple can

---

90. For the Jewish view see 4 Ezra 6:6–10, where the two ages are likened to the birth of Esau and Jacob, the latter holding the heel of the former. Compare 4QpPs37 2:9–11; 4 Ezra 7:75–99; 2 Bar. 14:12–13, 15:7–8, 21:22–25, 29–30, 44:12–15, 49–51; 57; 73; Aboth 6:9. See also Minear, *And Great Shall Be Your Reward*, 40–53.

91. Luke 16:9, 19:11–27, 20:34–36, 22:29–30, 24:21; Acts 1:6–7, 3:21.

92. See Krämer, *Parabel vom ungerechten Verwalter*, 138n240.

93. εἰς θεὸν πλουτῶν—Luke 12:21. See also Nolan, *Jesus before Christianity*, 46. There is no support in Luke for the view that the treasure is the kingdom itself. Matt 13:44 is the only place where this is clearly so, and the plural θησαυρούς in Matt 6:20 shows that treasure is not a fixed symbol even for him.

94. Tob 4:7–11, 12:8–9; Sir 29:9–13; compare Sir 3:3–6; Ps. Sol. 9:5; Cronbach, "Social Ideals of the Apocrypha and the Pseudepigrapha," 139–43.

95. Memorial—μνημόσυνον.

96. 2 Bar. 14:12, 24:1, 52:7; 4 Ezra 7:77, 83; Aboth 2:16.

97. Marmorstein, *Merits in Old Rabbinical Literature*, 19–20.

98. Against Sanders, *Palestinian Judaism*, 197, who thinks one can only talk of a treasure in heaven because reward is deferred to the age to come.

expect to meet with God's favor in both.⁹⁹ Acts 10:4, 31 shows that he is still influenced by the kind of thinking reflected in Tobit 12:12-14; just as Tobit is healed when the "memorial" of his good deeds comes before God, so when the "memorial" of Cornelius's alms deeds and prayers comes before God, Peter is sent forth to convert him. Thus, he meets with his reward prior to the judgment.¹⁰⁰

The Father's care which is promised to those who seek his kingdom should also be seen in this light. A "purse" suggests something which is to be in constant use, rather than a treasure which cannot be touched until the new age.¹⁰¹

Thus, the treasure spoken of in 33-34 is a store of favor with God which guarantees the disciple's wellbeing now and in the age to come.¹⁰² It can be gained by distributing one's possessions to the needy.¹⁰³ Such a treasure is "inexhaustible" because, in contrast to the perishables for which it is exchanged, it is both unchangeable and inexhaustible (being the attitude of God).¹⁰⁴ To have one's heart fixed on it is to have it fixed on God himself.¹⁰⁵ Hence the result of acting in accord with 33-34 will be identical to the attitude demanded in 22-31: confidence in the Father who guarantees the kingdom to disciples and who promises to care for all their needs in the meantime.

---

99. Luke 18:29-30. Luke's attitude is not so different from the idea in *Peah* 1:1, that for deeds of loving-kindness a person enjoys the fruits in this world while the capital is laid up for him in the world to come (against Schnackenburg, *Moral Teaching*, 154).

100. Compare Luke 7:4-5; *T. Naph.* 8:5.

101. "Purse" = βαλλάντιον. Luke 12:22-34. Compare Luke 10:4, 22:35.

102. The same double thought is present in 1 Tim 6:17-19.

103. A striking parallel is to be found in *B. Bat.* 11a. King Monobazus answers those who criticized him for disbursing in alms the treasures his fathers accumulated. "My fathers stored up below and I am storing above ... My fathers stored in a place that can be tampered with, but I have stored in a place which cannot be tampered with, as it says, 'Righteousness and judgment are the foundation of his throne'... My fathers gathered for this world, but I have gathered for the future world." Righteousness (צדק) is used repeatedly in this passage in the sense of "benevolence." Thus Monobazus's almsdeeds are seen as absolutely secure because they are the foundation of God's throne.

104. "Inexhaustible" = ἀνέκλειπτος. In a similar way wisdom is said to be ἀνέκλειπτος (Wis 7:14) and the source of inexhaustible wealth.

105. Compare Clement, *Stromateis* IV.6.33.

4.4 APPLICATION OF LUKE 12:13-34

There is nothing situational in this passage which would cause us to think that Luke did not intend the whole discourse to be applied directly to his readers. The problems of greed and anxious striving after material things are universal. Luke saw them as recurrent obstacles to the progress of the Christian mission. Paul and Silas are beaten and imprisoned in Philippi for removing a source of revenue from the masters of a demon-possessed girl.[106] In Ephesus an attack on the Christians is instigated by people who thought Paul's preaching was interfering with their trade.[107] The venality of Felix is blamed for Paul's long imprisonment in Caesarea.[108] Luke relates the first two of these stories with a touch of irony, for although the manifest cause of the trouble is money, in neither case is this the charge which is brought against the Christians; greed cloaks itself in concern for righteousness and piety. Within the Christian movement there is the case of Judas, as well as the attempt of Ananias and Sapphira to defraud the church. Paul has to work with his hands to give the Ephesian elders an example.[109] Such troubles from within and without would go a long way towards explaining the strength of Luke's warning against greed.

The background of potential persecution presupposed in the second part of the discourse is common to the Christian movement at all times, in that believers place themselves at risk with respect to society by their radical reorientation towards Jesus and the kingdom. This would certainly have been the case in Luke's day, whether or not active persecution was being experienced. The passage would also have been relevant to folk whose trades were incompatible with the Christian way and whose livelihood would therefore be threatened were they to embrace Christianity.

Luke refers verses 13-21 to those within and without the church; the primary focus of 22-34 is to disciples, though they are equally relevant to those attracted to the Christian movement but troubled by anxieties about the social and economic consequences of becoming fully identified. He would seriously warn everyone about the catastrophic judgment which is soon to fall on all who seek their life in possessions and fail to lay

---

106. Acts 16:16-24.
107. Acts 19:23-27.
108. Acts 24:26.
109. Luke 22:5; Acts 1:18, 5:1-11, 20:33-35. Paul's letters show a sensitivity to the problem of greed as a possible motive for preaching (1 Thess 2:5-6; 2 Cor 2:17; 11:7-15). Compare 2 Pet 2:1-3, 14; *Did.* 11:4-6, 9, 12.

hold of "that life which is life indeed."[110] He would exhort those who are already disciples, or thinking of it, that the Father who has given them the kingdom is well able to care for all their earthly needs. They can devote themselves fully to the kingdom, giving testimony to their new citizenship by exchanging the currency of the old order for a credit balance with God by means of generous and carefree contributions to the poor.

4.5 MAMMON AND THE KINGDOM, LUKE 16:1-13

The parable of the unjust steward with its attached sayings dominates the longest section on the theme of possessions in Luke-Acts, and is therefore vitally important to our study of Luke's attitudes. In addition to the overall thrust of the parable, which reveals an interesting relationship between eschatology and the ethics of money, we encounter the expression "mammon of unrighteousness," which promises to reveal much about Luke's fundamental attitude to money and possessions.

4.5.1 Literary Structure

Most scholars are of the opinion that the parable has attracted to itself at some point in its transmission a series of free sayings, but opinion is divided on where the parable ends and the attracted sayings begin. Jülicher thought the parable closed with verse 8; Dodd was undecided whether it ended with 7 or 8a; Jeremias thinks with 8a.[111] All three see the subsequent verses as later interpretations;[112] originally the parable was a call for wisdom and prudence on the part of disciples (Jülicher), or decisive action in view of the eschatological crisis (Dodd, Jeremias). Verse 9 represents a misunderstanding of the parable; perhaps Luke or his source mistook the κύριος (lord) in verse 8 for the Lord Jesus, and added a new interpretation of the parable (Jülicher).

The problem with the last view is well expressed by Wellhausen:

---

110. 1 Tim 6:19.

111. Jülicher, *Gleichnisreden*, 505. Dodd, *Parables of the Kingdom*, 30–31. Jeremias, *Parables*, 45–46.

112. Also Descamps, "Composition littéraire de Luc 16:9–13," 47–53; he thinks the parable ends with v. 8.

Remarkable that that which is most emphasized should have no significance.[113]

Accordingly, a number of scholars have argued convincingly that verse 9 is an integral part of the parable.[114] Jülicher's view that 9 is a genuine saying of Jesus brought from another context is certainly untenable, for the saying corresponds too closely to the action of the steward in the parable.[115] Jeremias admits that verse 9 must have been composed with reference to 4, and postulates the voice of a primitive preacher seeking to drive home the force of the parable.[116] This is no doubt possible, though he hardly substantiates the need for such a solution.[117] In any case, the parable would have come to Luke with verse 9 already governing its interpretation, for it is unlikely that he would have composed a conclusion with such obscurities and barbarisms.

It is impossible to say whether 10–13 were gathered into their present location by Luke, or whether they were already associated with the parable before him.[118] In any case it is clear that they are not integral to its understanding but rather represent a continuation of the theme which it introduces (the right use of possessions).[119]

113. "Merkwürdig, dass das was am meisten hervorgehoben wird, nichts zu bedeuten haben soll": Wellhausen, *Lucae*, 87. Weiss, *Schriften*, 486.

114. Bigo, "Richesse comme intendance," 267–71; Hiers, "Eschatological Proletariat," 31–33; Krämer, *Parabel vom ungerechten Verwalter*, 132–34; compare Goulder, "Characteristics of the Parables," 64, especially n1.

115. Jülicher, *Gleichnisreden*, 505–06. V. 9 corresponds to v. 4 at every point: ποιήσατε φίλους, μαμωνᾶς τῆς ἀδικίας, ἐκλίπῃ, δέξωνται, αἰωνίους σκηνάς (make friends, mammon of unrighteousness, it fails, they will receive you, eternal tents) No better setting could be found for the saying than the parable itself!

116. Jeremias, *Parables*, 47.

117. It is unthinkable to him that the κύριος of v. 8 could be the master of the parable. Thus, there is a distinction between vv. 8 and 9. However, it is possible that the master's unexpected judgment was meant to provoke shock in the hearers (compare Luke 19:24–25) and thus to invite them to closer consideration of the steward's actions. Foerster, "Gleichnis von den anvertrauten Pfunden," 48, points out that parables often contain something which does not fit a strict analysis of the story, but which thereby points to a beyond with which the parable is concerned. Degenhardt, *Evangelist der Armen*, 116–17, argues convincingly that the κύριος is the master.

118. Feuillet, "Riche intendants du Christ," 31–32, argues for the unity of vv. 1–12; Luke has added v. 13.

119. Various attempts have been made to apply the parable to something other than possessions, but they are unconvincing and confused. Maass, "Gleichnis vom ungerechten Haushalter," 173–84, sees it as an appeal for a forgiving attitude (it praises "ungerechten" [unrighteous] forgiveness). This seems far-fetched for the original

4.5.2 The Unjust Steward, Luke 16:1–9

The parable tells of a steward who was caught in a crisis, but who through swift and prudent action secured himself a future when his life was about to dissolve around him. The surprise, which catches attention today and no doubt would have done so when the parable was told, is that the steward is praised for his action. This surprise remains whether or not the amounts which the steward remitted to his master's debtors corresponded to his own potential profit,[120] or to interest which had been unlawfully charged on the loans.[121] In either case the money was already lost to the steward, and altering the promissory notes would have led to loss on the master's part.[122] The surprise invites us to consider closely the

---

parable, and impossible in its Lukan setting. Topel, "Injustice of the Unjust Steward," 216–27, who follows Maass, holds the strange view that Luke understands the parable as an appeal for forgiveness *and* almsgiving. Lunt, "Interpretation of the Parable of the Unjust Steward," 335–37, and Lunt, "Parable of the Unjust Steward," 132–36, sees the parable with ch. 15 as an appeal to the leaders of Israel to lessen the legal burden on the people. To do this he is forced to brush aside other Lukan accretions (vv. 1, 9). A similar view is argued by Kamlah, "Parabel vom ungerechten Verwalter," 276–94, on the ground that "steward" naturally connotes the spiritual hierarchy. Bailey, *Poet and Peasant*, 86–110, thinks the point of the parable is that the steward placed his total trust in the quality of mercy shown by the master when he did not jail him at the outset. To arrive at this interpretation, however, he has to read a great deal into the parable, stress points that the parable does not stress, and ignore v. 9 by grouping it with the following verses as a separate discourse. Williams, "Is Almsgiving the Point of the 'Unjust Steward'?" 293–97, argues that the main point of the parable has to do with the use of possessions.

120. First suggested by Gibson, "Parable of the Unjust Steward," 334, and followed by Hampden-Cook and Dutton, "Unjust Steward," 44; Steele, "Unjust Steward," 236–37, and Gächter, "Dishonest Steward," 121–31.

121. See also Firth, "Unrighteous Steward," 93–95. Derrett, "Parable of the Unjust Steward," 63–64, 72–73, thinks the master was in the position of having to own up to usurious practices or to accept what the steward had done and suffer financial loss. In praising him he takes the credit for having cancelled the interest. This is ingenious, but one hesitates to build so much on unspoken assumptions. Bailey, *Poet and Peasant*, 92–93, dismisses Derrett's assumptions and introduces a new set of his own! It is doubtful that the first hearers and readers of the parable would have inferred so much as either of these suggests, even with the benefit of background knowledge. Sherwin-White, *Roman Society and Roman Law*, 141–42, notes the conspicuous absence of money-lenders in Galilee in the period of Jesus and thinks the Jews were generally faithful to the law against usury.

122. According to Gächter, "Dishonest Steward," 130, the incoming steward would have been the real loser.

action of the steward and leads in verse 8b to a statement of the nature of the comparison which is required.

The action of the steward illustrates the greater degree of prudence shown by "the children of this age" than by "the sons of light." However, it is a prudence "in their own generation,"[123] which in the present comparative context probably has the sense of "among their own kind" or "in their own frame of reference."[124] Men of the world[125] show amazing insight and wisdom in their own affairs. A businessman caught in a financial crisis will bring all his wits to bear on his problem and will act decisively to minimize his losses and maximize his gains. The children of light belong to a different "generation." They have a different set of realities, different horizons, and different ways of acting. The parable accuses them of being less prudent in their world than the businessman in his.

The crisis motif, so common in the parables and teaching of Jesus,[126] shows that more is intended than a mere exhortation to prudence. The disciples found themselves in the midst of an eschatological emergency: the kingdom, judgment, and salvation are being proclaimed and Jesus is calling for decisive action.[127] This is the crisis that pertains to their "sphere of life" (Lebensgebiet), but they do not seem to have grasped its urgency; they are urged to take a lesson from a steward who was caught in an analogous situation.[128]

Thus far we can agree with Dodd and Jeremias, but we must go further to ask what kind of decisive action the parable recommends. The crisis motif occurs in other parables, as does the master-servant motif,

---

123. εἰς τὴν γενεὰν ἑαυτῶν.

124. Krämer, *Parabel vom ungerechten Verwalter*, 156-63, argues for the temporal meaning of "in ihrer Generation, nämlich in dieser Entscheidungsgeneration" (in their generation, namely, in this decisive generation)" (162). The comparative material he adduces clearly points in this direction, but his conclusion does not fit the present context where ἑαυτῶν (their own) implies a separate generation of the sons of light. There is thus a realm (or race) corresponding to the present aeon (compare Acts 2:40) and another corresponding to the children of light (compare Phil 2:15). Leaney, *Luke*, 222, translates γενεά as "society."

125. See pages 170-72, below.

126. In this section of Luke see 12:54-59, 13:6-9.

127. Bornkamm, *Jesus*, 87-89. Against the idea that death is in view see pages 172-74, below.

128. The parable is not an allegory, though certain elements lend themselves to this. The story must be understood as a scene from life and then carried over to "ein andres Lebensgebiet" (another sphere of life) (Weiss, *Schriften*, 485.)

particularly in relation to some sort of reckoning or judgment.[129] The steward is also a common figure. The only novel feature of the parable is the steward's remarkable evasive action. It is this, therefore, which should be taken as key to the parable. Verse 9 makes it clear that, in Luke's eyes at least, this is where the real point lies: the steward's stratagem, employing the remaining hours of his oversight of the master's possessions to provide for himself friends who will welcome him into their homes when he is cast from his job. This is applied by way of analogy to disciples faced with the end of the age.

4.5.3 Friendship and Mammon

Mamōnās (μαμωνᾶς) is a Greek transliteration of the emphatic form of the Aramaic *mamōn* (ממון), a general term for possessions which can have an ethically positive, negative, or neutral sense, depending of the context.[130] It is likely that the early Christian community was responsible for this transliteration since the word is not found in Greek before or after the New Testament except in reference to its use in the Gospels.[131] Jesus' use of the term was probably distinctive and invited transliteration rather than translation. In Luke 16:13 (Matthew 6:24) mammon is almost personified as a potential rival to God.[132] With this one mammon saying extant, there may have been a tendency to preserve others.[133]

Various suggestions have been given as to the meaning of "mammon of unrighteousness."[134] One frequently meets with the suggestion that it is equivalent to the common Aramaic expression *mamon dishkar*.[135]

---

129. See Kamlah, "Parabel vom ungerechten Verwalter," 276–94.

130. For examples see TDNT IV.388–89. For neutral uses approximately contemporary with the NT, see 1QS 6:2; CD 14:20 and probably 1QMyst 1.2.5 (DJD I.105). In *Exod. Rab.* 31:15 ממון של אמת (wealth [mammon] of truthfulness) is contrasted with) ממון של שקר (wealth [mammon] of falsehood).

131. *Mammon* is rendered χρυσίου (gold) in Sir 31(34):8, suggesting that it had not at that stage made its way into Greek as a loan word. Its use in 2 Clem 6:1 is dependent on the Gospels.

132. In Aristophanes's *Plutus*, wealth is portrayed as a blind god.

133. Luke 16:9, 11.

134. μαμωνᾶς τῆς ἀδικίας.

135. ממון דשקר - gain acquired by fraudulent means. TDNT IV, 390; Billerbeck II, 220. However there are other possible equivalents: ממון דרשע = mammon of wickedness (TgHab 2:9; MT - בצע רע = πλεονεξίαν κακήν = evil greed; compare CD 6:15 הון הרשעה = wealth of wickedness); הון חמס = gain from violence (1QS 10:19); נכסי שקר =

Verse 9 would then be telling people what to do with ill-gotten gains.[136] However, it is improbable that Luke would have addressed a word with such narrow application to disciples. Moreover, his reference to the *failure* of mammon indicates that all wealth is regarded as "mammon of unrighteousness."[137]

A second view regards "mammon of unrighteousness" as expressing the essential evilness of possessions. Thus Herbert Braun infers: "The third gospel understands possessions as something fundamentally evil which must be given up in view of the approaching judgment."[138] This interpretation falls foul of the fact that of all the evangelists Luke is the only one who indicates a positive appreciation of the constructive role which possessions can play. The point of the parable of the unjust steward does not lie in urging disciples to flee possessions, but in persuading them to use them wisely and constructively in the light of their eventual "failure." They are called upon to be "faithful with unrighteous mammon,"[139] an odd turn of phrase if what Luke means is that possessions are to be shunned as inherently evil. He obviously intends that the poor are to be advantaged by the reception of alms, and is proud of the early church's achievement in abolishing want. The leaders of the early church are not pictured abandoning wealth, but carefully administering it for the good of the community.[140]

Others have suggested that possessions are characterized as "unrighteous" because of their tendency to corrupt, or because they are so often tainted with unrighteousness through their acquisition and use[141] or because of their idol-like potential.[142] These are all possibilities. However,

---

property of falsehood (χρήμασιν ἀδίκοις - Sir 5:8); אוצרין דרשע = treasures of wickedness (TgMic 6:10; MT - אצרות רשע). Compare 1 Enoch 63:10.

136. Schleiermacher, *Luke*, 213-14, saw it as a justification of tax collectors who were following Jesus and using their ill-gotten gains to help their countrymen.

137. ὅταν ἐκλίπῃ—when it fails.

138. "Das dritte Evangelium versteht den Besitz als etwas grundsätzliches Böses, welches angesichts des nahen Gerichtes aufzugeben ist." Braun, *Radikalismus*, II.74.

139. ἐν τῷ ἀδίκῳ μαμωνᾷ πιστοί.

140. Acts 4:34-35, 37, 6:1-6, 11:29-30.

141. Hauck, *Arbeit und Geld*, 86; *TDNT* IV.390.

142. Krämer, *Parabel vom ungerechten Verwalter*, 95, thinks Jesus used such an expression to express his estimation of riches as "eine der Haupttriebkräfte der gottfremden und gottfeindlichen Weltzeit (one of the main driving forces of the godless and God-hating world-age)." Dupont, *Béatitudes*, III.168-72 thinks people have appropriated what is God's and not their own (ἀλλότριον—belonging to another) and

I incline to the suggestion of Hans Kosmala, that *adikia* (ἀδικία—unrighteousness) is used here in the sense in which the Qumran documents use "*perversion*" and "*wickedness*": "as a technical expression for evil and its mastery in the end-time."[143] "Mammon of unrighteousness," would then mean mammon that belongs to the sphere of *adikia*, i.e., to the realm of Satan. "The steward of unrighteousness" in verse 8 and "the judge of unrighteousness" in Luke 18:7 are not being described as unjust, but as belonging to this evil age.[144] Kosmala thinks that "mammon of unrighteousness" is equivalent to "wealth of unrighteousness" in the Scrolls.[145] This suggestion seems to me not only to be sound, but to illuminate both the attitude of the Qumran community to possessions, and the fundamentally different outlook of Luke (Jesus).

Those who entered the covenant of the community were to be "careful to act according to the exact tenor of the law in the time of wickedness,[146] to separate themselves from the sons of the pit, and to keep themselves from the unclean riches of iniquity, in vow, in anathema, and in property of the sanctuary."[147] It is not easy to be certain of the meaning of the last part of this passage. Dupont-Sommer translates it as "(got) with a vow or anathema or by robbing the goods of the sanctuary"; Lohse has "which is unclean through a vow or an anathema or the possession of the temple."[148] However, it is difficult to see how property could be fraudulently obtained or rendered unclean through vows, or what "wealth of the sanctuary" would mean if this were so. Charles also runs foul of this last phrase. He made it an idol.

---

143. עול and רשעה. "Als technische Ausdruck für die Bosheit und ihre Herrschaft in der Endzeit." Kosmala, *Hebräer—Essener—Christen*, 195. ἀνομία (lawlessness) is the normal equivalent of עול and is used in Matt, the writings of Paul, and 1 John. It is avoided by Luke, who prefers ἀδικία (unrighteousness) (compare Luke 13:27 with Matt 7:23).

144. ὁ οἰκόνομος τῆς ἀδικίας and ὁ κρίτης τῆς ἀδικίας. Compare Acts 8:23 where σύνδεσμον ἀδικίας (bond of unrighteousness) seems to denote Satanic bondage. Kosmala's view is followed by Jeremias, *Theology*, 222, and Ellis, *Luke*, 199. Krämer, *Parabel vom ungerechten Verwalter*, agrees for the expression "steward of unrighteousness" (43, 149–50), but disagrees for "mammon of unrighteousness" because he thinks there is no comparable term in the DSS (93).

145. הון הרשעה CD 6:15; 8:5; 19:17.

146. לקץ הרשעה.

147. CD 6:14–16: ולהנזר מהון הרשעה הטמא בנדר ובחרם ובהון המקדש

148. "... der unrein ist durch ein Gelübde oder einen Bannfluch oder Besitz des Tempels."

thinks the sectary was to place himself under a vow and a curse to hold aloof from the unclean wealth of wickedness. To make any sense of "with wealth of the sanctuary" he must amend it to "from wealth."[149]

In my opinion, it is more likely that covenant members are here prohibited from accepting offerings from non-sect members and from taking any share of temple offerings. The many priests of the community would have stood to be beneficiaries of vows and votive offerings, and would have had rights to a share in temple offerings.[150] All this they are called to "renounce."[151] If this is correct, "unclean wealth of unrighteousness"[152] is "unclean" and "unrighteous," not because of the way it has been obtained, but because it comes from the realm of evil outside the sect. The unfaithful sectaries who defiled themselves with this "wealth of unrighteousness" were probably guilty of conducting illicit business outside the sect[153] or of accepting the offerings of non-sect members.

This view is consistent with what else we know of the sect's attitude to possessions. Members voluntarily separated themselves from "the assembly of men of perversity,"[154] i.e., men who belong to the realm of Satan, the sons of darkness, to become a community in the law and with regard to property. Within the community property was clean and undefiling;[155] outside it was unclean.[156] Thus it might appropriately be characterized as ""wealth of unrighteousness" since it belonged to the sphere of evil and defilement.[157]

149. ומהון המקדש to ובהון המקדש. Charles, *Pseudepigrapha*, 813–14. Hvidberg, *Menigheden af den nye pagt i Damascus*, 112, notes this problem and thinks wealth is unclean because it belongs to the Temple, which is defiled.

150. In this very passage community members are forbidden to take any part in the temple cult (CD 6:11–14). See Ginzberg, *Unknown Jewish Sect*, 117; Vermes, *Qumran in Perspective*, 180–82.

151. להנזר.

152. הון הרשעה הטמא.

153. CD 8:5; 19:17. Obviously it was impossible for them totally to cut themselves off from dealings with the outside world, but they strictly controlled what business they did conduct. See 1QS 5:14–20; CD 13:14–16; and 3 John 7.

154. מעדת אנשי העול —1QS 5:1–2. Compare οἱ υἱοὶ τοῦ αἰῶνος τούτου—the sons of this age—Luke 16:8.

155. Hence the care taken over "mingling" the property of a new member (1QS 6:13–23), and the prohibition of mingling the possessions of the men of deceit with that of the community (1QS 9:8–9).

156. 1QS 5:20.

157. Note the expression גבול רשעה (realm of wickedness) in 1QH 3:24.

In contrast to the outlook of Qumran, Luke 16:9 demands that disciples *make use* of the mammon of unrighteousness.[158] Though they are the sons of light, it is not possible for them to separate themselves from the realm of evil and establish a community with its own internal system of purified mammon. All mammon is "of unrighteousness"; i.e., it belongs to this evil age.[159] They must use it, but if they are wise there is a way by which it may be converted into the kind of wealth which is appropriate to the kingdom of God.

If the above argument is correct, the clause "when it fails" at once falls into place. This age with all that belongs to it is about to pass away,[160] and mammon will soon cease to have any value.[161] As the steward found himself with a brief period before his control of his master's goods would end, so the disciple finds himself with possessions which, with the coming of the kingdom, will become valueless.[162] The only wise course is to make some use of them while they still have value, which will contribute

---

158. In my opinion Kosmala in his later paper ("Parable of the Unjust Steward in the Light of Qumran," 115–16) misuses his own insight: "Mammon is part and parcel of the world and, therefore, damnable. *For the sake of one's salvation one should not have anything to do with it.*" (Emphasis mine). But this is just where Qumran and Luke part company.

159. This view coalesces with what a number of scholars have felt instinctively, that "mammon of unrighteousness" simply denotes "worldly wealth." See Jülicher, *Gleichnisreden*, 506; Jalland, "Note on Luke 16:1–9," 504.

160. Compare 2 Bar. 44:8–12.

161. Compare Zeph 1:18. Degenhardt's suggestion that the failure of mammon could refer to the voluntary renunciation of the disciples (*Evangelist der Armen*, 123) destroys the parallel between vv. 4 and 9, and removes the crisis motif from the application.

162. I am conscious that this interpretation departs from the majority view that v. 9 has in mind the individual's death. The earliest witness to this view is the textual variant ἐκλίπητε (you fail, come to an end) Dupont, *Béatitudes*, III.118–22, argues that death is meant on the grounds that ὅταν μετασταθῶ (when I am removed) in v. 4 suits the thought of death better than the final judgment, and on the analogy of v. 9 with Luke 12:33. I have already shown with respect to Luke 12:33 that "treasure in the heavens" does not denote what is to be enjoyed in heaven after death, but the favor of God which is experienced now and in the age to come. The former argument seems to have little weight. It might be pointed out that in Luke 12:46 (compare 19:11–27) we find a steward being ejected from office where the parousia is clearly in mind. More telling is the crisis motif in the parable (ταχέως—quickly). Death is never represented as an urgent crisis in the Gospels. For further criticism of Dupont's thesis see Ernst, *Perspektiven der lukanischen Eschatologie*, 78–88, who argues that Luke has not replaced a two aeons eschatological scheme with a vertical Platonic conception.

to his position in the age to come. He should use them to make friends who will welcome him into "the eternal tents."

Again, I take exception to the majority viewpoint, that "eternal tents" is a figure for heaven.[163] Well before the Schweitzer revolution H. A. W. Meyer argued that *aiōnios* (eternal) was an unsuitable description of the state after death.[164] The chambers to which the righteous departed after death were conceived in early Jewish literature only as temporary resting places for those awaiting the new world.[165] Admittedly the early Christians had a more positive appreciation of the state of the believer after death than the Jews, but still their hope continued to be focused on the general resurrection and the revelation of Jesus Christ, not on a state of bliss after death. It was still possible for them to conceive of the state after death as a period of waiting, albeit in the presence of God.[166]

"Eternal tents" was probably not a standard eschatological term, for it is not attested elsewhere in biblical or Jewish literature.[167] It may well have been produced in relation to this particular parable. Nevertheless, the idea of the righteous inhabiting "tents" in the new age is not unattested. In Isaiah 33:20 where the Masoretic Text describes the Jerusalem of the age to come as "a tent that shall not be removed," the Septuagint has "tents which shall not be shaken."[168] Thus, it was possible to visualize the new age as a restored Jerusalem whose inhabitants dwelt in secure dwellings (tents).[169]

---

163. αἰωνίους σκηνάς. Often equated with the μοναὶ πολλαί (many rooms) of John 14:2; e.g., Friedel, "Parable of the Unjust Steward," 346.

164 Meyer, *Mark and Luke*, II.224-25.

165. See 1 En. 22; 4 Ezra 4:35-43, 7:75-101; 2 Bar. 21:23, 30:2-3; also Charles, *Pseudepigrapha*, 567, on 4 Ezra 4:35.

166. Rev 6:9-11.

167. 4 Ezra 2:11 and *Aboth* 20 are probably influenced by Luke 16:9.

168. σκηναὶ αἵ οὐ μὴ σεισθῶσιν.

169. Compare CantR 1.5.1 (Soncino 55) and MidrPs 118:14 with Ps 118:15. This disposes of the view that *skēnai* represent something impermanent, which has led some to give v. 9 an ironical meaning (McFayden, "Parable of the Unjust Steward," 535-39; Steele, "Unjust Steward"; Pautrel, "Aeterna Tabernacula," 307-27). In Acts 15:16 σκηνή (סכה) is used of the Davidic dynasty. Michaelis (*TDNT* VII.371-72) thinks אהל came to have a more stable connotation because it was used to translate משׁכן (dwelling place: the tabernacle; the words share three consonants). In any case אהל could be used as a solemn expression for "hearth and home," and "the dwelling places of a whole people are summed up as their *'ohalim*, 'tents'" (*TDOT* I.120-21).

Various other suggestions regarding the background of "eternal tents" have been made. Godet, *Luke*, 166: a glorification of Canaan of the patriarchal period; Oesterley,

In Luke 16:9 the new age is depicted in concrete terms of a new era of life upon earth, where people will live in dwellings, much as they do now.[170] The all-important thing is to be received into the fellowship of that society, to find a reception in the homes of the inhabitants of the new age.[171] The parable and its application want to say that it is possible to make such friends now by the generous use of possessions.

The parable of the rich man and Lazarus shows that in Luke's understanding this is to be achieved preeminently by acts of mercy to the poor. No doubt he would have wanted to include the actions of the many women who supported Jesus and his disciples during their mission,[172] and, by implication, the financial backers of the later Christian mission. It is unnecessary to use the parable to place any restriction on the scope of charitable activity; the antisectarian outlook of Jesus and Luke would regard any needy person as potentially an inhabitant of the age to come. Chapter 2 exposed the error in assuming that the kingdom is seen as populated primarily by the poor, so that only those who help the poor might expect to be received by them.[173] Nor should it be inferred that a restriction of almsgiving to the believing community is desired,[174] though it is easy to see how the parable might have been used with particular

---

"Parable of the Unjust Steward," 280; Ps 61:4; Meyer, *Mark and Luke*, 225; the tabernacle of the wilderness wanderings. With regard to this last suggestion Hos 12:9 (on which it is based) is not referred in rabbinic tradition to the messianic age but to the period immediately prior when the Messiah would again dwell with his people in the wilderness (*Num. Rab.* 11:2; *Cant. Rab.* 2.9.3; *Ruth Rab.* 5:6; compare Jeremias, *Parables*, 46n88). However, there is a tradition based on Isa 4:5-6 that in the age to come Israel would again dwell in tents as at the feast of Tabernacles (*Gen. Rab.* 48:10; *Num. Rab.* 14:2; compare *Midr. Ps.* 13:4; *Eccl. Rab.* 11.1.1; *Mekilta de-Rabbi Ishmael* 14:15-17; Rev 7:15-16). RuthR 3:4 envisages each person in the new age having a "canopy" (גנון).

170. Though the fact mammon is no longer valued points to a radical difference in the societies before and after the judgment.

171. This is the most natural way to take δέξωνται (they will receive) in v. 9. To make the subject "angels" or "God" (Creed, *Luke*, 205; Menoud, "Richesse injustes et biens véritable," 13) destroys the analogy with the parable; so does the idea suggested by Fiebig (see Krämer, *Parabel vom ungerechten Verwalter*, 130-31) and Williams, "Almsgiving," 295-96 that the friends are personified almsdeeds. In *Exod. Rab.* 31:2 a man's friends point out his good works before God; in 31:14 the angels do the same.

172. Luke 8:1-3.

173. The view of Hiers, "Eschatological Proletariat," 34, and F. J. Moore, "Parable of the Unjust Steward," 103-05; compare Bigo, "Richesse comme intendance."

174. Suggested by Ryrie, "Christ's Teachings on Social Ethics," 220-23.

application to the Christian community, in the service of an ethic such as is expressed in Galatians 6:10.[175]

4.5.4 Wealth of the World and Wealth of the Kingdom, Luke 16:10-12

What is not yet clear is whether verses 1-9 envisage a once and for all abandonment of all possessions to the poor, or a more controlled ongoing generosity. The note of urgency which pervades the parable suggests the former,[176] but it would be unwise to press a detail like this without further confirmatory indications; it might be meant to excite a radical reorientation towards wealth leading to an ongoing practice of charity. There are various pointers which suggest that this is more what is in Luke's mind. He is conscious of a considerable interval which has already passed without the parousia having arrived; he even gives it a theological basis.[177] He is prepared for the in-between time to continue and warns that disciples must exercise a constant and perhaps prolonged stewardship before the coming of the Lord.[178] The presence of the stewardship motif in the parable of the unjust steward suggests that a similar viewpoint may apply here.[179] This finds confirmation in the sayings which follow the unjust steward as well as in the parable of the rich man and Lazarus.

Various thought links between the parable and verses 10-12 indicate that they were not placed together haphazardly.[180] Whether we attribute this to Luke or his source, it is clear that these verses form a studied progression of thought from the parable, which Luke must have intended.

---

175. Further pages 224-25, below.

176. Luke 16:6: καθίσας τάχεως γράψον (sit down and immediately write).

177. Schneider, *Parusiegleichnisse im Lukas-Evangelium*, 95.

178. See Luke 12:35-46, 19:11-27, 21:9, 24, Acts 1:6-8; also Cadbury, *Making of Luke-Acts*, 290-96. Nevertheless, the sense of urgency over the nearness of the Parousia remains. See Cranfield, "Parable of the Unjust Judge," 297-301; Wilson, "Lukan Eschatology," 340-47.

179. Krämer, *Parabel vom ungerechten Verwalter*, 238-39 thinks Jesus called for complete renunciation (vv. 1-9), the early church for an ongoing use of goods to help poor Christian brothers (adding vv. 10-12), and that Luke took up the parable in this latter sense and added v. 13.

180. The stewardship idea, ἄδικος—ἀδικία, ἄδικος μαμωνᾶς.

Verse 10 states a general principle, and 11–12 apply it to the case of "unrighteous mammon," which is equated with "the least thing"[181] and "that which belongs to another,"[182] and contrasted with "what is your own."[183] Earthly possessions are declared to be of infinitesimal worth, and in some sense unreal. They create the illusion of security and wellbeing, but are soon to pass away. Even now, as the kingdom is proclaimed, they are being revealed as almost worthless. Nevertheless, disciples cannot escape having to deal with them. Verse 11 makes faithfulness with respect to wealth a precondition for receiving what is real.[184]

Josef Ernst understands "that which is real"[185] as "the word of truth": the ministry of the word cannot be undertaken by those who have acted unfaithfully with the community's money.[186] However, the equation of "the real" with "your own" would then be most inappropriate. Faithfulness in spiritual ministry was regarded by the early church as a testing leading to a greater reward,[187] just as the proper use of mammon is here. "The real" is better understood as "that which pertains to the kingdom" (compare 19:17), the wealth of the new age which is neither illusory nor passing.[188]

Earthly possessions are also declared to be "that which is another's" in contrast to "your own." Some think that behind this is the picture of inheritance: during his minority the son is tested with his father's

---

181. τὸ ἐλάχιστον.

182. τὸ ἀλλότριον.

183. τὸ ὑμέτερον. ἡμέτερον is read by a few mss (incl. B) but the weight of witness favors ὑμέτερον. "ἡμέτερον . . . has the appearance of being a later theological refinement (= belonging to the Father and the Son)," Metzger, *Textual Commentary*, 165.

184. The NEB captures the force of ἐγένεσθε (become): "If, then, you have not *proved* trustworthy with the wealth of this world, who will trust you with the wealth that is real?"

185. τὸ ἀληθινόν.

186. Ernst, *Lukas*, 467; following Hauck. Also, Descamps, "Composition littéraire de Luc 16:9–13," 52, who speaks of "déseschatologisation." For a critique of this view see Krämer, *Parabel vom ungerechten Verwalter*, 222–24.

187. 1 Cor 3:10–15, 4:1–5.

188. This is the only use of ἀληθινός in Luke-Acts. It probably carries the sense of "'divine' in contrast to human and earthly reality" (*TDNT* I.250) as often in John and Hebrews; it thus has an eschatological coloring. Feuillet, "Riche intendants du Christ," 41, says of its use in John that it designates "les grandes réalités permanentes et invisibles, en opposition avec celles qui passent et n'en sont que l'ébauche grossière (the great permanent and invisible realities, in opposition with those which pass and in which there is only the coarse outline)."

possessions, but when he inherits they become his own.[189] Others feel we are dealing with a stewardship motif: the steward must be faithful with that which is not his own (God's).[190] However, this makes the "that which is your own" problematical. How is the wealth of the new age any less God's than worldly mammon? Probably *to allotrion* (τὸ ἀλλότριον) signifies not "wealth which belongs to another" but "alien" wealth. In the Septuagint *allotrios* is a common equivalent of *nakar, nokri* (נכר, נכרי— strange) and describes the foreigner, "the strange woman," strange gods, etc.[191] The only other occurrence of the term in Luke-Acts is in reference to Israel's sojourn in Egypt as "in an alien (foreign) land."[192] This meaning would harmonize well with the dualistic thinking of verses 8-9. *To allotrion* is the foreign wealth[193] which belongs to this aeon, and not to the kingdom of the sons of light.[194]

4.5.5 Summary and Conclusion

We may sum up this section by saying that although, with the approaching eschatological crisis, possessions are about to become valueless—belonging as they do to the alien realm of *adikia* (i.e., to this age and not to the kingdom), they are nonetheless to be faithfully employed by the sons of light. In the framework of thought provided by 1–9, this can only mean that they are to be used in charitable acts. However, almsgiving is not simply a way of unloading possessions which might bar one's entrance to the kingdom. For Luke, possessions have a positive role, being

---

189. Thompson, *Luke*, 212, suggests this as a possibility.

190. See also *Gos. Thom.* 88 where the angels come to receive what is theirs. Also Plummer, *Luke*, 386; Marshall, *Luke: Commentary on the Greek Text*, 623-24.

191. Compare Ignatius, *Philadelphians* 3:3 (ἀλλοτρίᾳ γνώμῃ—strange doctrine); *Trallians* 6:1 (ἀλλοτρίας βοτάνης—strange plant [heresy]); *Romans, Inscription* (ἀλλοτρίου χρώματος—foreign stain)

192. Acts 7:6: ἐν γῇ ἀλλοτρίᾳ—in a foreign land.

193. ἀλλότριος also occurs occasionally in LXX with the Greek sense of "what does not truly pertain to one" (Isa 28:21; Wis 12:15; cf 1 Clem. 1:1). It is possible that this thought is also present. See Lagrange, *Luc*, 437; Bigo, "Richesse comme intendance," 269-70.

194. "Als Kinder des Lichtes haben wir kein Teil an dem was zu diesem Aeon gehört, für uns ist der Reichtum dieser Welt so fremd, wie diese Welt selber, das Unsre ist das Licht, das Reich, Das Leben (As children of light we have no part of what belongs to this Aeon, the riches of this world are so strange to us, like this world itself, ours is the light, the kingdom, the life)." Jülicher, *Gleichnisreden*, 509.

exchangeable for the currency of the new realm. In the friends who will afford a welcome into their eternal houses we have a vital clue as to how he conceives the character of the new age. It will not be a society in which value is measured in monetary terms, albeit a purified currency, as at Qumran; this form of wealth belongs to what is passing away. Value in the new age is measured in terms of relationships, and those who belong to it must begin to accumulate that sort of wealth now.

In the final saying (verse 13), which may have been brought into this location by Luke to overarch the whole of 1–12, mammon and God are depicted as two rival lords.[195] To serve both is an impossibility; the person who seeks to do so will end up hating and despising one or the other (by implication, God). Thus, disciples are warned against love of money; they must be single-minded in their adherence to God. In the present context this means using possessions to actualize the values of the kingdom by acts of humanitarian goodness in the present age. All this is applicable to the ordinary Christian, as well as to those faced with the challenge of discipleship.

Once again, we have failed to detect any ideal of poverty or renunciation ethic. What we have uncovered is a fundamental evaluation of possessions in the light of the kingdom, which will lead wise disciples to use their possessions in the service of the needy in a manner that takes the closeness of the kingdom so seriously that they begin now in this age to actualize its values and accumulate its wealth.

4.6 THE RICH AND THE POOR, LUKE 16:19–31

The parable of the rich man and Lazarus describes the opulent lifestyle of a certain rich man and the misery of a beggar named Lazarus who longed for scraps at his gate. Death brings each man into a new situation, which is described and interpreted. The difficulty lies in interpreting the interpretation. Some, focusing on verse 25, have discerned a doctrine of simple reversal: the rich are damned because they are rich, and the poor are blessed because of their poverty;[196] hence the claim that Luke has an

---

195. Greed is linked with idolatry in Jewish and Christian tradition. "Whoever turns away his eyes from charity is considered as if he were serving idols" (*B. Bat.* 10a); further, see Billerbeck IV.541n1 and Col 3:5. The rabbis understood בכל מאדך (with all thy might) in the *Shema'* as a demand to serve God with one's mammon (*b. Ber.* 61b).

196. de Wette, *Handbuch*, 100–101; Bolkestein, *Wohltätigkeit und Armenpflege*, 409.

Ebionite outlook or has made use of an Ebionite source. Others, shrinking from the apparent amorality of this, have sought to find something reprehensible in the rich man to justify his condemnation (that he did not work; his neglect of Lazarus)[197] and something correspondingly virtuous in Lazarus. A further approach has been to downgrade the significance of the first part of the parable and to find the sole point in the latter half of the story: an explanation for Jesus' refusal to grant signs,[198] or an appeal to Jews to believe in Christ.[199] It is vital for our study that we determine what precisely the parable does condemn. To do this we will first examine the parable as a whole, and then its setting in Luke 16.

4.6.1 Tradition and Redaction

In 1918 Hugo Gressmann drew attention to an Egyptian tale in which two dead men, one rich and the other poor, are seen in the afterlife (Amenti) with roles reversed. The poor man is sitting near Osiris dressed in the costly linen in which the rich man had been buried.[200] The rich man, in a different chamber, has the bolt of the door of Amenti fixed in his right eye.[201] The point of the story is that a person's good or evil deeds, not their affluence, determine their position in the afterlife. A related Jewish story is found in *p. Hag.* 2:2 (77d).[202] A poor *hasid* and a rich tax-collector die. The former is ignored in his burial except by his pious friend; the latter receives a splendid funeral. The disgruntled friend sees in a dream the positions of the two men reversed in the afterlife. The *hasid* wanders

---

197. Oesterley, *Gospel Parables*, 204. Bruce, *Parabolic Teaching of Christ*, 384–86; Bornhäuser, "Geschichte vom reichen Mann und armen Lazarus," 833–43. Smith, *Parables of the Synoptic Gospels*, 135, thinks Lazarus did not even get scraps.

198. Cadoux, *Parables of Jesus*, 123–28.

199. Evans, "Uncomfortable Words," 228–31, sees it as a comment on the Jewish mission.

200. Byssus; compare Luke 16:19.

201. Gressmann, *Vom reichen Mann und armen Lazarus*, 63–68, gives a German translation of the story of Khamuas and his son, Si-Osiris. For an English translation, see Griffith, *High Priests of Memphis*, 42–44.

202. The relatedness of the two stories is seen most clearly in the detail that in both the bolt on which the door of Hades swings was fixed, in the former in the eye, in the latter in the ear of one of the tortured victims. Gressmann thought the story travelled from Egypt to Palestine where it was adapted by the Jews. Various later versions of the story are extant. See Gressmann, *Vom reichen Mann*, 70–89.

amid streams of water in paradise,²⁰³ while the tax collector stretches out his tongue in vain to reach the water.

There is no question of literary dependence of the parable on this story, but it does appear to have been familiar to Jesus and his contemporaries; a detail from the Jewish version occurs also in the parable of the great banquet.²⁰⁴ Thus a comparison of the parable of the rich man and Lazarus with the Jewish-Egyptian story is not out of place.

The major difference which appears from such a comparison is that unlike the Egyptian and Jewish tales the parable brings the two main characters into relationship in this life.²⁰⁵ In the Jewish-Egyptian tale two men just happen to be buried on the same day; in Jesus' parable Lazarus had his accustomed place at the gate of the rich man.²⁰⁶ This is probably why the beggar is named. It is unlikely that Luke would intend his readers to draw any conclusions regarding the piety or ultimate destiny of the beggar from the etymology of his name. Lazarus is a shortened form of *Elazar* (God helps).²⁰⁷ Even less were they meant to identify him with Eliezer, Abraham's steward.²⁰⁸ *Lazaros* would then be the variant of a variant. The effect of naming him is to make him more than a "faceless" beggar; it gives him a place within the rich man's life. In contrast to the static institutionalized portrayal of the Jewish story (scholar, tax collector) and the Demotic tale (rich man, poor man), the parable presents us with a scene of relationship and dynamic interaction.

203. גנין גו פרדסין—gardens of inner paradise.

204. Luke 14:16-24; Matt 22:1-14. The tax collector's magnificent funeral is to recompense him for his one good deed: once he prepared a feast for the local dignitaries but they refused his invitation and he allowed the feast to be given to the poor.

205. See also Lorenzen, "Luke 16:19-31," 42; the same point was made by Bruce, *Parabolic Teaching of Christ*, 385, without reference to the Demotic tale. Gressmann's supposition (*Vom reichen Mann und armen Lazarus*, 50-51) that the Egyptian tale must originally have told of the poor man at the rich man's gate (hence the punishment meted out to the rich man) seems fanciful.

206. Notice the perfect ἐβέβλητο (he has been thrown) and the imperfect ἐπέλειχον (they used to lick) (v. 21).

207. אלעזר. Attempts to see Lazarus as a pious man often begin with the meaning of his name. See *RGG* I47; Jeremias, *Parables*, 185.

208. אליעזר. Suggested by Lightfoot, *Horae*, 165-66; developed by Derrett, "Dives and Lazarus," 85-92, who thinks Lazarus was sent on a mission to test the rich man's hospitality (compare Cave, "Lazarus and the Lukan Deuteronomy," 319-25.) Since, according to Derrett, Eliezer was one of the nine who entered paradise alive and was thus free to carry out such missions, it is odd that the parable should describe his death. For Eliezer in Jewish tradition see Rabinowitz, "Study of a Midrash," 143-61.

A second difference lies in the purpose of the stories. The parable is neither a revelation of the moral basis of one's standing in the afterlife, as the Demotic tale, nor a theodicy, as the Jewish stories. Rather it is a warning to the rich of the consequences of certain behavior.[209] Thus the rich man is unnamed;[210] he is a general character, though involved in a specific relationship with a certain poor man.[211] To the end he remains the main actor.

The third noteworthy difference is the end of the parable. Jeremias argues that because the first part of the story was familiar to Jesus' hearers, the emphasis must fall on the epilogue, though he does not deny the first part its point.[212] It is inevitable that verse 31 should have led some to regard 27–31 as a post-Easter addition to the parable, but there are grounds for doubting this conclusion. Bultmann adduces as background to the parable a Jewish legend in which a lad returns from hell with a description of tortures meant to produce repentance in the person to whom he is sent.[213] While I can see no close relationship between this story and the parable, it does show that a return from hell was not an unknown motif in storytelling. Christopher Evans notes that "coming from the dead" is not Christian resurrection language, but the language of folklore.[214] Perhaps verse 31 was reworded to give the parable an ironical twist in the light of the resurrection.

I see no reason, therefore, for regarding 27–31 as in any way separate from the rest of the parable. In fact, both the Demotic tale and the Jewish story have something similar. Si Osiris, it transpires, is on a mission from the underworld,[215] and in the Jewish story the scholar, having seen in a dream the condition of those in the underworld, is sent to confront Simeon b. Shetah and warn him of his fate, if he refuses to destroy the

209. Stanton, *Gospels*, II.235.

210. Conversely, in the Jewish story, which is addressed to the pious, the scholars are unnamed and the tax collector is named. The oldest ms of Luke (P^{75}) calls the rich man Νευης (Neves), but has probably been influenced by the Sahidic reading "Nineue." See Grobel, "'Whose Name was Neves," 373–82; also, Lefort, "Le nom du mauvais riche," 65–72; Cadbury, "A Proper Name for Dives," 399–402.

211. Compare Grobel, "Whose Name was Neves," 373.

212. As does Rimmer, "Parable of Dives and Lazarus," 215–16. See Jeremias, *Parables*, 186.

213. Bultmann, *History of the Synoptic Tradition*, 197. For the text and French translation, see Lévi, "Un recueil de contes juifs inédits," 76–81.

214. ἀπὸ νεκρῶν πορευθῇ (he should come). Evans, "Uncomfortable Words," 230.

215. See the Second Tale of Khamuas, 7 (Griffith, *High Priests of Memphis*, 65–66).

eighty witches living at Ashkelon. The scholar is even to perform a sign if Simeon refuses the warning. Thus, we should explore the possibility that the parable is a unified whole, keeping in mind what has been gained from comparing it with its "relations."

4.6.2 The Importance of Charity

It was a significant insight of Karl Bornhäuser which drew attention to Isaiah 58:7 in relation to the rich man's treatment of Lazarus.[216] According to this verse, behavior which pleases God is "to share your bread with the hungry, and to bring the homeless poor into your house; when you see the naked, to cover him; and not to hide yourself from your own flesh." Lazarus is all of these things, yet the rich man does nothing. He is hungry, "desiring to be filled,"[217] while the rich man is full, "enjoying himself sumptuously every day."[218] The only home of this *ptōchos* seems to be the rich man's gate, and there he remained.[219] His lack of covering could not be more horribly portrayed than with dogs coming to lick his sores, while the rich man is clothed in purple and linen. In addition to all this it is made abundantly clear in the irony of 24–25 that the two men are of the same flesh, since both call on Abraham as father.[220] Thus there can be no question of an amoral situation. The parable deals with a flagrant violation of "the law and the prophets." Moreover, it is an offence against that part of the law and the prophets which we have already had reason to suspect lay close in Luke's mind as what was required by way of repentance of those seeking the kingdom.

Once all this is seen, verse 25 can no longer be read as the basis of the reversal of fortunes in the afterlife.[221] Whatever it is, it can only be

216. Bornhäuser, "Geschichte vom reichen Mann und armen Lazarus," 835–36.
217. ἐπιθυμῶν χορτασθῆναι.
218. εὐφραινόμενος καθ' ἡμέραν λαμπρῶς.
219. ἐβέβλητο (he had been thrown).
220. Farrell, *Eschatological Perspective of Luke-Acts*, 216. Exploring the social background to the parable, Pax, "Der Reiche und der arme Lazarus," 258, makes the point that the rich man does not regard Lazarus as one of his clan, and therefore feels no responsibility towards him. In relation to this it is interesting to note that rabbinic interpretation took "not to hide yourself from your own flesh" as a reference to near relations (*b. Sheb.* 39a; *b. Ket.* 86a; compare *b. Yeb.* 62b–63a) or to a divorced wife (*Gen. Rab.* 17:3; *Lev. Rab.* 34:14).
221. Braun, *Radikalismus*, II.74–75n4, says "Der Reiche als Reicher kommt an den Ort der Qual, der Arme als Armer in Abrahams Schoss (The rich man comes as a rich

additional to the crime already established. Possibly it is designed to indicate to the rich man the appropriateness of his fate. It may indicate more. For "goods" is an idea which in Hebrew and Aramaic is used of material "good things," "profits," "pleasures," etc., but also of "good deeds," hence merits and heavenly capital.[222] Thus "you received your good things in your life" probably carries the notion that the rich man drew the whole of his capital during his lifetime, with the implication that he failed to lay up anything for himself in heaven, which he could easily have done had he acted charitably.[223] Thus, even in verse 25 there may be an implied condemnation of the rich man's lack of charity, which could have been apparent even to Greek readers with Jewish sympathies. Furthermore, the ultimate purpose of verse 25 was not to instruct the rich man, but to warn those in danger of making the same mistake. As a warning its meaning is clear: Do not hold all your capital for yourself now and be denied your consolation later;[224] invest something in the future (the kingdom). Verse 26 underlines the seriousness of this warning: there is what Otto Glombitza calls a "too late."[225]

If the above understanding of 19–26 is correct, verses 27–31 follow naturally and do not diverge to bring in any new theme.[226] The rich man's fate is sealed; there is no reprieve for him. But his story is meant as a warning to the living. His brothers are in danger of sharing his fate. Just as the anonymous scholar is sent to warn Simeon b. Shetah, the rich man asks that Lazarus be sent to warn his brothers to repent. It is important to emphasize, however, that it is not general repentance, nor repentance towards Christ, which is the issue in this parable,[227] but repentance over their neglect of the poor. The request is refused, the effect being to bring into sharp relief the role of the law and the prophets. The rich man had

---

man to the place of torment, the poor man as a poor man into Abraham's bosom)." Compare Percy, *Botschaft*, 102-03, who sees v. 25 as the condemnation of a life of riches, luxury and enjoyment, rather than a failure of brotherly love.

222. טיבותין ,טובות. See page 150n42, above. In *b Kidd.* 40b a person's טובות (goods) are his merit.

223. ἀπέλαβες τὰ ἀγαθά σου ἐν τῇ ζωῇ σου. For a similar use of this concept see Phil 4:17.

224. Compare Luke 6:24 with pages 97–98, above.

225. "Ein 'Zu spät'." Glombitza, "Reiche Mann und arme Lazarus," 166–80.

226. See also Percy, *Botschaft*, 104.

227. As Rimmer, "Dives and Lazarus," and Bartsch, *Entmythologisierende Auslegung*, 184–85, hold; also Degenhardt, *Evangelist der Armen*, 134–35, though he goes on to admit that Luke has the question of charity in mind.

clear warning during his own lifetime and so do the brothers in theirs.[228] If they ignore Moses and the prophets, they will not be convinced by a messenger from the dead; not even by the resurrection of Jesus himself, the parable adds wistfully.

4.6.3 Context and Application

We can now consider the parable in relation to its context. Luke 16:14–18 contain four elements which have often been noted for their apparent unrelatedness.[229] Some have sought with varying success to find a logical connection between them.[230] Many have noted the thought link between 19–31 and 14–15, 17.[231] In 14 the Pharisees react with mocking scorn to the parable of the unjust steward and the sayings which follow; their message, as we have seen, is that earthly possessions should be faithfully utilized for the benefit of others, particularly the poor. Jesus replies angrily to their mockery, accusing them of putting on a show before people while in the sight of God they are an abomination.[232] The parable of the rich man and Lazarus answers so well to this attack that Oesterley thought they fitted together, and that 19–31 had no relation to 16–18.[233] We may accept then that Luke saw 19–31 historically as a warning to the Pharisees. On the surface this seems strange since the Pharisees were not known for

---

228. However, the parable does not teach the rejection of the brothers (as in Johnson, "Possessions in Luke-Acts," 140–44, who thinks the brothers are the leaders of the Jews who reject the prophet Jesus), but seeks to warn them in the strongest terms.

229. Bruce, *Parabolic Teaching of Christ*, 378–79, thinks there is a natural connection between the two parables, and that 14–18 are a subsequently attracted miscellany. Bartsch, *Entmythologisierende Auslegung*, 184, argues from the disconnectedness of 14–18 and that 19–31 are free of redactional modifications.

230. Plummer, *Luke*, 388–89, thinks the argument has been so highly compressed that the connecting links have been lost. Nevertheless, he supplies a convincing outline of the argument. Compare Derrett, *Dives*, 83–55, 92–99.

231. E.g., Smith, *Parables of the Synoptic Gospels*, 141.

232. Dupont, *Béatitudes*, III.165, correctly denies that the Pharisees were seeking to pass off their wealth as proof of their righteousness, but then infers incorrectly that v. 15 has no relation to 14 and 19–31. It is rather that they sought to appear righteous by ostentatious keeping of the law, while, according to 15, their love of money exposed the true condition of their hearts. No more stinging rebuke of Pharisees can be imagined than βδέλυγμα (abomination), which puts God's loathing of their hypocrisy on a par with the defilement of idolatry. See *TDNT* I.598–600.

233. Oesterley, *Gospel Parables*, 203. Dupont, *Béatitudes*, III.167, thinks Luke composed v. 14 to introduce the parable.

their wealth and held a similar doctrine of charity to what Jesus is here espousing.[234] The accusation, however, is not that they are rich, but that they are money-lovers[235] and hypocrites. Nor is it a solitary accusation; in Luke 20:47 the scribes are accused of devouring widows' houses and making long prayers for a pretense, and in Luke 11:39 the Pharisees are accused of being inwardly full of extortion and wickedness.[236] The former of these is paralleled in Mark, the latter is a Q saying, so it cannot be argued that we are dealing here with Luke's special prejudice.

The point of verse 16 is clear enough: the Pharisaic era is over: the rule of the law and the prophets has come to an end and the kingdom is proclaimed, with the result that *all* (contrast the Pharisees) are pushing their way in. Nevertheless, the law is not nullified. The preaching of the kingdom transcends it, but does not do away with it. Its demands remain as long as the world exists (17). Verse 18 is an attack on the Pharisees' manner of ignoring the intention of the law while preserving its letter. To divorce in order to remarry differs from adultery in nothing but the bill of divorce which made it legal.[237]

It is now plain how verses 19-31 relate to 16-18. The Pharisees are warned to pay more serious heed to the Scriptures, which will turn them from love of money to an earnest and true brotherly care for their fellow Israelites.[238] Luke is not, of course, writing to Pharisees, but what was addressed to them is relevant to all who neglect the poor. The parable's application is not even to be limited to the rich. The Pharisees by and large were not rich like the main character in the parable, but the parable's strength is its description of a *relationship* which leads to perdition. Any reader, rich or otherwise, who is conscious of withholding help from a needy person is in such a relationship and will feel the sting of the parable.

Thus, the two parables in chapter 16 complement one another, the former challenging disciples to a consistent use of mammon in the face of the coming kingdom, the latter warning those who are not persuaded

---

234. Josephus, *Ant.* 17.12, though others have argued that only reasonably well-to-do people could afford to be Pharisees (Leipoldt, "Jesus und die Armen," 785; Hauck, *Arbeit und Geld*, 22-23). There are many examples of rich rabbis from later times.

235. φιλάργθροι (*philarguroi*).

236. ἁρπαγᾶς καὶ πονηρίας.

237. This position is argued with respect to Jesus' controversy with the Pharisees' easy system of divorce by Powers, *Sex and Marriage and Family Relationships*, 398.

238. See Jervell, *People of God*, 150n29.

and continue to value the things of this world more highly than the values of the new age, of the awful fate which awaits them if they do not pay heed to the law and the prophets and repent.

This raises the question of the relationship of 19–31 to the preaching of the kingdom. Does the parable "look forward to no other crisis than the hour of death," as B. T. D. Smith claims?[239] There is need for caution here, for it may not be the intention of the parable to offer any specific warning about the individual's death or the last judgment, but simply to emphasize the extreme seriousness and awful consequences of failing to act in a brotherly manner. That the medium chosen to convey this is a folktale in which a revelation of each man's state after death reveals the true state of affairs, does not necessarily imply that a parousia-centered eschatology has given way to a death-centered view.[240] The picture of the rich man in Hades and Lazarus in Abraham's bosom[241] is similar to the description in 1 Enoch 22 of the chambers in which the wicked and the righteous are to await the final judgment and the world to come.[242] Such a picture is not inconsistent with proclaiming the imminence of the kingdom. Thus, what might have been represented with the imagery of the Great Assize could as well be presented as here.[243]

A number of considerations suggest that the parable has not escaped from the framework of Luke's kingdom expectation. Luke 16:1–13 are, as we have seen, impregnated with eschatological terminology, which is best understood in relation to the coming kingdom. Verse 16 also brings the kingdom into view. The connection between verse 25 and Luke 6:24 indicates that the same eschatological view as is present in the beatitudes and woes is also operative in the parable of the rich man and Lazarus. Even more telling is the parable's demand for an Isaiah 58:7 style of repentance which we have already seen is integrally related to the coming kingdom.[244]

---

239. Smith, *Parables of the Synoptic Gospels*, 139.

240. As Dupont, *Béatitudes*, III.111–12, 173–75 argues.

241. Some think this expression means table fellowship with Abraham, hence the messianic age (compare Matt 8:11), but more probably it pictures Lazarus being comforted in Abraham's lap as a child with its mother (compare Num 11:12 and see Haupt, "Abraham's Bosom," 162–67; Zahn, *Lucas*, 586–87n16; Billerbeck II.225–27), which is hardly a picture of the new age.

242. See Grensted, "Use of Enoch in St Luke 16:19–31," 333–34, and Standen, "Parable of Dives and Lazarus and Enoch 22," 523.

243. See Matt 25:31–46.

244. Pages 51–53, above.

Once again, we have failed to find poverty ideal, renunciation ethic, or reversal doctrine. Nevertheless, we are clearly dealing with an extremely far-reaching demand for charity to the needy, which could have afforded little comfort to any of Luke's well-off readers. Luke is saying in no uncertain terms that the kingdom is forever closed to those who close their hearts against the needy. The reappearance here of the ethical pattern of Isaiah 58:7 suggests that this is more than incidental to his theological and ethical thinking. We are now in a position to explore this further.

4.7 ALMSGIVING AND CHARITY

The importance of almsgiving and practical charity in Judaism cannot be overemphasized. "Simeon the Just . . . used to say: By three things is the world sustained: by the law, by the (temple-) service, and by deeds of loving-kindness."[245] Almsgiving and charitable works gained one a treasure in heaven, i.e., the favor of God, in this world and in the world to come.[246]

The influence of this thought-system on Luke has been widely recognized. Surprisingly little attention, however, has been given to the specifically Christian element in his teaching on charity. Of course, it is generally assumed that he takes his high appreciation of the importance of love from Jesus and the early Christian movement, and it is often noted that he emphasizes the practical person-to-person dimension of this love. All this is true. What is lacking is a consideration of where charity fits into his wider theological thinking and how it relates to his eschatological understanding.[247] It will be the purpose of this section to bring together

---

245. *Aboth* 1:2.

246. Luke uses ἐλεημοσύνη in the sense of "alms" (מצות—meritorious acts; צדקה—righteousness), but also more widely probably to include the traditional גמילות חסדים (deeds of kindness: visiting the sick, housing strangers, etc.). See page 190n265, below; also Billerbeck IV.536.

247. In the major studies of the love theme this century Moffat, *Love in the New Testament*, gives three pages (187–89) to the eschatological dimensions of Paul's teaching on love; Warnach, *Agape: Die Liebe als Grundmotiv der neutestamentliche Theologie*, has a more general discussion in which he develops the idea of love as "das erste Motiv und das letzte Ziel des grossen Weltdramas (the initial motive and the final goal of the great world-drama," 435–43; Spicq, *Agape dans le Nouveau Testament*, I.98–155, discusses charity in Luke but does not touch on its relationship to eschatology; similarly Furnish, *The Love Command in the New Testament*, 84–90, though he presents some valuable insights in this area with respect to the teaching of Jesus (68–69).

and to develop some of the insights already gained, which are relevant to these questions.

In chapter 2 we examined the fusion of Isaiah 58:6 with Isaiah 61:1–2 in Luke 4:18–19 and saw that Luke was able to view the ethical demands of Isaiah 58 as equally descriptions of what God would do to save his people in the coming kingdom. On the other hand, the preaching of the Baptist showed that he also saw them as ethical requirements of those seeking to enter the kingdom. I suggested that we might be looking at an ethic of anticipatory realization of kingdom conditions: behavior is to mirror and anticipate the believer's expectation of salvation. If salvation means God will put an end to the oppression of his people (Luke 4:18–19), his people must cease to oppress one another (3:12–14); if it means an end to hunger and want (6:20–21), his people will share what they have now with the hungry and naked (3:1). The rich man of Luke 16:19–31 is forever excluded from the kingdom,[248] because he allows the continuance of a pattern of relationship between himself and Lazarus which is contrary to what the kingdom promises; he fails to act in an Isaiah 58:7 manner.

I would suggest, therefore, that if Isaiah 61:1–2 is seen as the focal point of Luke's understanding of Jesus' proclamation of the kingdom, the focus of his charity ethics is Isaiah 58:6–7.

This pattern of anticipatory realization is to be seen elsewhere in Luke. Walter Grundmann connects Jesus' demand for mercy in Luke 6:36 with Isaiah 58 and 61 in a similar manner to what I am suggesting.[249] Perhaps the petition "forgive us our sins, for we ourselves forgive everyone who is indebted to us" in the course of a prayer for the coming of the kingdom also reflects such an ethical pattern; the reconciliation which the kingdom promises is to be practiced among those who wait for it.[250] The juxtaposition of the parable of the great banquet, with the demand to invite the poor to your feasts, invites a similar understanding: God invites the poor to his banquet, so his children will do likewise.[251]

For Luke repentance means beginning to act in an Isaiah 58:6–7 manner. The fruit of repentance is the restoration of true brotherhood:

---

248. παράκλησις (comfort) indicates we are dealing ultimately with the kingdom.
249. Grundmann, "Bergpredigt nach der Lukasfassung," 186–87.
250. Luke 11:4.
251. Luke 14:16–24 and 12–14.

the end of oppression and extortion and radical openness to one's neighbor.[252] My neighbor is anyone I am in a position to help.[253] No doubt Luke understands the fruit-bearing which, according to the parable of the sower, is the true response to the word of God, in the same manner.[254]

It might be objected at this point that the command to feed the hungry and clothe the poor is an essential component of Jewish piety.[255] This is true, and Luke himself makes it clear that such behavior is no more than what is demanded by Moses and the prophets.[256] Nevertheless, for him it is more than simply "a sign of true adherence to the law."[257] It is appropriate "kingdom behavior," anticipating the arrival of the age to come and producing a foretaste of it now. It is not simply a way to accumulate merit, but is a living of the very life of the kingdom.[258] For in Jesus the powers of the age to come are already invading the present order. There is thus an earnestness and radicalness about the demand for charity in Luke which is not found in Jewish piety.[259] The tension between law and kingdom in Luke is similar to what is expressed in 1 John 2:7-8: love is an old commandment, but it is new "in him and in you, because the darkness is passing away and the true light is already shining."

Related to this is the emphasis on *reality* in Luke's ethical teaching. Charity must not be token or formal; it must flow from the heart. Jesus' attack on the Pharisees is leveled at their hypocrisy: they appear to be what they are not. Their scruples in tithing, and presumably almsgiving, do not reflect real brotherliness. Inwardly they are greedy and grasping,

---

252. Luke 3:8, 12-14, 19:1-10, 3:10-11, 16:19-31.

253. Luke 10:29-37.

254. Luke 8:15. Compare Luke 13:6-9, 20:10. In Isa 5:7 God seeks the fruit of משפט and צדקה (*mishpat* and *tsedakah*—justice and righteousness) but only finds משפח and צעקה (*mishpaḥ* and *tseʿakah*—bloodshed and a cry of distress).

255. See also Sahlin, "Früchte der Umkehr," 57. See Job 31:16-23; Ezek 18:7; Tob 1:16-17 4:16; 2 En. 9:1, 10:5, 42:7-9; 63:1. It is noteworthy that Job 31:16-23 and Ezek 18:7 are hardly mentioned in rabbinic literature; Isa 58:7 is frequently met.

256. Luke 10:26-28, 16:29.

257. Jervell, *People of God*, 140.

258. Moltmann, *Theology of Hope*, 121, says on the relationship of law and promise: "The commandments of the covenant, which point our hopes in the promise to the path of physical obedience, are nothing else but the ethical reverse of the promise itself. The promised life here applies as the life that is commanded."

259. Luke 3:11. Isa 58:7 has lost its eschatological flavor in rabbinic writings. In *B. Bat.* 9b and *Lev. Rab.* 34:11 Isa 58:8-9 is taken as a series of blessings which will fall upon the individual who gives the highest amount of money to a poor man.

and Jesus does not shrink from accusing them of outward acts of injustice and inhumanity.[260]

Comparison of Luke 11:39-41 and Matthew 23:25-6 is instructive. Luke has this saying in the course of a meal with a Pharisee. It is sparked by the Pharisee's amazement that Jesus did not wash before dinner. Jesus retorts—and here the Matthaean form of the saying is probably closer to the original—that while they are meticulous about cleansing the outside of vessels, the contents are rapaciousness and wickedness. This has frequently been taken to mean that the contents of their dishes have been gained by fraudulent means. More likely the cup and dish were meant as a picture of the Pharisee himself. He pays close attention to matters of external cleanliness but inside is full of wickedness.[261] This is clearly how Luke understands it,[262] for he fuses interpretation with the parable: "the outside of the cup and dish you cleanse, but the inside *of you* is full of robbery and wickedness."[263] Verse 41, then, cannot mean, as Degenhardt suggests, that they should give away the contents of their bowls to the poor.[264] It must mean something like, "Bring forth acts of mercy from your inward being and then you will be truly clean."[265] It thus forms a complement to Mark 7:20-23, where Jesus argues that defilement does not result from external contamination but flows from the heart.

Thus, the fruit of repentance, the lifestyle which is commensurate with the kingdom, means for Luke a return to real brotherhood, a compassionate generosity which flows from the center of a person's being towards all those whom he is in any position to help.

---

260. Matt 6:2-4; Luke 18:9-12. The accusation that they "devour the houses of widows" (Luke 20:47) is particularly stinging, since traditionally it was orphans and widows who were to be preeminently the objects of charity.

261. Compare Matt 23:27-28.

262. Leaney, *Luke*, 193.

263. τὸ ἔξωθεν τοῦ ποτηρίου καὶ τοῦ πίνακος καθαρίζετε, τὸ δὲ ἔσωθεν ὑμῶν γέμει ἁρπαγῆς καὶ πονηρίας.

264. Degenhardt, *Evangelist der Armen*, 57-59. He thinks the ὑμῶν (your) of v. 39 belongs with ἁρπαγῆς καὶ πονηρίας (robbery and evil).

265. This will be the meaning Luke intends whether or not he has mistranslated his source, as Wellhausen, *Lucae*, 61, suggests. Jervell, *People of God*, 140, thinks he has done so deliberately. ἐλεημοσύνη is wider than "alms" suggests. In LXX it renders חסד, צדקה, etc. as "benevolent activity," a better equivalent, though it can also have the technical meaning of "alms" for the poor. See *TDNT* II.485-87, and compare Acts 9:36.

The next important feature of Luke's concept of charity is that it has a positive function with respect to the kingdom. Money will have no value in the coming kingdom, and, since the kingdom has now been proclaimed, in a sense mammon has already lost its worth. The only sensible thing to do with it now is to convert it into something which will retain value beyond the changing of the aeons, namely the values of brotherhood and friendship.

Alternatively, one can speak, as in Judaism, of stockpiling treasure in heaven. However, there is a considerable difference between the way Luke and Judaism approached this. For the rabbis (Pharisees?) almsgiving was token and formal.[266] Whatever one gave to a poor person, be it the tiniest amount, was counted as a meritorious deed[267] and was accounted to their heavenly credit balance. Luke on the other hand demands total compassionate engagement with the poor man leading to unlimited generosity.[268] The parable of the rich man and Lazarus speaks to anyone who is in a position to help a needy person and warns them not to turn away. The degree to which help should be given is dictated by the need, and will even go further.[269]

In Luke's mind there is probably something demonstrative about this kind of charity. It is costly, and really only a possibility for those who have relinquished the present aeon in favor of the kingdom.[270] By going outside the conventional limits of the circle of friends, and those who might be expected to be able to repay in kind, it declares the reality of the kingdom and marks out those who are truly the "sons of the Most High."[271]

---

266. See *B. Bat.* 9b.

267. מצוה (*mitzvah*).

268. In Luke 21:1–4 a woman is highly praised for contributing a tiny amount to the temple treasury, but it is all she has and represents a real and total engagement with God.

269. Luke 10:35, 6:29.

270. Luke 6:20–36, 12:32–34.

271. Luke 6:30–36, 14:12–14. Note with respect to Luke 6:34–35 that such lending was regarded as more meritorious than simple almsgiving, being a way of giving without humiliating the recipient (*b. Shab.* 63a). Luke 6:36 sees God as preeminently οἰκτιρμῶν (compassionate) (compare Matt 5:48—τέλειος—perfect). In LXX God is frequently described as οἰκτιρμῶν καὶ ἐλεήμων (= רחום וחנון—compassionate and merciful—Exod 34:6).

4.8 THE LITERALLY POOR

Considering Luke's common reputation as a champion of the cause of the poor and underprivileged, there is very little in the Gospel and Acts which relates to the actual poor. As we have seen, outside the few passages where it characterizes "poor" Israel, *ptōchoi* denotes those who have insufficient resources to live without charitable assistance of some kind.[272] Even when we widen our vision somewhat to include traditional needy people such as widows, we still find only a few stories in the Gospel which involve folk who might be deemed economically deprived. Luke has probably added the story of the healing of the widow of Nain's son to counterbalance the healing of the centurion's servant, thus producing a clear expression of the all-embracing character of Jesus' mission. A greater contrast could hardly be imagined than the inevitably wealthy gentile centurion and the traditionally poor widow, deprived of her only son and last means of support.[273] Luke also records Mark's story of blind Bartimaeus, though, as we have seen, he overshadows it with the story of Zacchaeus.[274] Otherwise, in the Gospel we have only the traditional story of the poor widow.[275] The figure of Lazarus in Luke 16:19–31 is really only a backdrop to the story about the rich man. We could perhaps include the many sick people to whom Jesus ministered, but Luke does not concern himself with their economic circumstances, and in most cases there is no cause for us to think they existed socially necessarily among the lower strata of society.[276]

Luke gives more attention to Jesus' contacts with people of adequate to quite substantial means. We think of the fishermen, the centurion, Jairus, Mary and Martha, and the women—like the wife of Herod's steward—who provided for Jesus and his disciples.[277] His favorites are the tax collectors and sinners,[278] though not because there was anything particularly winsome about them, as we have seen,[279] but because they were the

272. Pages 32, above.
273. Luke 7:2–17.
274. Luke 18:35–19:10.
275. Luke 21:1–4.
276. The lepers and the Gerasene demoniac did, but this has nothing to do with their healing.
277. Luke 5:2–11, 7:2–10, 8:41–48, 10:38–42, 8:3.
278. Luke 3:12, 5:27–32, 7:29, 15:1–32, 19:1–10.
279. Page 138n218, above.

most unlikely people to have responded to Jesus, and for that reason most perfectly manifested the grace of God. It is not impossible that they may also have had something in common with Luke and his readers, if, as seems likely, they included within their ranks hellenized, cultured, cosmopolitan Jews who had ceased to make any real effort to keep the law.

The social milieu reflected incidentally in Jesus' teaching is consistent with this rather "middle-class" impression.[280] Examples range from the woman with a house, and savings amounting to ten drachmas, the man with one hundred sheep, the steward who will be in difficulties if he loses his job, even the farmer with a slave ploughing or keeping his sheep, to the wealthy landowner.[281] Parables dealing with rich people should probably not be pressed for social conclusions, since, when they are not negative, as the rich man who neglected Lazarus, they often portray God or the Son of Man.[282] On the other hand, there is nothing in the *teaching* in the third Gospel which could be said to reflect the milieu of the very poor. It depicts ordinary people of average to comfortable means doing ordinary things like planting and husbanding, doing business, preparing meals, entertaining friends, traveling, conducting lawsuits, and sleeping in their well-stocked houses.[283] More telling even than this is the cameo of life prior to the judgment of the land: one on the housetop with his goods in the house, another at work in the field, two together in bed, and two grinding meal.[284]

Thus, it is clear that the common picture of Luke and Jesus as champions of the dispossessed "proletariat" is nowhere near the truth. Nevertheless, it would be a mistake to conclude that Luke had no interest in the poor. He insists that the disciples have a practical compassionate concern for anyone in need. This is not only congruent with his portrayal of Jesus, who "went around doing good," but probably also reflects his

---

280. It is dangerous to use such terms of the NT period, for they can hardly correspond to their counterparts in an industrialized society. By using the term here, I would intend all those who were capable of supporting themselves without recourse to begging and other forms of charity. Where one would begin to speak of the upper class is more difficult. The priestly aristocracy and the Roman elite would be included, but for the rest the question would be complicated by religious considerations.

281. Luke 15:8-9 (note 15:3: τίς ἄνθρωπος ἐξ ὑμῶν—which one of you), 16:1-9 (note 17:7: τίς δὲ ἐξ ὑμῶν—who of you); 15:11-24.

282. Luke 7:41-43, 12:35-40, 14:16-24, 15:11-24, 20:9-18.

283. Further see McCormick, *Social and Economic Background of Luke*; Kilpatrick, "What John Tells Us about John," 75-77.

284. Luke 17:31-37.

understanding of salvation as the rescue of "poor" Israel. What God is to "poor" Israel the Israelite should be to his poor neighbor. The significance of the poor, maimed, lame, and blind in the parable of the banquet is that none are excluded from the kingdom except those who exclude themselves.[285] They are the most unlikely folk one would have thought to invite to such a feast.[286] Thus, in a sense, they function as a symbol of the needy in Israel—or even of needy humanity, if the trip to the highways and hedges is thought to have the gentiles in mind. It is appropriate, therefore, that disciples who have themselves experienced this grace towards their own "poverty" should extend their generosity towards those literally poor, maimed, lame, and blind.[287] The story of the rich man and Lazarus shows how seriously Luke regarded this. It is totally in accord with this picture that in Acts we find the Christians seeking to meet the needs of the poor in their community. Nevertheless, as in the Gospel, the focus of attention is not the poor themselves, but those who are ministering to them.[288]

4.9 STEWARDSHIP OF POSSESSIONS

The steward, familiar to us from some of Luke's parables, is the servant or slave entrusted with the oversight of his master's household, property or possessions.[289] According to Cadbury, it is particularly from Luke that modern ideas about the stewardship of wealth derive.[290] It will be useful, therefore, to examine to what extent Luke does have a concept of stewardship of possessions and to explore its implications.

We have already seen that what is often regarded as one of the clearest expressions of a doctrine of stewardship of possessions has quite a

---

285. Luke 14:16-24; Caird, *Luke*, 177.

286. The shepherds in the story of Jesus' birth probably foreshadow this pattern of thinking. According to rabbinic sources they were dishonest and disreputable (*Baba Qamma* 10:9; *M. Kidd.* 4:14; *b. Sanh.* 25b; *Midr. Ps.* 23:2; further see Billerbeck II.113-14). Thus, they are the last people one would have thought worthy to witness the birth of the Messiah and hear the angelic proclamation. Nevertheless, they do, standing as representatives of the *laos* (2:10) and all those of God's good pleasure (2:14).

287. Luke 14:12-14.

288. Acts 6:1-6; 9:36-41.

289. See Philo, *Prob.* 35 for a good description of the steward (ἐπίτροπος); also Judge, *Social Patterns of Christian Groups*, 30-39.

290. Cadbury, *Making of Luke-Acts*, 260.

different meaning.[291] The parable of the unjust steward represents a steward-master relationship, but its point (if one may allegorize to this extent) is that man's unfaithful stewarding of God's world has brought us to the point where God is about *to take our stewardship away*.[292] The desperate measures of his last hours in office hardly lay the foundation for a general doctrine of stewardship, especially when it is recalled that within the terms of the parable the steward's action is *against* his master. Nevertheless, the extension and application of the parable in verses 10–12 does imply a stewardship of money. God will only entrust someone with "the true" (wealth) who first shows themselves faithful in unrighteous mammon: this implies that possessions have been entrusted by God, and he expects the recipients to exercise a faithful stewardship.[293] In this context this means action like that of the steward in the parable, so indirectly the parable does have a bearing on Luke's stewardship concept.

The parable of the pounds also represents what amounts to a master-steward parable.[294] Ten slaves are each given a *mina*[295] and commanded to do business in the period of their master's absence. One of the difficulties in interpreting this parable is to determine the significance of the *minas*. Just because the parable has to do with trading does not mean that its application is to money. Most commentators interpret them as spiritual gifts of some kind: "the gifts of the Holy Ghost,"[296] the grace of God,[297] "the word of the kingdom."[298]

In the light of the similarity of the temporal outlook of this parable with Acts 1:6–8, these suggestions are not without force. However, it should be kept in mind that Luke has not limited this parable to the apostolic band, but imagines Jesus addressing all those who followed him. Flender, therefore, warns against an over-spiritual view of the parable:

---

291. Luke 16:12. See page 177, above.

292. Kamlah, "Parable der ungerechten Verwalter," unneccesarily limits stewardship to Israel's spiritual aristocracy. A wider concept is not unknown in first-century Judaism (see Philo, *Cher.* 107-119, *Spec. Laws* 1:295; *Aboth* 3:7; compare Wis 9:1–4).

293. Luke 16:13 has similar implications; God is to be the house-slave's (οἰκέτης) sole master, and money is to be strictly subordinate.

294. Luke 19:11–27.

295. Μνᾶ (*mna*).

296. Swete, *Parables of the Kingdom*, 140.

297. Oesterley, *Gospel Parables*, 146, 148; Godet, *Luke*, II.221-23.

298. Bruce, *Parabolic Teaching of Christ*, 221–22.

> In Luke 19:13 the work demanded of the disciples could easily be equated with missionary service. But as I see it, it means primarily action in the world . . . Luke wishes to emphasize the importance of secular activity.[299]

The echo of Luke 16:10-11 in 19:17 suggests that stewardship of possessions was not altogether absent from Luke's mind. Neither his use of "the least thing,"[300] nor the modest sums given in trust,[301] suggest that he was thinking primarily of spiritual graces, or the Holy Spirit, or the word of God.

A sounder approach, however, is to recognize that the parable is not concerned with the exact allegorical equivalent of the *minas* (or Luke would give us some indication of their meaning), but rather depicts the character of the relationship of servant to his master in the period of the latter's absence. Luke gives no indication that he regards the *minas* as a test.[302] The master is more interested in his money than the servants. To each he has given a small but tradable sum and commands them to do business in his absence. On returning he wants to know what each has earned. It is often argued that the final detailed interchange between the master and the third servant is the sole point of the parable. However, the fact that the first two servants are singled out from a field of ten, and their performances and rewards described in detail, shows that Luke was also concerned about the activities of the faithful servants. Thus verse 17 is a key interpretative comment applied explicitly to the first servant, but also implicitly to the second: the master rewards faithfulness in little things with great honor and responsibility.

The third slave is given special attention not because he is the point of the parable, but because the judgment passed on him is so unexpected.

---

299. Flender, *Theologian of Redemptive History*, 77.

300. ἐλαχίστῳ "Reichtum ist die allerkleinste Gabe, den Gott einem Menschen geben kann (Wealth is the smallest of all gifts which God can give to a person)." Luther, quoted by Uhlhorn, "Christenthum und das Geld," 142.

301. The *mina* was worth about 1/60 of a talent. However, it was not, as Creed, *Luke*, 233, suggests, "a trifling sum." The modern monetary equivalents normally given are quite misleading. An idea of the purchasing power of the mina (= 100 denarii) can be gained from considering that an average parcel of land might cost 120 denarii (Jeremias, *Jerusalem*, 140). Judas's thirty pieces of silver probably amounted to 120 denarii, with which it was possible to buy a field. Thus, it is clear that the servants were given modest but tradable sums.

302. As is suggested by Smith, *Parables*, 164, and others. Luke draws no attention to the equality of the sums trusted; this is incidental to the parable.

Triumphantly (though perhaps a little defensively), he declares that he has kept his master's *mina* safe.³⁰³ The others may have made greater gains but he has caused his master no loss. In the ensuing conversation the third servant effectively condemns himself. As excuse for his inactivity he says he was afraid because he knew his master to be "a severe man," who would not take kindly to loss.³⁰⁴ This, no doubt, is the aspect of his severity which inspired fear, but the servant spills over into a further description (probably a standard description of the *austēros* [αὐστηρός] man) which majors on his exacting character; he takes up more than he puts down, and reaps what he has not sown.³⁰⁵ Having said this the servant has condemned himself, for it should have frightened him not into inactivity, but into the most strenuous efforts.

The effect of this conversation is striking, for it emphasizes the character of the master as one who demands profit. The slave is not condemned for laziness, faithlessness, or for his insolence. He knew his master's character, yet failed to bring him a profit. This seemingly leads to such an offensive application that some have sought to tone it down. R. Winterbotham can only see Archelaus in the "austere" man, and recoils from any application of this thought to Jesus.³⁰⁶ Jacques Ellul uses the parable to establish the principle that God becomes for a person what his concept of him is.³⁰⁷ B. T. D. Smith dismisses the slave's description of his master as slander.³⁰⁸ However, the repetition makes it difficult to avoid applying it to Jesus. In fact, it is the attention-catching twist in the parable, underlined by the form of judgment passed: his *mina* is taken from him and given to the servant who has shown himself best able to make a profit—all this despite the protest of the onlookers.

The cases of the three servants establish a pattern of relationship, applicable to Jesus' disciples in his absence. They are to work for him as for

---

303. On the basis of the references cited by Billerbeck I.971–72 to the effect that burial of money was expected of a conscientious trustee, some scholars (e.g., Kamlah, "Parabel von den anvertauten Geldern," 31), comparing the parables in Luke and Matt, think Luke deliberately portrayed the slave as irresponsible. The parable, however, does not suggest this. Having the money wrapped in a napkin does not mean he necessarily carried it on his person, nor that it was not well concealed. Matthew may have introduced the idea of burial, consonant with his much larger sum.

304. ἄνθρωπος αὐστηρός. Compare 2 Macc 14:30.

305. See Plummer, *Luke*, 441; Brightman, "S. Luke 19:21," 158; Philo, *Hypoth*. 7:6.

306. Winterbotham, "Christ or Archelaus?" 338–47.

307. Ellul, "Les talents," 134–36.

308. Smith, *Parables*, 166.

a severe master who demands a high return for all that he has entrusted to them. They are also to realize that he is lavish in his rewards for those who serve him well. Once seen in this light, it becomes clear that nothing can be excepted from the stewardship relationship. Whatever the disciple may regard as being a trust from his Lord—and for Luke this includes possessions—he must diligently employ for a maximum return.[309] Thus the parable is probably deliberately vague as to the meaning of the *minas*. The question is not "What does the *mina* represent?" but "What may the disciple regard as a tradable trust from his Lord?"[310]

At this point we should note the eschatological framework of the parable. If it is true that Luke has here fused together two different parables, it is more accurate to say that he has blended the parable of the *minas* with that of the nobleman than vice versa, for it is the latter which is integral to the structure of his narrative. The story of the nobleman establishes Luke's theological understanding of the time in which he lived and wrote.[311] Contrary to the expectation of some, Jesus did not expect that the kingdom would be manifested on his arrival at Jerusalem.[312] There was to be a period of uncertainty in which the rule of the Messiah would be ratified before he came to settle accounts with servants and enemies.[313] This age was to be a period of diligent and faithful activity on the

---

309. It is usual to interpret Luke 12:41-48 in terms of spiritual ministry, but it is not at all clear that Luke would have been happy with such a restriction. Peter inquires whether the parable is intended for the apostles only, and is given an open-ended answer: the steward is the one who is doing the job when his master returns; it is a question of how much has been entrusted to him which is of importance. He is a steward to the extent that he has had something committed to him. Vv. 42, 45 lend themselves to an ecclesiastical interpretation, but the ministering of material possessions, whether for the church or privately, need not be excluded. It is even suggested by the proximity to vv. 13-34.

310. Compare Luke 10:29-37, where the question "Who is my neighbor?" is transformed into "To whom am I prepared to be a neighbor?"

311. Though he should not be credited with the invention of the parable. The outlook of the stewardship parable in Luke 12:42-48 is similar. Zerwick, "Parabel vom Thronanwärter," 654-74, argues convincingly that no one in the later church would have invented a story which likened Jesus to Archelaus.

312. ἡ βασιλεία τοῦ θεοῦ ἀναφαίνεσθαι (the kingdom of God to appear) refers to the final ἀποκατάστασις (restoration) of Israel; compare 1 En. 10:16–11:2 (Greek) with the note in Charles, *Pseudepigrapha*, 194.

313. There is nothing in the parable itself which justifies speaking of a delay of the parousia. Luke makes no mention of the nobleman being delayed, nor of any length of time (compare Matt 25:19) though εἰς χώραν μακράν (to a far country) suggests that he might remain away for some time. "Le thème n'est d'ailleurs de retard de la

part of disciples, which would issue in the manifestation of the Messiah's rule and the bestowal of great rewards for services rendered and profits gained. Insofar as possessions are concerned, the kind of profits which Luke would count as such are described in Luke 16:9.

4.10 CONCLUSIONS

This chapter has ranged over a wide variety of material. All of it presupposes people with possessions, or with problems over possessions. Little of it could be said to be very relevant to folk with nothing. We have not found an ideal of poverty, nor any call for ascetic renunciation of possessions. Nevertheless, Luke's attitude towards possessions can hardly be called positive; they exercise too great a power over people, binding them to this age and preventing them from embracing the promised kingdom. For all this, he does not treat possessions as evil in themselves, nor inveigh against them in an ascetic manner. Instead, he recognizes that disciples must live in and make use of the world. The important thing is that they live as children of the kingdom, behaving now in a manner which reflects the contours of their final hope. This will mean employing possessions in a total and unreserved manner to help the needy and create structures and relationships which embody the values and anticipate the blessings of the new age, and which can therefore be commended to God as "profit."

The following are some of the more important individual conclusions:

a. Jesus' message about the kingdom has given Luke a revolutionary outlook on possessions. They are of infinitesimal value in comparison with the riches of the kingdom and, with the approaching eschatological crisis, they are about to lose even the little value they still have.

b. Stockpiling of possessions is to be assiduously avoided both because it will keep one from finding real life in Jesus, and because all greedy people will be destroyed in the coming judgment.

---

parousie, mais la nécessité pour le Christ de s'éloigner avant de venir de juger (The theme is not as elsewhere the delay of the parousia, but the necessity for the Christ to go away before his coming to judge)." Lagrange, *Luc*, 491. Perhaps ἐν τῷ ἐρχομένῳ (while he is coming) of v. 13 has been influenced by parousia language. If so it suggests the imminence of the coming of the Son of Man.

c. Disciples' anxieties about sustenance and clothing are recognized. They should not let such fears keep them from confessing Christ and seeking his kingdom. God is pledged to providing them richly with what they need, so they should trust to his fatherly care and live lives of outgoing carefree generosity.

d. Although disciples are to be ready for the return of Jesus at any time, Luke does not expect him to return immediately. A period exists in which they are to be active and hardworking in serving and representing their Lord. This includes using possessions "profitably."

e. The values of the new age are not monetary but social. Disciples should use their money to help those in need and hence to create a fellowship which will extend into the age to come.

f. Acts of charity which flow from the heart and which break with convention in their magnitude and scope declare the reality of the kingdom in disciples' lives and actualize its values and powers in the world.

g. As God stands to the needy world with the gracious gift of salvation, so the disciple should stand to the poor of society in generous open-handedness.

h. Those who with an eye to the eschatological situation wisely employ their possessions in acts of mercy will be richly rewarded both here and in the age to come. Those who neglect the needy face the prospect of inevitable judgment.

From this it is very apparent that Luke's ethical thinking has been conditioned in a thoroughgoing manner by his belief in the kingdom. It is not true to say that he is not influenced by the expectation of an imminent end, nor to say that he expects the end at any moment and is therefore unconcerned in his ethics about anything but the immediate future. A truer appraisal of his stance would be to say that he is captivated by the kingdom as a *reality* which conditions all human values and activities. For Luke, discipleship means unreserved attachment to Jesus in hope of the coming kingdom; the Christian life means living now with that kingdom as the ultimate value and goal of one's life.

Chapter 5

Fellowship and the Church

5.1 INTRODUCTION

A GREAT DEAL HAS been written on the nature of the community life of the first church in Jerusalem. Luke's descriptions of its sharing of possessions have understandably been the subject of debate since the rise of socialism in the nineteenth century and have gained new impetus with the increased understanding of Essene communalism gained with the publication of the Dead Sea Scrolls. Little attention, however, has been given to the function of Luke's description of the life of the community in the overall purpose of Luke-Acts.

The main concern of this chapter will be to examine Luke's descriptions of the common life of the Jerusalem church in relation to his purpose in Luke-Acts. I will look first at some of the sharing motifs and show that Luke is not describing a formal community of possessions but commending the church to Hellenistic readers for whom such motifs were familiar. Second, the story of Ananias and Sapphira will be seen to lie within the framework of the "summaries" of the life of the early church and to be an expansion of a "fear" motif, and not, therefore, directly relevant to the question of possessions. Thirdly, I will digress to establish the significance of Luke's concern with the Jerusalem church, and then show how the motifs already considered relate to this. Finally, I will explore the possible connections between the third Gospel and Acts, and indicate what I think to be the ethical import of Luke's description of the church in Acts.

5.2 KOINŌNIA AND FRIENDSHIP, ACTS 2:42-47; 4:32-37

There will be occasion later to make a comparison of Luke's two descriptions of the common life of the Jerusalem church. For the moment we will direct our attention to the parallel statements in Acts 2:44 and 4:32: "they had everything common"[1] and "there was with them everything common."[2]

Various scholars have seen here the influence of a proverbial Greek saying about friendship: "*koina ta tōn philōn* (common are the things of friends)."[3] Haenchen draws particular attention to Aristotle's *Nicomachean Ethics* (9:8, 1168b) where a number of friendship proverbs are grouped together: "one soul" and "common the things of friends" and "friendship is equality" and "the knee is near the leg."[4] The first and second of these are reflected in Acts 4:32, though they are so widely spread through Greek literature that it is hardly necessary to think Luke's readers would have thought specifically of Aristotle (also "nothing one's own").[5]

1. εἶχον ἅπαντα κοινά (they had everything common—*hapanta koina*).

2. ἦν αὐτοῖς ἅπαντα κοινά.

3. κοινὰ τὰ (τῶν) φίλων. Preuschen, *Apostelgeschichte*, 27; *TDNT* II.794, 796; Cerfaux, "La première communauté chrétienne," 5–31; Haenchen, *Acts*, 231–33; Degenhardt, *Evangelist der Armen*, 171; Dupont, "Communauté des biens," 503–19; Mealand, "Utopian Allusions," 96–99. The saying is attributed to Pythagoras (*Diogenes Laertius* 8:19). Iamblichus's description of Pythagoras's views on common life (30:167–68) contain so many phrases reminiscent of Luke's summaries that von Schubert, *Kommunismus der Wiedertäufer in Münster*, 35–37, postulates Luke's dependence on Iamblichus's source (Timaeus, born 350 BC). Influence from Neopythagorean quarters on Luke (and the Essenes) is not impossible; the movement had its high point in the first and second centuries AD (*RGG* IV 1432–33; *ERE* IX.319–21; Chadwick, "Philo and the Beginnings of Christian Thought," 141). However, in the light of radical differences in ethos and practice between Christianity and Neopythagoreanism, the influence was more likely indirect, being mediated by Hellenistic culture which took up much of this terminology to its own end.

4. "μία ψυχή" καὶ "κοινὰ τῶν φίλων" καὶ "ἰσότης φιλότης" καὶ "γόνυ κνήμης ἔγγιον."

5. οὐδὲν ἴδιον—*ouden idion*. For κοινὰ τὰ φίλων see Plato, *Resp.* 4.424a, 5.449c; Aristotle, *Eth. Nic.* 8:9.1159b; *Pol.* 2:2.1263a; Euripides, *Andr.* 376–77; *Ores*, 735; *Fem. Phoe.* 243–44; Menander, *Adel.* 9K; Martial, *Epigrams* 2:43 (twice); Cicero, *De offic.* 1.16.51 (amicorum esse communia omnia); Philo, *Vita Mos.* 1:156; Seneca, *De benefic.* 7.4.1; Plutarch, *De frat. Am.* 20.490e; *Amat.* 21:9.767e; Dio Chrysostom, *Discourses*

This, however, only strengthens Haenchen's conclusion that "Luke is here suggesting that the primitive church ... realized the Greek communal ideal."[6]

In a more recent study of the question Mealand argues that "everything common" and "nothing one's own" are more closely related to the slogans of Greek utopianism than to the ideal of friendship.[7] Utopian expectations and humanitarian ideals are obviously related,[8] but it is not unimportant for our study that we distinguish whether Luke is presenting the Christians as having realized the ideal society in which private property ceases to exist, or a level of interpersonal relationships which answered to Hellenistic aspirations. A number of considerations weigh against Mealand's position:

a. It is doubtful if a Christian writer, as immersed in the Old Testament as Luke, would consciously have imitated pagan mythological conceptions in his presentation of the Christian movement. In the Gospel he does imply that money and earthly possessions will have no place in the coming kingdom, but, as we have seen, he does not infer from this that they should have no place in this age. There is nothing in the Gospel to suggest that he envisaged the age to come as egalitarian. He can even use the charge of various numbers of cities as a picture of future reward.[9] It need not be denied, however, that someone with a Hellenistic upbringing might have been unconsciously influenced by utopian pictures in the direction of a high appreciation of sharing and the social virtues, but this is different from consciously striving towards a specific utopian goal.

3:110, 37:7; Diogenes Laertius, *Lives* 6:72; 8:10; Terence, *Adelph.* 803–04. For μία ψυχή, see page 205n20, below. For οὐδὲν ἴδιον see page 203n7, below.

6. "Gemeinschaftsideal": Haenchen, *Acts*, 233.

7. πάντα κοινά and οὐδὲν ἴδιον. Compare 4:32. Mealand, "Utopian Allusions." For πάντα κοινά see Plato, *Critias* 110d; *Resp.* 5.464d, 8.543b; Strabo, *Geography* 7.3.9. For οὐδὲν ἴδιον see Plato, *Critias* 110d; *Tim* 18b; *Resp.* 3.416d; 8.543b; Euripides, *Androm.* 366–67; Diogenes Laertius, *Lives* 8:23; compare Epictetus, *Discourses* 2.10.4, but for his own view see 2.10.7. That an ideal of friendship is in view see Plümacher, *Lukas als hellenistischer Schriftsteller*, 16–18; Hengel, *Property and Riches in the Early Church*, 8–9.

8. One would judge from Plato that πάντα κοινά and οὐδὲν ἴδιον are derived from κοινὰ τὰ φίλων and φίλων οὐδὲν ἴδιον respectively. Compare Plutarch, *Coniug. Praec.* 34.143a; Lucian, *Merc. Cond.* 20.

9. Luke 19:17–19; compare 22:30.

b. Community of possessions as a practical utopian ideal is seriously expressed only in the writings of Plato,[10] and was subsequently criticized by Aristotle, and ridiculed by Aristophanes.[11]

c. Plato's communistic system was, in any case, partial. Only the "guardians" of his republic were to practice such community. Moreover, the feature of the system which receives most attention, from himself and from his critics, is the having in common of wives and children.[12] If the ideal society was what Luke had in view, one might have expected him to be more specific with his use of *panta koina* (πάντα κοινά).

d. That Acts tells us so little about the organization of the early church and fails even to mention their work makes it unlikely that he is trying to depict an ideal society.

On the other hand, there is much to be said for the view that Luke is attentive to the realization in the community of Hellenistic ideals of friendship.

a. In the period relevant to Luke's writing, the proverb "the things of friends are common" was widely used throughout the Hellenistic world. It described neither an ideal society nor a strict communism of goods, but had broken free of its Platonic connection to express in a general and imaginative way the openness and sharing of friends.[13] Cicero insists that those things which the laws treat as private property should remain so, the rest being shared in accordance with the proverb.[14] Plutarch quotes Theophrastus to the effect that if friends hold all in common, then friends of friends should surely

---

10. Especially *Critias* 110d of the Golden Age. *Tim.* 18b of the "guardians" of the state; also *Resp.* 3.416, 4.424, 5.449, 463–64. For other descriptions of the Golden Age see Virgil, *Georg.* 1.125–27. Ovid, *Metam.* 1:89–112; Seneca, *Ep.* 90:3, but note that only Plato uses the friendship language we are considering. Seneca does speak of the Golden Age as a time of fellowship (consortium). Diodorus Siculus (5:45) describes the island of Panchaeitis where not a thing except a home and garden may a person possess as his own. Further *TDNT* III.794; Hengel, *Property and Riches in the Early Church*, 1–8.

11. Aristotle, *Pol.* 2:1–2. Polybius, *Histories* (6.47.7) dismisses it as untried. Aristophanes, *Eccl.* esp. lines 589–90; compare Epictetus, *Discourses* 2.4.8.

12. Some continued to favor it. See Diogenes Laertius, *Lives* 6:72; 7:33.

13. Aristotle himself wants to retain the proverb as an ideal of virtue, not to be enforced by the state, but to be fashioned by education (*Pol.* 2:2. 1263a).

14. Cicero, *De offic.* 1.16.51.

be common.[15] Elsewhere he applies the proverb to the relationship of husband and wife.[16] Dio Chrysostom uses it in connection with a king whose circle of friends gives him the opportunity to be in many places and to experience many things at once.[17] Philo applies it to Moses's fellowship with God, whereby he was able to direct and control the elements like God.[18]

b. "One soul" is more congenial to a description of ideal friendship than to an ideal society. Dupont has shown that it too belongs to the Hellenistic friendship notion.[19] To the question "What is a friend?" Aristotle replies, "One soul living in two bodies."[20]

c. Rather than providing detailed descriptions of the organization of the community, Luke focuses attention on their unity[21] and joyful sharing.[22]

At this point it might be objected that since Luke makes no use of the term "friendship" (*philia*—φιλία) he could hardly be consciously presenting it as an ideal. But *philia* is not to be found anywhere in the New Testament with a positive sense.[23] Edwin Judge explores the reason for Paul's avoidance of the term, and concludes that it was because of the rigidly structured patronistic character of Greek and Roman friendship relationships.[24] No doubt Luke had similar problems. The side of

---

15. *De frat. Am.* 20.490e.
16. *Amat.* 21:9. 767e.
17. Dio Chrysostom, 3:104–15.
18. *Vita Mos.* 1:156
19. ψυχὴ μία—*psychē mia*. Dupont, "Communauté des biens," 513–14.
20. τί ἐστι φίλος; μία ψυχὴ δύο σώμασιν ἐνοικοῦσα. Diogenes Laertius 5:20. For further references and allusions see Euripides, *Ores.* 1045; Plutarch, *Amat.* 21:9.767e (with κοινὰ τὰ φίλων); Cicero, *De amicit.* 25.92, 21.81; *De offic.* 1.17.56; Aristotle, *Eth. Nic.* 9:8. 1168b; Iamblichus, Life of *Pythagoras* 30:167 (with κοινὰ φίλων).
21. ὁμοθυμαδόν—with one mind—Acts 1:14, 2:46, 4:24, 5:12.
22. Acts 2:46–47.
23. Jas 4:4 is the single occurrence, and it is negative.
24. Judge, "St. Paul as a Radical Critic of Society," 195–97. Compare Bolkestein, *Wohltätigkeit und Armenpflege*, 82–85, who explores the question of who might be denoted a friend and lists folk such as adherents (Anhänger) of a king, comrades, fellow citizens, guests, and business associates. He comments on how "friend" becomes a title in some political contexts. Compare John 19:12.

friendship which is idealized in the proverb is better expressed by the term "fellowship" (*koinōnia*—κοινωνία), precisely the term Luke uses.[25]

We turn, therefore, to Acts 2:42, and to a consideration of Luke's single use of *koinōnia*. Its strategic position in a fourfold summary of the essential character of the earliest Christian community highlights its importance.

J. Y. Campbell argues that in this context *koinōnia* has the limited sense of contributions of money as part of the liturgical life of the church, as in Hebrews 13:16.[26] Heinrich Seesemann objects to this limitation on the grounds that this is a specialized and infrequent sense of the word, and that Luke could not have expected his readers to discern this meaning without some additional indication of such limitation.[27] Seesemann discerns three meanings for *koinōnia* in the New Testament: contribution (Mitteilsamkeit), i.e., sharing of material possessions, participation (Anteilhaben), and fellowship (Gemeinschaft), the last of these being the sense intended in Acts 2:42.[28] Luke's readers could be expected to give the word its widest interpretation including within its scope contributions, table fellowship, and the general friendship and unity which characterized the community. Confirmation of this view, as well as important insights into Luke's purpose in presenting the early church in this way, is to be gained from a study of Philo's use of *koinōnia*. To my knowledge such a study has not been previously undertaken.

---

25. κοινωνία (*koinōnia*). καὶ οἱ παροιμία κοινὰ τὰ φίλων, ὀρθῶς· ἐν κοινωνίᾳ γὰρ ἡ φιλία—and the proverb, "things of friends are common," is true; for in fellowship is friendship. Aristotle, *Eth. Nic.* 8:9. 1159b. Bolkestein, *Wohltätigkeit und Armenpflege*, 432, says "κοινωνία wird nicht selten als synonym von φιλία gebraucht ('Fellowship' is not infrequently used as a synonym for 'friendship')." Dupont, "Communauté des biens," thinks Luke has substituted κοινωνία for φιλία, but he is unable to give any reason for Luke's avoidance of φιλία: "On a certaines raisons de penser, que dans sa description de la κοινωνία des premiers chrétiens, Luc opera une transposition de quelques thèmes littéraires grecs et hellénistiques relatifs à l'amitié (One has certain reasons to think that in his description of the koinōnia of the first Christians Luke employs a transposition of certain Greek and Hellenistic literary themes relating to friendship)," 518.

26. Campbell, "ΚΟΙΝΩΝΙΑ," 374–75. Similarly, Hort, *Christian Ecclesia*, 44; Reicke, *Glaube und Leben der Urgemeinde*, 131–32.

27. Seesemann, *KOINŌNIA im Neuen Testament*, 87–89. The same objections may be raised against the thesis of Scott ("What Happened at Pentecost?" 136–42; *The Fellowship of the Spirit*; "'Fellowship' or κοινωνία," 567) that *koinōnia* means "the Fellowship" and is equivalent to the חבורה (an association sharing common meals). For critiques see Seesemann, *KOINŌNIA im Neuen Testament*, 90–92; Wood, "Fellowship," 31–40.

28. Seesemann, *KOINŌNIA im Neuen Testament*, 24–26.

Koinōnia is a favorite term for Philo. He uses it to describe the fellowship of marriage,[29] business partnerships,[30] as well as the various affinities which exist between different things (e.g., crime and punishment,[31] body and soul,[32] various virtues[33]). He often speaks of the "fellowship of the body," usually referring to the harmony of its separate parts.[34] This affords us a concrete picture of his concept of "fellowship." It is close to "harmony" and "(vocal) harmony," which he often uses in connection with *koinōnia*.[35]

In the realm of human society *koinōnia* refers to the state of harmony, concord, and friendship which should exist between people. Its importance to Philo can be readily seen from a few examples. It is among "the best things in the world"[36] and is the complement of piety.[37] Moses's motive for giving the Israelites the law was that they might be prepared, on settling down, to follow the principles of justice "in harmony and fellowship and rendering to everyone their due."[38] It is clear for Philo that the law was to prepare people for fellowship,[39] though it is also taught by reason.[40] At this point we begin to see him using the word in a new way. *Koinōnia* becomes a virtue, the characteristic of an individual whose behavior is conducive to the state of *koinōnia* with his fellows. In the Loeb edition of Philo's works it is often translated "fellow feeling" or "sense of fellowship."[41] As such it is almost the same as *philanthropia* (love of humankind), of which Moses is the great exemplar:

> The next subject to be examined is humanity (*philanthropia*) the virtue closest akin to piety, its sister and its twin. The prophetic

29. *Op.* 152; *Ebr.* 48; *Abr.* 100, 248; *Dec.* 123; *Spec. Leg.* 1:109, 138; 3:23, 29.
30. *Mut.* 104; *Dec.* 171; *Spec. Leg.* 1:235, I2:75, 3:158, 4:30; *Gaium*, 47.
31. *Spec. Leg.* 3:182.
32. *Fuga* 55.
33. *Fuga* 112.
34. *Op.* 138; *Conf.* 194–95; *Spec. Leg.* 3:28, 4:83; *Aet.* 143; *Flacc.* 190. He sometimes comes close to using *koinōnia* in the sense of "system" *Abr.* 74; *Jos.* 160; *Dec.* 71, 150
35. ἁρμονία (*harmonia*) and συμφωνία (*symphonia*). *Sacr.* 75; *Dec.* 132; compare *Migr.* 178 (καί συμπαθείᾳ)
36. *Post.* 181; compare *Spec. Leg.* 2:7; *Virt.* 84, 119.
37. *Ebr.* 84; compare *Ebr.* 78; *Decal.* 109.
38. ἐν ὁμονοίᾳ καὶ κοινωνίᾳ καὶ διανομῇ τῶν ἐπιβαλλόντων ἑκάστοις. *Dec.* 14
39. *Dec.* 162; *Spec. Leg.* 1:295, 324; *Hyp.* 8.11.1.
40. *Dec.* 132; *Spec. Leg.* 3:103.
41. *Sacr.* 27; *Spec. Leg.* 2:167, 3:103.

legislator who perhaps loved her more than anyone else has done, since he knew that she was a high road leading to holiness, used to incite and train all his subjects to fellowship (*koinōnia*), setting before them the monument of his own life like an original design to be their beautiful model.[42]

I can find no clear case in Philo where one would wish to translate *koinōnia* as "contribution." The idea is always more general. If we were to find in Philo a statement to the effect that someone devoted himself to *koinōnia*, we would undoubtedly understand it either as the spirit of harmony and co-operation of the group,[43] or as the virtue which made such a state of affairs possible. In Acts 2:42 the definite article favors the former sense, as does the context and the parallel passage, where, instead of *koinōnia*, we find "one heart and soul."[44]

Having said this, it is important to realize that the sharing of material possessions is a significant component of Philo's concept of *koinōnia*. Speaking of those whom he calls *philanthropoi* he says:

> Others conceiving the idea that there is no good outside doing justice to men have no heart for anything but companionship with men.[45] In their desire for fellowship,[46] they supply the good things of life in equal measure to all for their use[47]

Philo's only critique of these people is that they "only come halfway in virtue," i.e., they lack piety, the complement of *philanthropia* (= *koinōnia*). The passage shows the high place he gives to *koinōnia*, and that the sharing of possessions is very much part of this. For Philo the perfect life consists of only two things, "piety"[48] and *koinōnia* (*philanthropia*). His description of people worthy of salvation also highlights the honor he pays to *koinōnia* and shows how integral it was to his idea of sharing. It also shows that having all things common can have a wider sense than formal community of property:

---

42. *Virt.* 51; compare *Virt.* 80.

43. It is interesting to find two cases in Philo where *koinōnia* comes close to carrying the modern psychological idea of "communication": *Vita Mos.* 2:190; *Spec. Leg.* 2:7.

44. καρδία καὶ ψύχη μία. Acts 4:32

45. ὁμιλίαν.

46. διὰ κοινωνίας ἵμερον.

47. *Dec.* 109

48. εὐσέβεια (*eusebeia*).

> ... men of peaceful disposition who cherish brotherly affection and good fellowship,⁴⁹ in whom envy has either found no room at all or has entered only to take its departure with all speed, because their will is to bring their private blessings into the common stock to be shared and enjoyed by all alike.⁵⁰

Philo is not saying that only those who dwell in formal communities like the Essenes are worthy of salvation. Nevertheless, the formal community does afford him a concrete illustration.

His proof to the Greeks that Judaism excels in inculcating *koinōnia* is crowned by his description of the Essenes with their complete community of goods.⁵¹ He concludes:

> Unable to resist the high excellence of these people, they all treated them as self-governing and freemen by nature and extolled their communal meals and that ineffable sense of fellowship, which is the clearest evidence of a perfect and supremely happy life.⁵²

If his contemporaries shared his view that *koinōnia* is the outward sign of inner perfection and happiness, it is understandable that in an apology for the Jewish faith Philo should have wished to demonstrate that Judaism excelled in this respect.⁵³ It also gives us a clue to the possible significance of this language for Luke. For both are addressing Hellenists. The amount of attention Philo gives to demonstrating Judaism's favorable record in inculcating *koinōnia* is related to the esteem with which this ideal was held in the Hellenistic world;⁵⁴ there is no

---

49. ὁμοφροσύνην καὶ κοινωνίαν.

50. *Praem.* 87; compare *Conf.* 48; *Spec. Leg.* 2:108; *Virt.* 140; *Fug.* 28–29.

51. Though it is clear that *koinōnia* refers more to the spirit manifested than to the communistic form it took.

52. τὰ συσσίτια καὶ τὴν παντὸς λόγου κρείττονα κοινωνίαν, ἣ βίου τελείου καὶ σφόδρα εὐδαίμονός ἐστι σαφέστατον δεῖγμα. *Quod omn.* 91

53. The Jews were accused of inhumanity and failing in the realm of *koinōnia* (*Spec. Leg.* 2:167). It is possible that the Wisdom of Solomon is responding to the same sort of accusations when it claims that wisdom is φιλάνθρωπος (1:6; 7:23), and that God taught his people "that the righteous person must be a φιλάνθρωπον." (12:19)

54. "Wollte man die Frage, welche menschliche Beziehung den Griechen als die wichtigste galt, nach der Zahl der darauf bezüglichen Aussprüche in der Literatur entscheiden, so würde ohne jeden Zweifel die Entscheidung zugunsten der Freundschaft ausfallen (If one wants to decide the question, which human relation was valued as the most important by the Greeks, according to the number of relevant sayings in the literature, doubtless the decision would turn out in favor of friendship)." Bolkestein,

significant Old Testament background to the idea.[55] Nor is it to be found in intertestamental literature. This raises the possibility that Luke's purpose may also be apologetic. He does not seem to have borrowed his concept of *koinōnia* from Paul,[56] who uses it for the most part of participation in salvation, ministry, etc.[57] It seems that Luke has taken the term independently from the Greek realm to convey to his Hellenistic readers a picture of the early church which they would understand and appreciate. He is seeking to commend Christianity, or perhaps the church itself, to people for whom *koinōnia* was a supreme virtue.

Thus, in highlighting the Hellenistic background to the idea of "all things common" and the ideal of *koinōnia*, we have uncovered a likely motive for Luke's description of the common life, meals, and material sharing of the Jerusalem church. At the same time, we have seen that words which to modern ears suggest a formal community of possessions may have suggested something quite different to his readers. There is, therefore, no need to speak of confusion in Luke's sources about whether the early church had a system of common ownership or to postulate a different understanding on the part of the author of the "summaries" to the other sources of the life of the primitive church.[58] Luke and his readers may well have understood the summaries to be perfectly in harmony with the remainder of the description, which, as the following considerations show, clearly implies the continuance of private property.[59]

Wohltätigkeit und Armenpflege, 82.

55. Κοινωνία occurs 3 times only, in LXX, and never in the sense we have discussed. (Lev 5:21 [6:2]; Wis 8:18; 3 Macc 4:6).

56. Paul does not use *koinōnia* to describe the communal life of the church. The nearest he comes to it is Gal 2:9; compare Phil 1:5. Only in 1 John (1:3, 7) do we find it in a similar sense to Acts 2:42.

57. See Seesemann, *KOINŌNIA im Neuen Testament*, 34–36.

58. For suggestions such as these see Schmiedel, "Gütergemeinschaft der ältesten Christenheit," 373; *BC* V.147–48; Conzelmann, *Geschichte des Urchristentums*, 24.

59. On the basis of these and other considerations a number of scholars have come to the conclusion that Luke does not mean to claim that the early church practiced a form of economic communism: Uhlhorn, *Christian Charity in the Ancient Church*, 73–74; Cobb, "Fellowship of Goods in the Apostolic Church," 17–34; Hort, *Ecclesia*, 48; Hicks, "Communistic Experiment," 21–32; Baumgarten, "Kommunismus im Urchristentum," 625–45; Dodd, "Communism in the New Testament," 55–61; Menoud, *Vie de l'Église naissante*, 32–33; Haenchen, *Acts*, 231; Greehy, "Community of Goods—Qumran and Acts," 230–40; Dupont, "Communauté des biens." The following think some formal system of sharing possessions existed: Holtzmann, "Gütergemeinschaft," 327–36; Knox, *St Paul and the Church of Jerusalem*, 4; Easton, *Early Christianity*, 92;

a. The example of Barnabas selling a field is a poor one if others were liquidating their whole estates to live from a common purse.[60]

b. Peter's reply to Ananias, "While it was still yours, did it not remain yours, and when it was sold was it not at your disposal?" presupposes the continuance of private property.[61] Moreover, the description "sold a possession" hardly suggests the disposal of their whole estate.[62] *Chōrion* (χώριον) in this context probably means "a piece of land."[63]

c. Luke describes a central fund whereby the needy were assisted, not a communal fund on which all drew.[64]

d. The mention of the house of Mary and the maid Rhoda in Acts 12:12–13 implies the continued existence of private property, and, outwardly at least, of normal societal roles.

We may conclude, then, that Luke did not intend in his summary descriptions to claim a formal community of possessions for the early church; nor would his readers have understood them in this way. What he is describing is a spirit of openness and sharing which constituted true *koinōnia* friendship. As Dupont[65] points out, this makes perfect sense of Acts 4:32: "No one *was saying* any of his possessions was his own."[66]

Reicke, *Glaube und Leben der Urgemeinde*, 56–58, 60–61, 85–87; Kümmel, *Introduction to the New Testament*, 167. Only Holtzmann argues the case, which rests for him on a highly suspect interpretation of Acts 5:4: "Blieb dir nicht ein Rest und war es denn nach dem Verkauf in deiner Gewalt? (Wasn't there a balance, and after the sale was it then in your power?)" (331). This idea is supported by Scheidweiler, "Zu Act 5:4," 136–37, who amends the text to read οὐχ ὅ instead of οὐχί to alleviate the difficulty of Holzmann's translation. The following take an intermediate position: *DThC*, III.578–79; Marshall, *Luke: Historian and Theologian*, 207–209; Hengel, *Property and Riches in the Early Church*, 31–34 (following E. Bloch).

60. Acts 4:37. Haenchen, *Acts*, 233. Hengel's suggestion (*Property and Riches in the Early Church*, 33) that Barnabas is singled out because he was known to the church in Antioch does not remove the difficulty.

61. οὐχὶ μένον σοὶ ἔμενεν καὶ πραθὲν ἐν τῇ σῇ ἐξουσίᾳ ὑπῆρχεν; Acts 5:4.

62. ἐπώλησεν κτῆμα. Acts 5:1.

63. Acts 5:3; compare 1:18–19; 4:34.

64. In Acts 6 it is a deprived group, the widows, who were being neglected. Had Luke been describing a formal community of possessions as at Qumran, he would have used aorists in 2:45 and 4:34–35 instead of imperfects (ἐπίπρασκον, ἔφερον, ἐτίθουν—they were buying, they were bringing, they were carrying) which suggest an ongoing or occasional activity.

65. Dupont, "Communauté des biens," 508.

66. Καὶ οὐδὲ εἰς τι τῶν ὑπαρχόντων αὐτῷ ἔλεγεν ἴδιον εἶναι.

Accordingly, the actual details of the church's organization and common life cannot be reconstructed exactly and in detail, though certain things are clear. There was a remarkable degree of sharing through common meals, the practice of hospitality, worship, and the sharing of material possessions. No barriers existed to the Christians' fellowship.[67] There was a central fund organized at an early stage[68] from which the needy were supported through the provision of meals and probably clothes.[69] It was established from voluntary contributions, many of them substantial gifts from well-off Christians who sold property to meet the general need. There was no compulsion or obligation, but the spontaneous generosity was such as to cause it to be long remembered. Even the ideal that there should be no poor among God's people was fulfilled.[70]

There are no serious reasons for doubting that what Luke pictures in his description of the Jerusalem church is essentially what he believed to be true, and, despite some idealization, represents the actual historical situation.[71] That he is not purposely "playing up" to Hellenistic ideals and aspirations[72] is shown by the absence from Acts of the notion of "equality,"[73] which, along with sharing, is a standard component of the

---

67. This is especially significant in view of the socio-religious fragmentation of Jewish society in the first century. That Pharisees would join in regular table fellowship with common folk was no mean achievement. The ἀφελότης καρδίας (simplicity of heart) that characterized their meals (Acts 2:46) may be related to their putting aside complex antisocial scruples (compare Philo, *Abr.* 117).

68. The historicity of this has been challenged on the ground that an organized system of charity among the Jews obviated any need for such a fund until a later period. In a short note, "Was There Organized Charity in Jerusalem before the Christians?" I questioned the existence of such a Jewish system at this period and defended the appropriateness of what Luke describes.

69. Acts 9:39.

70. Compare Deut 15:4 with Acts 4:34. This is the only occurrence of ἐνδεής (needy) in the NT.

71. His frank treatment of the problem with the widows of the Hellenists and the story of Ananias and Sapphira show that he is not deliberately presenting an overfavorable picture.

72. Holtzmann, "Gütergemeinschaft der Apostelgeschichte," 25-60, thought the author of Acts, writing about AD 110-120, was reading his own ideals back into the early church.

73. ἰσότης (*isotēs*). Several authors assume its presence: Hicks, "Communistic Experiment," 27; Dupont, "Communauté des biens," 512, 517-18; Lietzmann, *An die Korinther I.II*, 134-35. Its absence is noted in *NIDNTT* I 642.

Greek ideal of friendship.[74] Philo makes particular use of this concept.[75] Josephus commends the Essenes for their equality in matters of property and dress, though in terms of their ranking within the order they seem to have been anything but equal.[76]

Thus, I find it difficult to think Luke would have made no mention of equality among the Christians had there been a real attempt to create a leveled society of no rich and no poor, or if he was simply playing to Greek expectations or projecting his own ideals back into the life of the earliest church. Such a claim would have been most appropriate in connection with Acts 4:32 or 4:34–35 where he is piling up friendship ideas. But there is no hint of it, and this agrees well with the picture given in Acts 6 where a deprived class is still in existence.[77]

Thus, Luke is not trying to "sell" the Jerusalem church to Hellenists as having achieved the ideal society, nor even all their ideals of friendship. His emphasis on *koinōnia* is all the more significant for this. He is exploiting a point of genuine correspondence between Greek and Christian viewpoints.

5.3 ANANIAS AND SAPPHIRA ACTS 5:1-11

The parallel nature of the two summaries of the church's life in Acts 2:42–47 and 4:32–35 is too well recognized to require any defense. What has not been recognized is that the second summary in fact continues to 5:16 and constitutes not just a repetition but an expansion of the first.[78] This can best be seen by lining up the two passages with their corresponding

---

74. Aristotle, *Eth. Nic.* 9:8. 1168b (ἰσότης φιλότης—friendship is equality); 8:10. 1159b (ἡ δ'ἰσότης καὶ ὁμοιότης φιλότης—friendship is equality and similarity); Diogenes Laertius, *Lives* 8:10 (φιλίαν ἰσότητα); compare Ps. Sol. 17:41; Dio Chrysostom, *Discourses* 17:9 (quoting Euripides); also *TDNT* III.347.

75. *Spec. Leg.* 1:295, 4:187; *Quod omn* 79, 84; *Conf.* 48; *Dec.* 162.

76. Josephus, *War* 2.122, 140, 150.

77. Compare Gal 2:10. Rom 15:26 implies that there were poor and those who were not poor among the Jerusalem Christians. See Keck, "The Poor among the Saints in the New Testament," 119. Little is made of the idea of equality elsewhere in the NT. In 2 Cor 8:14–15 Paul's intention seems to be to relieve need, not to create a technical equality, though he is appealing to Greek ideals of equality.

78. Benoit, "'Summaries' in Acts 2, 4 and 5," 94–103, treats Acts 5:12–16 as a third summary, not recognizing that 5:1–11 is an expansion of one of the motifs that occurs in the first summary. Significantly, he hints that 5:11 can almost be considered part of the third summary.

sections in parallel. The first summary is presented in order; the second has been rearranged. The original order of the second summary is indicated with alphabetical lettering.

Acts 2:42–47	Acts 4:32–5:16
Apostles' teaching, fellowship, breaking bread, prayers (2:42)	No parallel
Fear came on every soul (2:43a)	e. Ananias and Sapphira: great fear on all who heard (5:1–11) h. None dared join them (5:13a)
Signs and wonders (2:43b)	f. Signs and wonders (5:12a) k. Miraculous healings (5:15f)
All who believed ἐπὶ τὸ αὐτό (at the same place) (2:44a) Had everything in common (2:44b)	a. Believers were καρδία καὶ ψυχὴ μία (one heart and soul—4:32a) b. No one said his possessions his own, everything common (4:32b)
Possessions sold and distributed to needy (2:45)	d. No needy, possessors sold land, etc., distribution to needy; Barnabas (4:34–7)
Continued daily in temple with one accord (2:46a)	g. With one accord in Solomon's Porch (5:12b)
Breaking bread at home with gladness and simplicity, praising God (2:46b–47a)	No parallel
Having favor with the whole people (2:47b)	i. The people magnified them (5:13b)
The Lord added those being saved (2:47c)	j. Multitudes added to the Lord (5:14)
No parallel	c. Apostles witness with power (4:33)

The jumbled order of the second summary with respect to the first suggests Luke is not employing a written source at this point but composing freely.⁷⁹ The most satisfactory explanation for the high degree of correlation in subject matter between them is that Luke had in his mind various characteristics of the primitive church which he outlines once and then repeats at the appropriate time and in an expanded form, with suitable examples introduced from the tradition.⁸⁰

The foregoing analysis implies that the main purpose of the Ananias and Sapphira story is to give illustration and content to the idea that fear surrounded the primitive community. This must now be justified.

It makes little sense to see the point of the story as a negative aspect of the sharing of goods.⁸¹ Why would Luke, who has just given two glowing and commendatory accounts of the generosity of the first Christians, want to spend even more space recounting their faults? The conclusion to the story (repeated from 5:5) is surely indicative of its main purpose: "Great fear came upon the whole church [meeting?] and upon all who heard these things."⁸² When this is compared with 2:43 (fear came upon every soul),⁸³ and it is seen that both statements are followed by descriptions of signs and wonders worked by the apostles, little doubt can remain that we are dealing in some manner with the theme of fear.⁸⁴

The particular crime of Ananias and Sapphira was their collusion to defraud the community.⁸⁵ Peter's question shows that they were not

---

79. Compare Haenchen, *Acts*, 195, who thinks that the summaries "flow entirely from the pen of Luke."

80. Acts 2–5 are not intended as "biography" of the primitive church. They are theological proclamation. Luke presents his material in two cycles (miracle—proclamation—response—description of community), the second cycle being interrupted by a new cycle (arrest—proclamation—result) which then takes over (5:17-42). The theory of Johnson, "Possessions in Luke-Acts," 198–211, that the second summary is meant to establish symbolically the authority of the apostles in the church ("the disposition of possessions is a direct symbol of the disposition of the self," 202) demands too much ingenuity on the part of Luke's readers.

81. As in Dibelius, "Style Criticism in the Book of Acts," 15–16.

82. καὶ ἐγένετο φόβος μέγας ἐφ' ὅλην τὴν ἐκκλησίαν καὶ ἐπὶ πάντας τοὺς ἀκούοντας ταῦτα. Acts 5:11.

83. ἐγίνετο δὲ πάσῃ ψυχῇ φόβος. Notice the same motif in Acts 19:13–17.

84. See also Harrison, *Expanding Church*, 94.

85. For details of the story see Derrett, "Ananias, Sapphira, and the Right of Property," 225–32. His view that that they withheld Sapphira's *ketubah* (wife's deed of settlement in case of divorce or husband's death) is fanciful. Nor is there foundation for his view that what they sold was *all* they had, and that Ananias had vowed on entering the community that *if* he sold his property he would do so in favor of the church (also Scheidweiler, "Act 5:4," 137). Menoud, "Mort d'Ananias et de Saphira," 146–54, thinks

obliged to sell the piece of land for the benefit of the community, nor, in the event of sale, to contribute the whole amount, or any. The story only makes sense if the couple had previously declared their intention to donate the land to the community.[86] Luke assumes, having just related the story of Barnabas, that his readers will understand "he sold a field" to imply "for the community."[87] This is confirmed by Peter's question in verse 8: "Tell me if you sold the land for such and such?"[88] In publicly donating the land to the community the previous owners apparently undertook to look after the sale. In holding back some of what they obtained they were embezzling the community's central fund.[89] The public esteem and gratitude which their original action might be expected to attract was thus fraudulently obtained.[90]

This act of deception is branded as "lying to the Holy Spirit." What was ostensibly against a human community was in fact against God, and the couple's death is related in such a way as to imply it is God who judged them. The effect of the story is to underline heavily the holiness of the community: "The church is a holy, one could say, power-laden realm; it is taboo. Whoever touches the holy, without themselves being holy, dies."[91] This community has been brought into being by God's Spirit and is jealously guarded by him. Whoever touches the church touches God; "whoever fights against her fights against God."[92]

We meet this idea elsewhere in Acts. Paul also attempts to harm the church, and his attack is revealed to be against the Lord Jesus himself.[93] It is also futile; he only damaged himself: "It is hard for you to kick against the goads."[94] Luke takes obvious delight in relating Gamaliel's caution to

---

the story evolved from an account of the first two deaths in the church. His conjecture that Luke invented the sin of which they were guilty is highly dubious. Would Luke invent such a blemish on the fellowship of the church?

86. BC IV.50. Attention is here drawn to a possible analogy in the system of *corban* whereby property could be dedicated to God in advance.

87. Acts 5:1.

88. εἰπέ μοι, εἰ τοσούτου τὸ χωρίον ἀπέδοσθε.

89. ἐνοσφίσατο ἀπὸ τῆς τιμῆς (he misappropriated from the price).

90. See also Rackham, *Acts*, 65–66.

91. "Die Kirche ist ein heiliger, sozusagen mit Macht geladener Bereich; sie ist tabu. Wer Heiliges anrührt, ohne selbst heilig zu sein, kommt um." Conzelmann, *Geschichte des Urchristentums*, 22.

92. "Wer gegen sie kämpft, kämpft gegen Gott." Lohfink, *Sammlung Israels*, 87.

93. Acts 9:4–5.

94. Acts 26:14. Paul echoes this theme in 1 Cor 3:16–17; compare Käsemann,

the Sanhedrin: "If it is from God you will not be able to destroy it, you may even be found to be fighting against God."[95]

The sin of Ananias and Sapphira, however, is not the same as Paul's. His is an external attack, while theirs arises from within. Significantly, Peter characterizes their sin as "tempting the Spirit of the Lord." With one exception the idea of tempting God has to do, in the Old Testament, with Israel putting God to the test in the wilderness.[96] Even the term "Spirit of God" sounds like conscious imitation of Old Testament language.[97] The suggestion is strong that Luke sees Ananias and Sapphira's sin in the same light as the rebellion of the Israelites in the wilderness. As then, so now God breaks forth with judgments to protect the purity of the nascent community (*ekklēsia*). The story of Achan, which probably is in Luke's mind as he records this story, is one specific instance of this.[98]

The fate of Ananias and Sapphira inspires great fear in all who hear of it.[99] It is the same fear as is mentioned in Acts 2:43, "religious awe at the self-manifestation of the divine."[100] God is near to, and jealously guards, the new community, which is his own possession.[101] For the first time in Acts we encounter the word *ecclēsia* (ἐκκλησία—meeting, church). Thus, we must conclude that the primary function of Acts 5:1-11 is to demonstrate the holiness of the primitive community. Luke hardly imagines that everyone who subsequently transgressed against the church met with instant death. Such things as he describes belonged to the period

---

"Sentences of Holy Law," 66-88.

95. εἰ δὲ ἐκ θεοῦ ἐστιν, οὐ δυνήσεσθε καταλῦσαι αὐτούς, μήποτε καὶ θεομάχοι εὑρεθῆτε. Acts 5:39. Luke's presentation of this theme (attack on community = attack on God, therefore futile) may have been influenced by the similar theme in Euripides's *Bacchae* where Pentheus seeks to persecute the worshipers of the new god Dionysus, but is himself destroyed. See Dibelius, "Literary Allusions in the Speeches in Acts," 188-91; compare Lohfink, *Sammlung Israels*, 86-87.

96. Exod 17:2; Deut 6:16; Ps 78:18, 41, 56, 95:8-9. The exception is Isa 7:12. In the NT see Matt 4:7 par; 1 Cor 10:9; Heb 3:8, 9.

97. Elsewhere in Luke-Acts at Luke 4:18 (quoting Isa 61:1) and Acts 8:39 (an allusion to the taking up of Elijah?) Compare 1 Kings 18:12; 2 Kings 2:11, 16).

98. Compare Josh 7:1 (LXX) with Acts 5:2-3. See *BC* IV.50; Haenchen, *Acts*, 237.

99. Acts 5:11.

100. Haenchen, *Acts*, 192. Compare the story in Acts 19:13-17. For the idea of people being gripped with fear before a manifestation of divine power see Luke 1:12, 65, 2:9, 5:26, 7:16, 8:37, 9:34.

101. Brown, *Meaning and Function of Acts* 5:1-11: "What the author is seeking to illustrate in this melodramatic story is the dogmatic belief that the Holy Spirit is essentially and immediately present in and judge over the Christian congregation" (236).

of the church's establishment, when God was demonstrating his possession of the new community. In this sense the parallel with the wilderness congregation is apt.

It would be foolish, however, to say that the story has no relevance to the question of possessions. It provides another clear example of the destructive power of greed.[102] Though Luke does not expect that everyone who thus sins will meet with instantaneous judgment, it nonetheless provides clear warning to the greedy of God's impending judgment, and thus forms a fitting counterpart to the parable of the rich fool.

5.4 THE CHURCH IN ACTS 2-5

We have now examined two aspects of Luke's characterization of the life of the primitive church: its *koinōnia* and the holy fear which it inspired. In this section I wish to present these as part of a wider whole and view them in connection with Luke's purpose in the early part of Acts. Van Unnik warns us against definitions of Luke's purpose which only cover part of his material, but also against vague and summarizing definitions such as "the spread of the gospel from Jerusalem to Rome."[103] Taking his lead, I shall not concern myself here with *the* purpose of Acts but will deal with one constitutive part.[104] For it seems to me that the two parallel "summaries" already examined provide a clue to an aspect of Luke's purpose which is widely overlooked.

In discerning Luke's purpose, attention is often rightly focused on Acts 1:8, leading to statements of his aim in terms of the progress of the gospel to Rome, the missionary activity of Christ, the Holy Spirit, etc.[105] Attention is inevitably concentrated in the area of Christology and soteriology. Reicke, however, suggests that the purpose of Acts should *also* be seen in terms of ecclesiology.[106] This certainly seems to be correct for the

---

102. See page 163, above.

103. Van Unnik, "Confirmation of the Gospel," 31-32.

104. "The large number of well-grounded proposals concerning the purpose of the book make it questionable whether an unequivocal answer to this question (of purpose) is possible," Kümmel, *Introduction to the New Testament*, 163-64. Minear, "Kerygmatic Intention of Acts," 132, speaks of "multiple 'intentions.'"

105. E.g., Menoud, "Plan des Actes des Apôtres," 44-51.

106. Reicke, "Risen Lord and His Church," 157-69. He does not grapple with *why* Luke develops this theme. A few others recognize that the church is a significant theological entity in its own right in Acts. Lampe, *Luke and the Church of Jerusalem*, sees

early chapters, especially considering the amount of space which Luke gives to the second summary. It appears that he is concerned not only with continuing his presentation (proclamation) of Jesus and his salvation, as in the Gospel (now he is proclaimed as Lord, Christ, prophet), but also in commending the community itself as a separate entity.[107]

Such an intention would be very understandable if Luke was addressing readers who were perhaps troubled by the newness of the Christian churches. It would be even more understandable if, as we have had reason to suspect, they had sympathies with Judaism.[108] For unlike the church, the synagogue had the claim to tradition, antiquity, and continuity.[109] What I am suggesting, therefore, is that Luke is presenting an apology for the church.[110]

This appears to be the best explanation of the curious fact that in the place where he is most concerned with giving a picture of the church he goes out of his way to avoid the term *ekklēsia*,[111] employing various other words and circumlocutions instead.[112] He seems to be trying to avoid

---

the Jerusalem church as "center and headquarters of (Christianity's) witness to the whole world" (18); Lohfink, *Sammlung des Israels*, 85–92, shows that the church in Acts possesses "eine Tiefendimension (a depth-dimension)": Luke's concern is to show its origin in God.

107. The Gospel gives us nothing like a commendation of Jesus' disciples; quite the opposite!

108. I am influenced here by Nolland, "Luke's Readers," who argues that Luke is addressing gentile God-fearers who were attracted to the Christian faith. Van Unnik, "Confirmation of the Gospel," 59, cites the work of Mulder for a similar opinion. Compare McCormick, "Social and Economic Background of Luke," 206–07; Dahl, "Purpose of Luke-Acts," 96–97.

109. Dahl, "Purpose of Luke-Acts," 95. Compare the comments of Chadwick, "Ephesians," 980, on the purpose of Ephesians.

110. Lampe, *Luke and the Church of Jerusalem*, 12, asks concerning Acts 21:21 whether Luke is defending the church against Jewish propaganda. In "Grievous wolves," 253–68, he argues that the church suffered a serious counter-mission from the Jews in the late first to early second centuries. It was directed at their claim to be the true Israel.

111. It occurs first in Acts 5:11. Notice, too, the absence of *mathētai* (disciples) until 6:1. It is frequent from then on.

112. "Brethren"—Acts 1:15; "every soul" and "all that believed"—2:43–44; "the men"—4:4; "thy servants"—4:29; "the multitude of them that believed"—4:32. The phrase ἐπὶ τὸ αὐτό (at the same [place], 1:15; 2:1, 44, 47) looks suspiciously like a circumlocution for ἐκκλησία. Compare 1 Cor 11:20, 14:23, and see Bruce, *Acts*, 75. Wilcox, *Semitisms of Acts*, 93–100, thinks it corresponds to the Hebrew יחד, much used at Qumran. One might also have expected *ekklēsia* at 2:41.

anything which might suggest that Christianity is a sectarian party.[113] By the time he writes the *ekklēsia* stands over against the synagogue, and Christianity has inevitably come to be seen as a sect.[114] His sensitivity is plain to see in Paul's reply to Tertullus's accusation that the movement is a sect.[115] Luke prefers to style the movement as "the Way."[116]

It is especially instructive to study the manner in which Luke relates the Christians to the *laos* (*people*) in the early chapters of Acts. The converts are not removed from the *laos*, only "from this crooked generation."[117] Unlike the Pharisees and Essenes—strictly circumscribed parties with complex entry conditions and customs, which held them aloof from the people—the Christians are thoroughly immersed in the *laos*, following God's declared will for the people and seeking to draw the rest along with them.[118] Far from being separate, they are the true *laos*. For the prophet of whom Moses spoke has been revealed, "and it shall be, that every soul which shall not hearken to that prophet, shall be utterly destroyed from among the *laos*."[119] Luke seeks to emphasize both the distinctiveness of

---

113. Degenhardt, *Evangelist der Armen*, 167, and Glöckner, *Verkündigung des Heils*, 80–82, make similar observations in relation to the continuance of the Christians in the temple, though Glöckner dismisses any apologetic motive on the grounds that it would have been irrelevant when Luke wrote.

114. αἵρεσις. See Acts 28:22. Eltester, "Israel im lukanischen Werk und die Nazareth-perikope," 126–29, thinks Luke is sensitive to the specifically Christian coloration of *ekklēsia*: "ἐκκλησία ist zur Zeit des Lukas nicht mehr dasselbe, was es einst gewesen war, wo seine alttestamentliche Wurzel noch deutlich empfunden wurde (At the time of Luke *ekklēsia* is no longer the same as it once had been, when its OT root was still clearly felt)." According to Eltester, this is the reason for his avoidance of the term as an "Allgemeinbegriff" (general term) to describe the whole Christian movement. Luke's purpose is to stress the continuity of the Christian community with the old covenant people. Blevins, "The Early Church: Acts 1–5," 463–74, stresses the sectarian nature of the church. Historically he is no doubt correct, but he entirely overlooks Luke's discomfort with the idea. Contrary to Blevins (468–70), Luke never presents Christianity as the *new* Israel. Had he done so the sectarian label would have been unavoidable. For Luke it is *true* Israel, not *new* Israel.

115. Acts 24:14.

116. See Flew, *Jesus and His Church*, 156–59; Wilcox, *Semitisms of Acts*, 105–06.

117. ἀπὸ τῆς γενεᾶς τῆς σκολιᾶς. Acts 2:40.

118. See Acts 2:47, 3:9–10, 4:2, 21, 5:12, 20, 25. Note how the people are addressed as "men of Israel" and "brethren," and regarded as children of the covenant (2:22, 36, 3:12–13, 17, 26, 5:31).

119. Acts 3:23. However, this destruction is God's activity and belongs to the future; for the moment all the people remain the sons of the prophets and of the Abrahamic covenant (3:25).

the Christians,[120] *and* their solidarity with the rest of the people. This tension is evident in 5:12–14 where none dares join them because of the holy fear surrounding them, yet multitudes are added (to what?) from an admiring *laos*.

The non-sectarian character of the Christian movement is underlined further by Luke's portrayal of the opposition. The apostles' second confrontation by the Jewish leaders is attributed to the "jealousy" of "the sect of the Sadducees."[121]

Finally, it should be noted how and where Luke does introduce the term *ekklēsia*. Having described an internal attack on the integrity of the Christian body in terms reminiscent of the wilderness period, he relates the fear that fell on the whole *ekklēsia*.[122] Shortly afterwards, as Stephen builds an impressive apologetic bridge between the people's rejection of Moses's leadership and their reaction to Jesus, he adds, "This is he that was in the *ekklēsia* in the wilderness . . ."[123] The legitimacy and true identity of the Christian *ekklēsia* is thenceforth established; it stands under the leadership of the prophet of whom Moses spoke, in direct continuity with the *ekklēsia* which was with Moses in the wilderness. From 8:1 on, Luke uses the term freely. Correspondingly, he gives no further attention to the internal life of the churches, and his interest turns to other matters, such as the expansion of the gospel beyond Judaism.

---

120. ἐπὶ τὸ αὐτό.

121. αἵρεσις. Acts 5:17.

122. Acts 5:11. Note, however, that the term is ambiguous in this context. It could mean simply "the meeting," for it retained its secular meaning even in Luke's day (Acts 19:32, 39, 41). Compare Judge, *Social Patterns of Christian Groups*, 45–46. Luke may have intended the ambiguity, quietly introducing the term in preparation for 7:38.

123. Acts 7:38. Most commentators pass over this important verse. Killgallen, *The Stephen Speech*, does not mention it. But see Bruce, *Acts*, 172; Neil, *Acts*, 112. It should not be taken for granted that *ekklēsia* would automatically be used of the assembly in the wilderness. קהל (assembly) is more frequently translated συναγωγή (assembly). It is informative to compare this part of Stephen's speech with Luke's portrayal of the early church. On his return (7:35; compare 2:36), Moses a) led them out having performed τέρατα καὶ σημεῖα (signs and wonders), b) predicted that God would raise up a prophet like himself, c) was in the *ekklēsia* in the wilderness, d) received living oracles. The early community is characterized by τέρατα καὶ σημεῖα (4:30, 5:12, 6:8, cf. 2:19, 22) done in the name of Jesus, who is identified as the prophet like Moses (3:22). Those who refuse him will be cut off from the *laos* (3:23); the Jerusalem church is the true *ekklēsia* of the prophet like Moses. It is a time of revelation, the word of God being constantly spoken (2:42, 3:23, 4:4, 20, 29, 31, 6:2). For further evidence of Luke's concern with the Mosaic character of the early church see Daube, "A Reform in Acts and Its Models," 151–63.

It is now possible to appreciate Luke' descriptions of the community's common life and the story of Ananias and Sapphira as part of the matrix of his wider purpose. The task he has set himself is not just to proclaim Jesus, as he does in the Gospel; he must also legitimate and commend the new community, the church, which is claiming to be the true people of God. He presents the story of its origins in such a way as to show that it is no breakaway movement from Judaism, nor even a possible alternative within Judaism (*hairesis*), but the faithful *laos* in communion with the true prophet. Everything points to its legitimacy and solidarity with the *ekklēsia* of Moses. Through the name of the prophet "signs and wonders" are worked in the congregation, which is jealously guarded by the Spirit, and surrounded by an aura of fear. The account of the community's *koinōnia* is then best understood as Luke's attempt to show that the church's character was congruent with God's work in it.[124] It had a reality and a beauty which marked it out, even to gentiles, as the sphere of God's activity. It was truly bearing fruit that befitted repentance.[125]

5.5 CONCLUSIONS: ACTS AND THE GOSPEL

We are now in a position to draw the significant, though negative, conclusion that it was not Luke's primary purpose to say anything ethical with the community descriptions and the story of Ananias and Sapphira. This accords well with the descriptive character of the "summaries"[126] and the fact that no motive is indicated for the church's activity.[127] What happened is merely related; *koinōnia*, fear, etc. are simply properties of the divinely-chosen, Spirit-filled community. Our examination of the

---

124. Not a symbolic manner of establishing its unity, as in Johnson, "Possessions in Luke-Acts," 199.

125. Note the occurrence of this concept in Acts 26:20.

126. Compare *Did.* 4:8 and *Barn.* 19:8, where such community ideas are turned into ethical injunctions. The nearest we come to explicit ethical teaching in Acts is 20:33–35.

127. The commonly fielded motives for the activity of the early community have little support from Acts: intense expectation of the end (Holtzmann, "Gütergemeinschaft," 334–35; *BC*, I.306; Dunn, *Jesus and the Spirit*, 158–63); the attempt to create, under the new conditions, as close an approximation to the common life of Jesus and his disciples as possible (Tillard, "Fondemont de la vie religieuse," 941). Nor does Luke link it particularly with the activity of the Spirit. Schnackenburg, *Moral Teaching*, 170–71, notes that in Acts "the Spirit was seen rather as a religious phenomenon, not as the fundamental moral force in Christian life."

koinōnia motif, especially the analogy with Philo, strongly suggests that Luke was addressing cultured Hellenistic readers for whom the church was suspect. Luke's primary objective in his summaries of the church's life is not a change of behavior on the part of his readers, but an acceptance of and commitment to the church as the divinely authenticated sphere of salvation.

Having established this, it still remains a matter of interest to explore the possible connections between the Gospel and Acts and thus to uncover something of the continuing relevance of gospel categories for Luke. For he surely sees continuity between the ministry and teaching of Jesus, and the life of the post-Pentecost church.

At this stage of the study we can quickly dispose of the idea that the primitive church represents the attainment of an ideal of poverty. The converse is the case.[128] The word *ptōchos* does not even occur in Acts. The "poor" theme (salvation for Israel) is continued in the offer of salvation and forgiveness to all believing Israelites,[129] and then extended to include the gentiles.

I have already discussed and rejected the argument of Simon Légasse that Luke saw a continuity between the renunciation demanded of the rich ruler and the sharing fellowship of the Pentecost church.[130] In fact, echoes of the renunciation motif are not at all obvious in Acts. The radical and "limitless" character of discipleship (from Luke 14:25-35) is demonstrated and consummated in faithfulness under trial and witness unto death.[131] The warning against allowing wealth to stand in the way of one's coming to Jesus (from Luke 18:18-30) is not developed or illustrated in Acts, which tends to confirm that the rich ruler was not intended as a general case.[132]

---

128. Acts 4:34.

129. Note particularly Acts 4:11-12, and compare Luke 7:23. The two are perhaps related through the idea of "the stone of stumbling" (Isa 8:14; compare *Tg. Isa.* 8:14; 28:16), rendered πέτρα σκανδάλου in Rom 9:33 and 1 Pet 2:8.

130. Pages 134-35, above. Compare Theriault, "Dimensions sociales," 228: "Cette communauté des biens n'est pas inspirée par une théorie sociale quelconque, mais par le souci de realizer l'appel du Seigneur au renoncement (This community of goods is not inspired by a social theory of any kind, but by the concern to realize the Lord's call to renunciation)."

131. Pages 121-23, above. Acts 4:19-20, 29-31, 5:42, 6:8-7:60, 14:22, 21:13-14. The story of Stephen is especially pertinent.

132. Pages 135-37, above. Compare Acts 19:19 for a related thought.

When we turn to consider the primitive community in the light of the concepts uncovered in chapter 4, many points of contact suggest themselves. The most obvious is between Luke 16:9 and the friendship motif of the Acts summaries. The idea of using money to make friends for eternal life is unique to this verse, and is a perfect ethical complement to the descriptive picture of the church. The activity and relationships of the early church are also the direct antithesis of what is displayed in the parable of the rich man and Lazarus. There was no needy person among them, for those who possessed houses and the like sold them to contribute to their needs. Every Lazarus was sharing food in the house of someone better off.[133] The open spontaneous generosity of the early church has the appearance of a consummate fulfillment of what we have seen of Luke's charitable ideals.[134] Conversely, the "greed" (*pleonexia*) against which Luke 12:15–21 warns is the absolute antithesis of the spirit which is manifested in the early community.[135] When it does rear its head in the church (Ananias and Sapphira), it is shown up for what it is and meets with the sudden judgment of God.

In discussion of Luke's ethics, we were able to uncover a strong eschatological factor, a partial "realization" of the kingdom, or at least an ethical anticipation of its social values and conditions. Disappointingly, Acts does not yield anything direct to confirm or deny this picture. Consistent with its non-ethical, evangelistic and apologetic purpose, it has nothing to say about the philosophical framework of the church's social activity. Having admitted this, I would now tentatively suggest that certain incidental statements are revealing of the Lukan outlook, and do suggest that he conceived the activity of the early church as an anticipatory realization of the life of the kingdom, in a manner consistent with the teaching of the gospel.

It is wrong to speak in Acts of "realized eschatology" in the sense in which Dodd coined the term.[136] Luke remains oriented to a definite historical return of Jesus to judge the living and the dead and to establish

---

133. Acts 4:34–37; 2:46.

134. Also to be seen in the raising of Tabitha (9:36–42) and the collection (11:27–30). The point of the latter is no doubt to establish the reality of God's work in the first Greek church. Compare 11:23–24 with the "summaries."

135. In Hellenistic thinking πλεονεξία and πάντα κοινά (everything common) are opposites; see Dio Chrysostom 17:7–9, and compare Seneca, *Ep.* 90:3.

136. See the critique of Cadbury, "Acts and Eschatology," 300–321.

the kingdom for Israel in the manner promised by the prophets.[137] It is in the face of future judgment and salvation that repentance is demanded.[138] Nevertheless, the Christian life involves more than just waiting for the future. Luke also speaks of salvation in a way that suggests a present reality. New converts are described as "those being saved."[139] Forgiveness and possession of the Holy Spirit are presently experienced realities, and the term *zōe* (life) is used in such a way as to suggest that the life of the new age is already being experienced by believers.[140] God has sent his apostle to open blind eyes and to turn Jews and gentiles from the darkness of Satan's realm (*exousia*) to the light of God's kingdom.[141] Thus "the true light is already shining"[142] and repentance is even now leading people into the light of the kingdom, to forgiveness of sins, and to "works worthy of repentance."[143]

It is probable that the "great grace" which rested upon the whole Christian community should also be understood in terms of the grace of salvation. We recall that Luke describes Jesus' proclamation of the kingdom in Luke 4:22 as "words of grace," that is, words about God's gracious offer of salvation.[144] In Acts 4:33 and 11:23 grace (*charis*) appears to be the divine favor and presence which rests upon the community and which is tangibly manifest. Derrett[145] thinks the sharing described in 4:34–35 is the evidence of this *charis*.[146] If this is so, it is a strong indication that Luke sees the church's sharing fellowship as part of its present experience of salvation,[147] and thus a pattern of societal activity which is congruent with, and in some ways anticipates, the life of the age to come.[148]

---

137. See Acts 1:6–7, 11, 2:20b, 3:19–21, 10:42, 14:22, 17:30–31, 24:15.

138. Acts 3:19–21, 17:30–31; cf. 2:20–21.

139. τοὺς σωζομένους. Acts 2:47.

140. Acts 5:20; cf. 11:18.

141. Acts 26:17–18, cf. 2:40.

142. 1 John 2:8.

143. See Acts 26:20, and the discussion of "fruits of repentance," pages 189–90, above.

144. Cf. Acts 13:43; 14:3; 20:24, 32.

145. Derrett, "Ananias, Sapphira, and the Right of Property," 231n2.

146. Note that sharing also takes place in relation to Acts 11:23 (11:27–30).

147. Mott, "Greek Ethics and Christian Conversion," 22–48, examines Titus 2:10–14 and 3:3–7 against the background of Philo and thinks "the end of salvation now at least includes the goal of virtue in Greek ethical philosophy" (30). The appearance of *charis* delivers through παιδεία (discipline) into the virtues (33).

148. The echo of Deut 15:4 in Acts 4:34 may be significant here. In Deut the absence

What flows from this? It is insufficient to say with Conzelmann[149] that Luke's presentation of the primitive church is an ideal which belongs to the initial period, but not to the present.[150] He is correct insofar as Luke demands no mechanical imitation of the form of the church's *koinōnia*. But if this is the kind of community which is a true consummation of the ethical vision of Jesus, and a historical anticipation of the age to come, it can scarcely be doubted that Luke would have wanted it to act as an ideal and incentive to those within and those entering the later church.

---

of poverty is a characteristic of the faithful people enjoying the blessing of God in the land; i.e., it is consonant with salvation. The reality is recognized in Deut 15:11: "The poor will never cease out of the land." Luke does not echo Jesus' words in Mark 14:7, "You always have the poor with you." Thus, in the summaries, and particularly in Acts 4:34, he may be saying that the Christians were enjoying the state of salvific blessing, and that their philanthropic activity was part and parcel of this.

149. Conzelmann, *Theology of Luke*, 233.

150. He is also opposed by Schmithals, "Lukas," 158.

Chapter 6

Luke's Message

THE CHIEF OBJECTIVE OF this study has been to discover what message or messages Luke wished to convey with the large amount of material on possessions and the poor which he incorporated into his Gospel and Acts. Related to this general quest were two subordinate questions concerning the consistency of outlook, and destination and purpose of this material. It is pointless here to repeat the many individual findings which have already been summarized and discussed in their separate chapters. We will content ourselves with bringing together and relating our major results.

Luke's material on the poor and possessions was found not to be the expression of a single theme, but to serve him in various separate though related departments of thought. His fundamental concern is to present Jesus in a faith-compelling manner as the promised Messiah, come to save his people Israel and, ultimately, through his apostles, people from all nations. Israel in its humiliating bondage to gentile powers and its suffering at the hands of the satanic ruler of this present age of wickedness is portrayed in traditional terms as "the poor." God has promised to save "the poor" and set them high, and with the appearance of Jesus these promises are being fulfilled. Jesus proclaims the end of all need and the dawning of peace, joy, freedom, plenty, and laughter.

The simplicity of this picture is disturbed by the fact that the one who claims to have come to inaugurate the kingdom does not appear to be in a state of salvation himself. Rather than being a glorious one who calls people to share his glory, he appears as a suffering one who asks them to identify with him in his rejectedness. Instead of moving Israel to repentance, he succeeds only in creating a division among the people: some believe his promise of the kingdom and are willing to identify with him and share his rejection; others—the leadership of the nation included—are unmoved, seeming to prefer the world as it is. Instead of the painful allegiance to the Son of Man, which will have its glorious reward in the revelation of the kingdom, they opt for the present order by clinging to the good things of this life. A concept of discipleship emerges in which disciples are seen as the true suffering people in solidarity with the Son of Man, and heirs therefore of the promise of the kingdom to "the poor." Israelites who refuse to repent at Jesus' proclamation of the kingdom are characterized as "rich" because they betray themselves as being satisfied and happy with their lot in this age. Luke warns his readers in no uncertain terms not to treat the good things of this age as "good enough" but to reach out for the kingdom, to come to Jesus, suffering for a while if need be, but ultimately inheriting the new age. Because Jesus is the one who brings the kingdom, and experiencing it apart from him is impossible, it is imperative that nothing be allowed to stand in the way of a person's coming to Jesus—especially not possessions—and that once he or she has become a disciple, nothing should be allowed to cause them to withdraw from following and confessing their Lord. In the extreme situation disciples may need to turn their back on possessions, family, and even life itself if they are to remain faithful. If they shrink back their discipleship is utterly worthless.

However, Luke does not imagine that disciples live all the time in such extreme circumstances; they are to pray constantly that they will be spared the time of trial! The extreme situation displays the limitless and unconditional character of commitment to Jesus, which in normal times will be expressed in less dramatic and less painful ways.

Jesus is no longer physically present with his people, but he has not left them in ignorance with nothing to do. He will be absent for an undisclosed period of time until the day when he returns to redeem Israel and openly manifest his kingship in the new age. During this time his people are to busy themselves with kingdom-related activity for which they will be amply rewarded on his return. Luke is captivated by the reality and inevitability of the coming kingdom and desires that human beings should live with it as a fact which changes and conditions their lives, regardless of whether it is to arrive tomorrow or after a long period of time. Such a stance is possible, for the ethic of the kingdom is no "Interimsethik" which is only valid over a short period of time but a making real of what is to be the life of all permanently in the new age. Nor is such an ethic of anticipatory realization of kingdom life completely foreign to Israel or the world; it is after all only what the law has always demanded and, in terms of interpersonal relationships, is not far removed from certain Greek ideals. What is new is the degree of unreserved engagement with God and the fact that what once might have been seen as lofty ideals are now promised realities which have already begun to appear with the coming of Jesus.

Insofar as possessions are concerned, the disciple is to realize that they belong to a passing age, and that value in the kingdom is measured in other terms. Because they are already anticipating the life of the kingdom and are thus committed to its values, disciples will want to transform the wealth of this age into what counts as wealth in the value system of the world to come. They will use their possessions, therefore, to help the needy and to foster fellowship and goodwill which will extend into the age to come.

The final result of this living for Jesus and his kingdom will be a glorious reception into the new age, which, after all, will only be the consummation and vindication of what disciples have longed for, prayed for, and lived for. In the meantime, they may be assured of the helping care of God to meet their needs and to enable them to live in the present time with an absence of anxious care. This is itself a foretaste of the promised future. People who in their desire for "the good life" cling to possessions for themselves instead of employing them generously in the service of others will find that they have failed to find the life they sought—a life which is available only through Jesus—and will be lost in the coming judgment.

But Luke's concern goes further than presenting Jesus and the kingdom: he has to convince his readers that the church, though seemingly a latecomer on the scene, is nonetheless the sphere of God's saving activity. He wants to show his readers that the Christian assemblies are the creation of the God of the Old Testament, who has sent his Messiah to save Israel and the nations. To this end he portrays the earliest Jerusalem church simply as faithful Israelites responding to the call of the prophet Jesus, being the object of the favor and admiration of the rest of the people (leaders excluded) and having all the marks of a community especially favored by God. In particular, it is surrounded by holy awe inspired by the manifest activity of the holy God in its midst and is characterized by such a caring, charitable fellowship that it appears in genuine beauty as the true resting place of the divine favor and as a worthy witness to the reality of the new age it proclaims.

Luke's purpose, however, is not just that his readers be convinced of the authenticity of the church; he wants them to *be* the church, which he sees as the community of the new age, even now experiencing the blessings and living the life of the age to come. The church is a societal embodiment of devotion towards God and open caring for others, which is of the essence of Jesus' ethical teaching. Luke desires that people should come to Jesus in an act of repentance which will radically reorient them towards the coming kingdom and hence to a present caring for others. He wants them to enter the church and begin living the life of the new age by ongoing faithfulness to the Messiah-Lord and unrelenting benevolence to their fellows.

Moving to our two specific questions, we are now able to affirm with confidence that Luke displays a consistency of outlook in his employment of poor-possessions material. We have found nothing ascetic in Luke-Acts: neither poverty ideal nor demand for renunciation of possessions for its own sake. Far from counseling a withdrawal from the world and its wealth, Luke demands positive engagement: money is to be used positively to good effect in accordance with the values of the kingdom. Luke's glowing statements about the glorious destiny of the poor and his warnings of the horrors coming upon the rich have turned out to be quite consistent with an orientation towards and concern for the well-to-do. His apparent demands for total renunciation have also been seen to be in accord with his teaching on the ongoing use of possessions. The appearance of contradiction is due on the one hand to our unfamiliarity with Jewish and Hellenistic thought forms and on the other to an over-readiness to make direct ethical applications of materials which Luke presents in such a way as to demand a more subtle and thoughtful application. It may also be noted at this point that we have had no cause to suspect that Luke is presenting a message which is seriously divergent from that of his sources.

The question of destination is more difficult, and we should not attempt to be dogmatic in a study as limited in its scope as this has been. Nevertheless, our inquiry has been fruitful in suggestions that Luke was writing to folk with a good knowledge and appreciation of Jewish ways of thinking, as well as some degree of sophistication in terms of classical Hellenistic culture. Much in our study has indicated that they were well-to-do and potentially had a lot to lose if they were to attach themselves to the Christian movement. We have found nothing which might suggest Luke was addressing the socially and economically disadvantaged.

As to Luke's purpose in writing, it is clear from much that I have written that I take it to be evangelistic. This is something about which it is difficult to be certain; books written to convert outsiders have often been of great service to those already in the church, and some written to encourage the faithful have proved fruitful in reaching outsiders. Nevertheless, there is much in Luke which "feels" like it is meant to convince the not-yet-convinced and to push the not-yet-committed rather than confirm and instruct the converted. The quantity of pure apologetic points this way (his redaction of the passion narrative to demonstrate Jesus' innocence; his demonstration of Christians' faithfulness to classical Jewish hopes, *and* his portrayal of its political innocence, *and* his concern to legitimate Paul and the gentile mission; his way of commending the church); so does the way he highlights the division of Israel, portraying people at the point of decision being challenged to all-or-nothing commitment. Luke's presentation of the story of the rich ruler and his arrangement of it with the story of Zacchaeus strongly suggested an evangelistic purpose.

This study would certainly add weight to the opinion that Luke was addressing well-to-do Hellenistic God-fearers who were attracted to the Christian movement, but hesitant as to whether such a newcomer on the scene as the church could possibly be authentic and afraid of what might be the cost to them socially and economically if they were to declare themselves publicly and unreservedly for Christ and his church.

Appendix

REVIEW OF SOME IMPORTANT STUDIES SINCE 1978

UNKNOWN TO ME, OTHERS were impelled by the rising social unease of the seventies to undertake studies of Jesus' teaching about the rich and poor. Some of these took it as axiomatic that any understanding which gave anything but a straight literal interpretation of "poor" on the lips of Jesus was an evil spiritualization in the service of Western affluence, which robbed the genuine poor of their gospel. So, without argument, Schottroff and Stegemann dismiss any symbolic or non-literal approach to the poor.

Luise Schottroff and Wolfgang Stegemann. *Jesus and the Hope of the Poor*. Eugene, OR: Wipf and Stock, 2009.

Jesus and the Hope of the Poor first appeared in German in 1978 (*Jesus von Nazaret: Hoffnung der Armen* [Kevalaer: Topos plus]) when the authors both taught in German universities. The first two chapters were written by Schottroff, the third by Stegemann; the English translation came in 1986. My own dissertation was submitted in 1978, so we worked unaware of each other. Schottroff and Stegemann examine the issue of poverty more widely than in Luke-Acts. They identify three levels: the earliest Jesus tradition, the beliefs of the supposed Q-community, and then of Luke. They do not think we can know much with certainty about the historical Jesus, and opt, therefore, to speak of the "earliest Jesus tradition" at the same time as they want to use the word "Jesus" as a theological term. Viewed in this manner one could say that over their three main chapters they have given us three "Jesuses." As to which is to be seen as authoritative or regulative they are not clear. Respecting the authority of the Bible becomes a "confrontation" and "conversation with human beings who have lived the faith before us."[1]

Working on the earliest Jesus tradition, they assert that Jesus comes from a poor background; his disciples are poor because they have renounced possessions and embraced poverty. They acknowledge that the word *ptōchos* means destitute, but then, surprisingly and in my view improbably, they include in this category paid employees of the tax office. So, although they set out insisting that we must understand "poor" literally, they end up with a broad category of people under this classification. As well as Jesus' favor towards the impoverished, what emerges is his "non-exclusiveness." "Now in the middle of the first century AD, in a time of terrible misery and destitution, poor Jews formed an association with tax collectors and sinners in Israel and claimed this Israel for its God" (37). This earliest tradition believes in a future reversal of the positions of rich and poor, when the poor will be compensated for their present deprivation.

The second layer of tradition, represented by the document Q, evidences the existence of a community of wandering "messengers of Jesus" who have appropriated Jesus' teaching in such a way that they resemble the ancient Cynics. They voluntarily place themselves at the bottom of the heap in society. They are against wealth in all its forms, yet desire the salvation of their enemies, so continue their wandering, society-challenging lifestyle. Jesus' instruction to the twelve for their mission is seen as the teaching of this Q group.

Schottroff and Stegemann move finally to a study of Luke-Acts—a third layer of tradition—and the community presupposed by these writings. It is a community without poor and with many well-to-do Christians. Luke is the "evangelist of the rich." He holds up the example of Jesus' disciples, who were literally required to renounce all possessions, though Luke does not ask this of the Christians of his community. His demand of them is conveyed in the story of Zacchaeus: they are to give away half of their possessions to the less well-off of their community and establish equality. They may use their wealth, but must avoid greed, practice almsgiving to the poor outside the church, and do "caritative activity" to those within. Luke intends the teaching of the Sermon on the Mount (after the Beatitudes) to address directly the members of his own community. Love

---

1. Schottroff and Stegemann, *Hope of the Poor*, viii.

of enemies and the teaching that follows means they are to lend to church members (who will hate them!) without expecting a return.

The strength of this study, if it be judged a strength, is that it solves some of the tensions in Luke and Acts by apportioning them to three strata of tradition. All along Schottroff and Stegemann insist that Jesus demanded absolute renunciation of possessions of all his followers, whereas the Q-Christians expected some to stay in their homes, and Luke expects members of his church to be comfortable, and comfortable in dealing with their possessions. But did Luke think that his readers would distinguish these three strata within his Gospel? In my view, the weakness of the study is the confusion it creates by its thee-layered approach. Luke states his intention clearly at the beginning of his Gospel. It is to relate the story surrounding Jesus with a view to his readers (hearers) gaining certainty—about Jesus! He gives no indication that he is surveying the beliefs of two separate communities along with a third, which is his own. He would surely know if Q (which he draws on copiously) was in fact the teaching of a later movement, and an idiosyncratic appropriation of an earlier Jesus tradition. Luke's convictions, in my opinion, are to be assayed from all the material he utilizes, not just that which is judged not to belong to two earlier layers of tradition. This study, therefore, hardly helps us towards a unified and coherent understanding of Luke's teaching. Although it wishes to say something to the modern world about poverty, it leaves us in confusion as to which, if any, of the three very different approaches is meant to be followed.

Walter Pilgrim. *Good News for the Poor*. Minneapolis: Augsburg, 1981.

At the time as I was doing my work in Cambridge, Walter Pilgrim was at work in Tübingen on a study leave project from Pacific Lutheran University, where he was a theology professor. *Good News for the Poor* (1981) was published shortly before my own dissertation. I was not aware of his work, nor did he interact with mine. He comes to the question of Luke and the poor out of his own conviction of the need for churches to engage with the world's poor. He focuses on Luke but introduces his study with two preliminary studies: a survey of the Old Testament and intertestamental writings, including the Dead Sea Scrolls and the rabbis, and then a short study of Jesus and the poor. His Old Testament survey is useful. In his discussion of the Psalms he is drawn to associate the *anawim* (poor) of the Psalms with the pious, an association which he carries into his study of Jesus. He thinks there was a distinct *anawim* mentality, a fusion of poverty and piety, in which Jesus was nurtured. This view is not original to Pilgrim and is not an uncommon claim. My own dissertation argues that this is fundamentally mistaken. It makes poverty a virtue, which the Gospels never do. Pilgrim also takes note of one psalm in which there is an identification of the "poor" with Israel up against its enemies, but neglects a number of others where the same understanding is present.[2] He also notes that the Dead Sea community applied this language to itself, but overlooks the possible significance of this for untying the knot of Jesus' preaching about the poor.

In chapter 3 Pilgrim turns his attention to Luke. The main issue is to determine who Luke means by "the poor." He struggles on the one hand with his determination not to "spiritualize" what Luke says about them, and on the other with his own holistic reading which suggests that Jesus addressed a broader audience than the economically deprived.[3] He attempts to solve the tension by extending the category of "poor." My own studies convinced me that the word *ptōchos* meant poor in the sense of indigent: paupers, who needed charity to subsist.[4] Pilgrim mentions this group, but only at the end of a catalog consisting of "multitudes," tax collectors, sinners, prostitutes, and day-laborers. Who does Pilgrim think are the poor? The poor "include those suffering from genuine poverty and need," but then he extends the idea to include "the sick and possessed ... outcasts and sinners, those excluded socially and religiously because of despised professions and immoral lives ... even the disciples of Jesus, who have left all in his service."[5] By this means he concludes that the majority of the population were "poor" and "on the mind of anyone who came to announce 'good news for the poor.'"[6] In my view Pilgrim takes a modern first-world view of the poor and projects it onto the world of Jesus: "The simple fact that Palestine was so poor, so that the poor

---

2. Psalm 74; Pilgrim, *Good News for the Poor*, 29–30.

3. This is a feature of Armitage, "Good News to the Poor," who, when considering Jesus' treatment of tax collectors, makes the striking observation, "'Good news is preached to the poor', yet it seems also that good news is offered to oppressors of the poor," 210.

4. Pages 32, above.

5. Pilgrim, *Good News for the Poor*, 83.

6. Pilgrim, *Good News for the Poor*, 44.

constituted the majority of the people, points to the poor masses as the chief human source of Jesus' appeal."[7] This is asserted, not demonstrated. I think it is wide of the mark.

Pilgrim's interpretive instincts are good. He knows that Jesus' gospel was not for a limited few—not just the literal poor. But he strains the bounds of clarity when he wants to include wealthy businessfolk as "poor" while insisting on a literal reading. At one point he comes close to my own thesis. Had he followed through he might have seen how some of his apparently ill-fitting groups actually do belong to a common category. Pilgrim and I were reading the same books at the same time, and I am encouraged that he saw clearly that the final fulfillment of Jesus' gospel awaits the coming in fullness of the new age.

In Part 2 of Pilgrim's study, the various passages dealing with possessions are examined with useful exegetical comment. The material is arranged under the themes of renunciation, the dangers of wealth, the right use of possessions, and the sharing community. He underlines Jesus' demand of all his followers that they abandon all their possessions, but follows Schottroff and Stegemann in concluding that this was limited to Jesus' own lifetime. Why, then, does Luke emphasize it? He rejects Degenhard's suggestion that it is meant as a demand of full-time Christian workers, and does not consider a background of persecution to be correct. Again, he follows Schottroff and Stegemann's theory that Luke is addressing the rich Christians of his own community about the danger of their possessions. In his warnings of the danger of greed Luke urges the wealthy Christians in his own church to consider the peril they are in. At times Pilgrim appears to want Christians in our own day to go all the way with renunciation of possessions—this is what his reading of the material seems to require—but he hesitates because of the considerable amount of teaching in Luke about the use of possessions. So, his chapter on the right use of possessions establishes that Luke wants those with wealth "to participate boldly in the worldly service of making friends with your wealth."[8] Zacchaeus "is the paradigm *par excellence* for Luke of how the rich can enter the kingdom of God."[9] Almsgiving, charity, lending *gratis*, inviting the poor to your banquet are what the wealthy Christian of

---

7. Pilgrim, *Good News for the Poor*, 51; 48–55.
8. Pilgrim, *Good News for the Poor*, 129.
9. Pilgrim, *Good News for the Poor*, 134.

Luke's time is enjoined to do. The survey finishes with a perceptive study of the ethical teaching of John the Baptist.

In this second part of his study Pilgrim works hard at drawing out the particular thrust of the teaching to the community of Luke's time. He introduces a similar confusion to that of Schottroff and Stegemann's study. What is reckoned to be the original teaching of Jesus is accorded great authority and importance, though much of it is reckoned to be inapplicable today. Luke's revision and reapplication is then treated as though *it* carries real authority for the present. The descriptions in Acts of the first Jerusalem church are intended as "a working vision of what every Christian community should be like, then and now." Pilgrim even wants to squeeze Luke to commend the practice of giving aid outside the Christian community. No doubt this is an admirable thing, but it can hardly be derived from Luke-Acts. There are obvious tensions in Pilgrim's approach. He betrays his discomfort when he insists that the kingdom is especially proclaimed to the economically poor—but then struggles to give the rich a place; and when he insists that the rich take the demand of renunciation seriously—but then draws back and affirms the legitimacy of Christians having possessions and even being rich.

Philip Francis Esler. *Community and Gospel in Luke-Acts: The Social and Political Motivations of Lucan Theology*. Cambridge, UK: Cambridge University Press, 1987.

Esler was a barrister of the New South Wales Supreme Court and a lecturer at Sydney University. Since writing "Community and Gospel" (an Oxford PhD dissertation, 1981) he has lectured in several English and Scottish universities and is a champion of social-scientific interpretation of biblical texts. He has the degree of Doctor of Divinity from Oxford University and is a Fellow of the Royal Society of Edinburgh. He describes his approach in *Community and Gospel* as "socio-redactional."[10] Chapter 7 is devoted to poverty and riches in Luke-Acts and is an elaboration of his main thesis.

Esler has a radical approach to redaction criticism. He thinks the traditional approach, where applications to life are drawn from an existing theology, needs to be turned on its head: "social and political exigencies played a vital role in the formation of Luke's theology, rather than

---

10. Esler, *Community and Gospel*, 5–6.

merely constituting the areas in which it was applied."[11] He thinks the social situation of Luke's community induced him to *formulate* theology. If this meant Luke selected from Jesus and the apostles what was especially relevant to his own context and re-expressed it for his own time, I would have no quarrel. But Esler means Luke actually invented incidents to create a theology to say what he wanted to say to his community.[12] For example, according to Esler, Luke's Nazareth story, the conversion of Cornelius, and the Jerusalem Council have all been invented by Luke to expound his theological purpose. So, "Luke's so strangely uniform and idealistic portrayal of the first Christian congregations is not an accurate reflection of the historical reality of their origins."[13] Thus, when Esler speaks of "the Lukan Jesus" he is speaking of a fiction, invented to sell his view of how Christians should behave towards the poor—at least, that is how I read Esler. One wonders what possible authority Luke's teaching could have for Christians today. Esler appears to think this is still a legitimate way to do theology: one invents it to meet current needs.

One must question whether Theophilus and Luke's community would have been aware that this was what Luke was doing, and what their attitude towards his theology was, if they were. Or did Luke hide it, only for it to be discovered by a twentieth-century barrister? In fact, what Esler suggests is flat contrary to the stated intention of Luke's preface, and would soon have disqualified his account from any serious consideration by those who knew.

That having been said, let me say something about Esler's view of Luke's community. The strength of his work is its clarity and argumentation. So, unlike many scholars, he gives *reasons* for dating Luke-Acts to about 85–95. However, his chief pointer, that Luke has historical knowledge of the fall of Jerusalem, is one not all will accept; it is a point on which scholars will forever be divided.

Having established a date for Luke-Acts, Esler reasons from their prominence in Acts that Luke's church was composed largely of God-fearers and Jews (in contrast to the many pagans in Paul's churches). Luke emphasizes their legitimacy (according to Esler) because they have been recently ejected from the synagogues and require reassurance. He views Luke's emphasis on the poor and the rich as a further example of

---

11. Esler, *Community and Gospel*, 1.
12. Against this see Dunn, *Neither Jew nor Greek*, 303–04.
13. Esler, *Community and Gospel*, 42.

social circumstances drawing forth creative theology. He has an excellent discussion of the stratification of Roman society in Hellenistic cities of the East,[14] from which he opines the presence of rich and poor together in Luke's church. Luke's prominent possessions theme arises, on the one hand from the many who were wealthy, and on the other from the difficult economic conditions in the empire and the membership of many poor people in his church. He states correctly that *ptōchos* meant a beggar.[15] He thinks the priority accorded them in Jesus' teaching (understand: the Lukan Jesus) indicates the practice of Luke's church, which "although it contained wealthy and influential members, the privileged places in it were reserved for the very dregs of Hellenistic society, especially the beggars and the physically disabled."[16]

The preference shown by "the Lukan Jesus" for the poor is intended by Luke to "legitimate" the poor. The rich, on the other hand, are severely warned: if they do not distribute some of their wealth to the poor they face eternal punishment.[17] Luke demands that they assist the poor. In this way the blessing of the poor, which in part belongs to the next world, is also experienced in the here and now: "The elimination of injustice, the alleviation of the sufferings of the poor and destitute, is not merely an eschatological reality, but is a vital constituent of Christianity in this world, here and now."[18] This is no doubt correct, but although emphasized by Luke, it is common to early Christianity and hardly Luke's invention.

S. John Roth. *The Blind, the Lame and the Poor: Character Types in Luke-Acts*. Sheffield, UK: Sheffield Academic Press, 1997.

"Why are the blind, lepers, the poor, and the deaf so prominent in the Gospel of Luke and all but absent in the Acts of the Apostles?"[19] With this perceptive question Roth opens his study. The language of poverty, he observes, which is so prominent in the Gospel of Luke, is nowhere found in Acts. This requires explanation, and Roth sets out to find it. Unlike many studies of our theme in Luke-Acts, including my own, Roth's study

14. Esler, *Community and Gospel*, 173–79.
15. Esler, *Community and Gospel*, 164, 180.
16. Esler, *Community and Gospel*, xv.
17. Esler, *Community and Gospel*, 197–98.
18. Esler, *Community and Gospel*, 193.
19. Roth, *Character Types*, 11.

is devoted to this one issue: who are the poor in Luke? He is critical of my own conclusion.

In 2011 Roth was made a bishop in the Evangelical Lutheran Church of America. His doctoral studies were done at Vanderbilt University and *The Blind, the Lame and the Poor* is an updated version of his 1994 dissertation. It approaches the inquiry in an audience-orientated literary direction, which makes use of the notion of "intertext." This is a text the author of the third Gospel assumes his readers will have knowledge of and will use to interpret—in this case—character types in his Gospel. "When directed to an intertext, readers fill out types by reading them through the lens of literary conventions established in the intertext."[20]

Roth contends that Luke assumes an audience familiar with the Septuagint version of the Old Testament, and steers them to learn from this "intertext" the identity of the blind, poor, etc. He conducts an inquiry into the meaning of these terms in the Septuagint and concludes that the poor, blind, lame, etc. are the needy who cannot help themselves. One interesting conclusion is that these people have no personality. For example: "The captive is not an actor, but is one who is acted upon."[21] Roth observes that this is also true in Luke.

In his study of the use of such terminology in Luke's Gospel (it is mostly absent from Acts) he concludes that they are character types lacking the capacity for moral action: "They display neither piety nor impiety, neither moral character or immoral character." Conforming to the Septuagint stereotype, "they are typically anonymous, powerless, vulnerable and a-responsible."[22]

The function of these characters in Luke is to confirm Jesus as God's eschatological agent, "whose ministry and fate express in narrative form God's end-time intervention to restructure the world."[23] "Those who experienced Jesus' presence before his ascension experienced the kingdom of God for a time.[24] In other words, they function christologically (not ethically). "Jesus fulfills the authorial audience's expectation that the 'coming one' will be the divine deliverer of the blind, the poor, and

20. Roth, *Character Types*, 79.
21. Roth, *Character Types*, 101.
22. Roth, *Character Types*, 215.
23. Roth, *Character Types*, 215.
24. Roth, *Character Types*, 215–16.

the lame."[25] They are absent from Acts because Jesus is no longer "God's earthly eschatological agent of salvation." He is now the ascended Lord, and there is "a new christological situation."[26]

Roth approves of my attention to the Old Testament background in *Possessions and the Poor*, but is critical of its attention to the Hebrew, allegedly at the expense of the Greek. But his insistence that the Septuagint alone should provide the answer to our question I see as problematic. I am in total agreement that Luke makes heavy use of the Septuagint, and assumes his readers will be familiar with it. It is an important "intertext" for study of Luke. However, to move from there to assuming it is the sole or primary source of their understanding of Greek terms, for readers who are conversant in the common Greek, and part of an international Hellenistic culture, seems to me quite wrong. As with most language it will be the context which is the primary guide to interpreting which of a range of possible meanings is correct. Furthermore, it is artificial to limit the readers' outside knowledge to the Septuagint alone, when they were involved in a movement which was led mostly by people with a Jewish and Aramaic language background and for whom Jesus was still a living memory. Albeit I (and he) focus our attention on Luke, and not Jesus, we should not lose sight of the fact that *Luke* focuses on Jesus. In his telling of the Nazareth story, for example, is Luke so unconcerned with what happened that his account is meant to be understood solely via the Greek Old Testament? Jesus did not address the synagogue in Greek, and I have shown at one point that the Hebrew background makes better sense of the thought-connections in his reading.[27]

Besides this, careful study of the Septuagint does not rule out the poor sometimes being used as a description of Israel in captivity, as Roth himself is forced to concede on one occasion,[28] though he calls my overall conclusion "extraordinary" and "inventive."[29] Extraordinary my conclusion may be, but it is not inventive; it is the most probable meaning

---

25. Roth, *Character Types*, 218.
26. Roth, *Character Types*, 220.
27. Pages 48–59, above.
28. 121n94. Roth argues against me on the basis of Psalm 71 (72), though I did not use this Psalm to support my case. Roth's exegesis here is sound. However, he concedes that "poor" may be used as a "cipher" for Israel in Psalm 73 (74), but does not consider this in relation to the other psalms where I find a similar characterization of Israel as "poor" (Psalms 9, 68, 76; possibly 132, 147, 102). See page 28, above.
29. Roth, *Character Types*, 46–47.

in Isaiah 61 and related passages. Furthermore, I discovered it in the literature of Jewish movements before, during, and after Jesus. Reliance on the Greek Bible alone—even if it did lead to Roth's conclusion—is far too limited.

His conclusion that the notion of the "poor" is absent from Acts because it is not required, as it is in the Gospel, to establish Jesus' eschatological credentials is not the only one that is possible. Of course, Jesus is not present in the same way to establish his credentials, but Acts is as concerned as the Gospel with his identity. If Roth's thesis were correct, the evangelistic speeches would have trumpeted Jesus' treatment of the poor and needy. Could it not be that the language of the poor features in certain passages in the Gospel on the lips of Jesus because this is actually one way he spoke to Israel's self-understanding? In the wider world of Acts such language was not used.

Kyoung-Jin Kim. *Stewardship and Almsgiving in Luke's Theology.* Sheffield, UK: Sheffield Academic Press, 1998.

In 1993 Kyoung-Jin Kim completed a doctoral dissertation at the University of Glasgow, which, with some revision, he published in 1998 as *Stewardship and Almsgiving in Luke's Theology.* He tackles most of the issues relating to the themes of wealth and poverty and rich and poor in Luke and Acts but focuses attention on the relationship of renunciation versus stewardship of possessions. Comparison with Mark suggests a different concept of discipleship on the part of Luke. Whereas for Mark the disciples are a limited group called to total renunciation of all possessions, in Luke they are a much larger group whom Kim sees belonging to two categories: itinerant and sedentary. Those who travelled with Jesus had to renounce everything material, while those who stayed at home were called only to renounce *ownership* of their possessions.

This leads Kim to the question of Luke's understanding of the relationship of disciples to their Master. According to Kim, the relation of teacher to learner is informed by that of master and slave. The disciple finds himself in the position of a steward, called to faithfully manage his master's goods. This is an important insight. I would only question whether it is applicable, as Kim suggests, only or especially to the wealthy in Luke's community. Surely it can have reference to all.

As to the question of how the steward is to discharge his trust, Kim points to the emphasis on almsgiving in Luke-Acts. Those with money are to help those who do not. He is uncertain whether this refers only to those within the Christian community or to the wider world of need.

As with most academic dissertations there is a wealth of material with which to agree or disagree. I am of the view that he has misplaced both Mark and Luke, the former in the midst of the Neronian persecution, the latter late in the century, but this has little effect on his major thesis. In focusing attention on the important themes of stewardship and almsgiving in Luke-Acts and tying these to a concept of discipleship, he has done a valuable thing.

John L. Topel. *Children of a Compassionate God: A Theological Exegesis of Luke 6.20–49.* Collegeville, MN: Liturgical Press, 2001.

In 2001 John L. Topel of Seattle University published this detailed study of Luke's "Sermon on the Plain." In answer to the question of who the poor are in Luke, he dismisses the idea that the poor are virtuous, along with other metaphorical interpretations, and the suggestion that "poor" might be an overarching generalization including all the categories of need mentioned in Jesus' Nazareth sermon. He contends that a literal, socio-economic reading is the only one tenable. Who are the poor? He acknowledges that *ptōchoi* are beggars and others unable to provide for themselves, but extends the category to include "the lowest segment of the artisan class, and the section of the peasant class teetering on the brink of foreclosure for debt."[30] In this way he includes an estimated 25 percent of the population. He also includes Jesus' disciples, who through renunciation of possessions have become voluntarily poor. He rejects approaches that see the blessing of the poor as belonging to the eschatological future.[31] What Jesus promises is for now. Having said this, he declares that the "reign of God" will not be complete in this age, but waits for Jesus' return. Topel mounts an interesting scenario whose conclusions to my mind reveal the improbability of his literal (but then extended) approach. Jesus announced the "reign of God" and called on all of his disciples to give away all their possessions to the poor and in so doing abolish poverty. This is the program of the "reign of God." It is seen to

30. Topel, *Children*, 78.
31. Topel, *Children*, 76.

become a reality in Acts where there is no mention of the "poor." In the latter section of his study, where he explores what motivation might make Jesus' "impossible ethic" possible, he goes as far as saying rich oppressors are longing to be liberated. It is their conversion which makes possible the relief of the poor and the reign of God in its present form: "Their dispossession and sharing is the material grounds for the human community of the reign coming to be. If they become poor by such generosity, they too will be fed by other rich people caught by the disciples' contagious love."[32]

This is a startling thesis. It raises the question of whether in his declaring the poor blessed Jesus had in mind an immediate social "program" which his ministry would bring about.[33] I think not.

If Jesus saw himself as executing a practical strategy to abolish poverty, I think we would find an amount of material in his gospel focusing on the benefits accruing to the poor as a result of the divestment of his better-off followers. There is nothing of this nature. The focus is entirely on the actions of wealthy disciples, and one does not feel there are many of these. Impoverished people joining the Jesus movement would certainly have been helped, but without evidence of an enduring system of support, it is unlikely their poverty could be said to be ended. Does Jesus himself not say, "The poor you will always have among you"? It is true that in the Jerusalem church poverty is addressed and alleviated for a time. It "shows the success of Jesus' program for the poor."[34] But for how long is impossible to say, and begs the question: "Why is there no mention of anything like this in the Gospels?"

Thomas E. Phillips. *Reading Issues of Wealth and Poverty in Luke-Acts*. New York: Edwin Mellen, 2001.

Issues of Wealth and Poverty is a fascinating study of a single theme in Luke-Acts, fascinating in part because it allows its reader to look into the mental processes of the study's author. Phillips employs a specific reading method which he has crafted from the reader-response theory of Wolfgang Iser. He reads Luke and then Acts sequentially, picking up the theme of possessions where it first occurs and making an initial judgment of its probable meaning. Reading on, he refines this judgment as he encounters

32. Topel, *Children*, 260.
33. Topel, *Children*, 86.
34. Topel, *Children*, 86.

material consistent with his initial judgment, or contradictory, or forcing an adjustment, or posing fresh questions to be answered later in the reading process. A "gestalt" (shape) emerges, which is progressively refined. The reader of the book is in a real sense hearing Phillips trying to make sense of an issue which superficially presents as contradictory.

He begins with Mary's Magnificat, where the "poor" are lifted up and the "rich" sent away empty, and poses the question of whether these terms are to be understood metaphorically or literally. He will chase this question through both of Luke's volumes, but makes a tentative judgment that the language must be metaphorical, because the earlier parts of the song are about human attitudes.[35] This is different from my own reading of the Magnificat and from that of many others.

Phillips insists on the openness of his reading at this point; it may need to be abandoned or refined. He comes next to the counsel of John the Baptist to those who ask what they should do. Less is required of them than members of the Qumran community; John simply "affirms the traditional Jewish values of generosity towards those in need . . . and refraining from greed."[36] As I applied Phillips's reading method to his own work, I began to wonder if he was not at this stage minimizing the radical nature of John's requirements in the interest of "taming" Luke's teaching.

According to Phillips, the theme of Jesus' reading in the Nazareth synagogue is forgiveness, so the language of preaching good news to the poor is again quickly taken as metaphorical.[37] This is confirmed for Phillips as God is seen helping both rich (Naaman) and poor (the widow). He proceeds through the rest of the Gospel and Acts building on his initial "gestalt" with an eminently sensible reading, though one which arouses the feeling that something may be getting left out.

Phillips divides the Gospel into four sections whose titles indicate his reading strategy: chapters 1–4, "Initial Frame of Reference"; 5–8, "Finding and Filling Gaps"; 9–14, "Encountering Negation"; 15–24, "Bringing Closure to the Reading." The primary "gap" to be filled is the question whether renunciation of possessions is required of all Christians; what does it mean that Peter and his associates "left all"? The reader (Phillips) is faced with the possible negation of the reading he has been developing.[38]

---

35. Phillips, *Wealth and Poverty*, 91.
36. Phillips, *Wealth and Poverty*, 94.
37. Phillips, *Wealth and Poverty*, 96–97.
38. Phillips, *Wealth and Poverty*, 101.

But he observes that Levi was not told to leave *everything* and later hosts a banquet in his house. "Leaving," then, must refer to quitting his employment: "his lucrative trade, and not the sum of possessions."[39] Furthermore, the disciples are not portrayed as experiencing literal privation, which confirms for Phillips that renunciation of possessions is not called for, nor is literal poverty adumbrated.[40]

The principal "negation" of his developing "gestalt" is the instruction Jesus gives to the Twelve and later the seventy-two as he sends them out on their mission. Are the rigorous requirements to travel without money and equipment meant for disciples at all times, so negating the reading to this point, or were they specific to a certain time and situation? Is a distinction to be made between the Twelve and "the receptive households, who share their resources with the Twelve"?[41] In the story of the feeding of the five thousand, which follows the return of the twelve, the disciples are portrayed "entertaining the possibility of buying food for the crowds."[42] They seem no longer to be subject to the "stern" conditions of the earlier mission. Phillips notes the sense of urgency that seems to accompany the later mission.[43]

Proceeding in this manner Phillips is able to establish that there is no general call for renunciation of possessions and no glamorization of poverty. The ethic demanded is generosity and avoidance of greed. He deals with the Gospel and then in a separate chapter with Acts. The reader (Phillips) ends up satisfied with a consistent answer to his original question.

However, another reader may wish to query certain of Phillips' consistency-making decisions and wonder whether his reading strategy may unconsciously be closing off possibilities so that the reader is left "comfortable."[44] With respect to the Magnificat the choice of metaphorical over literal begs the question of what the point of the metaphor might be. Phillips assumes it means an attitude of detachment from wealth. But

---

39. Phillips, *Wealth and Poverty*, 104.

40. Phillips has many valuable matter-of-fact observations which support his case that renunciation of possessions is not called for. Others are found in Armitage, "Good News for the Poor," 206–10.

41. Phillips, *Wealth and Poverty*, 129.

42. Phillips, *Wealth and Poverty*, 130.

43. Phillips, *Wealth and Poverty*, 132–33.

44. Phillips, *Wealth and Poverty*, 94.

what if the language is nationalistic (as abounds in Luke 1–2), and what if "poor" was a recognizable cipher for Israel, as I have argued?[45]

The reader (Phillips) is "comfortable" with the Baptist's "traditional Jewish values."[46] But why is there no attention to other Jewish boundary markers, to purity and sabbath-keeping, for example? I find myself asking why John's demands are focused where they are and not somewhere else. And where does John fit in relation to the developing story of Jesus? Are John and Jesus simply equal vehicles for expressing an ethic of possessions? What, for instance, is the place of the kingdom of God, something Phillips mostly ignores?

In my own approach to the issues of wealth and the poor in Luke-Acts I made the conscious decision not to carry conclusions from earlier passages on to others. I did this for fear that my modern Western presuppositions might produce a false conclusion, which, if carried forward, might vitiate the whole study. Only when I had studied each passage separately did I look for connections and possible consistency. This is not to deny the legitimacy of Phillips's reading strategy; it is the way people normally read, though not always the way they study.

I gained a great deal from reading Phillips. He is clear, logical, perceptive, insightful, and presents his material well. Yet he left me troubled. In picking up a single issue and reading it through the whole of Luke and Acts, Luke's bigger message is easily lost. How, for example, does the kingdom of God relate to what Luke says about possessions and the poor? Though early on Phillips recognizes that "poor" belongs with Luke's soteriological understanding, he does not explore this any further or connect it to the rest of the teaching. We are left then with the answer to a number of important questions (e.g., is renunciation a demand for all?) but somewhat decontextualized. His answers may be correct, but how does it fit with the rest of Jesus' mission?

This becomes strikingly clear when we come to the final chapter where Phillips looks at Seneca, Philo, and Clement of Alexandria for confirmation that Luke's ethic "fits into the Greco-Roman framework." Seneca was extremely wealthy but claims that he is not attached to his wealth; his happiness is independent of whether he is rich or otherwise. He has

---

45. In his review of the literature Phillips refers appreciatively to my study (26–30), but in the main body of his argument makes little reference to it, even where some of my conclusions were similar to his own, and some support his own case. It appears he may have read my work when his own was virtually complete.

46. Phillips, *Wealth and Poverty*, 94.

no concern for the poor. There is no thought of employing possessions for a higher goal (the kingdom of God, making friends for eternity). His generosity, though he views it as a virtue, is for the worthy, no one else. His ruling principle is the Stoic desire for an untroubled mind. This is far removed from Jesus' passionate quest for the kingdom. Yet Phillips sees Seneca and Luke sharing a similar ethic, similar to a common Western justification of wealth.[47]

C.-S. Abraham Cheong. *A Dialogic Reading of the Steward Parable (Luke 16:1–9)*. New York: Peter Lang, 2001.

C.-S. Abraham Cheong's study of the parable of the unjust steward was done as a PhD project at Sheffield University. I was drawn to this study as the parable is a key to how Luke understood a Christian should use his or her possessions. I was surprised, therefore, to find that Cheong thinks it is a critique of and appeal to the Pharisees and other like-minded people.

The first three chapters present a reading strategy derived from Wolfgang Iser and Mikhael Bakhtin. Unfortunately Cheong's presentation is obscure (to me at least). For example, "the text repeatedly *redefines* its own discourse, using multiple voices. These features of the Lukan parable are carnivalistic, and its language provides *social heteroglassia* which always scrutinizes a centripetal imposition" (his italics).

Consequently, in chapter 4 and 5 it is difficult to determine how well the method is applied to reading the parable. Chapter 5 is a collection of ancient examples mostly of debt remission, intended to provide contemporary background. Mostly they speak of rulers granting tax relief and the like, with the purpose of cementing alliances or building political influence. Cheong is right to see Luke's non-reciprocal approach to charity as quite different.

Cheong sees Luke 15 and 16 as a series of connected parables answering to the Pharisees' criticism of Jesus' behavior towards sinners. Thus, "Lukan Pharisees are frequently represented as a fairly rich class, who play the role of brokers . . . and community leaders. Within this framework, Luke tries to persuade those rich to care for the community . . . through benefaction and debt reduction."[48] The steward of the

---

47. Compare Phillips's approving appraisal of Seneca with Michael Green's critical view (Green, *Evangelism in the Early Church*), 145–46.

48. Cheong, *Steward Parable*, 174; compare 176.

parable is perceived as an intentional and praiseworthy practitioner of debt reduction.

I find all this odd when Luke has, firstly, given the Pharisees' criticism as a reason for the lost and found parables of chapter 15 but provided a different target—disciples—for the *steward* parable. Here the master's praise is directed at the steward's prudence, not to his meritorious reduction of debts.

Cheong concludes his study with a consideration of why the parable deals with debt *reduction* rather than debt *remission*, as Jewish precedents might suggest. In my view he has severely limited possible applications of the parable with his focus on debt-reduction. After all, Jesus does not advise making friends by reducing debts, but by an unspecified and therefore more general use of "the mammon of unrighteousness." Sophisticated reading strategies are no substitute for painstaking analysis of the text in its grammatical, historical, and literary context.

Christopher M. Hays. *Luke's Wealth Ethics: A Study in their Coherence and Character.* Tübingen: Mohr Siebeck, 2010.

Luke's Wealth Ethics is an expansion of a D. Phil. dissertation done at Oxford University. Richard M. Hays has researched in Britain, Germany, and USA. At present he is a missionary with the "Theological Education Initiative" of United World Mission. He serves as Professor of New Testament at the Fundación Universitaria Seminario Bíblico de Colombia in Medellín.

Luke's Wealth Ethics begins with a survey of scholarly opinion regarding this subject. (1–20) Hays classifies recent scholarship into four categories. "Bivocational solutions" deal with the tensions in Luke's wealth ethics by allocating different requirements to different target groups, viz professional and lay. "Interim solutions" are those which understand Luke's demand for renunciation as limited to the period of Jesus' ministry. He classifies my own study here, which is hardly correct; because I suggest a situational understanding of Luke 14:33 does not mean I limit its application to the time of Jesus. "Literary solutions" account for the diversity of outlooks in Luke by apportioning them to different sources. "Personalist solutions" accept the incoherence of Luke's ethics, and require the reader to decide how they will respond to Jesus' various teachings.

Hays then proceeds to state his thesis clearly and boldly: "Luke advocates the renunciation of all one's possessions, though that renunciation appears in a variety of forms determined by one's vocation and wealth." (24) By this means he will remove the incoherence felt by many scholars at Luke's Jesus at times demanding total abandonment of worldly goods, and at other times advocating behaviour which implies a continuing possession.

In his second and third chapters (25–69) Hays makes a helpful survey of a range of attitudes to wealth in ancient Jewish and Hellenistic writings, drawing attention at various points to possible links with Luke and Acts.

In chapter 4 ("The Coherence and Character of Lukan Wealth Ethics") Hays attends to the exegetical justification of his main thesis. Luke's wealth ethic, he contends is encapsulated in Luke 14:33. The "crucial principle is Jesus stark pronouncement, 'No one of you is able to be my disciple who does not renounce all his possessions.'" (133; Hays' translation) He is able to hold this position because he regards this verse as summarizing a number of former contingent manifestations of the principle. Everything from the first disciples' leaving all has led up to this, and, according to Hays, must be used to interpret the meaning and scope of what is meant by renouncing *everything*. So, he argues, "we might be expecting Jesus to be demanding less than the divestiture of all worldly goods." (135) He argues that the behaviour of exemplary characters like the first disciples, Levi, Jesus' female followers, Zacchaeus and the rest, defines the meaning of "renouncing all". He views renunciation, therefore, as an internal readiness, though he rejects the notion that one view this as readiness alone: defining "inaction" as "preparedness for action" mocks Luke's meaning. (137) "All" in "renounce all" is correctly seen as common Lukan hyperbole, and therefore, no objection to his thesis. But can "all" be given such a minimal interpretation in this context? Hays concludes that renunciation can take many forms depending on the hearer's situation.

However, to identify "renunciation of all" as Luke's underlying and overriding ethical stance, while redefining the idea of renunciation, and lessening the scope of "everything", arouses suspicion. In my own study I attempted a situational treatment of Jesus' words, not to limit their application to Jesus' time, as Hays seems to have understood me, but to make sense of them in his (Jesus') own context, prior to general application.[49] The application each of us (myself and Hays) finally reaches may not be very different, though I would judge the heart of Luke's concern, not to be renunciation of possessions, but unlimited commitment to discipleship (to Jesus), whatever the cost. To sustain his thesis Hays must reduce the force of hating family, and carrying one's cross, and he makes no comment on the seeming lessening of Jesus' demand implicit in renouncing possessions coming as a summing up of what appear to be much more stringent demands.

Hays treats the rich ruler as an example of what is required of every disciple. He rejects the idea that his story is a special case, and that what is asked of him is "specific to his unique situation." He is "nothing more than another would-be disciple." (172) Hays thinks that Luke has earlier in the Gospel "erected ethical scaffolding sufficient for providing a context" for understanding the demand made of the ruler. (172) This is just what is earlier required of the first disciples; radical disvestiture is a "fundamental requirement of discipleship." (169, 172) I argue that even Peter saw what Jesus demanded of the ruler as exceptional.[50]

However, Hays ameliorates this demand by himself suggesting a situational component to the ruler's case (he was called to itinerancy), and a lessening of the force of renouncing "all": "One need not think that Jesus categorically commands the Ruler to sell each solitary item he owned; it would likely have been acceptable if he kept a house from which to extend hospitality to Jesus and his disciples ... and for him to bring some basic accoutrements for the trip." (174) In identifying the "one thing" lacking in the Ruler as selling all and charity (not the "come follow me"), and seeing treasure in heaven as eternal life, Hays develops an interpretation very different to my own.[51]

When it comes to Luke's teaching about charity and the proper use of possessions, Hays has much to say that is valuable. Clearly Luke has a great sympathy for the poor and is adamant that they be helped by the generosity (almsgiving) of those well-off. The "steward of unrighteousness" teaches Christians to employ their wealth in the light of the coming

---

49. Seccombe, Poor, 105–23.
50. Seccombe, Poor, 134–37.
51. Seccombe, Poor, 123–27.

eschaton to help the needy; the recipients of their generosity will repay their kindness by welcoming them into the kingdom of God. (140–46) The parable of the Rich Man and Lazarus teaches that those who neglect the poor are guilty of ignoring "the law and the prophets" and will be excluded from the kingdom. (153–59)

Hays has a novel treatment of the eschatological discourse in Luke 17:22–37. (159–66) This passage is not normally considered part of Luke's ethical teaching, but Hays contends that it should be. The days of Noah and Sodom are invoked not as times of great wickedness, but to warn people not to become entangled in the everyday affairs of family and business. The warning is not about what to do in the final crisis, but how to live every day. Lot's wife is to be considered as one who hankered after her family and the wealth and luxury of Sodom. This is insightful exegesis, which will occasion scholarly discussion. Hays makes a good point.

His fifth chapter surveys the relevant material in Acts to determine whether there is a consistent wealth ethic in Luke-Acts. The most attention is given to the two descriptions of the sharing of the early Jerusalem church. Much of this is spent interacting with Brian Capper's argument that this early sharing was heavily influenced by Essene practice—indeed that the majority of first-generation Jerusalem Christians were Essenes living in the Essene quarter of Jerusalem, practicing formal communalism. Hays shows this to be running far ahead of, and contrary to the evidence. He contends rather, that Luke is portraying the Jerusalem church in terms of Hellenistic friendship ideals, (190–211) as I do myself.

Otherwise, Hays confirms from Acts the high value Luke places on charity and hospitality, and his antipathy to greed. In keeping with the major thesis of chapter 4, he affirms that various groups in their own way "do what is needed to renounce all ..." (210) He "asserts that Acts' teachings on possessions are essentially contiguous with what Luke wrote in the Gospel." (261) To my mind this is more assertion than conclusion. Nowhere do we find language or example in Acts corresponding to renunciation of all possessions.[52] Of course, having reduced "sell all" to a *willingness* to divest, albeit manifested in real acts of charity, he will not be far off in terms of ultimate application, but it throws a question mark over his bold contention that renouncing all possession is Jesus' demand of all disciples. In his conclusion to chapter 5 he restates this as "complete

---

52. Neither of the actions of Barnabas and Ananias and Sapphira is narrated by Luke under the rubric of renunciation.

commitment of their goods to the service of the Kingdom of God," (261) a sentiment I would not dispute, at the same time as I doubt it can be held up as equivalent to renouncing all, or made the central principle of Luke's wealth ethics.

Anthony Giambrone. *Sacramental Charity, Creditor Christology, and the Economy of Salvation in Luke's Gospel*. Tübingen: Mohr Siebeck, 2017.

Here is a solid and challenging study by another Roman Catholic scholar, originating as a PhD dissertation done at the University of Notre Dame in 2013–14. The question of Luke's theology of possessions will not go away! According to Giambrone, the legacy of Luther and the Reformation has cast suspicion on anything that looks like works-righteousness. This has distorted scholarship and led to adverse judgments on Judaism, Catholicism, and the notion of rewards for almsgiving. Luke, he maintains, had a different view of things than the Reformed consensus. Giambrone has a bold thesis: "Sola caritas . . . charity alone . . . saves from death."[53] After a thorough study of relevant literature, he focuses on three main areas where, he argues, the notion that salvation can be purchased by almsgiving and good works comes through strongly.

In chapter 2 he establishes that in Second Temple Judaism sin came to be seen as debt and argues that Luke held such a view. In the Lord's Prayer God *forgives sin* and the believer responds by *cancelling debts*, yet in the story of the woman who anointed Jesus' feet (Luke 7:36–50)—per Giambrone—forgiveness (salvation) is a *consequence* of her action, which he argues was an exercise of charity. Jesus becomes the divine creditor who is able to forgive sins. The sinful woman comes to him seeking forgiveness by her tears and good works. Giambrone argues his case even against a Roman Catholic scholar, Joseph Fitzmyer. Fitzmyer is clear that her action was gratitude for a forgiveness previously given; Giambrone says her tears and "hospitality" *merited* her forgiveness. Luke's thinking, he argues, is in line with Second Temple Judaism, which entertained a strong notion of repentance being granted to those who give alms. But this is hardly sufficient to outweigh the logic of the story, which demands that her action be seen as gratitude ("Who will love him most?"). Giambrone admits to a tension in the story between works done after salvation

---

53. Giambrone, *Sacramental Charity*, 230–31.

and works meriting salvation, but nonetheless contends that *"charity somehow secures this sinful woman's salvation."*[54]

He then gives attention to Luke 12:57–59, the parable about the two men on the road to judgment. Here he correctly identifies another example of "sin equals debt" and Jesus as the divine creditor who must be brought to terms before it comes to judgment. He moves from this to claim that the parable is part of a unified discourse on wealth ethics. By associating it with the parable of the rich fool he concludes that charity is the manner in which one satisfies God and escapes judgment. But it is questionable whether Luke 12:35–13:9 deals with wealth or is part of a section which does. It is characteristic of Giambrone's study to follow intertextual hints that lead to conclusions that are nowhere evident in the passage under examination. This is evident in his treatment of the woman who anointed Jesus' feet[55] and the appendix to chapter 2 on the Nazareth incident. Here the debt release idea is clearly present, and Jesus, "conforming well to the expectations of a beneficent regent . . . enters upon his reign with a massive pardon."[56] But it is on the basis of associations elsewhere of Satan (to whom Israel is in bondage) with greed that allows Giambrone to introduce an aspect of human action into Jesus' sermon that is not at all obvious: Israel is asked to perform "economic mercy."[57]

The focus of chapter 3 is the parable of the good Samaritan. Giambrone finds a link in Second Temple Judaism between love of neighbor (Lev 19:18) and almsgiving. He suggests the parable should be understood in this light. The lawyer's question ("What must I do to be saved?") is a reworking of Mark's "Which is the greatest commandment?" The word "commandment" was developing along the lines of "almsgiving" in the period. This allows Giambrone to claim the notion of almsgiving for the story of the good Samaritan. This is a long and fascinating study dealing with most aspects of the parable. Giambrone is drawn to the patristic allegorizing interpretation: in the end the Samaritan stands for Jesus, a view for which I have some sympathy, though Giambrone's argument, that the Samaritan is on the same road as Jesus and going in the same direction, is unsupportable. Luke could easily have said so had he intended such a connection. Other interesting allegorical touches are

---

54. Giambrone, *Sacramental Charity*, 118.
55. E.g., Giambrone, *Sacramental Charity*, 99.
56. Giambrone, *Sacramental Charity*, 138.
57. Giambrone, *Sacramental Charity*, 136–37.

suggested, like the lawyer standing for wealthy Pharisees who "rob" the poor (by failing to practice almsgiving) and are thus "complicit in the plundering of innocent people" and walk "right by the poor man robbed on the road."[58]

It is difficult to find an actual conclusion in this chapter, although Giambrone's feeling becomes evident later in the book. In the good Samaritan good works are the way to eternal life.[59] "As in the good Samaritan and the story of the rich ruler . . . the way to 'eternal life' in Luke requires a determined course of self-denial and charitable action—as patently demanded by the scriptures."[60]

In chapter 4 a connection is made between almsgiving and resurrection. Giambrone first establishes the influence of Proverbs 10:2 in Second Temple Judaism: "Almsgiving saves from death." He shows this is linked, both for the individual and Israel, to resurrection as well as rescue from dying. Then follows a strong case that Luke regarded almsgiving in the same way, as rendering an individual (and Israel) as worthy of resurrection. John the Baptist's demand, "ποιήσατε οὖν καρποὺς ἀξίους τῆς μετανοίας," is read as "bear fruit *worthy* of repentance" (rather than *befitting* repentance), meaning the kind of charity John goes on to mention acts as a kind of plea for the gift of repentance. This understanding is then connected with Luke 20:35, where, it is argued, Jesus requires merit for attaining resurrection ("a determined course of self-denial and charitable action").[61] With this Giambrone aligns the worthiness of the centurion of Capernaum, Tabitha, and the centurion Cornelius. It is characteristic of Luke to point out people's piety (Zechariah and Elizabeth, Simeon, Anna, the two centurions, Tabitha, Barnabas, etc.) in a manner that could suggest merit, though, in my view, it has another motive. One needs to distinguish between the good works of the faithful, which Luke certainly regards as entailing a reward (but is this the same as meriting?), and charity *aimed at* securing repentance and salvation. Giambrone is not always clear on this. His introduction of resurrection into the Cornelius story is fanciful: Cornelius falling at Peter's feet and being raised by him is seen as a picture of resurrection.

58. Giambrone, *Sacramental Charity*, 171.
59. Giambrone, *Sacramental Charity*, 221–22.
60. Giambrone, *Sacramental Charity*, 222.
61. Giambrone, *Sacramental Charity*, 222.

Chapter 4 deals with Luke 16, where Giambrone links in the prodigal son and sees "clues" that it too is about charity. Always in the background is Proverbs 10:2 ("Almsgiving saves from death"), though Luke never quotes it. The prodigal son, the unjust steward, and the rich man and Lazarus are *Schwestergeschichten* (sister-stories), all dealing with the theme of charity. Despite the alleged clues it is hard to see how the prodigal son can be dealt with this way; as Giambrone admits, the prodigal is on the receiving end of pure mercy and has nothing to give. However, he is right to find a positive ethic of almsgiving in the unjust steward and the rich man and Lazarus. His lengthy treatment especially of the unjust steward contains numerous valuable insights. Exchanging earthly treasure for heavenly is a frequent theme in Luke but receives a major adjustment in Luke 16 with the notion of "winning friends."[62] This is tied to the resurrection. "Rather than converting all charity into celestial coinage—as though giving alms were really no more than making a transaction with a heavenly banker—the one who acts with kindness here below can expect to receive *kindness* in return."[63] Giambrone is undoubtedly correct to see the story of the rich man as the converse of this, and the reason for the rich man's damnation not his being rich, but his failure to be charitable: "Wicked mammon inevitably fails the rich man on the day of wrath, *but metanoia (read charity) could have saved Dives from death* (cf. Prov 10:2)."[64] Thus, according to Giambrone, a door of repentance (read almsgiving) is opened for the rich,[65] though Lazarus's salvation is through the mercy of "the ultimate almsgiver."[66]

In his final chapter Giambrone discusses how Luke's charity notion might intersect with other theological *topoi*. His connections are at times difficult to follow; he ranges from Nicaea to Chalcedon, Augustine, the Reformation, and considers Christology, predestination, atonement, the gentile mission, salvation, the eucharist, and more. Contrary to much Lukan scholarship he is convinced that Luke sees the cross in atonement terms; almsgiving and the exercise of charity cohere with the atonement to the degree that they have atoning significance in their own right.

---

62. Giambrone, *Sacramental Charity*, 262.
63. Giambrone, *Sacramental Charity*, 263.
64. Giambrone, *Sacramental Charity*, 267.
65. Giambrone, *Sacramental Charity*, 279.
66. Giambrone, *Sacramental Charity*, 282.

With regard to the Reformation view of faith alone, Giambrone maintains that Luke "pushes back against any attempted erasure of merit theology or so-called 'works righteousness.'"[67] Nevertheless, he nuances his anti-Luther stance, admitting that at times, and especially for the poor (e.g., Lazarus), Luke sees salvation stemming entirely from the mercy of God. At one point he even speaks of two ways of salvation, one for the poor (through "God's preferential predilection"), in the other "the redemption of the rich operates on the plane of their active works."[68]

There is much to learn from this study, and much to challenge the Reformed thinker. Without doubt Luke is passionately concerned that Christians learn to be generous. However, Giambrone's tendency to see repentance as good works rather than a turning to God for mercy, and "works befitting repentance" as meriting salvation (even meriting repentance) brings an amount of confusion into the study.

David J. Armitage. *Theories of Poverty in the World of the New Testament*. Tübingen: Mohr Siebeck, 2016.

———. "'Good News Is Preached to the Poor': Economic Aspects of the Gospel Message in Luke-Acts." In *The Bible and Money: Economy and Socioeconomic Ethics in the Bible*, edited by Markus Zehnder and Hallvard Hagelia, 198–216. Sheffield, UK: Sheffield Phoenix, 2020.

David Armitage presented his doctoral dissertation at Nottingham University in 2015. He works currently for Tyndale House Cambridge.

Poverty is a universal problem. Based on his doctoral dissertation, *Theories of Poverty* is an important study of various understandings and attitudes current at the time the New Testament emerged. Armitage introduces his study with the emperor Julian the Apostate's complaint that no Jew has to beg, "and the impious Galileans support not only their own poor, but ours as well."[69]

Few have the time to trawl through all the sources of the Greek and Latin, classical and Hellenistic corpus, including also the Hebrew Bible and intertestamental and late second temple literature. Armitage has done it, and provided a precious resource for study. The available ancient literature is his focus, rather than non-literary studies of conditions in ancient societies. He explores its understanding of poverty and observes

---

67. Giambrone, *Sacramental Charity*, 304.
68. Giambrone, *Sacramental Charity*, 307.
69. Armitage, *Poverty*, 10.

its "vagueness and multidimensionsionality"⁷⁰ before settling on "material deprivation" in the New Testament world as the focus of his study.⁷¹

His exploration of the language of poverty in Greek, Latin, and Hebrew uncovers what to my mind is an important distinction born out in my own study: "The *ptōchos* is characterized as having nothing at all, whereas the *penēs* has a life characterized by hard toil and lack of surplus rather than total indigence."⁷²

According to Homer, Zeus has two jars from one of which he dispenses misery and the other blessings.⁷³ The gods may therefore be seen as the origin of poverty. However, Zeus is also seen as the protector of beggars.⁷⁴ (54–55)

Plutarch, however, refuses the superstitious attribution of poverty and evil to the gods, focusing on chance (*tuchē*). The Cynics and Stoics give more emphasis to fate (*heirmemene*), which may be a result of good or bad behavior. For Plutarch the human *telos* is "an escape from materiality, leaving behind the 'pleasure and pain' associated with bodily existence."⁷⁵

The Stoics believed the world contained all that was needed and fate ruled the world. What matters is how one reacts. According to Epictetus, "One's role in a play is determined by the author, and the actor's role is merely to act well in that role . . . 'Would you have me bear poverty? Bring it on, and you shall see what poverty is when it finds a good actor to play the part.'"⁷⁶ According to Armitage, "the logical consequence of this is that poverty—material deprivation—is simply not an evil."⁷⁷

In chapter 6 Armitage moves to the Hebrew Bible and finds a very different outlook. Materiality is good. Poverty is an evil, the result of human rebellion against God. "Life in the . . . world disordered by the divine curse for transgression . . . is characterized by vulnerability."⁷⁸ Wise living is called for, and compassion for those caught up in poverty.

70. Armitage, *Poverty*, 29.
71. Armitage, *Poverty*, 33–34.
72. Armitage, *Poverty*, 38.
73. Armitage, *Poverty*, 52.
74. Armitage, *Poverty*, 54–55.
75. Armitage, *Poverty*, 95.
76. Quoted in Armitage, *Poverty*, 112.
77. Armitage, *Poverty*, 127.
78. Armitage, *Poverty*, 143.

Discussing the Psalms and Isaiah, Armitage thinks the frequent association of poverty with the pious points to "spiritual poverty," a demeanor of humility before God.[79] The future of poverty is seen in terms of a new order without material need. Importantly, according to Armitage, "The *material* nature of this hope is not necessarily rendered figurative by the reworking of poverty language in the direction of 'religious' or 'spiritual' poverty: such alterations concern the recipients of the promised good, not its content."[80]

Coming to later Second Temple Judaism, Armitage examines the writings of Sirach, the book of Job, the Qumran writings, and Philo. Sirach appears not to believe in an afterlife. The pious poor must, therefore, have a good end. Circumstances are transitory and reversible: "What counts is one's condition at the point of death, when all that has gone before is quickly forgotten."[81] At Qumran the idea that material deprivation is evil and will be removed at the end, as found in the Hebrew Bible, is retained. The community termed itself the *'ebiōnim* (poor). In their vision of the future "it is the poor who will be delivered, and as a result it becomes desirable to be so designated."[82] Armitage sees in this "a shift in the connotation of 'the poor' away from simple material deprivation and towards piety and faithfulness."[83] In Philo, Armitage finds a fusion of ideas from the Hebrew Bible and Hellenistic conceptions. Philo comments at length on the laws of Moses, and so has a lot to say about philanthropy, but sees the future in Hellenistic terms as an escape from materiality.[84]

I have given only a taste of the riches of comment on poverty ideas which Armitage uncovers in his study of ancient literature bearing on the New Testament. His work will reward careful reading. It is a treasure store of ancient thought.

Coming to the New Testament, he sees "varied perspectives that potentially contribute to the inductive modeling of a theory of poverty," though not one that is anywhere set out in the New Testament.[85] Creation

---

79. Armitage, *Poverty*, 150–51. This is a view I discussed and rejected in my own study (pages 24–29, above).

80. Armitage, *Poverty*, 154.

81. Armitage, *Poverty*, 163.

82. Armitage, *Poverty*, 171.

83. Armitage, *Poverty*, 171. In *Possessions* I argued against this, seeing the shift being towards persecution, not piety (pages 27–28, above).

84. Armitage, *Poverty*, 175–90.

85. Armitage, *Poverty*, 205.

is in a state of futility "as a consequence of divine decision."[86] But this situation is temporary. The involvement of evil powers in inflicting poverty is not explicit, but may be implied.[87] The present world is viewed as flawed, unlike the Stoic insistence that it is as good as it can be.[88] However, a "great reversal" is coming, in favor of the poor ("or at least the *righteous poor*").[89] Because this transformation includes "a new earth," the basic goodness of materiality continues to be affirmed.

Armitage gives special attention to the writings of Luke, particularly Luke 4. He presents and expands this part of his thesis in "'Good News Is Preached to the Poor': Economic Aspects of the Gospel Message in Luke-Acts" (2020). He defines his inquiry with the following question: "Given the possible economic overtones of *euaggelisasthai ptōchois*, in what sense and to what extent is gospel proclamation, as presented by Luke, actually concerned with economic well-being?"[90] Exploring the link with Isaiah 61, he admits that "good news for the poor" is open to nationalistic or sectarian readings of "the poor" but thinks these are ruled out by the sequel in Luke 4, where Jesus points to the stories of Elijah and Elisha in which gentiles receive favor.[91]

Armitage has an important discussion of Jesus' involvement in the transformation of society. Against a number of modern writers, he points out that seldom are Jesus and his disciples seen alleviating poverty: people are healed and helped in various ways, but no one receives financial assistance: "The lack of interest in this matter is rather remarkable, and suggests that the *practice* of Jesus and his disciples in this area was not remembered as particularly distinctive."[92] Luke does not present Jesus as a "social innovator." The preaching of good news to the tax collectors, far from being an example of Jesus' focus on the poor, is rather an example

---

86. Armitage, *Poverty*, 208.
87. Armitage, *Poverty*, 211.
88. Armitage, *Poverty*, 215.
89. Armitage, *Poverty*, 219.
90. Armitage, *Poverty*, 203.
91. This is at variance with my own work where I argue that the mention of evangelizing the poor would have been understood by those in the synagogue as a reference to Israel. If the Nazareth incident was Luke's creation, what Armitage suggests could possibly be so, but if Luke is relating what actually took place, Jesus could rather be seen as warning his hearers of the danger of refusing the messenger and forfeiting Israel's promised salvation to others.
92. Armitage, *Poverty*, 228; "Good News," 210.

of his offer of salvation also to the "victimizers": "'Good news is preached to the poor', yet it seems it is also offered to the oppressors of the poor."[93] However, his insistence that aid for the poor is important and affects one's eternal destiny is a clear message, going back to the law and the prophets.[94] Importantly, Armitage points out that the only New Testament use of *endeēs* (ἐνδεής—needy) in Acts 4 (compare Deuteronomy 15:11) indicates that in Luke's understanding the eschatological reversal promised in the Hebrew Bible was becoming a reality in the church.[95] Armitage sees significant economic components in Luke's story, but they are embedded "in a wider narrative in which they are not of primary importance but rather are subordinate."[96] The wider narrative is the story of the inbreaking kingdom.

---

93. Armitage, "Good News," 209–10.
94. Armitage, *Poverty*, 229.
95. Armitage, *Poverty*, 225.
96. Armitage, "Good News," 206.

Bibliography

Ackroyd, Peter R. "Hosea and Jacob." *VetTest* 13 (1963) 245–59.
Adamson, James B. *The Epistle of James*. Grand Rapids, MI: Eerdmans, 1976.
Agouridès, S. "La tradition des béatitudes chez Matthieu et Luc." In *Mélanges Bibliques*, Fs. Béda Rigaux, edited by Albert Louis Descamps and André de Halleux, 9–27. Gembloux, Belgium: Duculot, 1970.
Aland, Kurt, et al., eds. *Greek New Testament*. 5th ed. Stuttgart: German Bible Society, 2014.
Albright, William Foxwell, and C. S. Mann. *Matthew*. AncB 26. Garden City, NY: Doubleday, 1971.
Allen, J. E. "Why Pilate?" In *The Trial of Jesus*, Fs. C. F. D. Moule, edited by Ernst Bammel, 78–83. London: SCM, 1970.
Allen, Willoughby C. *A Critical and Exegetical Commentary on the Gospel According to S. Matthew*. ICC. Edinburgh: T. & T. Clark, 1922.
Allison, John Philip. "The Concept of Wealth in Luke-Acts." PhD diss., New Orleans Baptist Theological Seminary, 1960.
Anderson, Fred C. "Luke 16:10." *ExpT* 59 (1947/48) 278–79.
Anderson, Hugh. "Broadening Horizons. The Rejection at Nazareth Pericope of Luke 4:16–30 in Light of Recent Critical Trends." *Interpr* 18 (1964) 259–75.
Armitage, David J. "'Good News Is Preached to the Poor': Economic Aspects of the Gospel Message in Luke-Acts." In *The Bible and Money: Economy and Socioeconomic Ethics in the Bible*, edited by Markus Zehnder and Hallvard Hagelia, 198–216. Sheffield, UK: Sheffield Phoenix, 2020.
———. *Theories of Poverty in the World of the New Testament*. WUNT 2/423. Tübingen: Mohr Siebeck, 2016.
Armstrong, Edward Allworth. *The Gospel Parables*. London: Hodder and Stoughton, 1967.
Athanasius. *Select Writings and Letters of Athanasius, Bishop of Alexandria*. Edited by Archibald Robertson. Oxford: Parker, 1892.
Aune, David E. "The Problem of the Messianic Secret." *NovTest* 11 (1969) 1–31.
Aytoun, R. A. "The Ten Lucan Hymns of the Nativity in Their Original Language." *JTS* 18 (1916/17) 274–88.
Bacher, Wilhelm. "Ein hebräisch-persisches Wörterbuch aus dem 15.Jahrhundert." *ZAW* 16 (1896) 201–47.
Bacon, Benjamin Wisner. "Jesus and the Law. A Study of the First 'Book' of Matthew (Mt. 3–7)." *JBL* 47 (1928) 203–31.

———. "Why Callest Thou Me Good?" *BW* 6 (1895) 334–50.
Baer, Heinrich. *Der Heilige Geist in den Lukasschriften*. BWANT 39. Stuttgart: Kohlhammer, 1926.
Bailey, Kenneth E. *Poet and Peasant. A Literary Cultural Approach to the Parables in Luke*. Grand Rapids, MI: Eerdmans, 1976.
Baily, M. "The Crib and Exegesis of Luke 2:1–20." *IER* 100 (1963) 358–76.
———. "The Shepherds and the Sign of a Child in a Manger." *IThQ* 31 (1964) 1–23.
Baird, J. Arthur. *Audience Criticism and the Historical Jesus*. Philadelphia: Westminster, 1969.
Bajard, J. "La structure de la péricope de Nazareth en Lc 4:16–30." *ETL* 45 (1969) 165–71.
Balch, David L. "Backgrounds of 1 Cor 7: Sayings of the Lord in Q; Moses as an Ascetic ΘΕΙΟΣ ΑΝΗΡ in 2 Cor 3." *NTS* 18 (1971/72) 351–64.
Bammel, Ernst. "The Baptist in Early Christian Tradition." *NTS* 18 (1971/72) 95–128.
———. "Crucifixion as a Punishment in Palestine." In *The Trial of Jesus*, Fs. C. F. D. Moule, edited by Ernst Bammel, 162–65. London: SCM, 1970.
———. "Erwägungen zur Eschatologie Jesu." *StudEv* III.3–32.
———. "Is Luke 16:16–18 of Baptist's Provenience?" *HTR* 51 (1958) 101–06.
———. "Israels Dienstbarkeit." In *Donum Gentilicium*, Fs. David Daube, edited by Ernst Bammel et al., 295–305. Oxford: Clarendon, 1978.
———. "Πτωχός." In *TDNT* VI.885–915.
Bardenhewer, O. "Ist Elisabeth die Sängerin des Magnificat?" *Biblische Studien* 6 (1901) 187–200.
Barnett, Paul W. "Under Tiberius All Was Quiet." *NTS* 21 (1975) 564–71.
Barns, T. "The Magnificat in Niceta of Remesiana and Cyril of Jerusalem." *JTS* 7 (1905/06) 449–53.
Barrett, Charles Kingsley. "The Acts and the Origins of Christianity." In *New Testament Essays*, 101–15. London: SPCK, 1972.
———. *A Commentary on the Second Epistle to the Corinthians*. BNTC. London: Adam and Charles Black, 1973.
———. "Der soziale Aspekt der urchristlichen Paränese von ihrem Ansatzpunkt her." *CV* 5 (1962) 255–60.
———. *The Holy Spirit and the Gospel Tradition*. London: SPCK, 1970.
———. "Stephen and the Son of the Man." In *Apophoreta*, Fs. Ernst Haenchen, 32–38. BZNW 30. Berlin: Töpelmann, 1964.
———. "ΨΕΥΔΑΠΟΣΤΟΛΟΙ (2 Cor 11:13)." In *Mélanges Bibliques*, Fs. Béda Rigaux, edited by Albert Louis Descamps and André de Halleux, 377–96. Gembloux, Belgium: Duculot, 1970.
Barth, Karl. "Poverty." In *Against the Stream*, 241–46. London: SCM, 1954.
Bartsch, Hans-Werner. *Entmythologisierende Auslegung*. Hamburg: H. Reich Evangelischer Verlag, 1962.
———. "Feldrede und Bergpredigt. Redaktionsarbeit in Luk. 6." *TZ* 16 (1960) 5–18.
Batey, Richard. *Jesus and the Poor*. New York: Harper and Row, 1972.
Batson Lloyd Ellis. "A Study of Jesus' Teachings on Possessions as Presented in the Gospel of Luke." PhD diss., Southern Baptist Theological Seminary, 1957.
Baudissin, Wolf Wilhelm. "Die alttestamentliche Religion und die Armen." *PrJ* 149 (1912) 193–231.
Baumgarten, J. M. "Der Kommunismus im Urchristentum." *ZkTh* 33 (1909) 625–45.

Baur, A. "Zur Auslegung von Matth. 19:23-6 (Marc. 10:23-9)." *ZwTh* 19 (1876) 300–304.
Behm, J. "Kommunismus und Urchristentum." *NKZ* 31 (1920) 275-97.
Belser, J. "Zu Lukas 4:23." *TQ* 89 (1907) 365-73.
Benko, Stephen. "The Magnificat. A History of the Controversy." *JBL* 86 (1967) 263-75.
Benoit, Pierre. "L'enfance de Jean-Baptiste selon Luc 1." *NTS* 3 (1956/57) 169-94.
———. "Some Notes on the 'Summaries' in Acts 2, 4, and 5." In *Jesus and the Gospel*, 94–103. London: Darton, Longman, and Todd, 1974.
Bernard, J. H. "The Magnificat." *Exp* VII.3 (1907) 193-206.
Best, Ernest. "The Camel and the Needle's Eye (Mk 10:25)." *ExpT* 82 (1970/71) 83-89.
———. "Matthew 5:3." *NTS* 7 (1960/61) 255-58.
Betz, Hans Dieter. *Nachfolge und Nachahmung Jesu Christi im Neuen Testament*. BhTh 37. Tübingen: Mohr, 1967.
Betz, Otto. "The Kerygma of Luke." *Interpr* 22 (1968) 131-46.
Bienert, Walther. *Die Arbeit nach der Lehre der Bibel*. Stuttgart: Evangelisches Verlagswerk, 1956.
Bigelmair, A. "Zur Frage des Sozialismus und Kommunismus im Christentum der ersten drei Jahrhunderte." In *Beiträge zur Geschichte des christlichen Altertums und der byzantinischen Literatur*, Fs. Albert Ehrhard, edited by Albert M. Koeniger, 73–93. Bonn, 1922.
Bigo, P. "La richesse comme intendance, dans l'Evangile. A propos de Lc 16:1-9." *NRT* 87 (1965) 267-71.
Billerbeck, Paul. "Ein Synagogengottesdienst in Jesu Tagen." *ZNW* 55 (1964) 143-61.
Birkeland, Harris. *'Ani und 'Anaw in den Psalmen*. Oslo: Jacob Dybwad, 1933.
Bishop, E. F. F. "Bethlehem and the Nativity: Some Travesties of Christmas." *AThR* 46 (1964) 401-13.
———. "A Yawning Chasm." *EvQ* 45 (1973) 3-5.
Black, Matthew. *An Aramaic Approach to the Gospels and Acts*. Oxford: Clarendon, 1967.
Blair, Hugh J. "Putting One's Hand to the Plough. Luke 9:62 in the Light of 1 Kings 19:19-21." *ExpT* 79 (1967/68) 342-43.
Blake, B. "'Good Master' (Mk 10:17)." *ExpT* 43 (1931/32) 334.
Blevins, William L. "The Early Church: Acts 1-5." *RExp* 7 (1974) 463-74.
Blinzler, Josef. "Die literarische Eigenart des sogenannten Reiseberichts im Lukasevangelium." In *Synoptische Studien*, Fs. Alfred Wikenhauser, 20–52. Munich: K. Zink, 1953.
———. "The Jewish Punishment of Stoning in the New Testament Period." In *The Trial of Jesus*, Fs. C. F. D. Moule, edited by Ernst Bammel, 147–61. SBT 2/13. London: SCM, 1970.
———. *The Trial of Jesus*. ET. Cork: Mercier, 1959.
Bochart, Samuel. *Opera Omnia, hoc est Phaleg, Canaan, et Hierozoicon*. Leiden, 1692.
Boehmer, Julius. "Die erste Seligpreisung." *JBL* 45 (1926) 298–304.
Boer, Harry R. *Above the Battle? The Bible and Its Critics*. Grand Rapids, MI: Eerdmans, 1977.
Bogle, A. N. "The Unjust Steward." *ExpT* 15 (1903/04) 475-76.
Bolkestein, Hendrik. *Wohltätigkeit und Armenpflege im vorchristlichen Altertum*. Utrecht: Oosthoek, 1939.
Bonino, José Miguez. "The Struggle of the Poor and the Church." *ER* 27 (1975) 36-43.

Bonnard, Pierre E. *Le second Isaie, son disciple et leurs editeurs Isaie.* Paris: Gabalda, 1972.

Bonsirven, J. *Textes rabbiniques des deux premiers siècles chrétiens.* Rome: Pontifical Biblical Institute, 1955.

Borgen, Peder. "Response to Barnabas Lindars, 'The Place of the Old Testament in the Formation of New Testament Theology.'" *NTS* 23 (1977) 67-75. *NTS* 23 (1977) 59-66.

Bornhäuser, Karl. "Zum Verständnis der Geschichte vom reichen Mann und armen Lazarus. Luk. 16:19-31." *NKZ* 39 (1928) 833-43.

Bornkamm, Günther. "Der Lohngedanke im Neuen Testament." In *Studien zu Antike und Urchristentum*, II.69-92. Munich: Chr. Kaiser, 1959.

———. *Jesus of Nazareth.* Translated by Irene and Fraser McLuskey and James M. Robinson. London: Hodder and Stoughton, 1960.

Borsch, Frederick Houk. "Jesus, the Wandering Preacher?" In *What About the New Testament?*, Fs. Christopher Evans, edited by Morna Dorothy Hooker and John Anderson Hickling, 45-63. London: SCM, 1975.

Boucher, Madeleine. *The Mysterious Parable.* CBQ MS 6. Washington: Catholic Biblical Association of America, 1977.

Bourke, M. M. "The Historicity of the Gospels." *Thought* 39 (1964) 37-56.

Bowker, John W. *Jesus and the Pharisees.* Cambridge, UK: Cambridge University Press, 1973.

———. "Speeches in Acts: A Study in Proem and Yelammedenu Form." *NTS* 14 (1967/68) 96-111.

Bowman, John Wick. "An Exposition of the Beatitudes." *JBR* 15 (1947) 162-70.

Box, G. H. *The Testament of Abraham.* London: SPCK, 1927.

Boyd, W. F. "The Parable of the Unjust Steward (Luke 16:1ff)." *ExpT* 50 (1938/39) 46.

Braude, William G. *The Midrash on Psalms* II. New Haven, CT: Yale University Press, 1959.

———. *Pesikta Rabbati.* New Haven, CT: Yale University Press, 1968.

Braun, Herbert. "Qumran und das Neue Testament. Ein Bericht über 10 Jahre Forschung (1950-1959)" *ThRu* 29 (1963) 142-76.

———. *Spätjüdisch-häretischer und frühchristlicher Radikalismus.* 2 vols. BhTh 24. Tübingen: Mohr, 1957.

Brightman, F. E. "S. Luke 19:21: αἴρεις ὃ οὐκ ἔθηκας." *JTS* 29 (1927/28) 158.

Brooks, A. "Salvation and Loss in the Story of Zacchaeus." *ExpT* 33 (1921/22) 286-88.

Brown, John Pairman. "Synoptic Parallels in the Epistles and Form-History." *NTS* 10 (1963/64) 27-48.

Brown, Paul B. "The Meaning and Function of Acts 5:1-11 in the Purpose of Luke-Acts." PhD diss., Boston University School of Theology, 1969.

Brown, Raymond E. "The Beatitudes According to Luke." In *New Testament Essays*, 265-71. London: Chapman, 1965.

———. *The Birth of the Messiah.* London: Chapman, 1977.

———. "The Meaning of the Manger. The Significance of the Shepherds." *Worship* 50 (1976) 528-38.

Brown, Schyler. *Apostasy and Perseverance in the Theology of Luke.* AnBib 36. Rome: Pontifical Biblical Institute, 1969.

Bruce, Alexander B. *The Parabolic Teaching of Christ.* London: Hodder and Stoughton, 1882.

Bruce, Frederick F. *The Acts of the Apostles*. London: Tyndale, 1962.
———. "The Book of Zechariah and the Passion Narrative." *BJRL* 43 (1961) 336–53.
———. *New Testament History*. London: Nelson, 1969.
Brun, Lyder. "Der Besuch Jesu in Nazareth nach Lukas." In *Serta Rudbergiana*, edited by Hans Holst and Henning Mørland, 7–17. Oslo: A. W. Brøgger, 1931.
———. *Segen und Fluch im Urchristentum*. Oslo: Dybvad, 1932.
Brunner, Emil. *The Divine Imperative*. Translated by Olive Wyon. London: Lutterworth, 1942.
Buchanan, George Wesley. "Jesus and the Upper Class." *NovTest* 7 (1964/65) 195–209.
Büchler, Adolf. "Ben Sira's Conception of Sin and Atonement." *JQR* 13 (1922/23) 303–35, 461–502; 14 (1923/24) 53–83.
———. *Der galiläische 'Am-ha'Ares des zweiten Jahrhunderts*. Wien: Olms, 1906.
Bultmann, Rudolf Karl. *The Gospel of John*. Translated by G. R. Beasley-Murray. Oxford: Basil Blackwell, 1971.
———. *History of the Synoptic Tradition*. Translated by John Marsh. Oxford: Basil Blackwell, 1972.
———. *Theology of the New Testament* I. Translated by Kendrick Grobel. London: SCM, 1952.
———. "Zur Geschichte der Lichtsymbolik im Altertum." *Philologus* 97 (1948) 1–36.
Bürki, Hans. "Die geistlich Armen." In *Abraham unser Vater*, Fs. Otto Michel, edited by Otto Betz et al., 58–64. Leiden: Brill, 1963.
Burkitt, Francis Crawford. *The Gospel History and Its Transmission*. Edinburgh: T. & T. Clark, 1907.
———. "Who Spoke the Magnificat?" *JTS* 7 (1905/06) 220–27.
Burrows, Millar. "The Origin of the Term 'Gospel.'" *JBL* 44 (1925) 21–33.
Buxtorfii, Johannis. *Lexicon Chaldaicum, Talmudicum et Rabbinicum*. London: Asher & Co., 1875.
Cadbury, Henry J. "Acts and Eschatology." In *The Background of the New Testament and Its Eschatology*, Fs. Charles Harold Dodd, edited by W. D. Davies and David Daube, 300–321. Cambridge, UK: Cambridge University Press, 1956.
———. "Luke's Interest in Lodging." *JBL* 45 (1926) 305–22.
———. *The Making of Luke-Acts*. London: SPCK, 1927.
———. "A Proper Name for Dives." *JBL* 81 (1962) 399–402.
———. *The Style and Literary Method of Luke*. HTS 6. 2 vols. Cambridge, MA: Harvard University Press, 1919–20.
Cadoux, Arthur Temple. *The Parables of Jesus*. London: James Clarke, 1930.
Caird, George B. "Eschatology and Politics. Some Misconceptions." In *Biblical Studies*, Fs. William Barclay, edited by Johnston R. McKay and James F. Miller, 72–86. London: Collins, 1976.
———. "Les eschatologies du Nouveau Testament." *RHPhR* 49 (1969) 217–27.
———. *The Gospel of St. Luke*. PNTC. London: Penguin, 1968.
———. *Jesus and the Jewish Nation*. London: Athlone, 1965.
———. "Redaction Criticism." *ExpT* 87 (1975/76) 168–72.
Calvin, John. *Institutes of the Christian Religion*. Edited by John T. McNeill, translated by Ford Lewis Battles. London: SCM, 1960.
Campbell, Colin. "Its Ebionite Tendency." In *Critical Studies in St. Luke's Gospel. Its Demonology and Ebionitism*, 171–318. Edinburgh: Blackwood, 1891.

Campbell, J. Y. "ΚΟΙΝΩΝΙΑ and Its Cognates in the New Testament." *JBL* 51 (1932) 352-80.

Candlish, R. "The Pounds and the Talents." *ExpT* 23 (1911/12) 136/37.

Capron, F. H. "'Son' in the Parable of the Rich Man and Lazarus." *ExpT* 13 (1901/02) 523.

Carcopino, Jerome. *Daily Life in Ancient Rome*. Translated by E. O. Lorimer. Hammondsworth, UK: Penguin, 1941.

Carpenter, S. C. *Christianity According to S. Luke*. London: SPCK, 1919.

Carr, A. "The Fellowship (Koinōnia) of Acts 2:42 and Cognate Words." *Exp* VIII.5 (1913) 458-64.

Cassidy, Richard J. "The Social and Political Stance of Jesus in Luke's Gospel." PhD diss., Berkeley Graduate Theological Union, 1976.

Catchpole, David R. "The Synoptic Divorce Material as a Tradition-Historical Problem." *BJRL* 57 (1974) 92-127.

———. *The Trial of Jesus. A Study in the Gospels and Jewish Historiography from 1770 to the Present Day*. SPB 18. Leiden: Brill, 1971.

Cave, C. H. "Lazarus and the Lukan Deuteronomy." *NTS* 15 (1968/69) 319-25.

———. "The Sermon at Nazareth and the Beatitudes in the Light of the Synagogue Lectionary." *StudEv* III.231-35.

Cerfaux, Lucien. "La composition de la première partie du Livre des Actes." *ETL* 13 (1936) 667-91.

———. "La première communauté chrétienne à Jérusalem (Acts 2:41-5:42)." *ETL* 16 (1939) 5-31.

Chadwick, Henry. "Ephesians." In *Peake's Commentary on the Bible*, edited by Matthew Black, 980-84. Edinburgh: Thomas Nelson, 1962.

———. "Philo and the Beginnings of Christian Thought." In *The Cambridge History of Later Greek and Early Medieval Philosophy*, edited by Arthur Hilary Armstrong, 133-92. Cambridge, UK: Cambridge University Press, 1970.

Charles, R. H. *The Apocrypha and Pseudepigrapha of the Old Testament*. Oxford: Clarendon, 1913.

Cheetham, F. P. "Acts 2:47: ἔχοντες χάριν πρὸς ὅλον τὸν λαόν." *ExpT* 74 (1962/63) 214-15.

Cheong, C.-S. Abraham. *A Dialogic Reading of the Steward Parable (Luke 16:1-9)*. Studies in Biblical Literature 28. New York: Peter Lang, 2001.

Classen, Carl Joachim. *Rhetorical Criticism of the New Testament*. WUNT 128. Boston: Brill Academic, 2002.

Clarke, A. K., and N. E. W. Collie. "A Comment on Luke 12:41-58." *JTS* 17 (1915/16) 299-301.

Clayton, J. W. "Who Was the Rich Young Ruler?" *ExpT* 39 (1927/28) 83-85.

Clemen, Carl. *Primitive Christianity and Its Non-Jewish Sources*. Edinburgh: Clark, 1912.

Clement of Alexandria. *Who Is the Rich Man That Is Being Saved?* Edited by Percy Mordaunt Barnard. London: SPCK, 1901.

Clement I, Pope. *Clementine Homilies*. Ante-Nicene Library 17. Edinburgh: T. & T. Clark, 1870.

———. *Clementine Recognitions*. Ante-Nicene Library 3. Edinburgh: T. & T. Clark, 1867.

Cobb, S. H. "The Fellowship of Goods in the Apostolic Church." *PRefR* 8 (1897) 17-34.

Comblin, J. "La Paix dans la théologie de Saint Luc." *ETL* 32 (1956) 439–60.
Combrink, H. J. B. "The Structure and Significance of Luke 4:16–30." *Neotestamentica* 7 (1973) 27–47.
Compston, H. F. B. "Friendship without Mammon." *ExpT* 31 (1919/20) 282.
Cone, James Hal. *God of the Oppressed*. Maryknoll, NY: Orbis, 1975.
Conzelmann, Hans. *Die Apostelgeschichte*. HbNT 7. Tübingen: Mohr, 1963.
———. *Geschichte des Urchristentums*. GNT 5. Göttingen: Vandenhoeck and Ruprecht, 1969.
———. *The Theology of St Luke*. Translated by Geoffrey Buswell. London: Faber and Faber, 1969.
Cook, S. A. "The Synagogue of Theodotos at Jerusalem." *Palestine Exploration Fund Quarterly Statement* 53 (1921) 22–23.
Coutts, J. "The Unjust Steward Lk 16:1–8a." *Theology* 52 (1949) 54–60.
Cox, S. "A New Parable. Luke 12:29." *Exp* I.1 (1875) 249–58.
Craddock, F. B. "The Poverty of Christ. An Investigation of II Corinthians 8:9." *Interpr* 22 (1968) 158–70.
Craghan, J. F. "A Redactional Study of Lk 7:21 in the Light of Dt 19:15." *CBQ* 29 (1967) 353–67.
Cranfield, C. E. B. *The Gospel According to Saint Mark*. Cambridge Greek Testament Commentary. Cambridge, UK: Cambridge University Press, 1959.
———. "The Parable of the Unjust Judge and the Eschatology of Luke-Acts." *SJT* 16 (1963) 297–301.
———. "Riches and the Kingdom of God St. Mark 10:17–31." *SJT* 4 (1951) 302–13.
Creed, John Martin. *The Gospel According to St Luke*. London: Macmillan, 1957.
Crehan, J. H. "The Purpose of Luke in Acts." *StudEv*, II.354–68.
Crockett, Larrimore C. "Luke 4:16–30 and the Jewish Lectionary Cycle: A Word of Caution." *JJS* 17 (1966) 13–46.
———. "Luke 4:25–27 and Jewish-Gentile Relations in Luke-Acts." *JBL* 88 (1969) 177–83.
———. "The Old Testament in the Gospel of Luke; with Emphasis on the Interpretation of Isaiah 61:1–2." PhD diss., Brown University, 1966.
Cronbach, A. "The Social Ideals of the Apocrypha and the Pseudepigrapha." *HUCA* 18 (1943/44) 119–56.
Crooke, W. "The Camel and the Eye of the Needle." *ExpT* 21 (1909/10) 283.
Cumont, Franz. *The Mysteries of Mithra*. Translated by Thomas J. McCormack. New York: Routledge, 1956.
Dahl, Nils Alstrup. *Das Volk Gottes*. Oslo: Dybwad, 1941.
———. "The Purpose of Luke-Acts." In *Jesus in the Memory of the Early Church*, 87–98. Minneapolis: Augsburg, 1976.
———. "The Story of Abraham in Luke-Acts." In *Studies in Luke-Acts*, Fs. Paul Schubert, edited by Leander E. Keck and James Louis Martyn, 139–58. New York: Abingdon, 1966.
Dahunsi, Emanuel A. "The Significance of the Account of the Nazareth Episode in the Gospel of Luke." PhD diss., Southern Baptist Theological Seminary, 1957.
Dalman, Gustav. *Sacred Sites and Ways*. London: SPCK, 1935.
Danby, Herbert. *The Mishnah*. Oxford: Oxford University Press, 1933.
Danker, F. W. "Luke 16:16—An Opposition Logion." *JBL* 77 (1958) 231–43.
Daube, David. *The New Testament and Rabbinic Judaism*. London: Athlone, 1956.

———. "A Reform in Acts and Its Models." In *Jews, Greeks and Christians*, Fs. William David Davies, edited by Robert Hamerton-Kelly and Robin Scroggs, 151–63. Leiden: Brill, 1976.

Davids, Peter H. "Themes in the Epistle of James That Are Judaistic in Character." PhD diss., University of Manchester, 1974.

Davies, J. G. "The Ascription of the Magnificat to Mary." *JTS* 15 (1964) 307–08.

Davies, J. H. "The Purpose of the Central Section of St. Luke's Gospel." *StudEv*, II.164–69.

Davies, William David. *The Setting of the Sermon on the Mount*. Cambridge, UK: Cambridge University Press, 1964.

Degenhardt, Hans-Joachim. *Lukas—Evangelist der Armen*. Stuttgart: Katholisches Bibelwerk, 1965.

Deissmann, Adolf. *Light from the Ancient East*. Translated by Lionel R. M. Strachan. London: Hodder and Stoughton, 1927.

De la Potterie, Ignace. "L'onction du Christ." *NRT* 80 (1958) 225–52.

Delcor, Mathias. *Le Testament d'Abraham*. Leiden: Brill, 1973.

Denney, James. "The Word 'Hate' in Luke 14:26." *ExpT* 21 (1909/10) 41–42.

Derrett, J. Duncan M. "Ananias, Sapphira, and the Right of Property." *DR* 89 (1971) 225–32.

———. "Dives and Lazarus and the Preceding Sayings." In *Law in the New Testament*, 78–99. London: Darton, Longman and Todd, 1970,

———. *Jesus' Audience*. London: Darton, Longman and Todd, 1973.

———. "Law in the New Testament: The Parable of the Talents and Two Logia." *ZNW* 56 (1965) 184–95.

———. "The Manger at Bethlehem: Light on St Luke's Technique from Contemporary Jewish Religious Law." *StudEv*, VI.86–94.

———. "The Manger: Ritual Law and Soteriology." *Theology* 74 (1971) 566–71.

———. "Midrash in the New Testament: The Origin of Luke 22:67–68." *StudTheol* 29 (1975) 147–56.

———. "Nisi Dominus Aedificaverit Domum: Towers and Wars (Lk 14:28–32)." *NovTest* 19 (1977) 241–61.

———. "The Parable of the Unjust Steward." In *Law in the New Testament*, 48–77. London: Darton, Longman and Todd, 1970.

———. "The Rich Fool: A Parable of Jesus Concerning Inheritance." *HeyJ* 18 (1977) 131–51.

Descamps, A. "La composition littéraire de Luc 16:9–13." *NovTest* 1 (1956) 47–53.

De Wette, Wilhelm Martin Leberecht. *Exegetisches Handbuch zum Neuen Testament*. Leipzig: Weidmann, 1839.

Dibelius, Martin. "Die Begpredigt." In *Botschaft und Geschichte* I, edited by Günther Bornkamm 79–174. Tübingen: Mohr, 1953.

———. *James*. Translated by Michael A. Williams. Hermeneia. Philadelphia: Fortress, 1976.

———. "Jungfrauensohn und Krippenkind." In *Botschaft und Geschichte*, edited by Günther Bornkamm I, 1–78. Tübingen: Mohr, 1953.

———. "Literary Allusions in the Speeches in Acts." In *Studies in the Acts of the Apostles*, translated by Mary Ling, 186–91. London: SCM, 1956.

———. "The Motive for Social Action in the New Testament." In *Jesus*, translated by Charles Baker Hedrick and Frederick Charles Grant, 137–66. London: SCM, 1963.

———. "Style Criticism in the Book of Acts." In *Studies in the Acts of the Apostles*, translated by Mary Ling, 1–25. London: SCM, 1956.
Dibelius, Otto. *Die werdende Kirche*. Hamburg: Furche, 1951.
Dinkler, Erich. "Comments on the History of the Symbol of the Cross." ET. *JTCh* 1 (1965) 124–46.
———. "Jesu Wort vom Kreuztragen." In *Neutestamentliche Studien für Rudolf Bultmann*. BZNW 21, 110–29. Berlin: Töpelmann, 1957.
Dodd, Charles Harold. *According to the Scriptures*. London: Collins, 1952.
———. "The Beatitudes: A Form-critical Study." In *More New Testament Studies*, 1–10. Manchester: Manchester University Press, 1968.
———. "Communism in the New Testament." *Interpreter* 18 (1921/22) 55–61.
———. *Gospel and Law*. Cambridge, UK: Cambridge University Press, 1951.
———. *Historical Tradition in the Fourth Gospel*. Cambridge, UK: Cambridge University Press, 1963.
———. *The Parables of the Kingdom*. London: Collins, 1941.
Dods, M. "Dives and Lazarus. Luke 16:19–31." *Exp* III.1 (1885) 45–59.
Dollinger, R. "Kreuz." *EvTh* 10 (1950/51) 433–50.
Douglas, E. H. "Blessed Are the Poor (Luke 6:20)." *MW* 55 (1965) 191–94.
Dover, Kenneth James. *Greek Popular Morality in the Time of Plato and Aristotle*. Oxford: Blackwell, 1974.
Drexler, H. "Zu Lukas 16:1–7." *ZNW* 58 (1967) 286–88.
Dreyer, Andries J. Gerhardus. *An Examination of the Possible Relation between Luke's Infancy Narratives and the Qumran Hodayot*. Amsterdam: A. A. A. Roter, 1962.
Drury, John. *Tradition and Design in Luke's Gospel*. London: Darton, Longman and Todd, 1976.
Dunkerley, R. "Lazarus." *NTS* 5 (1958/59) 321–27.
Dunn, James D. G. *Baptism in the Holy Spirit*. SBT 2/15. London: SCM, 1970.
———. *Jesus and the Spirit. A Study of the Religious and Charismatic Experience of Jesus and the First Christians as Reflected in the New Testament*. London: SCM, 1975.
———. "The Messianic Secret in Mark." *TynB* 21 (1970) 92–117.
———. *Neither Jew nor Greek: A Contested Identity*. Grand Rapids, MI: Eerdmans, 2015.
Dupont, Jacques. "Die individuelle Eschatologie im Lukasevangelium und in der Apostelgeschichte." In *Orientierung an Jesus. Zur Theologie der Synoptiker*, Fs. Josef Schmid, edited by Paul Hoffmann, 37–47. Freiburg: Herder, 1973.
———. "Introduction aux Béatitudes." *NRT* 98 (1976) 97–108.
———. "L'ambassade de Jean-Baptiste." *NRT* 83 (1961) 805–21, 943–59.
———. "La 'communauté des biens' aux premiers jours de l'Église." In *Études sur les Actes des Apôtres*. LD 45, 503–19. Paris: Cerf, 1967.
———. "La parabole des talents (Mat 25:14–30) ou des mines (Luc 19:12–27)." *RThPh* III.19 (1969) 376–91.
———. "Le salut des gentils et la signification théologique du livre des Actes." *NTS* 6 (1959/60) 132–55.
———. *Les Béatitudes*. 3 vols. Paris: Gabalda, 1969–73.
———. "Les pauvres en esprit." In *A la rencontre de Dieu*, Fs. Albert Gélin, 265–72. Le Puy, France: Xavier Mappus, 1961.

———. "Les πτωχοὶ τῷ πνεύματι de Matthieu 5, 3 et les עֲנָוֵי רוּחַ de Qumrân." In *Neutestamentliche Aufsätze*, Fs. Josef Schmid, edited by Josef Blinzler et al., 53–64. Regensburg: Friedrich Pustet, 1963.

———. "L'union entre les premiers chrétiens dans les Actes des Apôtres." *NRT* 91 (1969) 897–915.

———. "Renoncer à tous ses biens (Luc 14:33)." *NRT* 93 (1971) 561–82.

———. *The Sources of Acts*. Translated by Kathleen Pond. London: Darton, Longman and Todd, 1964.

Dupont-Sommer, André. *The Essene Writings from Qumran*. Translated by Geza Vermes. Oxford: Blackwell, 1961.

Durand, A. "L'origine du Magnificat." *RB* 7 (1898) 74–77.

Easton, Burton Scott. *Early Christianity: The Purpose of Acts and Other Papers*. Edited by Frederick C. Grant. London: SPCK, 1955.

———. *The Gospel According to St Luke*. New York: C. Scribner's Sons, 1926.

Edersheim, Alfred. *The Life and Times of Jesus the Messiah*. 2 vols. London, 1900.

Ehrhardt, Arnold. *The Acts of the Apostles*. Manchester: Manchester University Press, 1969.

———. "The Construction and Purpose of the Acts of the Apostles." *StudTheol* 12 (1958) 45–79.

Elliott-Binns, Leonard. *Galilean Christianity*. SBT 1/16. London: SCM, 1956.

Ellis, E. Earle. *The Gospel of Luke*. NCeB. London: Nelson, 1974.

———. "Present and Future Eschatology in Luke." *NTS* 12 (1965/66) 27–41.

Ellul, Jacques. "Der Arme. Eine Studie über die Verantwortung der Kirche und des Christen im Wirtschaftsleben." *EvTh* 11 (195/52) 193–209.

———. "Du texte au sermon 18: Les talents Matthieu 25:13–30." *ETR* 48 (1973) 125–38.

Eltester, Walther. "Israel im lukanischen Werk und die Nazareth-perikope." In *Jesus in Nazareth*, edited by W. Eltester et al., 76–147. BZNW 40. Berlin: de Gruyter, 1972.

Emmet, C. W. "Should the Magnifcat be Ascribed to Elizabeth?" *Exp* VII.8 (1909) 521–29.

Enslin, M. S. "The Christian Stories of the Nativity." *JBL* 59 (1940) 317–38.

Ernst, Josef. *Das Evangelium nach Lukas*. RNT. Regensburg: Friedrich Pustet. 1977.

———. *Herr der Geschichte. Perspektiven der lukansichen Eschatologie*. SBS 88. Stuttgart: Katholisches Bibelwerk, 1978.

Esler, Philip Francis. *Community and Gospel in Luke-Acts: The Social and Political Motivations of Lucan Theology*. SNTS MS 57. Cambridge, UK: Cambridge University Press, 1987.

Evans, Christopher F. "The Central Section of St. Luke's Gospel." In *Studies in the Gospels: Essays in Memory of R. H. Lightfoot*, edited by Dennis E. Nineham, 37–53. Oxford: Basil Blackwell, 1955.

———. "Uncomfortable Words—V. Luke 16:31." *ExpT* 81 (1969/70) 228–31.

Everson, A. J. "Isaiah 61:1–6 (To Give Them a Garland Instead of Ashes)." *Interpr* 32 (1978) 69–73.

Farmer, William Reuben. *Maccabees, Zealots, and Josephus: An Inquiry into Jewish Nationalism in the Greco-Roman Period*. New York: Columbia University Press, 1956.

———. "Matthew and the Bible: An Essay in Canonical Criticism." *LexTQ* 11 (1976) 57–71.

———. *The Synoptic Problem. A Critical Analysis.* Dillsboro, NC: Western North Carolina University Press, 1976.
Farrar, F. W. "The Camel and the Needle's Eye." *Exp* I.3 (1876) 369–80.
Farrell, Hobert Kenneth. "The Eschatological Perspective of Luke-Acts." PhD diss., Boston University Graduate School, 1972.
Fascher, Erich. "Jesus der Lehrer." *TLZ* 79 (1954) 325–42.
———. "Johannes 16:32. Eine Studie zur Geschichte der Schriftauslegung und zur Traditionsgeschichte des Urchristentums." *ZNW* 39 (1940) 171–230.
Feine, Paul. *Eine vorkanonsiche Überlieferung des Lukas in Evangelium und Apostelgeschichte.* Gotha, 1891.
———. *Theologie des Neuen Testaments.* Leipzig: Hinrichs, 1919.
———. "Ueber das gegenseitige Verhältniss der Texte der Bergpredigt bei Matthäus und bei Lukas." *JpTh* 11 (1885) 1–85.
Fenasse, J. M. "La force et la faiblesse dans la Bible." *BTS* 71 (1965) 6–7.
Fenton, John Charles. *The Gospel of St Matthew.* PNTC. London: Penguin, 1963.
Feuillet, A. "Les riches intendants du Christ." *RechSR* 34 (1947) 30–54.
Fiedler, P. "Die übergebenen Talente. Auslegung von Mt 25:14–30." *BiLeb* 11 (1970) 259–73.
Field, Frederick. *Notes on the Translation of the New Testament.* Cambridge, UK: Cambridge University Press, 1899.
———. *Origenis Hexaplorum.* Oxford: Clarendon, 1875.
Filson, Floyd Vivian. *St Paul's Conception of Recompense.* Leipzig: Hinrichs, 1931.
———. *Three Crucial Decades.* London: Epworth, 1964.
Finch, R. G. *The Synagogue Lectionary and the New Testament.* London: SPCK, 1939.
Finkel, Asher. "Jesus' Sermon at Nazareth (Luke 4:16–30)." In *Abraham unser Vater*, Fs. Otto Michel, edited by Otto Betz et al., 106–15. Leiden: Brill, 1963.
———. *The Pharisees and the Teacher of Nazareth.* AGSU 4. Leiden: Brill, 1964.
Finkelstein, Louis. *The Pharisees.* Philadelphia: Jewish Publishing Society of America, 1940.
Firth, C. B. "The Parable of the Unrighteous Steward (Luke 16:1–9)." *ExpT* 63 (1951/52) 93–95.
Fischel, H. A. "Martyr and Prophet." *JQR* 37 (1947) 265–80, 363–86.
Fitzmyer, Joseph A. "Further Light on Melchizedek from Qumran Cave 11." *JBL* 86 (1967) 25–41.
———. "The Story of the Dishonest Manager (Luke 16:1–13)." *TS* 25 (1964) 23–42.
———. "The Virginal Conception of Jesus in the New Testament." *TS* 34 (1973) 541–75.
Flender, Helmut. *St Luke. Theologian of Redemptive History.* Translated by Reginald H. Fuller and Ilse Fuller. London: SPCK, 1967.
Fletcher, D. R. "The Riddle of the Unjust Steward. Is Irony the Key?" *JBL* 82 (1963) 15–30.
Flew, R. Newton. *Jesus and His Church.* London: Epworth, 1938.
Flood, E. "The Magnificat and Benedictus." *CleR* 51 (1966) 205–10.
Flusser, David. "Blessed are the Poor in Spirit . . ." *IEJ* 10 (1960) 1–13.
Foerster, Werner. "Das Gleichnis von den anvertrauten Pfunden." In *Verbum Dei Manet Aeternum*, Fs. Otto Schmitz, 37–56. Witten: Luther-Verlag, 1953.
Ford, J. Massingbird. "'Crucify Him, Crucify Him' and the Temple Scroll." *ExpT* 87 (1975/76) 275/78.

———. "Money 'Bags' in the Temple (Mk 11:16)." *Bib* 57 (1976) 249–53.
———. "Zealotism and the Lukan Infancy Narratives." *NovTest* 18 (1976) 280–92.
Forestall, J. T. "Old Testament Background to the Magnificat." *MarSt* 12 (1961) 205–44.
France, Richard T. *Jesus and the Old Testament*. London: Tyndale, 1971.
———. "The Servant of the Lord in the Teaching of Jesus." *TynB* 19 (1968) 26–52.
Frankemölle, H. "Die Makarismen (Mt 5:1–12; Lk 6:20–23). Motive und Umfang der redaktionellen Komposition." *BZ* 15 (1971) 52–75.
Franklin, Eric. *Christ the Lord*. London: SPCK, 1975.
Freyne, Seán. *The Twelve: Disciples and Apostle*. London: Sheed and Ward, 1968.
Fridrichsen, A. "Ἀρνεῖσθαι im NT, insonderheit in den Pastoralbriefen." *CNT* 6 (1942) 94–96.
Friedel, L. M. "The Parable of the Unjust Steward Lk 16:1–13." *CBQ* 3 (1941) 337–48.
Friedrich, G. "εὐαγγελίζομαι." In *TDNT* II.707–37.
Frisch Ephraim. *An Historical Survey of Jewish Philanthropy*. New York: Macmillan, 1924.
Furnish, Victor Paul. *The Love Command in the New Testament*. London: SCM, 1973.
Gächter, Paul. "The Parable of the Dishonest Steward after Oriental Conceptions." *CBQ* 12 (1950) 121–31.
Galot, Jean. "Le fondement évangélique du voeu religieux de pauvreté." *Greg* 56 (1975) 441–67.
Gander, G. "Le procédé de l'économe infidel, décrit Luc 16:5–7, est-il répréhensible ou louable?" *VC* 7 (1953) 293–99.
Gasse, W. "Zum Reisebericht des Lukas." *ZNW* 34 (1935) 293–99.
Gaston, L. "The Lucan Birth Narratives in Tradition and Redaction." *SBL SP* 1976, 209–17.
Geldenhuys, Norval. *Commentary on the Gospel of Luke*. London: Marshall, Morgan and Scott, 1950.
Gélin, Albert. *The Poor of Yahweh*. Translated by Kathryn Sullivan. Collegeville, MN: Liturgical Press, 1964.
George, A. "La prédication inaugurale de Jésus dans la synagogue de Nazareth: Luc 4:16–30." *BVC* 59 (1964) 17–29.
Gerhardsson, Birger. "Einige Bemerkungen zu Apg 4:32." *StudTheol* 24 (1970) 142–49.
Gersdorf, Christof Gotthelf. *Beiträge zur Sprach-Characteristik der Schriftsteller des Neuen Testaments* I. Leipzig: Weidmann, 1816.
Geyser, A. S. "The Earliest Name of the Earliest Church." In *De Fructu Oris Sui*, Fs. Adrianus van Selms, edited by I. H. Eybers et al., 58–68. Leiden: Brill, 1971.
Giambrone, Anthony. *Sacramental Charity, Creditor Christology, and the Economy of Salvation in Luke's Gospel*. WUNT 2/439. Tübingen: Mohr Siebeck, 2017.
Gibbs, J. M. "Mark 1:1–15, Matthew 1:1–4:16, Luke 1:1–4:30, John 1:1–51. The Gospel Prologues and Their Function." *StudEv* VI.154–88.
Giblin, Charles H. "Reflections on the Sign of the Manger." *CBQ* 29 (1967) 87–101.
Gibson, M. D. "On the Parable of the Unjust Steward." *ExpT* 14 (1902/03) 334.
Ginsberg, M. *Perek Hashshalom: Chapter on Peace*. London: Soncino, 1965.
Ginzberg, Louis. *An Unknown Jewish Sect*. New York: Jewish Theological Society of America, 1976.
Glöckner, Richard. *Die Verkündigung des Heils beim Evangelisten Lukas*. Mainz: Matthias-Grünewald, 1975.

Glombitza, Otto. "Der reiche Mann und der arme Lazarus Luk 16:19-31. Zur Frage nach der Botschaft des Textes." *NovTest* 12 (1970) 166-80.

———. "Die christologische Aussage des Lukas in seiner Gestaltung der drei Nachfolgeworte Lukas 9:57-62." *NovTest* 13 (1971) 14-23.

Godet, Frédéric. *A Commentary on the Gospel of St Luke.* 5th ed. Edinburgh: T. & T. Clark, 1893.

Goguel, Maurice. "ΚΑΤΑ ΔΙΚΑΙΟΣΥΝΗΝ ΤΗΝ ΕΝ ΝΟΜΩΙ ΓΕΝΟΜΕΝΟΣ ΑΜΕΜΠΤΟΣ (Phil 3:6). Remarques sur un aspect de la conversion de Paul." *JBL* 53 (1934) 257-67.

———. "Le rejet de Jésus à Nazareth." *ZNW* 12 (1911) 321-14.

———. "Luke and Mark: With a Discussion of Streeter's Theory." *HTR* 26 (1933) 1-55.

Goldin, Hyman E. *Hebrew Criminal Law and Procedure: Mishnah: Sanhedrin-Makkot.* New York: Twayne, 1952.

Goodspeed, Edgar J. *Problems of New Testament Translation.* Chicago: University of Chicago Press, 1945.

Gordon, C. H. "Sabbatical Cycle or Seasonal Pattern?" *Orientalia* 22 (1953) 79-81.

Gould, Ezra P. *A Critical and Exegetical Commentary on the Gospel According to St. Mark.* ICC. Edinburgh: T. & T. Clark, 1907.

Goulder, Michael D. "Characteristics of the Parables in the Several Gospels." *JTS* 19 (1968) 51-69.

———. "The Chiastic Structure of the Lucan Journey." *StudEv* II.195-202.

———. *Type and History in Acts.* London: SPCK 1964.

Goulder, Michael D., and M. L. Sanderson. "St. Luke's Genesis." *JTS* 8 (1957) 12-30.

Gräßer, Erich. *Das Problem der Parusieverzögerung in den synoptischen Evangelien und in der Apostelgeschichte.* BZNW 22. Berlin: Töpelmann, 1977.

———. "'Der politisch gekreuzigte Christus'. Kritische Anmerkungen zu einer politischen Hermeneutik des Evangeliums." In *Text und Situation*, 302-30. Gütersloh: Mohn, 1973,

Grant, Frederick C. "The Economic Background of the New Testament." In *The Background of the New Testament and Its Eschatology*, Fs. Charles Harold Dodd, edited by W. D. Davies and David Daube, 96-114. Cambridge, UK: Cambridge University Press, 1956.

Grant, J. "The Unjust Steward." *ExpT* 16 (1904/05) 239-40.

Greehy, John G. "Community of Goods—Qumran and Acts." *IThQ* 32 (1965) 230-40.

Green, Michael. *Evangelism in the Early Church.* London: Hodder and Stoughton, 1970.

Grensted, L. W. "The Use of Enoch in St Luke, 16:19-31." *ExpT* 26 (1914/15) 333-34.

Gressmann, Hugo. *Das Weihnachts-Evangelium.* Göttingen: Vandenhoeck and Ruprecht, 1914.

———. *Vom reichen Mann und armen Lazarus.* Phil.-Hist. Klasse 7. Berlin: Abhandlungen der königlich preußischen Akademie der Wissenschaften, 1918.

Griffiss, J. E. "Some Current Literature on Political Theology." *AThR* 58 (1976) 217-28.

Griffith, Francis L. *Stories of the High Priests of Memphis.* Oxford: Clarendon, 1900.

Grobel, K. ". . . Whose Name was Neves." *NTS* 10 (1963/64) 373-82.

Grundmann, Walter. "Die Bergpredigt nach der Lukasfassung." *StudEv* I.180-89.

———. *Das Evangelium nach Lukas.* THK NT 3. Berlin: Evangelische Verlagsanstalt, 1961.

———. "Fragen der Komposition des lukanischen 'Reiseberichts.'" *ZNW* 50 (1959) 252-70.

Gryglewicz, Felicks. "Die Herkunft der Hymnen des Kindheitsevangeliums des Lucas." *NTS* 21 (1975) 265–73.
Guelich, Robert A. "The Matthean Beatitudes: 'Entrance-Requirements' or Eschatological Blessings?" *JBL* 95 (1976) 415–34.
Guilding, Aileen. *The Fourth Gospel and Jewish Worship*. Oxford: Clarendon, 1960.
Guillaumont, Antoine, et al., eds. *The Gospel According to Thomas*. Leiden: Brill, 1959.
Gunkel, Hermann. "Die Lieder in der Kindheitsgeschichte Jesu bei Lukas." In *Festgabe: Adolf von Harnack*, 43–60. Tübingen: Mohr, 1921.
Guthrie, Donald. "The New Testament Approach to Social Responsibility." *VoxEv* 8 (1973) 40–59.
Guttmann, Alexander. *Rabbinic Judaism in the Making*. Detroit: Wayne State University Press, 1970.
Haenchen, Ernst. *The Acts of the Apostles*. Translated by Bernard Noble and Gerald Shinn. Oxford: B. Blackwell, 1971.
———. "Das Gleichnis vom großen Mahl." In *Die Bibel und Wir*, 135–55. Tübingen: Mohr, 1968.
———. *Der Weg Jesu. Eine Erklärung des Markus-Evangeliums und der kanonischen Parallelen*. Berlin: Walter de Gruyter, 1968.
———. "Judentum und Christentum in der Apostelgeschichte." *ZNW* 54 (1963) 155–87.
Hahn, Ferdinand. "Das Gleichnis von der Einladung zum Festmahl." In *Verborum Veritas*, Fs. Gustav Stählin, edited by Otto Böcher and Klaus Haacker, 51–82. Wuppertal: R. Brockhaus, 1970.
———. "Pre-Easter Discipleship." In *The Beginnings of the Church in the New Testament*, edited by Ferdinand Hahn et al., translated by Iain and Ute Nicol, 9–39. Edinburgh: Saint Andrew, 1970.
Hall, S. G. "Swords of Offence." *StudEv* I.499–502.
Hampden-Cook, E., and E. G. Dutton. "The Unjust Steward." *ExpT* 16 (1904/05) 44.
Harnack, Adolf von. "Again the Magnificat." *ExpT* 42 (1930/31) 188–90.
———. "Das Magnifikat der Elisabet (Luk 1:46–55) nebst einigen Bemerkungen zu Luk 1 und 2." In *Studien zur Geschichte des Neuen Testaments und der alten Kirche* I.62–85. Berlin: Walter de Gruyter, 1931.
———. *Luke the Physician*. Crown Theological Library 20. London: Williams and Norgate, 1911.
———. *The Sayings of Jesus*. Translated by J. R. Wilkinson. London: Williams and Norgate, 1908.
———. *What is Christianity?* Translated by Thomas Bailey Saunders. London: Williams and Norgate, 1912.
Harrington, W. "The Visitation." *DoLi* 14 (1964) 411–15.
Harris, J. R. "Mary or Elizabeth?" *ExpT* 41 (1929/30) 266–67.
———. "Again the Magnificat." *ExpT* 42 (1930/31) 188–90.
Harrison, Everett Falconer. *Acts: The Expanding Church*. Chicago: Moody, 1975.
Harvey, Anthony E. *Jesus on Trial. A Study in the Fourth Gospel*. London: SPCK, 1976.
Haskin, Richard Webb. "The Call to Sell All: The History of the Interpretation of Mark 10:17–23 and Parallels." PhD diss., Columbia University, 1967.
Hatch, Edwin. *Essays in Biblical Greek*. Oxford: Clarendon, 1889.
Hauck, Friedrich. *Das Evangelium des Lukas*. THK NT 3. Leipzig: Deichert, 1934.

———. *Die Stellung des Urchristentums zu Arbeit und Geld*. Gütersloh: C. Bertelsmann, 1921.
Haupt, Paul. "Abraham's Bosom." *AJP* 42 (1921) 162/67.
———. "Magnificat and Benedictus." *AJP* 40 (1919) 64–75.
Hawkins, Robert Martyr. "An Enquiry into the Relationship between the Synoptic Record of the Teaching of Jesus and the Book of Isaiah, with Especial Reference to the Septuagint Version." PhD diss., Edinburgh University, 1927.
Hays, Christopher M. *Luke's Wealth Ethics: A Study in Their Coherence and Character*. WUNT 2/275. Tübingen: Mohr Siebeck, 2010.
Hebert, A. Gabriel. "The Virgin Mary as the Daughter of Zion." *Theology* 53 (1950) 403–10.
Heichelheim, F. M. "Roman Syria." In *An Economic Survey of Ancient Rome*, edited by Tenney Frank, 121–257. Baltimore: Johns Hopkins University Press, 1938.
Hemer, Colin J. "Luke the Historian." *BJRL* 60 (1977) 28–51.
Hengel, Martin. *Crucifixion*. Translated by John Bowden. London: SCM, 1977.
———. *Judaism and Hellenism*. Translated by John Bowden. London: SCM, 1974.
———. *Nachfolge und Charisma*. BZNW 34. Berlin: Töpelmann, 1968.
———. *Property and Riches in the Early Church*. Translated by John Bowden. London: SCM, 1974.
Hennecke, Edwin, and Walter Schneemelcher. *New Testament Apocrypha*. Translated by R. McL. Wilson. 2 vols. London: Lutterworth, 1975.
Herford, R. Travers. *The Pharisees*. London: George Allen and Unwin, 1924.
Hicks, E. L. "The Communistic Experiment of Acts II and IV." *Exp* VII.1 (1906) 21–32.
Hiers, Richard H. "Friends by Unrighteous Mammon: The Eschatological Proletariat (Luke 16:9)." *JAAR* 38 (1970) 30–36.
Hilgenfeld, Adolf. "Die Geburt—und Kindkeitsgeschichte Jesu Luc 1:5–2:52." *ZwTh* 44 (1901) 177–235.
———. "Die Verwerfung Jesu in Nazaret nach den kanonischen Evangelien und nach Marcion." *ZwTh* 45 (1902) 127–44.
Hill, David. *The Gospel of Matthew*. NCeB. London: Oliphants, 1972.
———. "The Rejection of Jesus at Nazareth (Luke 4:16–30)." *NovTest* 13 (1971) 161–80.
Hill, Edmund. "Messianic Fulfilment in St. Luke." *StudEv* I (1957) 190–98.
Hillmann, J. "Die Kindheitsgeschichte Jesu nach Lucas." *JpTh* 17 (1891) 192–261.
Hirsch, Emmanuel. *Frühgeschichte des Evangeliums*. Tübingen: Mohr, 1951.
Hofheinz, Walter Carlton. "An Analysis of the Usage and Influence of Isaiah Chapters 40–66 in the New Testament." PhD diss., Columbia University, 1964.
Holm-Nielsen, Svend. *Hodayot Psalms from Qumran*. Aarhus: Aarhus University Press, 1960.
Holtz, Traugott. *Untersuchungen über die alttestamentlichen Zitate bei Lukas*. TU 104. Berlin: Akademie-Verlag, 1968.
Holtzmann, Heinrich. "Die Gütergemeinschaft der Apostelgeschichte." In *Strassburger Abhandlungen zur Philosophie*, Fs. Eduard Zeller, 25–60. Tübingen: Mohr, 1884.
Holtzmann, Otto. "Studien zur Apostelgeschichte I. Die Gütergemeinschaft." *ZKG* 14 (1894) 25–60.
Holzmeister, U. "Das 'Angenehme Jahr des Herren' (Is 61:2 = Lk 4:19) und die Einjahr Theorie." *ZkTh* 53 (1929) 272–82.

Hooker, Morna. "In His Own Image?" In *What about the New Testament?* Fs. Christopher Evans, edited by Morna Hooker and Colin Hickling, 28–44. London: SCM, 1975.

———. *Jesus and the Servant*. London: SPCK, 1959.

Hooley, B. A., and A. J. Mason. "Some Thoughts on the Parable of the Unjust Steward (Luke 16:1–9)." *ABR* 6 (1958) 47–59.

Hort, Fenton John Anthony. *The Christian Ecclesia*. London: Macmillan, 1898.

Horton, Fred L. *The Melchizedek Tradition*. SNTS MS 30. Cambridge, UK: Cambridge University Press, 1976.

Houlden, J. L. *Ethics and the New Testament*. London: T. & T. Clark, 1973.

Hoyt, Thomas Jr. "The Poor in Luke-Acts." PhD diss., Duke University, 1974.

Humbert, Paul. "Le mot biblique 'ebyon." *RHPhR* 32 (1952) 1–6.

Huuhtanen, Pauli. "Die Perikope vom 'reichen Jüngling' unter Berücksichtigung der Akzentuierungen des Lukas." *SNTU* 2 (1977) 79–98.

Hvidberg, Fleming Friis. *Menigheden af den nye pagt i Damascus*. Copenhagen, 1928.

Iamblichus. *Iamblichus's Life of Pythagoras*. Translated by Thomas Taylor. London, 1926.

———. *Pythagoras, Griechisch und Deutsch*. Edited by M. Albrecht. Zürich: Artemis, 1963.

Irenaeus. *Sancti Irenaei Episcopi Lugdunensis Detectionis et Eversionis Falso Cognominatae Agnitionis seu Contra Omnes Haerses Libri Quinque*. Edited by A. Stieren. Leipzig: T. O. Weigel, 1853.

Isaacs, M. E. "Mary in the Lucan Infancy Narrative." *The Way* (Suppl) 25 (1975) 80–95.

Jacobé, F. "L'origine du Magnificat." *RHLR* 2 (1897) 424–32.

Jalland, T. G. "A Note on Luke 16:1–9." *StudEv* I.503–05.

Jeremias, Joachim. *Jerusalem in the Time of Jesus*. Translated by F. H. Cave and C. H. Cave. London: SCM, 1969.

———. *Jesus' Promise to the Nations*. Translated by S. H. Hooke. SBT 1/24. London: SCM, 1958.

———. *New Testament Theology*. Translated by John Bowden. London: SCM, 1971.

———. *The Parables of Jesus*. Translated by S. H. Hooke. London: SCM, 1972.

———. *The Sermon on the Mount*. Translated by Norman Perrin. London: Athlone, 1961.

Jervell, Jacob. *Luke and the People of God*. Minneapolis: Augsburg, 1972.

Johnson, Luke Timothy. "The Literary Function of Possessions in Luke-Acts." PhD diss., Yale University, 1976.

Jones, Douglas. "The Background and Character of the Lukan Psalms." *JTS* 19 (1968) 19–50.

Jones, D. C. "Who Are the Poor?" *CSR* 3 (1977) 62–72.

Jonge, M., and A. S. van der Woude. "11QMelchizedek and the New Testament." *NTS* 12 (1965/66) 301–26.

Joseph, M. "The Place of Charity or Almsgiving in the Old Testament." *ExpT* 21 (1909/10) 427–28.

Joüon, P. "La parabole du riche insensé." *RechSR* 29 (1939) 486–89.

———. "La parabole des mines (Luc 19:13–27) et la parabole des talents (Matthieu 25:14–30)." *RechSR* 29 (1939) 489–94.

Judge, Edwin A. *The Social Patterns of Christian Groups in the First Century*. London: Tyndale, 1960.

———. "St. Paul as a Radical Critic of Society." *Interchange* 16 (1974) 191–203.

Jülicher, Adolf. *Die Gleichnisreden Jesu.* Tübingen: Mohr, 1910.
Käsemann, Ernst. "The Problem of the Historical Jesus." In *Essays on New Testament Themes*, translated by W. J. Montague, 15-47. SBT 41. London: SCM, 1964.
———. "Sentences of Holy Law in the New Testament." In *New Testament Questions of Today*, translated by W. J. Montague, 66-81. London: SCM, 1969.
Kamlah, E. "Die Parabel vom ungerechten Verwalter (Luk 16:1ff) im Rahmen der Knechtsgleichnisse." In *Abraham unser Vater*, Fs. Otto Michel, edited by Otto Betz et al., 276-94. AGSU 5. Leiden: Brill, 1963.
———. "Kritik und Interpretation der Parabel von den anvertrauten Geldern Mt 25:14ff; Lk 19:12ff." *KuD* 14 (1968) 28-38.
Kandler, H. J. "Die Bedeutung der Armut im Schrifttum von Chirbet Qumran." *Jud* 13 (1957) 193-209.
Karris, Robert J. "The Lukan Sitz im Leben: Methodology and Prospects." *SBL Seminar Papers* (1976) 219-33.
Katz, Mordecai. *Protection of the Weak in the Talmud.* CUOS 24. New York: AMS, 1925.
Keck, Leander E. "The Poor among the Saints in Jewish Christianity and Qumran." *ZNW* 57 (1966) 54-78.
———. "The Poor among the Saints in the New Testament." *ZNW* 56 (1965) 100-129.
Kee, Howard Clark. *Community of the New Age. Studies in Mark's Gospel.* London: SCM, 1977.
Keim, Theodor. *The History of Jesus of Nazara.* 6 vols. London: Williams & Norgate, 1873-83.
Kieffer, R. "Wisdom and Blessing in the Beatitudes of St. Matthew and St. Luke." *StudEv* VI.291-95.
Kilgallen, John. *The Stephen Speech. A Literary and Redactional Study of Acts 7:2-53.* AnBib 67. Rome: Biblical Institute Press, 1976.
Kilpatrick, George D. "The Gentiles and the Strata of Luke." In *Verborum Veritas*, Fs. Gustav Stählin, edited by Otto Böcher and Klaus Haacker, 83-88. Wuppertal: R. Brockhaus, 1970.
———. "Scribes, Lawyers, and Lucan Origins." *JTS* 1 (1950) 56-60.
———. "What John Tells Us about John." In *Studies in John*, Fs. Jan Nicolaas Sevenster, edited by Jan Nicolaas Sevenster, 75-87. NovTestSuppl 24. Leiden: Brill, 1970.
Kim, Kyoung-Jin. *Stewardship and Almsgiving in Luke's Theology.* JSNTSuppl 155. Sheffield, UK: Sheffield Academic, 1998.
Kimbrough, S. T. "The Ethic of the Qumran Community." *RevQum* 6 (1967/69) 483-98.
King, A. "The Parable of the Unjust Steward." *ExpT* 50 (1938/39) 474-76.
King, N. Q. "The "Universalism" of the Third Gospel." *StudEv* I.199-205.
Kittel, Gerhard. *Die Probleme des palästinischen Spätjudentums und das Urchristentum.* Stuttgart: Kohlhammer, 1926.
Kittel, R. "Armengesetzgebung bei den Hebräern." In *Realencyklopädie für protestantische Theologie und Kirche*, 60-63. Leipzig: Hinrichs, 1897.
———. *Die Psalmen.* KAT 13. Leipzig: Scholl, 1922.
Klemm, Hans G. "Das Wort von der Selbstbestattung der Toten. Beobachtungen zur Auslegungsgeschichte von Mt 8:22 par." *NTS* 16 (1969/70) 60-75.
Klijn, Albertus Frederik Johannes. "The Question of the Rich Young Man in a Jewish-Christian Gospel." *NovTest* 8 (1966) 149-55.
Klijn, Albertus Frederik Johannes, and G. J. Reinink. *Patristic Evidence for Jewish Christian Sects.* Leiden: Brill, 1973.

Klostermann, Erich. *Das Lukasevangelium.* HbNT 5. Tübingen: Mohr, 1975.
Knox, Wilfred Lawrence. *The Sources of the Synoptic Gospels.* 2 vols. Cambridge University Press, 1953-57.
———. *St Paul and the Church of Jerusalem.* Cambridge, UK: Cambridge University Press, 1925.
Koch, Klaus. *The Growth of the Biblical Tradition.* Translated by S. M. Cupitt. London: A. and C. Black, 1969.
Koch, Robert. "Die Wertung des Besitzes im Lukasevangelium." *Bib* 38 (1957) 151-69.
Köbert, Raimund. "Kamel und Schiffstau: Zu Markus 10:25 (Par.) und Koran 7:40/38." *Bib* 53 (1972) 229-33.
Köhler, K. "Textkritische Bemerkungen zu der Perikope vom Sorgen im Lukasevangelium." *ThStKr* 86 (1913) 452-61.
Köstlin, H. A. "Das Magnificat Lc 1:46-55. Lobgesang der Maria oder der Elisabeth?" *ZNW* 3 (1902) 142-45.
Koolmeister, Richard. "Selbstverleugnung, Kreuzaufnahme und Nachfolge: Eine historische Studie über Mt 16:24." In *Charisteria Iohanni Köpp*, edited by J. Köpp, 64-94. Stockholm, 1954.
Koontz, J. V. G. "Mary's Magnificat." *BS* 116 (1959) 336-49.
Kosmala, Hans. *Hebräer—Essener—Christen.* SPB 1. Leiden: Brill, 1959.
———. "The Parable of the Unjust Steward in the Light of Qumran." *ASTI* 3 (1964) 114-21.
Krämer, Michael. *Das Rätsel der Parabel vom ungerechten Verwalter.* Zürich: PAS, 1972.
Krafft, E. "Die Vorgeschichten des Lukas." In *Zeit und Geschichte*, Fs. Rudolf Bultmann, edited by Erich Dinkler, 217-23. Tübingen: Mohr, 1964.
Kraft, Robert A., and Ann-Elizabeth Purintun. *Paraleipomena Jeremiou.* Missoula, MT: Scholars Press, 1972.
Krauss, Samuel. *Synagogale Altertümer.* Berlin: Georg Olms, 1922.
———. *Talmudische Archäologie.* 3 vols. Leipzig: G. Foch, 1910-12.
Kümmel, Werner Georg. *Introduction to the New Testament.* Translated by Howard Clark Kee. New Testament Library. London: SCM, 1975.
Kuschke, A. "Arm und reich in Altentestament mit besonderer Berücksichtigung der nachexilischen Zeit." *ZAW* 57 (1939) 31-57.
Lagrange, M.-J., *Evangile selon Saint Luc.* Paris: Gabalda, 1948.
Lamarche, Paul. *Zacharie IX-XIV. Structure littéraire et messianisme.*" Paris: Gabalda, 1961.
Lampe, Geoffrey William Hugo. "'Grievous Wolves' (Acts 20:29)." In *Christ and Spirit in the New Testament*, Fs. Charles Francis Digby Moule, edited by Barnabas Lindars and Stephen S. Smalley, 253-58. Cambridge, UK: Cambridge University Press, 1973.
———. "The Holy Spirit in the Writings of St. Luke." In *Studies in the Gospels. Essays in Memory of Robert Henry Lightfoot*, edited by Dennis E. Nineham, 159-200. Oxford: Blackwell, 1955.
———. "The Lucan Portrait of Christ." *NTS* 2 (1955/56) 160-75.
———. "Luke." In *Peake's Commentary on the Bible*, edited by Matthew Black, 820-43. Edinburgh, 1962.
———. *St Luke and the Church of Jerusalem.* London: Athlone, 1969.
Larkin, William J. "Luke's Use of the Old Testament as a Key to his Soteriology." *JEvThS* 20 (1977) 325-35.

Laurentin, René. *Structure et théologie de Luc.* 2 vols. Paris: Gabalda, 1957.
———. "Traces d'allusions étymologiques en Luc 1-2." *Bib* 37 (1956) 435-56; 38 (1957) 1-23.
Lauterbach, Jacob Z. *Mekilta de-Rabbi Ishmael.* Philadelphia: Jewish Publication Society of America, 1976.
Leaney, Alfred Robert Clare. "The Birth Narratives in St Luke and St Matthew." *NTS* 8 (1961/62) 158-66.
———. *A Commentary on the Gospel According to St. Luke.* BNTC. London: A. and C. Black, 1958.
———. *The Rule of Qumran and Its Meaning.* London: SCM, 1966.
Lebreton, J. "La doctrine du renoncement dans le Nouveau Testament." *NRT* 65 (1938) 385-412.
LeDéaut, R. "Miryam, soeur de Moise, et Marie, mère du Messie." *Bib* 45 (1964) 198-219.
Lee, G. M. "Mark 10:18." *Theology* 70 (1967) 167-68.
Lefort, L. Th. "Le nom du mauvais riche (Lc 16, 19) et la tradition copte." *ZNW* 37 (1938) 65-72.
Légasse, Simon. "Jésus a-t-il annoncé la conversion finale d'Israel? (A propos de Marc 10:23-7)." *NTS* 10 (1963/64) 480-87.
———. *L'appel du riche.* Paris: Beauchesne, 1966.
———. "Les pauvres en esprit et les 'volontaires' de Qumran" *NTS* 8 (1961/62) 336-45.
———. *Les pauvres en esprit. Evangile et non-violence.* LD 78. Paris: Cerf, 1974.
Legrand, L. "Christian Celibacy and the Cross." *Scrip* 14 (1962) 1-12.
———. "L'évangile aux bergers. Essai sur le genre littéraire de Luc 2:8-20." *RB* 75 (1968) 161-87.
Lehmann, J. "Assistance publique et privée d'après l'antique législation juive." *REJ* 35 (1897) 1-38.
Leipoldt, Johannes. *Der soziale Gedanke in der altchristlichen Kirche.* Leipzig: Kohler und Amelang, 1952.
———. "Jesus und die Armen." *NKZ* 28 (1917) 784-810.
Leivestad, R. "ΤΑΠΕΙΝΟΣ—ΤΑΠΕΙΝΟΦΡΩΝ." *NovTest* 8 (1966) 36-47.
Lemoine, F. M. "Législation et histoire de l'année jubilaire dans l'Ancien Testament." *VS* 344 (1949) 264-88.
Lévi, I. "Un recueil de contes juifs inédits." *REJ* 35 (1897) 65-83.
Levine, Étan. *The Aramaic Version of Ruth.* AnBib 58. Rome: Biblical Institute Press, 1973.
Levy, Isaac. *The Synagogue: Its History and Function.* London: Vallentine, Mitchell and Co., 1963.
Lewis, Agnes Smith. *A Translation of the Four Gospels from the Syriac of the Sinaitic Palimpsest.* London: C. J. Clay, 1894.
Lieberman, Saul. *Greek in Jewish Palestine.* New York: Feldheim, 1965.
Lietzmann, Hans. *An die Korinther I.II.* HbNT 9. Tübingen: Mohr, 1923.
———. "Jüdisch-griechische Inschriften aus Tell el Yehudieh." *ZNW* 22 (1923) 280-86.
Lightfoot, John. *Horae Hebraicae et Talmudicae.* Edited by R. Gandell. Oxford: Oxford University Press, 1859.
Lightfoot, Joseph Barber. *St Paul's Epistle to the Philippians.* London: Macmillan, 1898.
Lightfoot, Robert Henry. *The Gospel Message of St. Mark.* Oxford: Clarendon, 1950.

———. *History and Interpretation in the Gospels.* London: Hodder and Stoughton, 1935.
Lindars, Barnabas. *The Gospel of John.* NCeB. London: Marshall, Morgan and Scott, 1972.
———. "The Place of the Old Testament in the Formation of New Testament Theology. Prolegomena." *NTS* 23 (1977) 59–66.
Linnemann, Eta. *Parables of Jesus.* Translated by John Sturdy. London: SPCK, 1966.
Linton, O. "Le parallelismus membrorum dans le Nouveau Testament." In *Mélanges Bibliques*, Fs. Béda Rigaux, edited by A.-L. Descamps and André de Halleux, 489–507. Gembloux, Belgium: Duculot, 1970,.
Little, James C. "Parable Research in the Twentieth Century. III: Developments since J. Jeremias." *ExpT* 88 (1976/77) 71–75.
Loeb, I. "La literature des pauvres dans la Bible." *REJ* 20 (1890) 161–98; 21 (1890) 1–42, 161–206; 23 (1891) 1–31, 161–93.
Loewe, W. P. "Towards an Interpretation of Lk 19:1–10." *CBQ* 36 (1974) 321–31.
Lohfink, Gerhard. *Die Sammlung Israels. Eine Untersuchung zur lukanischen Ekklesiologie.* StANT 39. Munich: Kösel, 1975.
Lohmeyer, Ernst. *Das Evangelium des Markus.* KEK 1/2. Göttingen: Vandenhoeck and Ruprecht, 1953.
———. *Vom Begriff der religiösen Gemeinschaft.* Leipzig-Berlin: B. G. Teubner, 1925.
Lohse, Eduard. *Die Texte aus Qumran.* Munich: Kösel, 1971.
———. "Lukas als Theologe der Heilsgeschichte." *EvTh* 14 (1954) 256–75.
Loisy, Alfred. *Les évangiles synoptiques.* Ceffonds, 1907.
Lorenzen, T. "A Biblical Meditation on Luke 16:19–31." *ExpT* 87 (1975/76) 39–43.
Luce, Harry Kenneth. *The Gospel According to S. Luke.* Cambridge, UK: Cambridge University Press, 1949.
Lunt, R. G. "The Parable of the Unjust Steward (Luke 16:1–15)." *ExpT* 77 (1965/66) 132–36.
———. "Towards an Interpretation of the Parable of the Unjust Steward (Luke 16:1–18)." *ExpT* 66 (1954/55) 335–37.
Maass, F. "Das Gleichnis vom ungerechten Haushalter Lukas 16:1–8." *ThViat* 8 (1962) 173–84.
McCaughey, J. D. "The Intention of the Author. Some questions about the exegesis of Acts 6:1–6." *ABR* 7 (1959) 27–36.
McCormick, B. E. "The Social and Economic Background of Luke." PhD diss., Oxford University, 1960.
McCown, Chester Charlton. *The Genesis of the Social Gospel.* London: Williams and Norgate, 1929.
McCullock, W. "The Pounds and the Talents." *ExpT* 23 (1911/12) 382–83.
McFadyen, J. F. "The Parable of the Unjust Steward." *ExpT* 37 (1925/26) 535–39.
McGaughy, L. C. "The Fear of Yahweh and the Mission of Judaism: A Postexilic Maxim and Its Early Christian Expansion in the Parable of the Talents." *JBL* 94 (1975) 235–45.
Machen, J. Gresham. "The Hymns of the First Chapter of Luke." *PTR* 10 (1912) 1–38.
———. "The Origin of the First Two Chapters of Luke." *PTR* 10 (1912) 212–77.
———. *The Virgin Birth of Christ.* London: James Clarke, 1930.
MacMullen, Ramsay. *Enemies of the Roman Order.* Cambridge, MA: Harvard University Press, 1967.

McHugh, John. *The Mother of Jesus in the New Testament*. London: Doubleday, 1975.
McNeile, A. H. *The Gospel According to St. Matthew*. London: Macmillan, 1915.
MacNeill, H. L. "The Sitz im Leben of Luke 1:5–2:20." *JBL* 65 (1946) 123–30.
Maillot, A. "Réparer les coeurs brisés. Réunifier les vies en miettes." *RRef* 27 (1976) 97–103.
Malherbe, A. J. "The New Exodus in the Books of Luke." *NovTest* 2 (1958) 8–23.
Mann, Jacob. *The Bible as Read and Preached in the Old Synagogue*. 2 vols. New York: Ktav, 1971.
Manson, Thomas Walter. *The Sayings of Jesus*. London: SCM, 1950.
———. "The Work of St Luke." In *Studies in the Gospels and Epistles*, edited by Matthew Black, 46–67. Manchester: Manchester University Press, 1962.
Manson, William. *The Gospel of Luke*. MNTC. London: Hodder and Stoughton, 1948.
———. *Jesus the Messiah*. London: Hodder and Stoughton, 1944.
Marmorstein, A. *The Doctrine of Merits in Old Rabbinical Literature*. London: Jews' College, 1920.
———. "The Treasure in Heaven and upon Earth." *LQR* 132 (1919) 216–28.
Marshall, H. S. "The Parable of the Untrustworthy Steward (Luke 16:1–13). A Question Reopened." *ExpT* 39 (1927/28) 120–22.
Marshall, I. Howard. *Eschatology and the Parables*. London: Theological Students' Fellowship, 1963.
———. *The Gospel of Luke. A Commentary on the Greek Text*. Exeter, UK: Paternoster, 1978.
———. *Luke: Historian and Theologian*. Exeter, UK: Paternoster, 1970.
———. "Palestinian and Hellenistic Christianity: Some Critical Comments." *NTS* 19 (1972/73) 271–87.
Marshall, Laurence Henry. *The Challenge of New Testament Ethics*. London: Macmillan, 1946.
Martin, A. S. "Why callest thou me good?" *ExpT* 21 (1909/10) 137–38.
Martin, Hugh. *Luke's Portrait of Jesus*. London: SCM, 1949.
Martin, Ralph P. "Salvation and Discipleship in Luke's Gospel." *Interpr* 30 (1976) 366–80.
Martin-Achard, Robert. "Yahwé et les 'anawim.'" *TZ* 21 (1965) 349–57.
Masson, Charles. "Jésus à Nazareth." In *Vers les sources d'eau vive. Etudes d'exégèse et de théologie du Nouveau Testament*, 38–69. Lausanne: Librairie Payot, 1961.
Mattill, A. J. "The Good Samaritan and the Purpose of Luke-Acts—Halévy Reconsidered." *Encounter* 33 (1972) 359–76.
Mavrodes, G. I. "Jubilee—A Viable Model?" *RefJ* 28 (1978) 15–19.
Mealand, David L. "'As having nothing, and yet possessing everything': 2 Kor 6:10c," *ZNW* 67 (1976) 277–79.
———. "Community of Goods at Qumran." *TZ* 31 (1975) 129–39.
———. "Community of Goods and Utopian Allusions in Acts II–IV." *JTS* 28 (1977) 96–99.
———. "The Disparagement of Wealth in New Testament Times." PhD diss., Bristol University, 1971.
———. "'Paradisial' Elements in the Teaching of Jesus?" Paper presented at 6th International Congress for Biblical Studies, Oxford, 1978.

Menoud, Philippe H. "La mort d'Ananias et de Saphira (Actes 5:1–11)." In *Aux sources de la tradition chrétienne*, Fs. Maurice Goguel, 146–154. Paris: Delachaux and Niestlé, 1950.

———. *La vie de l'Eglise naissante*. Neuchâtel: Delachaux et Niestlé, 1952.

———. "Le plan des Actes des Apôtres." *NTS* 1 (1954/55) 44–51.

———. "Richesse injustes et biens véritables." *RThPh* 31 (1943) 5–17.

Merx, Adalbert. *Die Evangelien des Markus und Lukas nach der syrischen im Sinaikloster gefundenen Palimpsesthandschrift*. Berlin: de Gruyter, 1905.

Metz, Johann Baptiste. *Poverty of Spirit*. Translated by John Drury. New York: Newman, 1968.

Metzger, Bruce M. *A Textual Commentary on the Greek New Testament*. London: United Bible Society, 1971.

Meye, Robert Paul. *Jesus and the Twelve*. Grand Rapids, MI: Eerdmans, 1968.

Meyer, Arnold. *Jesu Muttersprache*. Leipzig: Mohr, 1896.

Meyer, H. A. W. *Critical and Exegetical Handbook to the Gospels of Mark and Luke*. Edinburgh: T. & T. Clark, 1880.

Michaelis, C. "Die Π-Alliteration der Subjektsworte der ersten 4 Seligpreisungen bei Mt, Lk und in Q." *NovTest* 10 (1968) 148–61.

Michaelis, Wilhelm. *Die Gleichnisse Jesu*. Hamburg: Furche-Verlag, 1956.

———. "Zelt und Hütte im biblischen Denken." *EvTh* 14 (1954) 29–49.

Michel, O. "Der Lohngedanke in der Verkündigung Jesu." *ZSTh* 9 (1931/32) 47–54.

Miller, M. P. "The Function of Isa 61:1–2 in 11QMelchizedek." *JBL* 88 (1969) 467–69.

Miller, W. D. "The Unjust Steward." *ExpT* 15 (1903/04) 332–34.

Minear, Paul S. *And Great Shall Be Your Reward*. New Haven, CT: Yale University Press, 1941.

———. *Commands of Christ*. Edinburgh: St. Andrew, 1972.

———. "Dear Theo. The Kerygmatic Intention and Claim of the Book of Acts." *Interpr* 27 (1973) 131–50.

———. *I Saw a New Earth*. Washington: Corpus Books, 1968.

———. "Jesus' Audiences, According to Luke." *NovTest* 16 (1974) 81–109.

———. "Luke's Use of the Birth Stories." In *Studies in Luke-Acts*, Fs. Paul Schubert, edited by Leander E. Keck and James Louis Martyn, 111–30. New York: Abingdon, 1966.

———. "The Needle's Eye." *JBL* 61 (1942) 157–69.

———. "A Note on Luke 22:36. *NovTest* 7 (1964/65) 128–34.

Miranda, José Porforio. *Marx and the Bible*. Translated by John Eagleson. New York: Orbis, 1974.

Moffatt, James. *Love in the New Testament*. London: Hodder and Stoughton, 1930.

Molitor, J. "Zur Übersetzung von μετεωρίζεσθε Lk 12:29." *BZ* 10 (1966) 107–08.

Moltmann, Jürgen. *Theology of Hope*. Tranlated by James W. Leitch. London: SCM, 1967.

Mommsen, Theodor. *Römisches Strafrecht*, Leipzig: Duncker and Humblot, 1899.

Moore, F. J. "The Parable of the Unjust Steward." *AThR* 47 (1965) 103–05.

Moore, George Foot. *Judaism*. 3 vols. Cambridge, MA: Harvard University Press, 1927–30.

Morris, Leon. *The Gospel According to St. Luke*. Grand Rapids, MI: Eerdmans, 1974.

———. *The New Testament and the Jewish Lectionaries*. London: Tyndale, 1964.

Moscato, M. A. "Current Theories Regarding the Audience of Luke-Acts." *CTM* 3 (1976) 335–61.
Mosley, A. W. "Historical Reporting in the Ancient World." *NTS* 12 (1965/66) 10–26.
———. "Jesus' Audiences in the Gospels of St Mark and St Luke." *NTS* 10 (1963/64) 139–49.
Mott, Stephen Charles. "Greek Ethics and Christian Conversion: The Philonic Background of Titus 2:10–14 and 3:3–7." *NovTest* 20 (1978) 22–48.
Moule, C. F. D. *The Birth of the New Testament*. BNTC 1. London: A. and C. Black, 1962.
———. "The Christology of Acts." In *Studies in Luke-Acts*, Fs. Paul Schubert, edited by Leander E. Keck and James Louis Martyn, 159–85. London: SPCK, 1968.
———. *An Idiom Book of New Testament Greek*. Cambridge, UK: Cambridge University Press, 1963.
———. "The Intention of the Evangelists." In *New Testament Essays. Studies in Memory of T. W. Manson*, edited by Angus John Brockhurst Higgins, 165–79. Manchester: Manchester University Press, 1959.
———. "Once More, Who Were the Hellenists?" *ExpT* 70 (1958/59) 100–102.
Moulton, James Hope. *A Grammar of New Testament Greek, Vol. III: Sytax*. Edinburgh: T. & T. Clark, 1963.
Mounce, R. H. "Synoptic Self-Portraits." *EvQ* 38 (1965) 212–17.
Mowinckel, Sigmund. *Psalmenstudien*. Amsterdam: Schippers, 1966.
Mowry, Lucetta. *The Dead Sea Scrolls and the Early Church*. South Bend, IN: University of Notre Dame Press, 1966.
Munch, P. A. "Einige Bemerkungen zu den עניים und den רשעים in den Psalmen." *MO* 30 (1936) 13–26.
Munck, Johannes. *The Acts of the Apostles*. AncB 31. New York: Doubleday, 1967.
Mussies, Gerard. *Dio Chrysostom and the New Testament*. SCH 2. Leiden: Brill, 1972.
Mussner, F. "Der Glaube Mariens im Lichte des Römerbriefs." *Cath* 18 (1964) 258–68.
———. "Die Mitte des Evangeliums in neutestamentlicher Sicht." *Cath* 15 (1961) 271–92.
———. "Lk 1:48f; 11:27f und die Anfänge der Marienverehrung in der Urkirche." *Cath* 21 (1967) 287–94.
Navone, John. *Themes of St. Luke*. Rome: Gegorian University Press, 1970.
Neil, William. *The Acts of the Apostles*. NCeB. London: Oliphants, 1973.
———. "Five Hard Sayings of Jesus." In *Biblical Studies*, Fs. William Barclay, edited by Johnston R. McKay and James F. Miller, 157–71. London: Collins, 1976.
Neill, Stephen. *Jesus through Many Eyes*. London: Lutterworth, 1976.
Neirynck, Frans. *The Minor Agreements of Matthew and Luke against Mark*. BETL 37. Leuven: Leuven University Press, 1974.
Nestlé, Eberhard. "Luc 4:18, 19." *ZNW* 2 (1901) 153–57.
Neuhäusler, E. "Mit welchem Massstab misst Gott die Menschen? Deutung zweier Jesussprüche." *BiLeb* 11 (1970) 104–13.
Neusner, Jacob. "First Cleanse the Inside." *NTS* 22 (1976) 486–95.
———. *From Politics to Piety*. Englewood Cliffs, NJ: Prentice-Hall, 1973.
———. "Pharisaic Law in New Testament Times." *USQR* 26 (1971) 331–40.
———. *The Rabbinic Traditions about the Pharisees before 70*. 3 vols. Leiden: Brill, 1971.
Noack, Bent. *Das Gottesreich bei Lukas. Eine Studie zu Luk 17:20–24*. Uppsala: Lund, 1948.

Nolan, Albert. *Jesus before Christianity*. London: Darton, Longman and Todd, 1976.
Nolland, John. "Luke's Readers—A Study of Luke 4:22–28; Acts 13:46; 18:6; 28:28 and Luke 21:5–36." PhD diss., Cambridge University, 1977.
Norden, Eduard. *Die Geburt des Kindes*. Leipzig: Teubner, 1924.
North, Christopher R. *The Second Isaiah*. Oxford: Clarendon, 1964.
Oesterley, William Oscar Emil. *The Gospel Parables in the Light of Their Jewish Background*. London: SPCK, 1936.
———. "The Parable of the 'Unjust' Steward (St. Luke 16)." *Exp* VI.7 (1903) 273–83.
Oliver, H. H. "The Lucan Birth Stories and the Purpose of Luke-Acts." *NTS* 10 (1963/64) 202–26.
Olsthoorn, M. F. *The Jewish Background and the Synoptic Setting of Mt 6:25–33 and Lk 12:22–31*. Jerusalem: Franciscan Press, 1975.
O'Neill, James C. "The Charge of Blasphemy at Jesus' Trial before the Sanhedrin." In *The Trial of Jesus*, Fs. C. F. D. Moule, edited by E. Bammel, 72–77. SBT 2/13. London: SCM, 1970.
———. "The Six Amen Sayings in Luke." *JTS* 10 (1959) 1–9.
———. *The Theology of Acts in Its Historical Setting*. London: SPCK, 1961.
Oppenheimer, Aharon. *The 'Am Ha-aretz*. Translated by I. H. Levine. Leiden: Brill, 1977.
Otomo, Yoko Takahashi. *Nachfolge Jesu und Anfänge der Kirche im Neuen Testament*. Mainz: Mainz University Press, 1970.
Owen, Huw P. "Stephen's Vision in Acts 7:55–56." *NTS* 1 (1954/55) 224–26.
Pargiter, F. E. "The Parable of the Unrighteous Steward." *ExpT* 32 (1920/21) 136–37.
Paterson, W. P. "The Example of the Unjust Steward." *ExpT* 35 (1923/24) 391–95.
Patterson, Richard Duane. "The Widow, the Orphan, and the Poor in the Old Testament and the Extra-Biblical Literature." *BS* 130 (1973) 223–34.
Paul, Geoffrey. "The Unjust Steward and the Interpretation of Luke 16:9." *Theology* 61 (1958) 189–93.
Pauly, August Friedrich von. *Real-Encyclopädie der classischen Altertumswissenschaft*. Stuttgart: J. B. Metzler, 1842.
Pautrel, R. "Aeterna Tabernacula (Luc 16:9)." *RechSR* 30 (1940) 307–27.
Pax, E. "Der Reiche und der arme Lazarus: Eine Milieustudie." *SBFLA* 25 (1975) 254–68.
Percy, Ernst. *Die Botschaft Jesu. Eine traditionskritische und exegetische Untersuchung*. LUA 49/5. Lund, Sweden: Gleerup, 1953.
Perles, Felix. "Zwei Übersetzungsfehler im Text der Evangelien." *ZNW* 19 (1919/20) 96.
Perrot, Charles. "Luc 4:16–30 et la lecture biblique de l'ancienne synagogue." In *Exégèse biblique et Judaisme*, edited by Jacques E. Ménard, 170–83. Strasbourg: Université des Sciences humaines de Strasbourg, 1973.
Pervo, Richard. *Profit with Delight: The Literary Genre of the Acts of the Apostles*. Philadelphia: Fortress, 1987.
Pesch, Wilhelm. *Der Lohngedanke in der Lehre Jesu*. MüThSt 1/7. Munich: Karl Zink, 1955.
———. "Zur Exegese von Mt 6:19–21 und Lk 12:33–34." *Bib* 41 (1960) 356–78.
———. "Zur Formgeschichte und Exegese von Lk 12:32." *Bib* 41 (1960) 25–40.
Pfleiderer, Otto. *Primitive Christianity*. 4 vols. Translated by W. Montgomery. London-New York: Fisher Unwin, 1906–11.

Phillips, J. B. *The New Testament in Modern English*. London: Geoffrey Bles and William Collins, 1958.
Phillips, Thomas E. *Reading Issues of Wealth and Poverty in Luke-Acts*. New York: Edwin Mellon, 2001.
Philo. *On the Virtues*. Translated by F. H. Colson. Loeb Classical Library 341. Cambridge, MA: Harvard University Press, 1984.
Pilgrim, Walter. *Good News for the Poor*. Minneapolis: Augsburg, 1981.
Plümacher, Eckhard. *Lukas als hellenistischer Schriftsteller. Studien zur Apostelgeschichte*. StUNT 9. Göttingen: Vandenhoeck and Ruprecht, 1972.
Plummer, Alfred. *A Commentary on St. Paul's Epistle to the Philippians*. London: R. Scott, 1919.
———. *A Critical and Exegetical Commentary on the Gospel According to S. Luke*. ICC. Edinburgh: T. & T. Clark, 1905.
Powell, W. "Parable of Dives and Lazarus (Luke 16:19–31)." *ExpT* 66 (1954/55) 350–51.
Powers, B. Ward. "The Ethical Teaching of the New Testament and Its Bases in Relation to the Spheres of Sex and Marriage and Family Relationships." PhD diss., London University, 1972.
———. "Marriage and Divorce. The Dispute of Jesus with the Pharisees and Its Inception." *Colloquium* 5 (1972) 34–41.
Prat, Ferdinand. *Jésus Christ: sa vie, sa doctrine, son oeuvre*. Paris: Beauchesne, 1953.
Preisker, H. "Lukas 16:1–7." *TLZ* 74 (1949) 85–92.
Preuschen, Erwin. "Das Wort vom verachteten Propheten." *ZNW* 17 (1916) 33–48.
———. *Die Apostelgeschichte*. Tübingen: Mohr, 1912.
Prevallet, E. M. "The Rejection at Nazareth: Luke 4:14–30." *Scrip* 20 (1968) 5–9.
Rabin, Chaim Menahem. *Qumran Studies*. Oxord: Oxford University Press, 1957.
Rabinowitz, Louis I. "The Study of a Midrash." *JQR* 58 (1967) 143–61.
Rackham, Richard Belward. *The Acts of the Apostles*. London: Methuen, 1910.
Ragg, Lonsdale. *St Luke*. London: Methuen, 1922.
Rahlfs, Alfred. עני *und* ענו *in den Psalmen*. Göttingen: Dieterich, 1892.
Reeves, David C. "Studies in the Ethics of Luke." PhD diss., Harvard University, 1971.
Reicke, Bo. *Diakonie, Festfreude und Zelos*. Uppsala: Lundequist, 1951.
———. *Glaube und Leben der Urgemeinde. Bemerkungen zu Apg. 1–7*. Zürich: Zwingli, 1957.
———. *The Gospel of Luke*. Translated by Ross Mackenzie. London: SPCK, 1965.
———. "Instruction and Discussion in the Travel Narrative." *StudEv* I.206–16.
———. "Jesus in Nazareth—Luke 4:14–30." In *Das Wort und die Wörter*, Fs. Gerhard Friedrich, edited by Horst Robert Balz and Siegfried Schulz, 47–55. Stuttgart: Kohlhammer, 1973.
———. "The New Testament Conception of Reward." In *Aux sources de la tradition chrétienne*, Fs. Maurice Goguel, 195–206. Paris: Delachaux and Niestlé, 1950.
———. "The Risen Lord and His Church." *Interpr* 13 (1959) 157–69.
Reid, J. "The Poor Rich Fool." *ExpT* 13 (1901/02) 567–68.
Reim, Günther. "John 4:44—Crux or Clue?" *NTS* 22 (1976) 476–80.
Reimarus, Hermann Samuel. *Reimarus: Fragments*. Edited by Charles H. Talbert, translated by Ralph S. Fraser. Philadelphia: Fortress, 1970.
Rengstorf, Karl Heinrich. *Das Evangelium nach Lukas*. NTD 3. Göttingen: Vandenhoeck and Ruprecht, 1958.
———. "μαθητής κτλ." In *TDNT* IV.390–461.

Rezevskis, J. "Die Makarismen bei Matthäus und Lukas, ihr Verhältnis zueinander und ihr historischer Hintergrund." *Stud Theol* (Riga) 1 (1935) 157–69.
Rice, E. P. "Fulfilled in Your Ears." *ExpT* 29 (1917/18) 45–46.
Rienecker, Fritz. *Das Evangelium des Lukas*. Wuppertal: R. Brockhaus, 1974.
Riesenfeld, Harold. *The Gospel Tradition*. Translated by E. Margaret Rowley and Robert A. Kraft. Oxford: Blackwell, 1970.
———. "The Meaning of the Verb ἀρνεῖσθαι." *CNT* 11 (1947) 207–19.
Riesner, Rainer. *Formen gemeinsamen Lebens im Neuen Testament und heute*. Basel: Brunnen, 1977.
Rimmer, N. "Parable of Dives and Lazarus (Luke 16:19–31)." *ExpT* 66 (1954/55) 215–16.
Robbins, Vernon K. *Exploring the Texture of Texts*. Harrisburg: Trinity International, 1996.
Robinson, Haddon W. *Expository Preaching: Principles and Practice*. Leicester: Intervarsity, 2001.
Robinson, John A. T. "The Most Primitive Christology of All?" In *Twelve New Testament Studies*, 139–53. SBT 34. London: SCM, 1962.
———. *Redating the New Testament*. London: SCM, 1977.
Robinson, William Charles. *The Way of the Lord. A Study of History and Eschatology in the Gospel of Luke*. Basel: Universität Basel 1960.
———. "The Theological Context for Interpreting Luke's Travel Narrative (9:51ff)." *JBL* 79 (1960) 20–31.
Rolsten, H. "Ministry to Need. The Teachings of Jesus Concerning Stewardship of Possessions." *Interpr* 8 (1954) 142–54.
Rostovtzeff, Michael. *The Social and Economic History of the Roman Empire*. Oxford: Clarendon, 1957.
Roth, S. John. *The Blind, the Lame and the Poor: Character Types in Luke-Acts*. JSNTSuppl 144. Sheffield, UK: Sheffield Academic Press, 1997.
Ruddick, C. Townsend Jr. "Birth Narratives in Genesis and Luke." *NovTest* 12 (1970) 343–48.
Rutherford, W. G. *The New Phyrnicus*. London, 1881.
Ryle, Herbert Edward, and Montegue Rhodes James. *The Psalms of Solomon*. Cambridge, UK: Cambridge University Press, 1891.
Ryrie, Charles Caldwell. "Perspectives on Social Ethics. III: Christ's Teachings on Social Ethics." *BS* 134 (1977) 215–27.
Sahlin, Harald. *Der Messias und das Gottesvolk*. Uppsala: Almqvist and Wiksells, 1945.
———. "Die Früchte der Umkehr. Die ethische Verkündigung Johannes des Täufers nach Lk 3:10–14." *StudTheol* 1 (1947) 54–68.
Salom, A. P. "Was Zacchaeus Really Reforming?" *ExpT* 78 (1966/67) 87.
Sandegren, C. A. "A Mostly Misunderstood Section of the Sermon on the Mount." *EvQ* 23 (1951) 134–38.
Sanders, Ed Parish. *Paul and Palestinian Judaism*. London: SCM, 1977.
———. "Priorités et dépendances dans la tradition synoptique." *RechSR* 60 (1972) 519–40.
———. *The Tendencies of the Synoptic Tradition*. SNTS MS 9. Cambridge, UK: Cambridge University Press, 1969.

Sanders, James A. "From Isaiah 61 to Luke 4." In *Christianity, Judaism and Other Greco-Roman Cults*, Fs. Morton Smith, edited by Jacob Neusner, 75-106. SJLA 12. Leiden: Brill, 1975.
Sanders, Jack T. *Ethics in the New Testament*. Philadelphia: Fortress, 1975.
Satake, Akira. "Das Leiden der Jünger 'um meinetwillen.'" *ZNW* 67 (1967) 4-19.
Sattler, W. "Die Anawim im Zeitalter Jesu Christi." In *Festgabe für Adolf Jülicher*, edited by Adolf Jülicher, 1-15. Tübingen: Mohr, 1927.
Scheele, Paul-Werner. "Maria in der Gemeinschaft und Geschichte Israels." *Cath* 29 (1975) 92-113.
Scheidweiler, Felix. "Zu Act 5:4." *ZNW* 49 (1958) 136-37.
Schelkle, Karl Hermann. *Die Passion Jesu in der Verkündigung des Neuen Testaments*. Heidelberg: Kerle, 1949.
Schlatter, Adolf. *The Church in the New Testament Period*. Translated by Paul P. Levertoff. London: SPCK, 1955.
———. *Die Evangelien nach Markus und Lukas*. Berlin: Evangelische Verlag, 1954.
———. *Der Evangelist Matthäus*, Stuttgart: Calwer, 1959.
———. *Das Evangelium des Lukas*. Stuttgart: Calwer, 1931.
Schleiermacher, Friedrich. *A Critical Essay on the Gospel of St. Luke*. London: John Taylor, 1825.
Schmeichel, W. "Christian Prophecy in Lukan thought: Luke 4:16-30 as a Point of Departure." *SBL Seminar Papers* (1976) 293-304.
Schmid, Josef. *Das Evangelium nach Lukas*. RNT 3. Regensburg: Pustet, 1960.
Schmidt, Karl Ludwig. *Der Rahmen der Geschichte Jesu*. Berlin: Trowitsch, 1919.
Schmidt, P. "Maria in der Sicht des Magnifikat." *GuL* 46 (1973) 417-30.
———. "Maria und das Magnificat." *Cath* 29 (1975) 230-46.
Schmiedel, P. W. "Die Gütergemeinschaft der ältesten Christenheit." *PrM* 2 (1898) 367-78.
Schmithals, Walter. "Lukas—Evangelist der Armen." *ThViat* 12 (1975) 153-67.
Schnackenburg, Rudolf. *The Church in the New Testament*. Translated by W. J. O'Hara. London: Burns and Oates, 1974.
———. "Das Magnificat, seine Spiritualität und Theologie." *GuL* 38 (1965) 342-57.
———. *The Moral Teaching of the New Testament*. Translated by J. Holland-Smith and W. J. O'Hara. London: Burns and Oates, 1975.
Schneider, Gerhard. *Das Evangelium nach Lukas*. ÖTK NT 3. Gütersloher Verlagshaus, 1977.
———. "Der Zweck des lukanischen Doppelwerks." *BZ* 21 (1977) 45-66.
———. *Parusiegleichnisse im Lukas-Evangelium*. SBS 74. Stuttgart: KBW, 1975.
Schneider, J. "Zur Analyse des lukanischen Reiseberichtes." In *Synoptische Studien*, Fs. Alfred Wikenhauser, 207-229. Munich: Zink, 1953.
Schniewind, Julius. *Das Evangelium nach Markus*. NTD 1. Göttingen: Vandenhoeck and Ruprecht, 1958.
———. *Das Evangelium nach Matthäus*. NTD 2. Göttingen: Vandenhoeck and Ruprecht, 1956.
Schoeps, Hans-Joachim. *Jewish Christianity*. Translated by Douglas R. A. Hare. Philadelphia: Fortress, 1969.
Schoonheim, P. L. "Der alttestamentliche Boden der Vokabel ὑπερήφανος Lukas 1:51." *NovTest* 8 (1966) 235-46.

Schottroff, Luise, and Wolfgang Stegemann. *Jesus and the Hope of the Poor.* Translated by Matthew J. O'Connell. Eugene, OR: Wipf and Stock, 1978.

Schramm, Tim. *Der Markus-Stoff bei Lukas.* SNTS MS 14. Cambridge, UK: Cambridge University Press, 1971.

Schubert, Kurt. *The Dead Sea Community.* Translated by John W. Doberstein. London: Black, 1959.

———. "The Sermon on the Mount and the Qumran Texts." In *The Scrolls and the New Testament,* edited by Krister Stendahl, 118–28. London: SCM, 1958.

Schubert, Paul. "The Structure and Significance of Luke 24." In *Neutestamentliche Studien für Rudolf Bultmann,* edited by Walther Eltester, 165–186. BZNW 21. Berlin: Töpelmann, 1957.

Schulz, Anselm. *Nachfolgen und Nachahmen. Studien über das Verhältnis der neutestamentlichen Jüngerschaft zur urchristlichen Vorbildethik.* StANT 6. Munich: Kösel, 1962.

Schulz, Siegfried. *Q. Die Spruchquelle der Evangelisten.* Zürich: Theologischer Verlag, 1972.

Schürer, Emil. *The History of the Jewish People in the Age of Jesus Christ (175 BC–AD 135).* Edited by Geza Vermes et al., translated by T. A. Burkill et al. 2 vols. Edinburgh: T. & T. Clark, 1973–79.

———. *A History of the Jewish People in the Time of Jesus Christ.* Edinburgh: T. & T. Clark, 1896–1901.

Schürmann, Heinz. *Das Lukasevangelium.* HThK 3/1. Freiburg: Herder, 1969.

———. "'Der Bericht vom Anfang'. Ein Rekonstruktionsversuch auf Grund von Lk 4:14–16." *StudEv* II.242–58.

———. "Eschatologie und Liebesdienst in der Verkündigung Jesu." In *Ursprung und Gestalt,* 279–98. Düsseldorf: Patmos, 1970.

———. "Sprachliche Reminisznezen an abgeänderte oder ausgelassene Bestandteile der Spruchsammlung im Lukas und Matthäusevangelium." *NTS* 6 (1959/60) 193–210.

———. *Traditionsgeschichtliche Untersuchungen zu den synoptischen Evangelien.* Düsseldorf: Patmos, 1968.

———. "Zur Traditionsgeschichte der Nazareth-Perikope Lk 4:16–30." In *Mélanges Bibliques* (= Fs. Beda Rigaux), edited by Albert-Louis Descamps and André de Halleux, 187–205. Gembloux, Belgium: Duculot, 1970.

Schütz, Frieder. *Der leidende Christus. Die angefochtene Gemeinde und das Christuskerygma der lukanischen Schriften.* BWANT 89. Stuttgart: Kohlhammer, 1969.

Schwarz, Günther. "Ihnen gehört das Himmelreich." *NTS* 23 (1977) 341–43.

———. "'... lobte den betrügerischen Verwalter'? (Lukas 16:8a)." *BZ* 18 (1974) 94–95.

———. "Lukas 6:22a, 23c, 26. Emendation, Rückübersetzung, Interpretation." *ZNW* 66 (1975) 269–74.

———. "ἰῶτα ἓν ἢ μία κεραία (Matthäus 5:18)." *ZNW* 66 (1975) 268–69.

Schweizer, Eduard. "The Disciples of Jesus and the Post-Resurrection Church." In *Neotestamentica,* edited by Eduard Schweizer, 239–53. Zürich: Zwingli, 1963.

———. "Formgeschichtliches zu den Seligpreisungen Jesu." *NTS* 19 (1972/73) 121–26.

———. *Lordship and Discipleship.* SBT 28. London: SCM, 1960.

Scott, Charles Archibald Anderson. "The 'Fellowship' or κοινωνία." *ExpT* 35 (1923/24) 567.

———. *The Fellowship of the Spirit*. London: J. Clarke, 1921.
———. "What Happened at Pentecost?" In *The Spirit*, edited by Burnett Hillman Streeter, 117–57. London: Macmillan, 1919.
Scroggs, Robin. "The Earliest Christian Communities as Sectarian Movement." In *Christianity, Judaism and Other Greco-Roman Cults*, Fs. Morton Smith, edited by Jacob Neusner, 1–23. SJLA 12. Leiden: Brill 1975.
Seccombe, David. "Luke and Isaiah." NTS 27 (1981) 252–59.
———. "Was There Organized Charity in Jerusalem before the Christians?" JTS 29 (1978) 140–43.
Sedgwick, W. B. "Covetousness and the Sensual Sins in the New Testament." ExpT 36 (1924/25) 478–79.
Seesemann, Heinrich. *Der Begriff KOINΩNIA im Neuen Testament*. Giessen: Töpelmann, 1933.
Seitz, Oscar J. F. "Gospel Prologues: A Common Pattern?" JBL 83 (1964) 262–68.
Selwyn, Edward Gordon. "St Luke 12:27, 28." Theology 16 (1928) 163–64.
Seng, Egbert W. "Der reiche Tor: Eine Untersuchung von Lk 12:16–21 unter besonderer Berücksichtigung form—und motivgeschichtlicher Aspekte." NovTest 20 (1978) 136–55.
Senior, D. "Religious Poverty and the Ministry of Jesus." ABenR 26 (1975) 169–79.
Sherlock, W. "The Visit of Christ to Nazareth. A Study in the Synoptic Gospels, Matt 13:54–58; Mark 6:1–6; Luke 4:16–30." JTS 11 (1909/10) 552–57.
Sherwin-White, A. N. *Roman Society and Roman Law in the New Testament*. Oxford: Clarendon, 1963.
Shurden, Robert Marshall. "The Christian Response to Poverty in the New Testament Era." PhD diss., Southern Baptist Theological Seminary, 1970.
Sidebottom, E. M. "The So-called Divine Passive in the Gospel Tradition." ExpT 87 (1975/76) 200–204.
Simpson, J. G. "The Parable of the Pounds." ExpT 37 (1925/26) 299–303.
Sloman, A. "'Blessed are the poor in spirit' Matt 5:3; cf. Luke 6:20." JTS 18 (1916/17) 34–35.
Smend, Rudolf. *Die Weisheit des Jesus Sirach*. Berlin: Georg Reimer, 1906.
Smith, Bertram Tom Dean. *The Parables of Synoptic Gospels*. Cambridge, UK: Cambridge University Press, 1937.
Sperber, Daniel. "Social Legislation in Jerusalem during the Latter Part of the Second Temple Period." JSJ 6 (1975) 86–95.
Spicq, Ceslaus. *Agape dans le Nouveau Testament*. 3 vols. Paris: Gabalda, 1958–66.
Spitta, Friedrich. "Jesu Weigerung, sich als 'gut' bezeichnen zu lassen." ZNW 9 (1908) 12–20.
Stagg, Frank. *The Purpose and Message of Acts*. RExp 44 (1947) 3–21.
Stamm, Johann Jakob. "Ein Vierteljahrhundert Psalmenforschung." ThRu 23 (1955) 1–68.
Standen, A. O. "The Parable of Dives and Lazarus and Enoch 22." ExpT 33 (1921/22) 523.
Stanton, Graham Norman. *Jesus of Nazareth in New Testament Preaching*. SNTS MS 27. Cambridge, UK: Cambridge University Press, 1974.
———. "On the Christology of Q." In *Christ and Spirit in the New Testament*, Fs. C. F. D. Moule, edited by Barnabas Lindars and Stephen S. Smalley, 27–42. Cambridge, UK: Cambridge University Press, 1973.

Stanton, Vincent Henry. *The Gospels as Historical Documents.* 3 vols. Cambridge, UK: Cambridge University Press, 1909-23.
Stauffer, Ethelbert. *Jerusalem und Rom im Zeitalter Jesu Christi.* Bern: Franke, 1957.
Steele, J. "The Unjust Steward." *ExpT* 39 (1927/28) 236-37.
Steiner, Anton. "Warum lebten die Essener asketisch?" *BZ* 15 (1971) 1-28.
Stenning, John Frederick. *The Targum of Isaiah.* Oxford: Clarendon, 1953.
Stewart, G. W. "The Place of Rewards in the Teaching of Christ." *Exp* VII.10 (1910) 97-111, 224-41.
Stock, E. "The Pounds and the Talents." *ExpT* 22 (1910/11) 424-25.
Stone, Michael E. *The Testament of Abraham.* Missoula, MT: SBL, 1972.
Stonehouse, Ned Bernard. *The Witness of Luke to Christ.* London: Tyndale, 1951.
Strecker, Georg. *Der Weg der Gerechtigkeit. Untersuchung zur Theologie des Matthäus.* FRLANT 82. Göttingen: Vandenhoeck and Ruprecht, 1962.
———. "Die Makarismen der Bergpredigt." *NTS* 17 (1970/71) 255-75.
Strobel, August. "Armenpfleger 'um des Friedens willen' (Zum Verständnis von Act 6:1-6)." *ZNW* 63 (1972) 271-76.
———. "Das apokalyptische Terminproblem in der sogen. Antrittspredigt Jesu (Lk 4:16-30)." *TLZ* 92 (1967) 251-54.
———. "Die Ausrufung des Jobeljahrs in der Nazarethpredigt Jesu." In *Jesus in Nazareth*, edited by Walther Eltester et al., 38-50. BZNW 40. Berlin: de Gruyter, 1972.
"Structures of Captivity and Lines of Liberation. Some Theological Reflections." *ER* 27 (1975) 44-47.
Stuhlmacher, Peter. *Das paulinische Evangelium. I: Vorgeschichte.* FRLANT 95. Göttingen: Vandenhoeck and Ruprecht, 1968.
Sukenik, Eleazar Lipa. *The Dead Sea Scrolls of the Hebrew University.* Jerusalem: Hebrew University Press, 1955.
Swete, Henry Barclay. "An Introduction to Acts." *RExp* 71 (1974) 437-49.
———. *Literary Patterns, Theological Themes, and the Genre of Luke-Acts.* SBL MS 20. Missoula, MT: SBL, 1974.
———. *The Parables of the Kingdom.* London: Macmillan, 1921.
Swete, Henry Barclay, ed. *The Psalms of Solomon with the Greek Fragments of the Book of Enoch.* Cambridge, UK: Cambridge University Press, 1899.
Talbert, Charles H. "An Introduction to Acts." *RExp* 71 (1974) 437-49.
———. "Literary Patterns, Theological Themes, and the Genre of Luke-Acts." SBL MS 20. Missoula, MT: SBL, 1974.
———. *Luke and the Gnostics.* Nashville: Abingdon, 1966.
Tannehill, Robert C. "The Magnificat as Poem." *JBL* 93 (1974) 263-75.
———. "The Mission of Jesus According to Luke 4:16-30." In *Jesus in Nazareth*, edited by Walther Eltester et al., 51-75. BZNW 40. Berlin: de Gruyter, 1972.
———. *The Sword of His Mouth.* Philadelphia: Fortress, 1975.
Tarelli, C. C. "A Note on Luke 12:15." *JTS* 41 (1940) 260-62.
Tatum, W. Barnes. "The Epoch of Israel: Luke 1-2 and the Theological Plan of Luke-Acts." *NTS* 13 (1966/67) 184-95.
Taylor, Vincent. *Behind the Third Gospel.* Oxford: Clarendon, 1926.
———. *The Gospel According to St. Mark.* London: Macmillan, 1952.
———. "The Origin of the Markan Passion-Sayings." In *New Testament Essays*, 60-71. London, 1970.

———. *The Passion Narrative of St Luke*. Edited by O. E. Evans. SNTS MS 19. Cambridge, UK: Cambridge University Press, 1972.
Teicher, Jacob L. "The Dead Sea Scrolls—Documents of the Jewish-Christian Sect of Ebionites." *JJS* 2 (1951) 67–99.
Temple, P. J. "The Rejection at Nazareth." *CBQ* 17 (1955) 229–42.
Theissen, Gerd. *The First Followers of Jesus*. Translated by John Bowden. London: SCM, 1978.
———. "Itinerant Radicalism: The Tradition of Jesus' Sayings from the Perspective of the Sociology of Literature." *Radical Religion* 2 (1975) 84–93.
Theriault, J. Y. "Les dimensions sociales, économiques et politiques dans l'oeuvre de Luc." *ScEs* 26 (1974) 205–31.
Thiering, Barbara. "The Biblical Source of Qumran Asceticism." *JBL* 93 (1974) 429–44.
———. "Suffering and Asceticism at Qumran, as Illustrated in the Hodayot." *RevQum* 8 (1972/75) 393–405.
Thiessen, H. C. "The Parable of the Nobleman and the Earthly Kingdom." *BS* 91 (1934) 180–90.
Thomas, D. W. "Some Observations on the Hebrew Root חדל." In *Volume du Congrès*. VetTestSuppl 4, 8–16. Leiden: Brill, 1957.
Thomas, K. J. "Liturgical Citations in the Synoptics." *NTS* 22 (1976) 205–14.
Thompson, George H. P. *The Gospel According to Luke*. Oxford: Clarendon, 1972.
Thompson, P. J. "The Infancy Gospels of St. Matthew and St. Luke Compared." *StudEv* I.217–22.
Thornton, L. S. *The Common Life in the Body of Christ*. London: Dacre, 1941.
Thurian, Max. *Mary: Mother of the Lord, Figure of the Church*. Translated by Neville B. Cryer. London: Mowbray, 1963.
Tillard, J. M. R. "Le fondement évangélique de la vie religieuse." *NRT* 91 (1969) 916–55.
Tischendorf, Constantin. *Novum Testamentum Graece*. Leipzig: Tauchnitz, 1869.
Tolbert, Malcolm O. "Contemporary Issues in the Book of Acts." *RExp* 71 (1974) 521–31.
Topel, L. John. *Children of a Compassionate God: A Theological Exegesis of Luke 6:20–49*. Collegeville, MN: Liturgical Press, 2001.
———. "On the Injustice of the Unjust Steward: Lk 16:1–13." *CBQ* 37 (1975) 216–27.
Torm, Frederik. "Die erste christliche Gemeinde in ihrem Verhältnis zum Judentum." *ZSTh* 13 (1936) 403–28.
Toy, Crawford Howell. *Quotations in the New Testament*. New York: Scribner's Sons, 1884.
Trench, Richard Chevenix. *Notes on the Parables of Our Lord*. London: Kegan Paul, 1870.
Tresmontant, Claude. *L'enseignement de Ieschoua de Nazareth*. Paris: Seuil, 1970.
Troadec, H. "La vocation de l'homme riche." *VS* 557 (1969) 138–48.
Trocmé, André. *Jesus and the Nonviolent Revolution*. Independence, MO: Herald, 1973.
Trocmé, Etienne. *Le "Livre des Actes" et l'histoire*. Paris: Presses Universitaires de France, 1957.
Troeltsch, Ernst. *The Social Teaching of the Christian Churches*. Translated by Olive Wyon. London: Allen and Unwin, 1931.
Truhlar, K. "The Beatitudes and the Kingdom." *Conc* 9 (1968) 18–23.
Tsuchiya, H. "The History and the Fiction in the Birth Stories of Jesus." *AJBI* 1 (1975) 73–90.

Turner, Nigel. "The Relation of Luke I and II to Hebraic Sources and to the Rest of Luke-Acts." *NTS* 2 (1955/56) 100–109.

Uhlhorn, Gerhard. *Christian Charity in the Ancient Church*. Edinburgh: T. & T. Clark, 1883.

———. "Das Christenthum und das Geld." In *Sammlungen von Vorträgen* 7 (1882) 119–57.

———. "Die Motivierung der Feindesliebe in Lukas 6:32–35." *NovTest* 8 (1966) 284–300.

———. "Jesus the Christ." *NTS* 8 (1961/62) 101–16.

———. "The Teaching of Good Works in 1 Peter." *NTS* 1 (1954/55) 92–110.

Van Cangh, J. M. "Fondement évangelique de la vie religieuse." *NRT* 95 (1973) 635–47.

Van der Woude, Adam S. "Melchisedek als himmlische Erlösergestalt in den neugefundenen eschatologischen Midraschim aus Qumran Höhle XI." *OTS* 14 (1965) 354–73.

Van der Ploeg, Johannes. "Les pauvres d'Israel et leur piété." *OTS* 7 (1950) 236–70.

Van Goudoever, Jan. *Biblical Calendars*. Leiden: Brill, 1959.

Van Leeuwen, Cornelis. *Le développement du sens social en Israel avant l'ère chrétienne*. Assen, Netherlands: Van Gorcum, 1955.

Van Segbroeck, Frans. "Jésus réjeté par sa patrie (Mt 13:54–58)." *Bib* 49 (1968) 167–98.

Van Unnik, W. C. "The 'Book of Acts': The Confirmation of the Gospel." *NovTest* 4 (1960) 26–59.

Vermes, Geza. *The Dead Sea Scrolls in English*. Harmondsworth, UK: Penguin, 1966.

———. *The Dead Sea Scrolls: Qumran in Perspective*. London: SCM, 1977.

Vielhauer, Philipp. "Das Benedictus des Zacharias." *ZThK* 49 (1952) 255–72.

———. *Geschichte der urchristlichen Literatur*. Berlin: Walter de Gruyter, 1975.

Vincent, Marvin R. *Epistles to the Philippians and to Philemon*. Edinburgh: T. & T. Clark, 1897.

Violet, Bruno. *Die Esra-Apokalypse (IV Esra)*. Leipzig: Hinrichs, 1910.

———. "Zum rechten Verständnis der Nazareth-Perikope Lc 4:16–30." *ZNW* 37 (1938) 251–71.

Vogels, W. "Le Magnificat, Marie et Israel." *EeT* 6 (1975) 279–96.

Vogt, E. "Peace among Men of God's Good Pleasure." In *The Scrolls and the New Testament*, edited by Krister Stendahl, 114–17. London: SCM, 1958.

Vogt, J. "Ecce Ancilla Domini: Eine Untersuchung zum sozialen Motiv des antiken Marienbildes." *VigChr* 23 (1969) 241–63.

Völter, D. *Die evangelische Erzählungen von der Geburt und Kindheit Jesu*. Strasburg: Heitz, 1911.

Von Campenhausen, Hans. "Early Christian Asceticism." In *Tradition and Life in the Church*, translated by A. V. Littledale, 90–122. London: Collins, 1968.

Von der Osten-Sacken, Peter. "Zur Christologie des lukanischen Reiseberichts." *EvTh* 33 (1973) 476–96.

Von Pöhlmann, Robert. *Geschichte der sozialen Frage und des Sozialismus in der antiken Welt*. Munich: Beck, 1925.

Von Schubert, Hans. *Der Kommunismus der Wiedertäufer in Münster und seine Quellen*. Phil.-Hist. Klasse. Heidelberg: Sitzungsberichte der Heidelberger Akademie der Wissenschaften, 1919.

Wagner, M. "Der Lohngedanke im Evangelium." *NKZ* 43 (1932) 106–12, 129–39.

Wagner, W. "In welchem Sinne hat Jesus das Prädikat ΑΓΑΘΟΣ von sich abgewiesen?" *ZNW* 8 (1907) 143–61.

Wainwright, A. W. "Luke and the Restoration of the Kingdom to Israel." *ExpT* 89 (1977/78) 76–79.

Walter, Nikolaus. "Zur Analyse von Mc 10:17–31." *ZNW* 53 (1962) 206–18.

Walvoord, John F. "Christ's Olivet Discourse on the End of the Age: The Parable of the Talents." *BS* 129 (1972) 206–10.

Wansbrough, Henry. "St Luke and Christian Ideals in an Affluent Society." *NBI* 49 (1968) 582–87.

Wansey, J. C. "The Parable of the Unjust Steward: An Interpretation." *ExpT* 47 (1935/36) 39–40.

Warfield, Benjamin B. "Jesus' Alleged Confession of Sin." *PTR* 12 (1914) 177–228.

———. "Messianic Psalms of the New Testament." *Exp* III.2 (1885) 301–09, 321–27.

Warnach, Viktor. *Agape: Die Liebe als Grundmotiv der neutestamentlichen Theologie.* Düsseldorf: Patmos, 1951.

Watson, Nigel M. "Was Zacchaeus Really Reforming?" *ExpT* 77 (1965/66) 282–85.

Weiss, Bernhard. *A Commentary on the New Testament.* New York: Funk and Wagnalls, 1906.

———. *Die Evangelien des Markus und Lukas.* KEK 1/2. Göttingen: Vandenhoeck and Ruprecht, 1901.

Weiss, Johannes. *Die Schriften des Neuen Testaments.* Göttingen: Vandenhoeck and Ruprecht, 1907.

———. "Zum reichen Jüngling Mk 10:13–27." *ZNW* 11 (1910) 79–83.

Wellhausen, Julius. *Das Evangelium Lucae.* Berlin: de Gruyter, 1904.

Wendt, Hans Hinrich. *The Teaching of Jesus.* Translated by John Wilson. 2 vols. Edinburgh: T. & T. Clark, 1909, 1911.

Wernberg-Møller, Preben. *The Manual of Discipline.* Leiden: Brill, 1957.

Westermann, Claus. *Isaiah 40–66.* Translated by David M. G. Stalker. London: SCM, 1969.

Whiteley, D. E. H. "Christ's Foreknowledge of His Crucifixion." *StudEv* I.100–114.

Whybray, Roger N. *Isaiah 40–66.* London: Oliphants, 1975.

Wieder, N. "Notes on the New Documents from the Fourth Cave of Qumran (The Term תלה חי)." *JJS* 7 (1956) 71–72.

———. "The Term קץ in the Dead Sea Scrolls." *JJS* 5 (1954) 22–31.

Wilcox, Max. "A Forward to the Study of the Speeches in Acts." In *Christianity, Judaism and Other Greco-Roman Cults,* Fs. Morton Smith, edited by Jacob Neusner, 206–25. SJLA 12. Leiden: Brill, 1975.

———. *The Semitisms of Acts.* Oxford: Clarendon, 1965.

Wilder, Amos N. *Eschatology and Ethics in the Teaching of Jesus.* New York: Harper, 1950.

———. "Social Factors in Early Christian Eschatology." In *Early Christian Origins,* Fs. Harold R. Willoughby, edited by Allen Paul Wikgren, 67–76. Chicago: Quadrangle, 1961.

Wilkens, W. "Die theologische Struktur der Komposition des Lukas-evangeliums." *TZ* 34 (1978) 1–13.

Willcock, J. "St Luke 19:8." *ExpT* 28 (1916/17) 236–37.

Williams, Francis E. "Is Almsgiving the Point of the 'Unjust Steward'?" *JBL* 83 (1964) 293–97.

Williams, J. "The Rich Young Ruler and St Paul." *ExpT* 41 (1929/30) 139–40.
Williams, R. R. "Church History in Acts: Is It Reliable?" In *Historicity and Chronology in the New Testament*, edited by Dennis E. Nineham, 145–60. TheolColl 6. London: SPCK, 1965.
Wilson, R. McL. "Some Recent Studies in the Lucan Infancy Narratives." *StudEv* I.235–53.
Wilson, S. G. "Lukan Eschatology." *NTS* 16 (1969/70) 330–47.
Winter, Paul. "Magnificat and Benedictus—Maccabaean Psalms?" *BJRL* 37 (1954) 328–47.
———. *On the Trial of Jesus*. SJ 1. Berlin: de Gruyter, 1974.
———. "The Proto-Source of Luke I." *NovTest* 1 (1956) 184–99.
———. "Some Observations on the Language in the Birth and Infancy Stories of the Third Gospel." *NTS* 1 (1954/55) 111–21.
Winterbotham, R. "Christ or Archelaus?" *Exp* VIII.4 (1912) 338–47.
Wood, I. F. "Τῆς δούλης in the Magnificat, Luke 1:48." *JBL* 21 (1902) 48–50.
———. "Two Biblical Attitudes toward Riches; James 5:1–6; Matt 19:23–26." *BW* 33 (1909) 408–13.
Wood, W. S. "Fellowship." *Exp* VIII.21 (1921) 31–40.
Wrege, Hans-Theo. *Die Überlieferungsgeschichte der Bergpredigt*. WUNT 9. Tübingen: Mohr, 1968.
———. "Jesusgeschichte und Jüngergeschick nach Joh 12:20–33 und Hebr 5:7–10." In *Der Ruf Jesus und die Antwort der Gemeinde*, Fs. Joachim Jeremais, edited by Eduard Lohse, 259–88. Göttingen: Vandenhoek and Ruprecht, 1970.
Wright, Christopher J. H. "Family, Land and Property in Ancient Israel." PhD diss., Cambridge University, 1976.
Yadin, Yigael. "Pesher Nahum (4QpNahum) Reconsidered." *IEJ* 21 (1971) 1–12.
Yoder, John Howard. *The Politics of Jesus*. Grand Rapids, MI: Eerdmans, 1975.
Young, Franklin W. "A Study of the Relation of Isaiah to the Fourth Gospel." *ZNW* 46 (1955) 215–33.
Zahn, Theodor. *Das Evangelium des Lucas*. KNT 3. Leipzig: A. Deichert, 1913.
———. *Introduction to the New Testament*. Translated by John Moore Trout et al. Edinburgh: T. & T. Clark, 1909.
Zeitlin, Solomon. "The Am Haarez." *JQR* 23 (1932/33) 45–61.
———. "The Tefillah, the Shemoneh Esreh: An Historical Study of the First Canonization of the Hebrew Liturgy." *JQR* 54 (1964) 208–49.
Zerwick, M. "Die Parable vom Thronanwärter." *Bib* 40 (1959) 654–74.
Ziesler, John A. *Christian Asceticism*. London: SPCK, 1973.
Zimmerli, Walther. "Die Frage des Reichen nach dem ewigen Leben." *EvTh* 19 (1959) 90–97.
Zimmerli, Walther, and Joachim Jeremias. *The Servant of God*. London: SCM, 1957.
Zimmermann, H. "Evangelium des Lukas Kap. 1 und 2: Ein Versuch der Vermittlung zwischen Hilgenfeld und Harnack." *ThStKr* 76 (1903) 247–90.

Index of Modern Authors

Agouridès, S., 29n37
Aland, Kurt, 5n2
Anderson, Hugh, 73n287
Armitage, David J., 236n3, 247n40, 258–62
Aytoun, R. A., 76n309

Bacon, B. W., 125
Bailey, Kenneth E., 166n119, 166n121
Baird, J. Arthur, 105n11
Bajard, J., 73n285
Bammel, Ernst, 26n16, 43, 54n181, 67, 70n266, 117n92
Bardenhewer, O., 77n313
Barns, T., 77n313
Barrett, C. K., 82n337
Bartsch, Hans-Werner, 34n72, 90n371, 91–92, 96, 183n224, 184n229
Batey, Richard, 29n34
Baudissan, Wolf Wilhelm, 25n10, 28n25, 39n98
Baumgarten, J. M., 210n59
Behm, J., 13n3
Bengel, John, 50
Benko, Stephen, 78n313
Benoit, Pierre, 213n78
Bernard, J. H., 78n313
Best, Ernest, 33n64
Betz, Hans Dieter, 104n7
Betz, Otto, 66n249
Bienert, Walther, 155n70, 158n81
Bigo, P., 165n114, 174n173, 177n193
Billerbeck, Paul, 29, 49, 50n159, 123n126, 126, 129n160, n161, 168n135, 178n246, 178n195, 186n241, 187n246, 194n286, 197n303
Birkeland, Harris, 25n8, n11, 26n16, 28n25
Black, Matthew, 96n406, 122
Blake, B., 129n160
Blevins, William L., 220n114
Blinzler, Josef, 118n96
Bloch, E., 211n59
Boehmer, Julius, 41n112
Bolkestein, Hendrik, 27n18, 178n196, 205n24, 206n25, 209n54
Bornhäuser, Karl, 179n197, 182
Bornkamm, Günther, 108n32, 131n172, 132n178, 140n226, 167n127
Braun, Herbert, 31n51, 103n1, 169, 182n221
Brightman, F. E., 77n313, 197n305
Brown, John Pairman, 95n406
Brown, Paul B., 217n101
Brown, Raymond E., 25n5, 31, 79n317, n318
Bruce, Alexander, B., 179n197, 190n205, 184n229, 195n298
Bruce, F. F., 157, 219n112, 221n123
Buchanan, George Wesley, 32n59
Büchler, Adolf, 30, 30n38, 30n43, 31, 49n154, 50
Brun, Lyder, 73n288, 99n416
Bultmann, Rudolf, 4, 25n5, 64n241, 96n406, 103n2, 104n7, 105, 115, 116n85, 152, 181
Burkitt, Francis Crawford, 12, 77n313

INDEX OF MODERN AUTHORS

Cadbury, Henry, 14n8, 65n243, 175n178, 181n210, 194, 224n136
Cadoux, Arthur Temple, 179n198
Caird, George B., 34, 49, 66n246, 90n372, 91n374, 110n51, 114n76, 146n16, 150n43, 157n79, 194n285
Calvin, John, 125n136
Campbell, Colin, 13
Campbell, J. Y., 206
Campenhausen, H., 103n1, 134n188
Cave, C. H., 49n157, 51, 57n202, 190n208
Cerfaux, Lucien, 202n3
Chadwick, Henry, 202n3
Charles, R. H., 28n30, 170–71, 171n149, 173n165, 198n312
Cheong, C.-S. Abraham, 249–50
Clarke, A. K., 151n49
Classen, Carl Joachim, 8
Cobb, S. H., 210n59
Collie, N. E. W., 151n49
Combrink, H. J. B., 64n241
Cone, James Hal, 31n51
Conzelmann, Hans, 1, 71n276, 114n76, 143, 155n68, 210n58, 216n91, 226
Cox, S., 156n72
Cranfield, C. E. B., 125, 129n160, 175n178
Creed, John Martin, 54n179, 76n311, 78n316, 94n392, 110n51, 122n121, 137n210, 155n70, 174n171, 196n301
Crockett, Larrimore C., 36n85, 39, 40n104, 50n164, 53n176, 71n278
Cronbach, A., 161n94

Dahl, Nils Alstrup, 28n25, 40n109, 219n108, n109
Daube, David, 96–97, 221n123
Davies, J. G., 78n313
Davies, J. H., 113n64, 114n72
Degenhardt, Hans Joachim, 14–16, 21, 33n61, 33n64, 34n73, 93n389, 103n3, 106–10, 119n105, 120–21, 127n150, 128n158, 132n177, 133n182, 137n210, 153–54, 160n87, 165n117, 172n161, 183n224, 190n264, 202n3, 220n113
De la Potterie, Ignace, 53n176
Denney, James, 112–15
Derrett, J. Duncan M., 30n44, 114n77, 119n103, n104, 150n42, 166n121, 190n208, 184n230, 215n85, 225
Descamps, A., 164n112, 176n186
De Wette, Wilhem Martin Leberecht, 122n122, 178n196
Dibelius, Martin, 24–25, 28n30, 30n44, 101n418, 134n188, 215n81, 217n95
Dodd, Charles Harold, 74n296, 110n49, 122n117, 164, 167, 210n59, 224
Drury, John, 46n139, 71n276
Dunn, James D. G., 222n127, 239n12
Dupont, Jacques, 16, 27n21, 32n55, 33n64, 35–36, 65n242, 74n293, 75n302, 90n369, n373, 93n389, 94n396, n397, 95, 96, 97n408, 99n414, 103n2, 105, 120n111, 121–22, 126n146, 148, 149n39, 152, 169n142, 172n162, 184n232, n233, 186n240, 105, 205n19, 206n25, 211
Dupont-Sommer, André, 55–56, 57n204, 62, 170, 202n3, 210n59, 212n73
Durand, A., 77n313
Dutton, E.G., 166n119

Easton, Burton Scott, 34, 90n370, 95n406, 110n52, 127n151, 210n59
Elliot-Binns, Leonard, 114n76
Ellis, E. Earle, 33n60, 92n385, 127n153, 137n210, 148n36, 177n144
Ellul, Jacques, 197
Eltester, Walther, 220n114
Emmet, C. W., 78n313
Ernst, Josef, 130n167, 146n22, 172n162, 176
Esler, Philip Francis, 238–40

Evans, Christopher F., 137n212, 179n199, 181
Everson, A. J., 40n108

Farrell, Hobert Kenneth, 182n220
Fascher, Erich, 108, 133n185
Feine, Paul, 13
Feuillet, A., 165n118, 176n188
Fiebig, Paul, 174n171
Field, Frederick, 42n118, 133n185
Finch, R. G., 50
Finkel, Asher, 50n164, 73n285, 122n121
Firth, C. B., 166n121
Fitzmeyer, Joseph, 254
Flender, Helmut, 71n276, n277, 92n387, 119n106, 131n174, 143, 196n299
Flew, R. Newton, 220n116
Flood, E., 80n322
Flusser, David, 33n64
Foerster, Werner, 165n117
Ford, J. Massingbird, 87
France, Richard T., 62n229
Frankemölle, H., 29n34
Franklin, Eric, 66n246, 75n301, 99n416, 124n133, 143
Friedel, L. M., 173n163
Friedrich, G., 69
Frisch, Ephraim, 28n28
Furnish, Victor Paul, 178n247, 187n247

Gächter, Paul, 166n120, 122
Galot, Jean, 103n3, 124n133, 133n187
Gasse, W., 113n64
Gaston, L., 75n301
Geldenhuys, Norval, 25n6, 125n136, 155n70
Gélin, Albert, 25n9, 27n23, 28n25, 79n318
George, A., 73n288
Giambrone, Anthony, 254–58
Gibbs, J. M., 88n366
Gibson, M. D., 166n120
Ginzberg, Louis, 171n150
Glöckner, Richard, 66n246, 71n276, 72n276, 72n281, 73n288,
75n301, 81n330, 138n214, 220n113
Glombitza, Otto, 183
Godet, Frédéric, 34n68, 91, 92n384, 93n389, 138n218, 145n15, 152n56, 160n87, 173n169, 195n297
Goguel, Maurice, 13
Goodspeed, Edgar J., 133n185
Gould, Ezra, P., 127
Goulder, Michael, D., 75n288, 131n174, 165n114
Greehy, John G., 210n59
Green, Michael, 249n47
Grensted, L. W., 186n242
Gressmann, Hugo, 179
Griffith, Francis I., 179n201, 181n215
Grobel, K., 181n210, n211
Grundmann, Walter, 71n276, 90n370, 110n51, 121n126, 123n130, 131n169, 149n39, 188
Gryglewicz, Feliks, 76n309
Guilding, Aileen, 51
Guelich, Robert A., 99n416
Gunkel, Hermann, 76, 81n335
Guttmann, Alexander, 30

Haenchen, Ernst, 49n152, 71n278, 124n133, 135–36, 202–203, 210n59, 211n60, 215n79, 217n98, n100
Hampden-Cook, E., 166n120
Harnack, Adolf von, 25n6, 75, 81
Harrison, Everett Falconer, 215n84
Haskin, Richard Webb, 123n131
Hatch, Edwin, 31
Hauck, Friedrich, 13, 19n23, 169n141, 176n186, 185n234
Haupt, Paul, 186n241
Hays, Christopher M., 250–54
Hebert, A. Gabriel, 79n317
Hengel, Martin, 85n360, 108–109, 112, 115n80, 116n84, 117n92, 203n7, 204n10, 211n59, 211n60
Hicks, E. L., 210n59, 212n73
Hiers, Richard H., 165n114, 174n173
Hill, David, 53n176, 71n278, 73n287
Hillman, J., 75n297

INDEX OF MODERN AUTHORS

Hirsch, Emmanuel, 124n135, 151
Holm-Nielsen, Svend, 55–56
Holtz, Traugott, 41n113
Holtzmann, Heinrich, 210–11n59, 212n72, 222n127
Holzmeister, U., 59n210
Hort, Fenton John Anthony, 206n26, 210n59
Horton, Fred L., 56n194
Hoyt, Thomas Jr, 140n227
Hvidberg, Fleming Vriis, 171n149

Isaacs, M. E., 25n5, 79n317, n318

Jacobé, F., 77n313
Jalland, T. G., 172n159
James, Montague Rhodes, 59n213
Jeremias, Joachim, 29n34, 30, 53n175, 73n287, 90n369, 119n103, 140n226, 147n24, 149, 164–65, 167, 170n144, 174n169, 180n207, 181, 196n301
Jervell, Jacob, 91n375, 99n415, 130n166, 185n238, 189n257, 190n265
Johnson, Luke Timothy, 18–19, 20n30, 20n31, 126n146, 184n228, 215n80, 222n124
Jones, D. C., 36n85,
Jones, Douglas, 79n317, 85n355
Jonge, M., 65n194
Joüen, P., 144n12, 149n39
Judge, Edwin A., 194n289, 205, 221n122
Jülicher, Adolf, 119n105, 147n24, n25, 149n39, 164–65, 172n159, 177n194

Kamlah, E., 166n119, 168n129, 195n292, 197n303
Kandler, H. J., 33, 43
Karris, Robert J., 14n8
Käsemann, Ernst, 216n94
Keck, Leander E., 213n77
Keim, Theodor, 13
Kilgallen, John, 221n123
Kilpatrick, George D., 193n283
Kim, Kyoung-Jin, 243–44

Kittel, Gerhard, 25n6, 110n51
Kittel, Rudolf, 38n96
Klostermann, Erich, 48, 151n47
Knox, Wilfred Lawrence, 90n373, 104n8, 122, 123n130, 210n59
Koch, Robert, 31n52, 34n72
Koontz, J. V. G., 80n322
Kosmala, Hans, 170, 172n158
Krafft, E., 78n314
Krämer, Michael, 161n92, 165n114, 167n124, 169n142, 170n144, 174n171, 175n179, 176n186
Kümmel, Werner Georg, 211n59, 218n104
Kuschke, A., 25n8, 26n13, n16

Lagrange, M. -J., 110n51, 119n106, 120, 132n180, 133n184, 146n16, 199n313
Lampe, G. W. H., 49, 218n106, 219n110
Laurentin, René, 76–78, 79n317
Lauterbach, Jacob Z., 26n12
Leaney, A. R. C., 35, 41n112, 49, 78n314, 98n411, 110n52, 113n70, 122n122, 167n124, 190n262
Lebreton, J., 137
LeDéaut, R., 80
Lefort, L. Th., 181n210
Légasse, Simon, 33n64, 43n126, 59n214, 124n133, 132n178, 133n187, 134–35, 223
Legrand, L., 136n207
Leipoldt, Johannes, 185n234
Leivestad, R., 26n14
Lemoine, F. M., 57n203
Lessing, G. E., 3
Levi, I., 181n213
Lietzmann, Hans, 212n73
Lightfoot, John, 190n208
Lightfoot, Joseph Barber, 126n140,
Lightfoot, Robert Henry, 73n286, 118
Linnemann, Eta, 4
Linton, O., 104n7
Lohfink, Gerhard, 107n25, n27, 109n42, 110, 216n92, 217n95, 219n106

Lohmeyer, Ernst, 117n88, 124n133, 126n145, 128–29, 133n186
Lohse, Eduard, 113n70, 170
Loisy, Alfred, 46n139, 90n369, 151n47
Lorenzen, T., 180n205
Luce, Harry Kenneth, 152n54
Lunt, R. G., 166n119

Maas, F., 165n119
Machen, J. Gresham, 75–76
McCormick, B. E., 138, 193n283, 219n108
McFayden, J. F., 173n169
McHugh, John, 41n112, 75n301, 79n317
Maillot, A., 65n242
Mann, Jacob, 50–51
Manson, T. W., 28n30, 90n370, 96n406, 104n6, 152n54
Manson, W., 25n6, 65n243, 110n52, 122n120, 128, 133n182
Marmorstein, A., 161n97
Marshall, I. Howard, 71n276, 80n321, 89n367, 113n64, 138n214, 139n223, 148n36, 177n190, 211n59
Martin-Achard, Robert, 27n24
Mealand, David L., 154–55, 202n3, 203–204
Menoud, Philippe, H., 174n171, 210n59, 215n85, 218n105
Metzger, Bruce M., 149n39, 176n183
Meyer, H. A. W., 173, 174n169
Michaelis, C., 97n408, 149n39, 173n169
Miller, M. P., 51n170
Minear, Paul S., 75n301, 92n385, n386, 94n393, 97n407, 99n416, 105n11, 107n25, 109n41, 128n158, 153n59, 155n68, 156n74, 161n90, 218n104
Moffatt, James, 178n247, 18n247
Molitor, J., 156n72
Moltmann, Jürgen, 189n258
Mommsen, Theodor, 115n82
Moore, F. J., 174n173
Moore, George Foot, 30n38, 31

Morris, Leon, 25n6, 50n164, 127n153
Mosely, A. W., 105n11
Mott, Stephen Charles, 225n147
Moule, C. F. D., 15n11, 81n335, 151n48
Munch, P. A., 25n8, 25n10, 27n19
Mussner, F., 80n322

Navone, John, 41n112, 79n318, 106n18, 140n227, 148n36
Neil, William, 221n123
Noack, Bent, 71n275, 131n169
Nolan, Albert, 31, 136n202, 161n93
Nolland, John, 73n289, 219n108

Oesterley, William Oscar Emil, 144n10, 173n169, 179n197, 184, 195n297
Oliver, H. H., 75n301
Olsthorn, M. F., 154n63
O'Neill, James C., 47n142
Oppenheimer, Aharon, 29n35, 30n38, 30n40, 30n43
Otomo, Yoko Takahashi, 108n36, 109n45

Pauly, August Friedrich von, 116n84
Pautrel, R., 173n169
Pax, E., 182n220
Percy, Ernst, 14, 25n11, 28n26, 34n72, 35n78, 42n121, 91, 104n7, 124n133, 133n187, 159n85, 183n221, n226
Perrot, Charles, 50–51, 53
Pervo, Richard, 7
Pesch, Wilhelm, 151n47, 157, 158n82
Pfleiderer, Otto, 13
Phillips, J. B., 120n112
Phillips, Thomas E., 245–49
Pilgrim, Walter, 235–38
Plümacher, Eckhard, 203n7
Plummer, Alfred, 13, 34, 48n147, 82n335, 110n52, 114n76, 122n120, 125n136, 126n140, 132n178, 144, 146n16, 146n19, 152n56, 177n190, 184n230, 197n305
Powers, B. Ward, 185n237

Prat, Ferdinand, 57n202
Preuschen, Erwin, 202n3

Rabinowitz, Louis, I., 180n208
Rackham, Richard Belward, 216n90
Rahlfs, Alfred, 25, 26n12
Reicke, Bo, 65n242, 91, 113n66, 211n59, 218–19
Reimarus, Hermann Samuel, 3
Rengstorf, Karl Heinrich, 78n315, 95n398, 107–108, 122n119, 123n130, 145n15, 147n23
Rezevskis, J., 13, 90n373
Rice, E.P., 71n276
Rienecker, Fritz, 29n36, 94n394, 125n136, 145n15, 160n87
Rimmer, N., 181n212, 183n224
Robinson, William Charles, 71n276, 113n64
Roth, S. John, 240–43
Ryle, Herbert Edward, 59n213
Ryrie, Charles Caldwell, 174n174

Sahlin, Harold, 78n314, 79n317, 81n330, 189n255
Sandegren, C. A., 154n62
Sanders, Ed Parish, 31n49, 124n135, 161n98
Sanders, James A., 61, 62n229, 72
Sattler, W., 24–25
Scheele, Paul-Werner, 80n322
Scheidweiler, Felix, 211n59, 215n85
Schlatter, Adolf, 115, 121n116, 145n15, 155n70
Schleiermacher, Friedrich, 169n136
Schmid, Josef, 78n313, n314, 80n322, 82n335
Schmiedel, P. W., 210n58
Schmithals, Walter, 17–18, 226n150
Schnackenburg, Rudolf, 78n315, 79n319, 80n322, 133n182, 162n99, 222n127
Schneemelcher, W. 125n137
Schneider, J., 113n66, n70, 175n177
Schniewind, Julius, 25n6, 127n152
Schoeps, Hans-Joachim, 13
Schoonheim, P. L., 80n322
Schottroff, Luise, 233–35

Schramm, Tim, 47, 124n135
Schubert, H., 202n3
Schubert, Karl, 33, 43
Schulz, Anselm, 103n3, 104n7, 105–106, 108, 110n51, 116n85
Schürer, Emil, 59n214
Schürmann, Heinz, 34n73, 35–36, 47, 59n215, 88–89, 90n369, 91n380, 92n384, 96n406, 110, 117n89, 149n39, 152n55
Schütz, Frieder, 18n18, 74n295, 112n59, 114n74, n76
Schwarz, Günther, 97n410
Schweitzer, Albert, 3, 4, 173
Schweizer, Eduard, 95n401, 98n412, 109n39
Scott, Charles Archibald Anderson, 206n27
Scroggs, Robin, 30n42
Seccombe, David Peter, 37, 212n68, 252n49–51
Seesemann, Heinrich, 206, 210n57
Selwyn, E. G., 152
Seitz, Oscar J. F., 88366
Sherwin-White, A. N., 118n94, 166n121
Sidebottom, E. M., 148
Smith, B. T. D., 179n197, 184n231, 186, 196n302, 197
Spicq, Ceslaus, 178n247, 187n247
Spitta, Friedrich, 129n162
Standen, A. O., 186n242
Stanton, Graham Norman, 47n146, 65n245, 73n291, 103n3, 181n209
Steele, J., 166n120, 173n169
Stegemann, Wolfgang, 233–35
Steiner, Anton, 34n65, 45n137
Stonehouse, Ned B., 36n85, 37n87, 113n64
Strack, H. L., 29
Strecker, Georg, 96n404
Strobel, August, 57–58
Stuhlmacher, Peter, 67n256, 70n267
Sukenik, Eleazar Lipa, 56n193
Swete, Henry Barclay, 195n296

Talbert, Charles H., 131n174

INDEX OF MODERN AUTHORS

Tannehill, Robert C., 46n139, 48–49, 53, 79n318, 155n70, 158n81
Tarelli, C. C., 145
Tatum, W. Barnes, 75n301
Taylor, Vincent, 124n135
Taylor, William, 9–10
Theissen, Gerd, 32n59, 107n22, 114n77
Theriault, J. Y., 223n130
Thiering, Barbara, 33n62, 43n129
Thompson, George H. P., 66n246, 71n274, 177n189
Thurian, Max, 79n317
Tillard, J. M. R., 133n187, 222n127
Topel, L. John, 166n119, 244–45
Toy, Crawford Howell, 65n242
Trench, R. C., 148
Troadec, H., 124n134, 133n187
Trocmé, André, 57–59
Turner, Nigel, 82n335

Uhlhorn, Gerhard, 196n300, 210n59

Van Cangh, J. M., 132n178, 133n187
Van der Ploeg, Johannes, 25n10
Van der Woude, Adam, S., 56n194
Van Goudoever, Jan, 51n172, 58n205, 59n210
Van Leeuwen, Cornelis, 27n19, 28n29, 37n88, 38, 40n111
Van Unnik, 71n274, 73n291, 218, 219n108
Vermes, Geza, 56n195, 171n150
Vielhauer, Philipp, 99n417
Vincent, Marvin R., 125n139
Violet, Bruno, 72n279, 73n287, 80n328

Vogels, W., 79n317, 80, 82n335

Wagner, W., 128n157, 129n162
Wainwright, A. W., 65n243
Warfield, B. B., 82n337, 128n157
Warnach, Viktor, 178n247, 187n247
Watson, Nigel M., 138n218
Weiss, Johannes, 31n52, 114, 124n135, 152n55, 165n113, 167n128
Wellhausen, Julius, 92n384, 123n130, 164, 190n265
Whybray, Roger N., 111n54
Wilcox, Max, 219n112, 220n116
Willcock, J., 138n218
Wilder, Amos N., 113n70
Wilkens, W. 77n310
Williams, Francis E., 166n119, 174n171
Wilson, S. G., 175n178
Winter, Paul, 76n309, 85n354, 118n94
Winterbotham, R., 197
Wood, I. F., 76n309
Wood, W. S., 206n27
Wrege, Hans Theo, 31n51, 94n397
Wright, Christopher J. H., 38n91

Yoder, John Howard, 57–59

Zahn, Theodor, 14n8, 77n313, 92n385, 109n42, 110n52, 125n136, 139n222, 151n45, 155n70, 186n241
Zeitlin, Solomon, 30n38, 59n214
Zerwick, M., 198n311
Zimmerli, Walther, 127n150, 131n172
Zimmermann, H., 75n299

Index of Scriptural and Other References

OLD TESTAMENT

Genesis

1:2	64
13:6	120n109
25:5	120n109
29:31, 33	110n53
29:31	45n138 29:31
35:9–10	51
39:4–6	120n109
45:18	120n109
49:13	64n237

Exodus

2:23–25	82
6:6	83n339
15:6	62n225
15:16	83n339
15:21	84n348
17:2	217n96
34:6	191n271

Leviticus

5:21 [6:2]	210n55
16	51n172
16:31	51n172
19:18	255–56
23:23–32	51n172
23:27	51
23:29, 32	51n172
25:13	51n170, 58

Numbers

10:35	84n349
11:1	84n348
11:12	186n241
12:3	26n16
16:46	62n226
17:11–15	62n226
24:17	62n225

Deuteronomy

3:24	83n339
4:34	83n339
5:15	83n339
6:16	217n96
6:21	83n339
7:8, 19	83n339
9:26, 29	83n339
11:2	83n339
15	28n29
15:2	58
15:4	212n70, 225n148
15:7	50
15:11	226n148
21:15–17	110n53
22:13, 16	111n55

(Deuteronomy continued)

24:3	111n55
26:7	80n323
28:33	80n323, 62n226
29:2	83n339
32:34	150n42

Joshua

7:1	217

Judges

14:16	111n55
15:2	111n55

1 Samuel (1 Kingdoms)

1:11	80
2:5, 7	87
12:4	66n247
12:23	129n163
25:25, 38–39	148n31

2 Samuel (2 Kingdoms)

4:10	68n259
13:13	147n29
13:15	111n55
18:20, 26	68n259

1 Kings (3 Kingdoms)

8:36	129n163
18:12	217n97
22:17	154n65

2 Kings (4 Kingdoms)

2:11, 16	217n97
14:26	80n323
17:36	83n339

2 Chronicles

6:24	62n226
6:27	129n163

Nehemiah

9:9	80n323
9:20	129n162

Esther

5:11	87

Job

2:3–4	120n109
5:3–5	147n29
11:16–17	64n237
17:7	64n237
24:4	26n13
27:8–23	147n28
30:8	147n29
31:16–23	189n255
40:7(12)	83n344

Psalms

9	28, 242n28
9:14	80n327
9:29(10:8)	86n360
12:5	27
13(14):7	60n217
14:1,	148n30
17(18)	84
Ps 17(18):27	84n351
19(20):2	81n331
22:24	27n22
24(25):18	80n327
25:8	129n162
25:16	27n21
33	27n22
33(34):11	86n360
34:6	27n20
35:10	27n22
37:10–11	45
37:11	26n18, 44
39:6	147n26
43(44):3	83n340
53:1,	148n30
61:4	174n169
62(63):8	81n331
67(68):1	84n349
68	242n28
68:10	28
68(69):29	81n331
69:14	55
69:29	27n22
69:32–36,	60n217

INDEX OF SCRIPTURAL AND OTHER REFERENCES 307

69:33–34	55n187
69:35	55n187
70:5	27n22
71 (72)	242n28
72	27n19, 28n25
73 (74)	242n28
74	236n2
74:19	28n27
74:21	28n27
74:22	148n30
76	242n28
76:9	28n27
76(77):15	83n340
77(78):52, 70–72	154n65
78:18, 41, 56,	217n96
79:11	60n216
82:1–2	51n170
84(85):1	60n217
86:1	27n20
88(89):10, 1	83n340
88:16	27n21
88(89):43	81n331
95:8–9	217n96
102	242n28
102:17	28n27
102:18–22	60n216, n217
107:4–9	85n357
107:10, 14, 20	65n245
109:16	27n22
109:22	27n22
113:7	27n18
117(118):13	81n331
118:15	173n169
119:68	129n162
125(126)	94n396
125(126):1	60n217
132	242n28
132:15	28n27
135(136):12	83n340
135(136):23	80n327
136(137):1	94n396
140:12	27n22
143:10	129n162
147	242n28
147:6	28n27
149:4	28n27

Proverbs

3:34	26n12, n16, 83n344
8:36	111n57
9:13–18, 14–16	147n29
10:2	256
13:24	111
14:21	26n14
15:32	111n57
16:19	26n14
19:18	111n57
29:24	111n57
19:29	147n29
30:23	110n53

Ecclesiastes

2:14–17, 24	147n27

Isaiah

1:17	38n93
1:18	49n153
1:27	60n217
2:10	62n225
2:12	83n344
3:14–15	37n89
3:15	38
4:5–6	174n169
5:1–8	37n89
5:7	189n254
6:15	110n53
7:12	217n96
8:14	223n129
8:22–9:2	64n237
8:23–24	93
9:1–2	63n235
9:17	38n92
10:1–2	37n89
11:1–5	38n94
11:4,	26
14:4–20	83n345
14:12	66
14:13	84n350
14:29–32	38n95
14:32	84n352
18:7	39n97
25:1–5	39n97
26:6	26n13, 84n352
28:12	85n358

(Isaiah continued)

28:21	177n193
29:17–21	38n95
29:19	26
29:20	83n344
30:19	94n396
32:1–8	38n94
32:5–8	147n29
32:6	85n358
32:7	26n15
33:20	173
33:24	49n153
35:10	94n396
40–66	35, 81
40–55	38, 60
40	83
40:2	80n323
40:9–11	68
40:10	83n341, n342
40:11	154n65
41:8–20	39
41:8–9, 13–14	81n334
41:8–9	81n332
41:8	61
41:13–14	81n332
41:27	68
42:1	81n332, n334
42:7	62
42:22	38n96
43:1–21	51
49:8	55–56
49:9–10	85n357
49:10	86
49:13	38, 84n352
49:24–25	66–67
49:26	81n332
50:6	98n411
50:7	114n72
51:5, 9	83n342
51:17–20,	81n332
51:22	81n334
52:7	51n170, 58, 68–69
52:9–10	83n341
52:20	60n216
53:1	83n342
53:11	64n237
53:12	67
54:6	11n55
54:11	84n352
55:1–3	85n358
55:1	39n102
55:7	49n153
57:15–58:14	50
57:15	50n162
58	51, 188
58:4–7	40n105
58:5	51n171,
58:6	52, 48–55, 62, 178, 188
58:7	54, 182, 186–87, 189n255, n259
58:8–9	189n259
58:10	63
58:12	52n174
59:1	54n183
59:9–10	63
59:16–20,	81n332
59:16	81n334, 83n341
60:1–3, 14–21	40n110
60:1–3, 19–20	63n235
60:4	40n107
60:6	68
60:10	55
60:19–20	62n232
61	94
61:1–2	24, 36, 46, 48–55, 178, 188
61:1	26, 35–36, 40, 40n111, 44
61:2–62:2	51
61:2–3, 7	94n396
61:3	40
61:4	52n174
61:8	40n109
62:1–12	40n110
62:1	63n235
62:4	40n108
62:8–9	85
62:8	40n106
63:5, 12	83n341
63:5	81n332, n334
63:11–12	81n338
63:12	63n342
63:19	63
65:13–14	40n109
66:10	94n396

Jeremiah

5:1–5	38n92

INDEX OF SCRIPTURAL AND OTHER REFERENCES

6:16	129n163
13:17, 20	154n65
17:11	148n29
23:1–6	154n65
31(38):10–13	94n396
38(31):10	154n65
39(32):21	83n339

Lamentations

3:1–2, 5–7	64n237
3:45	44n130

Ezekiel

18:7	189n255
20:33–34	83n341
34:12, 31	154n65

Daniel

9:15	83n339
9:24–27	57–58

Hosea

5:11	62n227

Amos

2:7	26
4:1	66n247
8:4	26n15

Micah

2:12	154n65
4:8	154n65
5:3(4)	154n65
6:8	129n163

Habbakuk

2:17	44

Zephaniah

1:18	172n161
2:3	26
3:12	26n13

Zechariah

7:1–7	51n172
8:18–19	51n172
9:9	26n13
9:11–12	60n217
10:3	154n65
11:7, 11	41
11:11	45, 157, 157
13:7	

Malachi

1:2–3	111n58

New Testament

Matthew

4:7	217n96
4:13	47
4:15–16	93n391
4:19	131n171
4:25	93n391
5–6	86n359
5:3	33n64
5:6	86n359
5:11–12	96
5:13	105, 121
5:48	191n271
6:2–4	190n260
6:19–21	152n55, 158n82
6:20	161n93
6:24	168
6:26	157n79
6:34	146n76
7:23	170n143
8:11	186n241
8:21–22	109
10	151n46
10:37–39	104
12:35	159n86
13:44	161n93
13:52	159n86
16:6	144
16:21–28	116n87
22:1–14	180n204
23:25–6	190
23:27–28	190n261
24:25	151n46
25:19	198n312

309

310   INDEX OF SCRIPTURAL AND OTHER REFERENCES

(Matthew continued)

25:31–46	186n243
26:31	42n119
27:9–10	42n119

Mark

1:14–15	57
1:14	117n91
1:15	59n212
1:17–20	108n37
1:17	131n171
2:14	108n37
2:15	106n14, 108
2:17	126n145
3:6	117n91
3:7–8	94n392
3:8	93n391
3:9–10	94n395
4:10	106n14
4:17	18n20
4:19	155n67
4:26–29	137n212 4
6:14–29	117n91
6:17–29	18n20, 137n212
6:34	154n65
6:46	120n111
7:20–23	190
7:22	83n344
8:15	144
8:31–38	116n87
8:34	116n86, 117n88
9:11–13,	137n212
9:41–10:52	137n212
9:49–50	122
9:59–62	133
10:17, 21, 24, 30	124n135
10:21	126
10:22	135n197, 138n216
10:23–24	135n199
10:23	130n168
10:28	132n181, 133
10:29–30	135n194
10:30	18n20
10:35–45	114n76
10:46	139
11:12–14	137n212
11:20–21	137n212
12:28–34	137n212

14:1–2	118n96
14:7	32n57, 226n148
14:10–11	118n95

Luke

1–2	88
1:6	127n148
1:12, 65	217n100
1:17	112n62
1:36	77n311
1:46–55	**74–89**
1:50	87
1:51–53, 1:54–5	97n407
1:68–75	87n363
2:7, 12, 16	98n413
2:9,	217n100
2:10	71n273, 194n286
2:11	79n320
2:12, 16, 20	77n312
2:14	194n286
2:25	127n148
2:34–35	99n415
3:1	57n201, 188
3:8, 12–14	189n252
3:10–14	54n181
3:10–11	189n252
3:11–14	54n179
3:11	189n259
3:12–14	188
3:12	192n278
3:22	65
4:14–15	46
4:14	94n395
4:16–30	**46–74**, 98, 261n91
4:16	59n211
4:18–19	24, **46–66**, 178, 188
4:18	23n1, 217n97
4:19, 24	53
4:20	99
4:22, 23–29	47
4:22	72n284
4:23	47, 73
4:24	47, 93n387
4:43–44	70
4:43	70n268
4:44	94n392
5:1–11, 27–28	108n37
5:2–11	192n277

INDEX OF SCRIPTURAL AND OTHER REFERENCES

5:11, 28	137n210	8:3	192n277
5:26	217n100	8:8	92n387
5:27–32	192n278	8:13	18n20
5:30	108	8:14	155n67
5:33–34	95n399	8:15	18n21, 129n159, 189n254
6:1–5	95n399	8:22	108n34
6:9	146n18	8:37	217n100
6:13–14	109n38	8:41–48	192n277
6:17–49	90–100	8:41	126n147
6:17–19	93	9–19	8
6:17	93, 108n35	9:3	95n399
6:20–36	191n270	9:6	70
6:20–21	54n184, 188	9:14, 18	108n34
6:20–26	93–100	9:22–27	116n87
6:20	23, 91, 95–96	9:23	116
6:21	34n69	9:24	146n18
6:24–26	134n191	9:34	217n100
6:24	183n224, 186	9:35	92n387
6:25	94n397	9:45	114n74
6:27–38	112n60	9:46–50	114n76
6:27	91, 92, 93,	9:49	108n34
6:29	98n411, 191n269	9:50–62	109n40
6:30–36	191n271	9:51–57	113n68
6:30	148n33	9:51–10:24	113n65
6:34–35	191n271	9:51	114n72
6:36	188, 191n271	9:57–58	98n413
6:39	91	9:61	120n111
6:40	109n43	10:1	109n40
6:45	129n159, 159n86	10:4	162n101
6:46–9	109n43	10:5–6	7n294, 96
6:47–49	92, 99n415	10:17–24	132n175
7:1	91, 92	10:17	114n75, 155n68
7:2–17	192	10:18	66
7:2–10	192n277	10:25–42	132n175
7:4–5	162n100	10:25–37	131n174, 255
7:16	217n100	10:25, 29	127n149
7:17	94n392	10:25	130
7:21–22	94n395	10:26–28	189n256
7:22–23	73–74	10:29–37	189n253, 198n310
7:22	23	10:35	191n269
7:23	223n129	10:38–42	113n66, 192n277
7:29–30	139n225	10:38	113n68
7:29	192n278	11:4	188n250
7:34	95n399	11:11–13	112n60
7:36–50	140n227, 254–55	11:15	126n147
7:41–43	193n282	11:21–22	66–67, 134
8:1–3	108n34, 174n172	11:29	113n69 12:1, 13, 54
8:1	70	11:39–41	190

INDEX OF SCRIPTURAL AND OTHER REFERENCES

(Luke continued)
11:39	185
11:53–12:1	151n50
12:1–13:9	149n40, 150, 151
12:1, 13, 54	113n69
12:1	114n75, 144n6, n7,
12:1–9, 51–53	151n46
12:1, 13, 41	151n51
12:1, 15, 22, 54	151n52
12:4–34	152
12:4–12	118, 156–57
12:7, 24	156n76
12:9	118n97
12:12	156n76
12:13–34	144–64, 151, 198n309
12:14	59n208
12:15–21	224
12:16–21	147–50
12:21	159n86
12:22–34	150–62
12:22–23,	146n18
12:32–34	191n270
12:32	42n119, 154n65
12:33–34	151n46, 152n55
12:33	172n162
12:35–13:9	255
12:35–46	175n178
12:35–40	193n282
12:35–38.	151n46
12:41–48	154n64, 198n309
12:42–48	198n311
12:44	120n109
12:45–46	18n19
12:46	172n162
12:49–50	113n71
12:54–9	150n43, 167n126
12:57–59	151n46, 255
12:58	126n147
13:1–9	150n43
13:1	151n51
13:2	151n52
13:5	149
13:6–9	167n126, 189n254
13:16	66n248
13:22–35	113n67
13:22, 33	113n68
13:22	113n65

13:27	170n143
13:31–33	117n91
13:33–35	113n71
13:35–48	150
14:1	126n147
14:12–14	191n271, 194n287
14:13–14, 21	32n55
14:15–24	123, 131
14:16–24	180n204, 188n251, 193n282, 194n285
14:18–20	135n201
14:25–35	103, **104–123**, 140–41, 223
14:26	136n207, 146n18
14:33	250–51
15:1–32	192n278
15:1–2	140n226
15:1	104
15:3	193n281
15:8–9	193n281
15:11–24	193n281, n282
15:32	146n21
16	257
16:1–13	**164–78**, 186
16:1–9	**166–75**, 193n281
16:9	161n91, 199, 224
16:10–12	195–96
16:13	195n293, 199n313
16:14–18	184–85
16:14–16	139n225
16:16–17	131n173
16:18	112n60
16:19–31	178–88, 189n252, 192, 253
16:20–21	32n54
16:29–31	130n165
16:29	189n256
17:3	144n6
17:7	193n281
17:11	113n65, n68
17:21	131n169
17:22–37	253
17:26–37	18n19
17:31–37	193n284
17:33	146n18
18:9–19:10	137
18:9–14	139n224
18:9–12	190n260

INDEX OF SCRIPTURAL AND OTHER REFERENCES   313

18:9	137n212	22:30	203n9
18:14, 17, 24, 29, 42	138n213	22:35–56	59n210
18:15–17	131n169	22:35–38	155
18:15	137n212	22:35	162n101
18:18–30	103–4, **123–137**, 140–41, 223, 252	22:36	155n69
		22:45	118
18:20	112n60	22:46	118n98
18:27	139	22:53	67
18:29–30	18n20, 162n99	22:57;	118n97
18:31–34	113n67, 137	23:13	107n26, 126n147
18:35–19:10	192	23:50	127n148, 129n159
18:35	113n65, 139	24:21	65, 161n91
18:36	113n68, n69		
18:38–43	139n225	## John	
18:42	138n214	1:11	133n185
19:1–10	**137–40**, 189n252, 192n278	1:46	73
		2:17	55n187
19:1	114n76, 138n217	6:35	86n359
19:9	131n169, 138n213, 140n227	8:3–11	126n144
		10:10	126n21
19:10	139n223	12:25–26	115n79, 116n87
19:11–27	113n67, 161n91, 172n162, 175n178, 195–99	12:25	110n49
		12:32–33	117n90
		12:38	83n343
19:11, 28	113n65	13:29	32n58
19:17–19	203n9	14:2	173n163
19:17	129n159, 176, 196	15:25	55n187
19:24–25	165n117	16:32	133n185
19:28, 36	113n68	18:31	118
19:37, 39	110n48, 113n69	18:32	117n90
19:37	108n35, 114n75	19:12	205n24
19:41	95n399		
20:1	70	## Acts	
20:9–18	193n282		
20:10	189n254	1:6–8	175n178, 195
20:34–36	161n91	1:6–7, 11	225n137
20:46	144n6	1:6–7	65, 161n91
20:47	185, 190n260	1:8	218
21:1–4	191n268, 192	1:14	205n21
21:2	32n54	1:15	219n112, 219n112
21:3	155n67	1:18–19	211n63
21:9, 24	175n178	1:18	163n109
21:19	146n18	1:20	55n187
21:34–36	18n21	2–5	215n80, 218–22
21:34	144n6	2:1, 44, 47	219n112
22:5	163n109	2:19, 22	221n123
22:24–30	114n76	2:20–21	225n138
22:29–30	161n91	2:20	225n137

(Acts continued)		5:12, 20, 25	220n118
2:22, 36	220n118	5:12	205n21, 221n123
2:27	146n18	5:17–42	215n80
2:28	146n21	5:17	221n121
2:31	107n25	5:18 (D)	133n185
2:36	221n123	5:20	146n21
2:40	167n124, 220n117, 225n141	5:31	79n320
2:41	219n112	5:35	144n6
2:42–47	202–13, 213–15	5:39	217n95
2:42	221n123	5:42	223n131
2:43–44	219n112	6:1–6	169n140, 194n288, 211n64, 213
2:46	95n400, 205n21, n22, 212n67, 224n133	6:1	219n111
2:47	220n118, 225	6:2	221n123
3:9–10	220n118	6:8–7:60	223n131
3:15	146n21	6:8,	221n123
3:19–21	225n137, 225n137, 225n138	6:12	107n26
		7:6	177n192
3:21	161n91	7:27, 35	126n147
3:22, 23	221n123	7:35	221n123 2:36
3:23, 25	220n119	7:38	221n122, n123
3:23	221n123	8:1	221
4:2, 21	220n118	8:23	54n182, 170n144
4:4, 20, 29, 31	221n123	8:35	70n271
4:4	219n112	8:39	217n97
4:11–12	223n129	9:4–5	216n93
4:19–20, 29–31	223n131	9:36–41	194n288, 224n134
4:24	205n21	9:36	190n265
4:25, 27	107n25	9:39	212n69
4:29	219n112	10:4, 31	162
4:30	221n123	10:14	31n47
4:32–5:16	213	10:35	53
4:32–37	**202–13**	10:36	70
4:32, 35	134	10:37–42	65
4:32	219n112	10:42	225n137
4:34–37	224n133	11:18	146n21
4:34–35, 37	169n140	11:27–30	225n144
4:34–35	95n400	11:23	225
4:34	211n63, 223n128, 225n148, 226n148	11:23–24	224n134
		11:24	129n159
4:36–37	135n195	11:27–30	224n134
5:1–11	163n109, 213–18	11:29–30	169n140
5:1	211n62	12:12–13	211
5:3	211n63	13:23	79n320
5:4	211n59, n61	13:43	225n144
5:11	221n122	14:3	225n144
5:12–16	213n78	14:5	126n147
5:12–14	221	14:18	133n185

INDEX OF SCRIPTURAL AND OTHER REFERENCES

14:22	223n131, 225n137
15:14	107n25
15:16	173n169
16:16–24	163n106
16:19	126n147
17:30–31	225n137, 225n138
17:31	150n43
18:10	107n25
18:18, 21	120n111
19:13–17	215n83, 217n100
19:19	223n132
19:23–27	163n107
19:32, 39, 41	221n122
20:10, 24, 20:24, 32	146n18
	225n144
20:28–29	154n66
20:28	144n6
20:29–35	18n22
20:33–35	163n109, 222n126
21:6	133n185
21:13–14	223n131
21:21	219n110
21:30, 40	107n26
22:3	126n139
22:12	127n148
23:5	126n147
24:14	220n115
24:15	225n137
24:26	163n108
26:14	216n94
26:17–18	225n141
26:17	107n26
26:20	222n125, 225n143
27:10, 22	146n18
28:22	2220n114
28:26	107

Romans

1:30	84
2:5	159n86
7:14–20	126n141
7:15	111n56
9:13	111n56
9:33	223n129
15:3	55n187
15:26	32n56, 213n77

1 Corinthians

3:10–15	176n187
3:16–17	216n94
4:1–5	176n187
4:13	44n130
7:12–16	136n207
7:32–33	155n67
9:5	136n207
10:9	217n96
11:20	219n112
14:23	219n112
16:2	159n86

2 Corinthians

2:13	120
2:17	163n109
8:9	33
8:14–15	213n77
11:7–15	163n109
12:14	159n86

Galatians

1:14	126n139
2:9	210n56
2:10	32n56, 213n77
6:10	175

Philippians

1:5	210n56
2:15	167n124
3:6	125
4:17	183n222

Colossians

3:5	178n195

1 Thessalonians

2:5–6	163n109

1 Timothy

6:17–19	162n102
6:19	146n21, 164n110

2 Timothy

3:2	83n344

Titus

2:10–14	225n147
3:3–7	225n147

Hebrews

1:9	111n56
3:8, 9	217n96
13:16	206

James

2:2	32n56
2:6	66n247
4:4	205n23
4:6	83n344
4:9	96n403
5:1	96n403, 97n408

1 Peter

2:8	223n129
5:2	154n66
5:5	83n344

2 Peter

2:1–3, 14	163n109
3:7	159n86

1 John

1:3, 7	210n56
2:7–8	189
2:8	225

3 John

7	171n153

Jude

23	111n56

Revelation

2:6	111n56
3:5	55n187
3:17	32n56
6:9–11	173n166
7:15–16	174n169
7:16–17	86

APOCRYPHA AND PSEUDEPIGRAPHA

Testament of Abraham

20	173n167

Assumption of Moses

10:1	61

1 Baruch

1:12	64n237
2:11	83n339.
2:18	64n237, 85
4:26	154n65
5	60n218

2 Baruch

14:12–13	161n90
14:12	161n96.
15:7–8	161n90
21:22–25, 29–30	161n90
21:23	173n165
24:1	161n96
30:2–3	173n165
44:8–12	172n160
44:12–15, 49–51	161n90
46:6	69n264
48:50	64n237
52:7	161n96
57	161n90
67:7	84n350
73	161n90

1 Enoch

1:8	63n235

INDEX OF SCRIPTURAL AND OTHER REFERENCES 317

5:6	63n235
10:16–11:2	198n312
22	173n165, 186
38:4	63n235
45:4	63n235
46:7–8	86n360
58:4–6	63n235
63:10	169n135
90:35	63n236
94:6–10	86n360
97:8–10	147n28, 150n41
97:9–10	86n360
98:9–10	148n29
102:9–10	86n360

2 Enoch

9:1	189n255
10:5	189n255
42:7–9	189n255
63:1	189n255

4 Ezra

2:11	173n167
3:35–6	126n145
4:35–43	173n165
4:35	173n165
6:6–10	160n90
7:75–101	173n165
7:75–99	160n90
7:75, 78	148n33
7:77, 83	161n96
9:38–10:59	80
9:45	80n328
11:42–43	84n348

Protevangelium of James

20:2	45n138

Jubilees

Jubilees	58n205

Judith

6:19	80n323
13:14	62n225
13:20	80n323

2 Maccabees

9:11	83n345
14:30	197n304

3 Maccabees

1:27	83n345
4:6	210n55
5:13	83n345
6:4	83n345

4 Maccabees

4:15	83n345
9:30	83n345

Paraleipomena Jeremiou

9:20	86

Sirach

3:3–6	161n94
4:2	85n358
5:1, 3	147
5:8	169n135
10:14–15	84–85
10:14	26n13
11:18–19	147n26
11:23–28	147n28
13:19	86n360
14:11–19	147n26
29:9–13	161n94
30:24—31:2	155n71
31(34):8	168n131
39:26	123n127
41:1	120n109
42:9	111n55

Psalms of Solomon

2	83
2:22	42n122
4:6	29n32
4:15	29n32
5	28, 85n356
7:8, 10	42n122
9:5	161n94
9:11	42n122
10	44

Index of Scriptural and Other References

(Psalms of Solomon continued)

10:1–3	42
10:5, 6, 8	95n398
10:6	29, 41
11	56n197, 59
11:1–9	42n122
11:1	60n218, 68
11:3	95n398
12:4	29n32
12:6	42n122
14:5	42n122
14:10	95n398
15:1	28n31
16:13–15	29
17:15(13)	83–84
17:21–22, 45	42n122
17:22	62n225
17:35	95n398
17:40	154n65
17:41	213n74
18:1–5	42n123
18:2	28n31

Testament of Asher

5:3	63n236

Testament of Benjamin

5:2	66n252

Testament of Dan

5:10–13	61

Testament of Joseph

2:4	62n231, 64n237
8:5	62n231
9:1	62n231

Testament of Levi

5:6	61

18:12	66n252
19:1	63n236

Testament of Naphtali

8:5	162n100

Testament of Simeon

6:6	66n252

Testament of Zebulun

9:8	61n222

Gospel of Thomas

31	47n140
88	177n190

Tobit

1:16–17	189n255
4:7–11	161n94
4:7	161
4:16	189n255
12:8–9	151n94
12:12–14	161, 162

Wisdom

1:6	209n53
6:15	155n71
7:14	162n104
7:23	155n71, 209n53
8:18	210n55
9:1–4	195n292
12:15	177n193
12:19	209n53
15:8	148n33
16:16	83n339

QUMRAN WRITINGS

War Scroll (1QM)

2:5	55n188
11:7–13	44n131
12:13–15	94n396

13:13–16	44n131	13:36–9	64n238
14:4–8	44n131	14:13	55n188
14:5–7	44n131	15:14–17	55
14.7	33n64	18:12–15	44
17:7–8	94n396	18:14–15	69n262, 94n396
18:14	55n188	18:19	63n236
		21:14–15	69n262
		Fragment 9	56

Manual of Discipline (1QS)

3:24	171n157
4:6–7	94n396
5:1, 9, 10	55n188
5:1–2	171n154
5:6	44n134
5:14–20	171n153
5:20	171n156
6:2	168n130
6:13–23	171n155
8:4	44n134
8:6	55n188
8:10,	55n188
8:13–14	60n219
9:4	55n188
9:8–9	171n155
9:13, 15	55n188
10:8	58n205, n206
10:19	168n135
11:3–5	63n236
11:18	55n188

Hodayot (Hymns 1QH)

1:8, 10, 15	55n188
2:31–37	43n128
3:23–28	43n128
4:5–6, 27	63n236
4:32–3	55n188
5:4	55n188
5:11–15, 20	43n128
5:21–22	44n130
5:32–34	63
5:36–39	64
7:19	55
9:8	60n220
9:23–26;	94n396
9:26–28	64n237
10:2, 6, 9	55n188
11:9	55n188
11:19–22	94n396

Damascus Document (CD)

1:9–10	63n236
2:14	63n236
2:21	55n188
3:3	55n188
3:4–19	45n137
6:11–14	171n150
6:14–16	170n147
6:15	168n135, 170n145
8:5	170n145, 171n153
11:4	55n188
13:9–10	62n227
13:14–16	171n153, 154n65
14:20	168n130
16:3	58n205
19:7–9	41, 154n65
19:9–10	45n136
19:17	170n145, 171n153
20:27–34	94n396

1QpHabbakuk

1QpHab	43n128
7:2, 12	58
12	44

1QMyst

1.2.5	168n130

1Q34bis

1–6	56

4QpPs37

1:8–10	26n17, 44n133
2:5–6	154n65
2:9–12	26n17, 44n133
2:9–11	160n90

11QPs^a

154:18	45n137

11QMelchizedek

11QMelch	44n135, 51, 56n197, 56, 57, 58, 59, 60, 69

RABBINIC WRITINGS

Mishnah

Peah 1:1	162n99
Dem. 2:3	31
Hor. 5:8	29n35
Meg. 4:4	49n157, 51n169
Meg. 4:18	49n158
Kid. 4:14,	194n286
BK 10:9	194n286
Aboth 1:2	178, 187
Aboth 2:16	161n96
Aboth 3:7	195n292
Aboth 6:9	161n90

Tosefta

Meg. 4:18	49n158
Meg. 4:19	50n159

Babylonian Talmud

Ber. 28b	128n156
Ber. 47b	31n46
Ber. 61b	178n195
Sheb. 39a	182n220
Shab. 63a	191n271
Pes. 94a	83n345
Taan. 24b	129n160
Meg. 15b	87n362
Meg 31a	51
Hag. 13a	83n345
Yeb. 62b–63a	182n220
Ket. 66b	123n128
Ket. 86a	182n220
Kidd. 40b	183n222
B. Bat. 9b	189n259, 191n266
B. Bat. 10a	178n195
B. Bat. 11a	162n103
Sanh. 25b	194n286
A Z 20b	26n12
Men. 53b	129n161
Bek. 8b	123n126
Nid. 31a	123n128

Jerusalem Talmud

Meg. 4:3	49n154
Hag. 2:2	179

Midrashim

Gen. Rab. 17:3;	182n220
Gen. Rab. 48:10	174n169
Gen. Rab. 56:3	115n80
Gen. Rab. 71:1	45n138
Gen. Rab. 97	64n237
Exod. Rab. 31:15	168n130
Exod. Rab. 31:2	174n171
Exod. Rab. 51:8	111
Lev. Rab. 34:11	189n259
Lev. Rab. 34:14	182n220
Num. Rab. 11:1	45n138
Num. Rab. 11:2	174n169
Num. Rab. 14:2	174n169
Ruth Rab. 3:4	174n169
Ruth Rab. 5:6	174n169
Midr. Ps. 9:12	45n138
Midr. Ps. 12	41n114
Midr. Ps. 13:4	174n169
Midr. Ps. 18:23	83
Midr. Ps. 23:2	194n286
Midr. Ps. 27:1	63n235
Midr. Ps. 60:3	45n138
Midr, Ps. 68:11	45n138
Midr. Ps. 118:14	173n169
Eccl. Rab. 11.1.1	174n169
Cant. Rab. 1.5.1	173n169
Cant. Rab. 2.9.3	174n169
Mekilta de-Rabbi Ishmael 14:15–17	174n169

Pesikta Rabbati

36	45n138, 63n235

Midrash Tanhumah

	50–51

EXTRA-CANONICAL WORKS

Derek Erez Rabbah

2:20	94n396

Perek Hashshalom

59b	69

Shemoneh Esreh

59n214, 84n348, 80, 84n348

Targums

Exod 15:1, 21 (TJ I&II)	84n347
Exod 15:2 (TJ I&II)	85n356
Exod 15:21 (TO)	84n348

1 Sam 2	86–87
1 Sam. 2:5	80–81
Isa	60n218
Isa 8:14	223n129
Isa 9:1	63n235
Isa 28:16	223n129
Isa 41:27	68
Isa 42:7	62n130
Isa 50:10	64n237
Isa 52:7	68
Isa 60:1	63n235
Isa 61:1	63
Mic. 6:10	169n135
Hab 2:9	168n135

JOSEPHUS

The Jewish War

2.122	34n66, 213n76
2.140	213n76
2.150	213n76
2.166	30n40
2.253	117n93
2.308	117n93

Antiquities

17.12	185n234
17.295	115n82
18.23	115n82
18.228	68

Philo

Op. 138	207n34
Op. 152	207n29
Leg. All. III.104–06	159n86
Cher. 107–119	195n292
Sacr. 27	207n41

Sacr. 75	207n35
Post. 181	207n36
Ebr. 48	207n29
Ebr. 78	207n37
Ebr. 84	207n37
Conf. 48	208n50, 213n75
Conf. 194–95	207n34
Migr. 178	207n35
Fug. 28–29	209n50
Fug. 55	207n32
Fug. 79	159n86
Fug. 112	207n33
Mut. 104	207n30
Abr. 74	207n34
Abr. 100, 248	207n29
Abr. 117	212n67
Jos. 160	207n34
Jos. 250	68n258
Vita Mos. 1:156	202n5, 205
Vita Mos. 2:190	208n43
Dec. 14	207n38
Dec. 71, 150	207n34

(Philo continued)

Decal. 109	207n37, 208n47
Dec. 123	207n29
Dec. 132	207n35, n40
Dec. 162	207n39, 213n75
Dec. 171	207n30
Spec. Leg. 1:109, 138	207n29
Spec. Leg. 1:235	207n30
Spec. Leg. 1:295	195n292, 207n39, 213n75
Spec. Leg. 1:324	207n39
Spec. Leg. 2:7	207n36, 208n43
Spec. Leg. 2:108	209n50
Spec. Leg. 2:167	207n41, 209n53
Spec. Leg. 3:23, 29	207n29
Spec. Leg. 3:28	207n34
Spec. Leg. 3:103	207n40, n41
Spec. Leg. 3:158	207n30
Spec. Leg. 3:182	207n31
Spec. Leg. 4:30	207n30
Spec. Leg. 4:83	207n34
Spec. Leg. 4:187	213n75
Spec. Leg. I2:75	207n30
Virt. 41	68n258
Virt. 51	208n42
Virt. 80	208n42
Virt. 84, 119	207n36
Virt. 90	159n86
Virt. 140–41	159n86, 209n50
Praem. 87	209n50
Quod Omn. 35	194n289
Quod Omn. 76	159n86
Quod omn. 77, 87	34n66
Quod omn 79, 84	213n75
Quod omn. 91	209n52
Aet. 143	207n34
Flacc. 190	207n34
Hyp. 7:6	197n305
Hyp. 8.11.1	207n39
Gaium, 47	207n30
Gaium 231	68n258

Christian Fathers

Athanasius, Life of Anthony	123–24
1 Clement 1:1	177n193
2 Clement 6:1	168n131
Barn. 19:8	222n126
Ignatius, Philadelphians 3:3	177n191
Ignatius, Trallians 6:1	177n191
Ignatius, Romans, Inscription	177n191
Did. 4:8	222n126
Did. 11:4–6, 9, 12	163n109
Clement Alex. Rich Man	124, 132n176
Stromateis 4.6.34	145
Stomateis 4.6.35	139n222
Stromateis 4.6.33	162n105
Clementine Homilies 2.1; 3.63–65, 71–72	139n222
Clementine Recognitions 3.65–71	139n222
Origen, Comm. Matt 15:14	125n137

GREEK AND ROMAN WRITINGS

Aristophanes

Eccl.	589–90
Plutus	168n132

Aristotle

Eth. Nic. 8:9.1159b	202n5, 206n25
Eth. Nic. 8:10.1159b	213n74
Eth. Nic. 9:8. 1168b	202, 205n19, 213n74
Pol. 2:1–2	204n11
Pol. 2:2.1263a	202n5, 204n12

Cicero

De amicit. 21.81	205n19
De amicit. 25.92	
De offic. 1.16.51	202n5, 204
De offic. 1.17.56	205n19

INDEX OF SCRIPTURAL AND OTHER REFERENCES

Dio Chrysostom

3:104–15	205
3:110, 37:7	202n5
17:7–9	224n135
17:9	213n74

Diodorus Siculus

5:45	204n10

Diogenes Laertius

5:20	205n19
6:72	203n5, 204n12
7:33	204n12
8:10	203n5, 213n74
8:19	202n3
8:23	203n7

Epictetus

Discourses 2.4.8	204n11
Discourses 2.10.4	203n7
Discourses 2.10.7	203n7
Discourse 4.1.172	148n33
Enchiridion 11; 4	148n33

Euripides

Andr. 366–67	203n7
Andr. 376–77	202n5
Bacchae	217n95
Fem. Phoe. 243–44	202n5
Ores, 735	202n5
Ores. 1045	205n19

Iamblichus

30:167–68	202n3, 205n19

Lucian

Merc. Cond. 20	203n8

Martial

Epigrams 2:43	202n3

Menander

Adel. 9K	202n3

Ovid

Metam. 1:89–112	204n10

Plato

Critias 110d	203n7, 104n10
Resp. 3.416d	203n7, 204n10
Resp. 4.424a	202n5, 204n10
Resp. 5.449c	202n5, 204n10
Resp. 5.463–64	204n10
Resp. 5.464d	203n7
Resp. 8.543b	203n7
Tim. 18b	203n7, 204n10

Plutarch

Amat. 21:9.767e	202n5, 205–6
Coniug. Praec. 34.143a	203n8.
De frat. Am. 20.490e	202n5, 204

Polybius

Histories 6.47.7	204n11

Seneca

De benefic. 7.4.1	202n5
Ep. 90:3	204n10, 224n135

Strabo

Geography 7.3.9	203n7

Terence

Adelph. 803–804	203n5

Virgil

Georg. 1.125–27	204n10

www.ingramcontent.com/pod-product-compliance
Lightning Source LLC
Chambersburg PA
CBHW052145300426
44115CB00011B/1526